Carl Menger and his legacy in economics

Carl Menger and his legacy in economics

Annual supplement to volume 22,

History of political economy

Edited by Bruce J. Caldwell

Duke University Press

Durham and London 1990

Contents

vi   Contents

IV. General themes

Preface and acknowledgments

Eve L. Menger donated the papers of her grandfather Carl to Duke University in 1987. The following spring Craufurd Goodwin and Neil de Marchi of Duke asked me to serve as the director of a conference to commemorate the acquisition. It was also decided that this would be the first in a series of such events to be held annually at Duke. The conference took place on the weekend of 15–17 April 1989. The papers gathered here are the result.

In addition to the authors of the articles, the following scholars attended the conference as discussants: Jack Birner, Mark Blaug, Stephan Boehm, Peter Boettke, William Butos, Greg Christiansen, Earlene Craver, Wade Hands, Richard Langlois, Kurt Leube, Peter Rosner, John Whitaker, and Larry White. Axel Leijonhufvud presented a delightful and insightful set of extemporaneous remarks at the closing luncheon. This was a distinguished group indeed, and the quality of their contributions was uniformly high. Three sets of comments were so apposite that I chose to include them in the volume, one of them in the form of a paper.

None of this would have been possible without funding from a number of sources. The Olin Foundation and the Sloan Foundation were magnanimous in their support. Additional funding was provided by Duke University Press and by the History of Economic Thought Workshop of the Duke Economics Department. The Government of Austria generously supported the travel of the Austrian participants. The University of North Carolina at Greensboro provided me with a generous phone budget. Finally, some of the participants were able to arrange alternative funding for travel or bore part of the expense themselves.

A number of individuals made my job as conference director considerably less onerous. Craufurd Goodwin, who provided his sound and calming advice and handled innumerable logistical problems before, during, and after the event, tops the list. Bob Byrd and Mason Barnett created an inviting display of Menger's papers which set just the right mood for the opening reception. Paula Schofield minimized the traumas produced by a last-minute change of venue. Neil de Marchi provided valuable suggestions, criticisms, and support. And the following members of Neil's History of Thought Workshop served dutifully as guides for their guests: Peter Dohlman, Jinbang Kim, Mike Lail, Robert Leonard, and Jeff Roggenbuch. To each I extend my heartfelt thanks.

Carl Menger and his legacy in economics

Editor's introduction

Bruce J. Caldwell

The conference organizers originally envisioned a set of papers which would deal with three episodes in the development of subjectivist economics. That vision was laid out in the general invitation which was sent to each of the participants. The invitation read as follows:

> Participants at the conference are asked to consider one of three episodes in the development of the Austrian tradition in economics. The first episode, quite properly, is the period in which Menger made his contributions. The second is the period in the 1920s and 1930s when Austrian ideas (soon to be followed by the economists themselves) were spread to the English-speaking world. The final episode marks the renaissance of interest in Austrian economics, which began in the 1970s and continues today.
>
> Though there already exists a literature on Menger's contributions to economics and to social science methodology, it is also clear that there are many gaps in our knowledge. For example, Hayek notes that we still know relatively little about the period prior to the publication of the *Principles* in 1871, so that we have been forced to conjecture about the origins of his ideas. One way, then, to organize the first session of the conference would be to ask: What questions concerning Menger and the development of his ideas might we hope to find answered once the archives have been thoroughly examined? What significant gaps in our knowledge presently exist? Another way of approaching the organization of this session might be to ask: What do we need to know about Menger and his times in order to make the best use of the materials in the archive? Since we are also interested in his legacy, we should address the question: What is the essence (he would probably approve of the use of that term) of Menger's contribution? Perhaps most important, and also most controversial: Which aspects of his thought should be retained, which should be discarded, and why?
>
> In the next section, the transmission of subjectivist thought from Vienna to the English-speaking world would be examined. A key issue here is to account for the meteoric rise and equally precipitous decline of Austrian influence during the 1930s. Some have recently argued that it was during this period that a distinctively

3

Austrian brand of economics emerged. Is such an interpretation correct? In tracing the Mengerian legacy, we must also ask: Who among the many different economists who worked within the Austrian tradition during this period were the true heirs of Menger? With whose ideas would Menger be greatly pleased? Would any earn the derision which Menger heaped on Böhm-Bawerk's theory of capital, that "greatest error ever committed"? Finally, in what ways was the development of neoclassical economics changed by the contributions, and later, by the criticisms of the Austrians?

The final episode to be examined is the resurgence of interest in subjectivist economics which took place over a century after the publication of the *Principles,* and after nearly four decades of studied indifference or outright hostility from the rest of the economics profession. Again we must ask: What caused this movement to emerge, and why has it succeeded to the extent that it has? Does subjectivist economics have a future? What strands in the current Austrian tradition would be recognizable by Menger? How would he feel about radical subjectivism, about apriorism, about interpretative or hermeneutical economics? Does any new work in mainstream economic theory hold promise for the reintegration of Austrian economics with neoclassicism? These are the sorts of questions that we hope will be addressed in the papers delivered at the conference and during discussions which take place there.

The conference program was set up to reflect this theme of "three episodes in Austrian economics." But in retrospect it seems better to arrange the papers around *four* general headings. There is little change in the first topic, which investigates the origins and substance of Menger's contribution. The second focuses more broadly on the work of the next two "generations" of Austrians rather than on the narrow theme of the transmission of subjectivist ideas to the English-speaking world. The third area is new, consisting of evaluations and reconstructions of Menger's methodology. It surely must appear ingenuous for the editor of this volume to express shock that a number of participants should address Menger's methodological contribution. But as all can plainly see, there was no explicit invitation to treat this subject in the call for papers. A plausible alternative explanation is simply to note that Menger's methodology virtually cries out for evaluation and reconstruction. In any case, the methodology section is a result of human action rather than of design, and no student of Menger's could willfully subvert such an organically emergent phenomenon. The final section contains papers on broader themes: one on Menger's work as a whole, one on matters of interpretation, and one on the Austrian revival.

I. *Origins and economic policy*

There already exists a substantial literature on Menger's work in economic theory. The four papers in the first section cover less traveled territory: the origins of his ideas, and his views on economic policy.

Erich Streissler's first contribution could itself be considered two papers, since it really addresses two themes. The first is the well-documented assertion that Menger borrowed heavily from what is dubbed the German "protoneoclassical" tradition. Those familiar with Streissler's earlier work will recognize this theme, but on the basis of new evidence it is stated more strongly here than it has been before. The second theme is tantalizingly developed; the author has the gifts of a storyteller. Streissler first constructs a chapter outline which a "representative" textbook writer in the German protoneoclassical tradition might follow. (It is important to note that the protoneoclassicals were principally writers of textbooks.) It turns out that the outline is the same as the one followed by Alfred Marshall, another textbook writer of some repute! Though Streissler never directly states that Marshall expropriated the organizational scheme of his German predecessors, the paper is filled with fascinating and suggestive indirect evidence. For example, one of the most important members of the earlier group, K. H. Rau, drew a downward-sloping demand curve in 1841, and in doing so he put price on the vertical axis. For years I have blamed Marshall for this outrageous trick on our students. Perhaps now I can tell them that it was all Rau's fault.

Paul Silverman uses Emil Kauder's interpretation of Menger as a foil in his paper. Kauder argued for a direct Aristotelian influence on Menger and the early Austrians, one which was transmitted through their studies of Aristotle and through the Greek philosopher's influence on *fin de siècle* Austrian culture. Silverman shows that the evidence for Kauder's claims is virtually nonexistent. His alternative interpretation is that the Aristotelianism in Menger entered indirectly through the influence of Menger's predecessors in economics. Much of the paper is taken up with describing how Aristotelian categories (the means-ends framework, the emphasis on the search for "the good life") entered the concepts of the cameralists, who wrote textbooks on economic policy and were contemporaries of the mercantilists. After Adam Smith's book was discovered, a generation of "Smithian cameralists" produced works which contained a variety of ideas which later popped up in Menger. Silverman also offers an intriguing explanation of Menger's account of "objective needs," an account which later generations of Austrians (who were more thoroughly subjectivist in outlook) found disturbing. The explanation is simple: the notion of objective needs is the result of

Menger's combining objective elements in Smith's theory of value with an Aristotelian emphasis on finding the specific content of "the good life."

The second two papers, one by Israel Kirzner and the other by Erich Streissler, address the same question: What were Menger's views on economic policy? As Streissler points out, we know little about Menger's policy views because of the institutional arrangement of Austrian economics departments at the turn of the century. Menger taught *theory,* not policy. The latter was the province of another professor, and Menger accordingly wrote relatively little about it. For those who have cringed when reading the pronouncements of theoretical economists concerning matters outside of their area of expertise (doctrinal history comes to mind), the thought of such a well-observed division of labor is appealing indeed. But in this case the losses outweigh the gains, for it reduces our knowledge of what a leading figure of economics thought about policy issues. The key question is this: How much scope for government intervention in the economy would Menger allow?

After a careful review of the literature, Kirzner notes that one can find support for a variety of theses concerning Menger's policy views. His own interpretation contains an interesting twist. Kirzner asserts that *in his policy writings* (the few that exist on the topic) Menger recognized both the efficacy of markets and specific instances in which government intervention would be beneficial. But his *theory* contains a case for free markets which is much stronger. In Kirzner's view, Menger and some of the early Austrians may not have recognized all of the implications their theories contained for the question of the propriety of government intervention. Those implications had to be spelled out by later generations of Austrians.

Streissler's thesis is based on the recent discovery of a set of notes recording the lectures given by Menger to Crown Prince Rudolph. The notes were periodically reviewed and corrected by Menger, so we can safely surmise that they accurately reflect the content of his instruction. As is appropriate given that the student was the presumptive future ruler, most of the lectures deal with policy. On the basis of these notes Streissler claims that Menger was if anything a more fervent advocate of laissez faire than were the classical economists, whose views are echoed throughout the manuscript. With the occasional exception of policies which either counteract the presence of negative external effects or promote the production of goods with positive externalities, Menger permitted virtually no scope for governmental action. Furthermore, in those rare moments when Menger mentioned anything relating to the theory of value, the crown prince again got the classical story rather than Menger's own theories. Because the lecture notes reflect what Menger said to a student, a number of symposium participants challenged whether it was legitimate to infer that they contain what Menger actually thought about policy. (Anyone who has taught introductory students can see the sense of this objection.) Alternate scenarios explaining why Menger might take a classical approach were hypothesized. To his credit, in the revision published here Streissler meets these alternative explanations head on. One suspects that the final chapter on Menger's policy views remains to be written.

II. *Successors*

Roger Garrison brings exceptional clarity to a murky subject in his review of some of the early controversies in Austrian capital theory. He details Menger's contributions to our understanding of the topic, then turns his attention to the Austrian who is best known for his work on capital theory, Eugen Böhm von Bawerk. Menger did not have much use for Böhm's contribution in this area, and modern Austrians are *very* Mengerian in this respect. Drawing on Ludwig Lachmann's distinction between subjectivist and formal modes of analysis, Garrison argues that Böhm's major error was to deviate from the subjectivism which permeated Menger's work. By straddling the fence between subjectivism and formalism, Böhm opened the door to criticisms from the likes of J. B. Clark and Frank Knight. Even worse was Wicksell's "correction" of errors in Böhm's presentation, a correction which led to the even greater error (from the perspective of a modern subjectivist) of an Austrian theory of capital that is formalized and expressed in a Walrasian framework. Garrison's solution is to recommend a return to the subjectivism of Menger.

Lionel Robbins was the person most responsible for bringing Hayek to the London School of Economics in the early 1930s. At the time he was also instrumental in getting certain books by Austrians translated into English. Thus Robbins might well be viewed as the proximate cause of the introduction of Austrian ideas to England and to the English-speaking academic community. As Robbins's biographer, D. P. O'Brien is superbly qualified to trace the impact of Austrian theorizing on the development of the Englishman's thought. O'Brien investigates the Austrian influence on both Robbins's microeconomics and his macroeconomics. He advances a dual thesis: the influence was less direct but more lasting in the first area, and more direct but less lasting in the second. A comment by Mark Blaug is also included. Blaug dislikes O'Brien's use of the label "general equilibrium theorist" to describe Robbins, because it suggests that he might be a Walrasian—which Robbins emphatically was not. Blaug recommends the more felicitous phrase "total equilibrium theory" for describing the analyses of economists (like Robbins and the Austrians) who demonstrate a concern with market interdependencies but reject the belief that such relationships are best modeled as systems of simultaneous equations. In the second part of his comment Blaug discusses Austrian capital theory and its role in Hayek's and Robbins's views on the trade cycle. The conclusions he draws are quite different from those of the previous paper. Blaug also raises what must be viewed as one of the most puzzling questions to come out of the 1930s: Why did Hayek and Robbins respond so anemically to the Keynesian onslaught?

Most modern Austrians take their subjectivism seriously; some would even prefer that the phrase "subjectivist economics" replace "Austrian economics." On the other hand, some Austrians have warned about the dangers of taking subjectivism too far. The specter of "radical subjectivism," a term associated with the work of G. L. S. Shackle and his Austrian defender Ludwig Lachmann, is typically invoked by those who fear the ever-forward movement of subjectivist ideas. Jeremy Shearmur engages this topic in a brilliant paper examining certain decidedly non-subjectivist concepts found in the work of Menger and Hayek. Shearmur addresses two broad questions, one in the area of welfare economics and the other in the methodology of the social sciences, but the range of the paper is much wider. In his view the biological domain holds the key to limiting subjectivism: it is the middle ground existing "between the physical and the meaningful." Shearmur urges that we explore this domain. His arguments are compelling and challenge the common wisdom that the best way forward for Austrians is always to expand rather than to limit subjectivism. His demonstration that such beliefs can look to at least some of the writings of Menger and Hayek for support may pose problems for subjectivists who adhere to an "original intent" thesis in doctrinal matters.

The three papers and the comment contained in this section address very different topics. But they aptly illustrate the variety of opinions which exist concerning the Austrian movement, as well as differing historiographical approaches. O'Brien gives us the straight stuff: he examines the sources judiciously to find what influence the Austrians had on Robbins and states his conclusions with scholarly caution. With its emphasis on the primacy of subjectivism, Garrison's work exemplifies modern Austrian historiography. Thus we find that early Austrians reasoned correctly when they hewed to the subjectivist line and erred when they wandered from it. The proper opponent for Garrison is Blaug, who finds the Austrians deficient when their views cannot be expressed within the more formal neoclassical framework. Interestingly enough, Blaug and Garrison would probably often agree in their assessments of attempts to express Austrian tenets in neoclassical language.

Most such attempts have not met with success. But whereas Blaug would conclude so much the worse for the Austrians, Garrison would say so much the worse for neoclassicism! Finally, Shearmur's paper represents a new iconoclasm in Austrian interpretation. Shearmur opposes the unquestioned march towards subjectivism, but his critique is not based on formalistic foundations. The tensions produced by the clash of all of these competing approaches can be fruitful. They may well be the harbingers of a new era in Austrian interpretation.

III. *Methodology*

A twentieth-century reader might be forgiven if he did not find Menger's methodological writing to be a paradigm of lucid exposition. Menger began by describing a number of "orientations" or methodologies appropriate for the investigation of different types of social phenomena. Some of these doctrines were taken as representative of the views of the German Historical School, Menger's principle opponent. After criticizing these doctrines Menger proposed an alternative approach. Certain elements of Menger's methodology (after transmittal by Hayek) survive in the writings of modern-day Austrians. These include his criticisms of historicism and his endorsements of methodological individualism, the compositive method (in which complex phenomena are built up from their constituent parts), and invisible-hand explanations (in which beneficient institutions emerge as the result of human action but independent of human design). Two Mengerian themes which are mentioned in the secondary literature but which have few analogues in contemporary Austrian thought are his essentialism and his distinction between real and exact theories. The symposium papers focus on these less familiar themes.

Karl Milford presents a detailed account of both the critical and the positive aspects of Menger's methodology. He then turns to the real-exact dichotomy. He interprets Menger as saying that "real types" refer to individuals or particulars, whereas "exact types" refer to universals. A problem in Menger's formulation is then revealed: How are the strictly universal terms, laws, and theories which constitute Menger's exact types to be justified? We think that such laws are true because in the past the laws have always held. But how can we prove them to be true? This is Hume's problem: universal generalizations cannot be justified inductively. And as Milford easily shows, Menger's few words on the subject (basically an appeal to man's "laws of thinking") do not provide an adequate solution. He concludes that Menger's methodology is inadequate on this point.

Milford nowhere announces that he is the follower of any particular philosopher of science. But the pedigree of his thought is revealed when he cites Karl Popper at critical junctures of his argument and when he praises the hints of Popper's critical rationalism which are to be found in Hayek's methodology. Popper is relevant in this context because he claims to have solved (or at least to have avoided) the problem of induction which plagues Menger's methodology. But as Jack Birner shows, Popper's solution encounters problems of its own when it is applied within the social sciences. Some background may help us to understand Birner's argument better.

Popper's answer to the question of how to justify universal claims is simplicity itself: drop the requirement that knowledge claims be justified! Universal generalizations cannot be proven to be true, they cannot be justified. But they can, if testable, be falsified. Science does not produce justified knowledge. But it can, if we are lucky, eliminate error.

Popper's solution was developed with the natural sciences in mind, where our intuition tells us that true, universal laws exist, even though we cannot prove them to be true. But other, less intuitively reasonable "theories" are also based on universal generalizations: for Popper these included Freudian psychology and Marxism. Since neither the laws of physics nor the laws of motion of the capitalist system can be proven true, should they be viewed as equally plausible?

Such a result was unacceptable for Popper. But his solution to the problem of induction also provided a means of resolving this dilemma, of demarcating science from nonscience. Whereas pseudoscientific theories are unfalsifiable, scientific generalizations are falsifiable: they are capable of being submitted to the most severe of tests. Since neither Marxism nor Freudian psychology yielded testable predictions, they did not qualify as scientific theories. Of those theories which did qualify as scientific, we should accept (though we cannot prove as true) those generalizations which have survived numerous attempts at refutation. Of course, those which are falsified are rejected.

Of course. But this is precisely where economics runs into trouble. Birner argues that the analogue to a universal law in economics is the statement that all agents act rationally. (People disagree about how best to define rationality, a point we shall ignore here.) But as Popper himself recognized, the rationality principle when interpreted empirically is false. If Birner's argument is correct, the most successful social science (the one Popper recommended as the model for the other social sciences) employs a universal law which is demonstrably false. Even worse, Popper's response to this dilemma is to endorse as a general methodological rule that the rationality principle never be rejected! Birner's next move is truly brilliant. Following the suggestions of one of the least appreciated Popperians, Noretta Koertge, he shows how her program for empirically identifying deviations from rational action was anticipated by certain remarks by Menger. If Milford's point was to demonstrate that Menger's problem with induction has been resolved by Popper, Birner's response is to show how Popper's difficulties with the rationality principle are overcome by Menger.

The origins of Menger's Aristotelianism are addressed by Paul Silverman in an earlier part of this volume. Its implications for his methodology are taken up at this point by Barry Smith. Smith reconstructs via a series of theses the common Aristotelian ground that Menger shared with many of his contemporaries. The variant of Austrian Aristotelianism specific to Menger emerges as the list grows longer. Smith's next step is to clarify two alternative approaches to apriorism, which he labels reflectionist and impositionist. The reflectionist view, which Menger embraced, is fully compatible with the search for constancies which exist in the underlying structure of reality. The impositionist view holds that the mind imposes its own structure, so that a priori knowledge is knowledge of the structure of our own minds. This second view, especially when it is linked to the thesis that knowledge of the a priori categories is incorrigible, is decidedly problematical. Ludwig von Mises's great error was to construct an elaborate methodological edifice on an impositionist foundation. Smith goes on to say that if we focus on Mises's practice rather than on his explicitly methodological pronouncements, our assessment of him improves. (This kind of divergence between pronouncement and practice is unfortunately unremarkable in methodology.) Mises contributed a large number of primitive concepts which provide the building blocks for a theory of the structure of reality.

Uskali Mäki is an advocate of the philosophical position known as scientific realism. In his paper he proposes a realist reconstruction of Menger's methodology. The choice of Menger makes sense: one of the "Austrian Aristotelian" theses mentioned by Smith is that the world is knowable via both commonsense realism and scientific realism. Barry Smith's paper shows how Menger and Mises provided the building blocks for a realist reconstruction of economics. If we complete the metaphor, Mäki provides the architectural blueprints for the project. He uses Menger as a vehicle for laying out a sophisticated realist account of such categories as the nature of universals and of essences; the concept of causal power, which applies not only to agents but also to things; and the meanings to be attached to such terms as existence and necessity. Mäki's paper will be hard going for many readers. The topics discussed will not be familiar to those who have been brought up in the logical empiricist or Popperian traditions. But the effort will be well worth it. Realism is currently the ascendent movement in the philosophy of science, and for good reason: it resolves many of conundrums which plagued earlier views. It also has the potential to cause significant change within economics. As Smith hints at the end of his paper, realism might provide the vehicle for a rapprochement between Austrian economics and neoclassicism.

Though there was substantial debate at the conference among the proponents of these various interpretations, it is not at all clear that one must make a choice among these Popperian, Aristotelian, and realist investigations of Menger's methodology. No choice is necessary if the various protagonists are pursuing different goals, which appears to be the case. The Popperians (Milford and Birner) want to identify and correct errors in Menger's presentation from the perspective of non-justificationist philosophy of science. Smith (and in a different context Silverman) wishes to reconstruct the Aristotelian elements which underlie Menger's contribution. For Mäki, Menger's work provides an example in a project which is much larger, the examination of what an economics founded on scientific realism would look like. These are very different endeavors. It is a tribute to Menger that his work is sufficiently rich to support this diversity of approaches.

IV. *General themes*

Max Alter's paper is probably the most controversial, and certainly the most ambitious, of the entire group. Alter first offers an overview and criticism of the secondary literature on Menger. He then produces what he feels are damning criticisms of Menger's methodological and economic contributions. Alter asserts that Menger's methodology allows introspection as the only source of knowledge of the social world. In the economic sphere, he argues, Menger's analysis contains an unresolvable "transformation problem." A few of the conference participants had an almost visceral negative reaction to the tone of the paper and to the absence of substantiation when provocative claims were being advanced. (Alter has a book forthcoming on Menger, and he frequently advises his readers that the arguments are presented in more detail there.) The paper is followed by an equally provocative comment from Larry White. In his discussion White rebuts Alter's claims point for point. Whatever one's opinion of this exchange, White's concession that Alter has provided a service by putting forward a host of bold conjectures is surely correct. Many of Alter's assertions are testable, and because they are controversial they will provide both an impetus and a target for those who will mine the archives.

The hermeneutical exegesis of texts, and of Menger's texts in particular, is the nominal topic of Don Lavoie's paper. But it is quickly apparent that he wants to explore bigger themes. He posits three levels of hermeneutical analysis: the exegetical level (How do we understand texts?), the agent level (How do we understand each other, and how do we model the communication of agents?), and the social level (How do we understand large-scale social interactions?). A crucial element of his approach is that there are common elements to the "exegesis" of "texts" among all three levels. Trying to understand a text is like trying to understand someone else in a conversation: conversations, the intentions of others, and the economy are all "texts" to be understood. Lavoie focuses his attention on the first two levels of hermeneutical analysis. First he explicates Hans-Georg Gadamer's critique of "copy theories" of knowledge and of communication. Then he details an alternative account of the process of understanding. He also anticipates and responds to potential objections to the hermeneutical approach. For example, he answers the complaint that hermeneutics reduces to an "anything goes" philosophy by invoking a Mengerian spontaneous order within interpretative communities which acts as a constraint on textual misinterpretations. The hermeneutical message has been clarified considerably by this paper.

In the final paper, Karen Vaughn traces the Mengerian roots of the Austrian revival. This is a piece of contemporary history told by a participant observer. The revival began in the early 1970s, when the marginal revolution was "dehomogenized" and Menger's work was shown to be different in significant respects from that of his co-founders. Vaughn briefly summarizes some of the prominent themes in Menger, then documents the introduction of Austrian economics to the English-speaking world by Hayek and Mises. She emphasizes the importance of the socialist calculation debate for the development of Hayek's ideas, and notes that it was Mises who was largely responsible for bringing Austrian thought to America. Though an increase in Mengerian scholarship and the awarding of the Nobel Prize to Hayek in the early 1970s both played a role in the revival, Vaughn chooses to emphasize the South Royalton Conference in 1974 as the key to the renaissance. It was there that a new generation of scholars were brought together and committed themselves to the study of Austrian ideas. Vaughn's closing remarks on the nature of the renaissance and of its future prospects will be viewed as controversial by some, but all will agree that they provide food for thought. Her musings are a fitting conclusion for a volume which contains so many divergent viewpoints.

It should be evident that some of the questions posed in the invitation to the participants were answered at the conference, while others were not. In some instances the answers were controversial; in others multiple answers were offered. Perhaps most important, new questions which were not anticipated in the invitation have emerged. Those who soon will begin working in the Menger archives will have plenty of hypotheses to test.

Let me close with a personal note. I did not know a lot about Menger when I organized the conference, but I knew *some*. I had read the English versions of his books and a bit of the secondary literature. In making the hard decisions about whom to invite, I decided to choose people whose past work had been excellent, even if it had not always necessarily been on Menger.

I was not at all prepared for the outcome. I was stunned at the conference by how much I did not know about Menger. The schedule we kept was unrelenting, and I remember feeling at the time that the sheer amount of new information that was being transmitted was staggering. Rereading the final versions of the articles confirms this initial impression. There are some superb papers in this collection, and there is a wealth of information. No editor can wish for more than that.

The Papers of Carl Menger in the Special Collections Department, William R. Perkins Library, Duke University

Mason Barnett

In 1985 the Duke University Manuscript Department, now the Special Collections Department, in conjunction with the University's Department of Economics, began a program aimed at preserving the correspondence, writings, and related papers of a select number of distinguished economists. The papers of Carl Menger (1840–1921), consisting of approximately 7,500 items and occupying eleven linear feet of shelf space, were donated to the University in 1987 by his granddaughter, Eve L. Menger. Copyright interests in the papers are reserved to his heirs under the provisions of U.S. copyright law (Title 17, U.S.C.). Further information about the collection or access to it may be obtained from the Special Collections Department, William R. Perkins Library, Duke University, Durham, North Carolina 27706, USA (telephone: (919) 684–3372).

Scope and content

The Carl Menger Papers span the years 1857 to 1985. Although the collection includes material from Menger's early professional life as well as some items from his brothers, Anton and Max, and his son, Karl, it is primarily composed of manuscripts and correspondence relating to his mature academic career. The contents are extremely dense and complex; they are also essential to an understanding of the mind of Carl Menger. Not only do the papers reflect Menger's mind, they also document his methods of work. He was a copious note-taker and read voraciously. He kept bound notebooks with reflections and excerpts from his current reading, especially in the early years when he was constructing the *Grundsätze*. Later he made notes and revisions on loose sheets, having some of them copied into a clear hand, and on those sheets too he made revisions. Menger also wrote directly in the printed text. For example, his papers include two copies of the *Grundsätze* (a third similar copy is in the Hitotsubashi University Library with the rest of Menger's library) with blank pages interleaved among the pages of

15

text. In each of these successively Menger made extensive notes and changes. Although it is frequently impossible to date his manuscripts precisely, one can get a sense of the development of his thought in some cases from the progression of his notes and from holographic evidence. The collection has been organized into series which reflect both Menger's style of work and his major areas of research. The series include research notebooks; manuscripts and notes on economic principles, money, and methodology; teaching materials; and correspondence.

Menger's work on political economy, on the nature of his subject, and on its appropriate research method typifies changes in the intellectual frontier in fin-de-siècle Vienna and Europe as a whole. Some of his most explicit thoughts on these subjects are evident in his lecture notes. Although he taught for more than thirty years, the collection contains only a small amount of material from this aspect of his career. What one discerns from the lecture notes, however, is a personal sense of the teacher and his high degree of moral commitment to his work. Menger clearly thought it important to articulate his thoughts on the distinction between political economy and jurisprudence—since that was the faculty in which he taught—and the method and aims of the discipline.

The bulk of the collection consists of Menger's notes and revisions on economic and theoretical topics. The series on general economic principles contains material relating to his first major work, *Grundsätze der Volkswirthschaftslehre,* which he published in 1871. Despite the lack of an extant full-length, coherent manuscript for this book, his background work can be discerned from a set of extensive notebooks he kept. These contain extracts of works he read, as well as his reactions and reflections. The range of works shows familiarity with classical authors, particularly Aristotle and Plato, through to his own contemporaries. He showed special interest in writers on law, political economy, and theories of knowledge, such as Grotius, Malthus, J. S. Mill, Ricardo, J. B. Say, Roscher, Descartes, Francis Bacon, Locke, Kant, Fichte, Hegel, and Savigny. Many of the notebooks date from the late 1860s and thus, in the absence of more explicit information from Menger about his development, serve the function of intellectual diaries. Early versions of the actual manuscript of the *Grundsätze* exist in fragmentary form, mostly heavily revised. A table of contents, dated 1870, provides a useful comparison for later revisions and schemas.

The collection contains extensive materials on the subjects of money, the gold standard, and capital theory. The work on money, which is some of the best-ordered in the collection, Menger produced as an article for the second edition of *Handwörterbuch der Staatswissenschaften* in 1900, with substantial revisions for the third edition in 1909. Yet even after the latter edition, he continued to make changes and notations. His work on monetary reform grew out of an appointment to an Austrian state commission on currency studying the use of a single or double bullion standard. Newsclippings of the reports have been maintained in the printed matter series.

Although not direct concerns in the *Grundsätze,* capital and interest received much attention from Menger, particularly in his refutation of his colleague Eugen Böhm-Bawerk's work of 1885, *Geschichte und Kritik der Kapitalzinstheorien.* Holographic evidence suggests that after dealing with this subject extensively in the late 1880s, Menger did not return to it again until the second decade of the twentieth century, when he was no longer teaching. At that point he resumed his considerations of capital and interest but looked additionally at credit and property.

The series in the collection which seems more opaque and less easily classified by subject deals with Menger's speculation and theories about the goals and methods of research, specifically for political economy, and the classification of knowledge. The appearance of *Untersuchungen über die Methode der Socialwissenschaften, und der Politischen Oekonomie insbesondere* in 1883 provoked sharp criticism from Gustav Schmoller, representing the younger German Historical School. Their dispute came to be known as the *Methodenstreit.* In the following year Menger replied to Schmoller with his *Irrthümer des Historismus in der Deutschen Nationalökonomie.* After this he published no further major works, although he continued to produce articles and book reviews for many years. His notes and manuscripts indicate that his research came to an end only with his death.

Menger's professional contacts with respected colleagues such as Emil Sax, Eugen Philippovich, and Böhm-Bawerk demonstrate that although he refused to publish further, he did not work in isolation. The incoming correspondence shows a lively exchange of information about university teaching and politics, news of the profession, and current research. Letters also refer frequently to works of others in the profession. Menger's library of some 25,000 volumes attests as well that he kept abreast of contemporary literature. Few drafts of Menger's own letters exist in the collection. A large proportion of these seem to be addressed to Böhm-Bawerk.

Processing

The original order of this collection is completely lost. Karl Menger had possession of the papers immediately after his father's death in 1921. He used much of the material now in the series on economic principles and some of the material from the series on money for the publication of a second edition of his father's best-known work, *Grundsätze der Volkswirthschaftslehre.* A number of years later Friedrich v. Hayek ordered several of the folders containing notes and manuscripts. His numbers are visible on the outside upper left corner of a number of the hardcover folders. From time to time he also made notes about the content of a particular folder, but none of these notes is extensive. In the 1970s Albert Zlabinger was permitted access to some of the papers, primarily the material on money. His careful work and notations allow for the reconstruction of the development of Menger's article on money for *Handwörterbuch der Staatswissenschaften* and its subsequent revisions.

Carl Menger did not date all, or even most, of his work, and because he made frequent emendations to his own notes and text, dating is hazardous at best. For this reason all loose manuscript material has been arranged topically. Almost all material belonging to a particular folder, however, has been kept together. Folders have been retained. The only materials which lent themselves to something approximating original order are the bound notebooks which Menger himself numbered. Correspondence has been arranged chronologically.

The majority of the paper in this collection has an extremely high acid content, although it is not overly brittle. Many sheets are crumpled badly, especially at the edges, but little text has been lost. All newspaper clippings have been photocopied on acid-free paper.

Description of series

Notebooks, ca. 1867–1920 (box nos. 1–3).

Contain excerpts from works on political economy, definitions of economic terms, philosophy, and the nature of science. Many entries are Menger's notes from readings, but approximately one-third are his own musings and reactions. Not all notebooks are dated, but they fall into two periods, one in the late 1860s, the second in the 1910s. Arranged chronologically.

Notes on economic principles, ca. 1870–1919 (box nos. 3–9).

Copious revisions of the *Grundsätze* (unpublished during Menger's lifetime), arranged according to topic in roughly the same order as presented in the first edition of the *Grundsätze;* some notes from Karl Menger along with sections he chose to include in the posthumous second edition of the *Grundsätze.* Other topics covered extensively in this series are capital and interest, particularly in relation to Böhm-Bawerk's theories, and ownership and property.

Notes on money, ca. 1890s–1919 (box nos. 9–13).

Contains revisions of Menger's article on money in the second and third editions of the *Handwörterbuch der Staatswissenschaften.* This section is arranged roughly in the order of the second edition article. Where possible, folders have been labeled to indicate where the material would belong in either or both editions. Some of these manuscripts were used by Menger's son Karl in the second edition of the *Grundsätze*. There are also several folders on monetary reform, especially from Menger's service on an Austrian government commission to reform the currency and evaluate its relation to bullion standards.

Teaching materials, 1872, 1884–94, and n.d. (box no. 13).

Lecture notes from several semesters; one folder of student papers on the term "capital." Arranged chronologically.

Notes on methodology, 1860s–1919 (box nos. 14–20).

Notes and revisions for the *Untersuchungen,* material on the ensuing *Methodenstreit,* G. Schmoller, and Menger's subsequent refutation, *Irrthümer;* notes for the article on the *Klassifikation der Wissenschaften* and material refuting Wundt; many general notes and partial manuscripts, apparently for a book on methodology and the aims of research which would have included material on the inductive vs. deductive method and the importance of theory in research. Arranged topically.

Correspondence, 1863–1918, 1921–85 (box no. 20).

Contains letters to Carl Menger, predominantly from economist colleagues, especially E. Böhm-Bawerk, J. Conrad, E. Philippovich, E. Sax, and F. Wieser, concerning professional matters. Menger's drafts are in the minority; most seem to be to E. Böhm-Bawerk. Several letters concern early professional matters, Menger's association with Rudolf, the crown prince of Austria, and his appointment at the University of Vienna. The series also includes letters to Karl Menger, dating primarily from the 1920s and 1930s, although a small number date from the 1960s to the mid-1980s, from economists such as F. Hayek, L. Mises, O. Morgenstern, R. Schuller, J. Schumpeter, K. Wicksell, and R. Zuckerkandl. Matters covered include Karl Menger's publication of the second edition of his father's *Grundsätze* and his later work on the Austrian School.

Biographical and personal materials, 1860s– (box no. 21).

Contains a biographical sketch by F. Hayek which appeared in volume one of the Collected Works of Carl Menger (Series of Reprints of Scarce Tracts in Economic and Political Science, London School of Economics and Political Science, 1934) and various lists for a curriculum vitae of Menger. A valuable but short (48 leaves) diary which Menger kept from 1875 to 1893–94 lists major events since his birth in 1840 but deals primarily with Menger's health, his appointments as a journalist, employment in the press section of the Austrian prime minister's office, his association with Crown Prince Rudolf, university politics, and academic research. A folder contains notices of celebrations for Menger's seventieth and seventy-fifth birthdays, and obituaries.

There is one undated postcard/photograph of Menger and a friend fishing.

Related family materials (box nos. 22–23).

Contains an unidentified register of railways and financial institutions; a tribute to Anton Menger by K. Grünberg; various articles by Anton Menger; a diary, 1861–70, and obituaries of Max Menger; an article by Karl Menger; and articles by others.

Miscellaneous, undated (box no. 23).

Notes; bibliographical references on topics other than economics or methodology; partial catalog of Carl Menger's library arranged alphabetically.

Printed matter (box nos. 24–26).

A. Books and articles by Menger, many with his annotations; some proofs of items in press.

B. Reviews of Menger's works; articles sent to him by other authors.

C. Clippings on the Austrian university students' uprisings.

D. News clippings concerning articles by Menger and others.

Container list

Notebooks

Box 1
25 undated notebooks, ca. 1860s

Box 2
"Geflügelte Worte"
Excerpts to 1899
Unmarked, 1870
5 notebooks
6 notebooks, ca. 1909–18
4 notebooks, 1917
6 notebooks, 1918–20

Box 3
8 notebooks, 1903, 1917–19
4 notebooks, 1902–19, 1919–20

Notes on economic principles

Excerpts from English works; Sonnenfels and others
Miscellaneous notes

Box 4
"Excerpte"
"Theoretisches Repertorium," 1867
Grundsätze, table of contents, 1870

"Einleitung." Zusammenhängende aber nicht abgeschlossene Darstellung der theor. Nationalök. Seit 1871 aus dem Jahre 1889.
Einleitung I
"Güter Wesen"
Güter
"Oekon. Güter"

Box 5
"Arten der Güter"
"Ad Gut" (*Grundsätze*, ch. 2)
"Gut"
"Wirtschaft"
"Complicationen der menschlichen Wirtschaft"
"Gangbarkeit"; Wirtschaft und Güter
Wirtschaft, 2 folders
Subjekte der Wirtschaft
"Wirtschaft, 1907." Includes material on Bedürfnisse
"Wirtschaft, 1906–1907." Also, material for introduction to a 2d ed. Dates from ca. 1899.

Box 6
"Wirtschaft"; includes material on etymology, Güter, and an introduction to a 2d ed.
"Volkswirtschaft"
Vermögen
Notes on goods and needs, includes material from 1st ed. and Karl Menger's notes for 2d ed.
Notes on value, human demand, needs
Bedürfnisse
Misc. notes on needs, ca. 1912–16
"Bedürfnisse"

Box 7
"Bedürfnisse, 1907" [1898–1910] (2 folders)
Wert der: (1) Grundstücke und Bodennutzungen; (2) Arbeitsleistung
Wert (Problemestellung der Productivität des Capitals)
"Ad subjektive Wertlehre"
Wert
Wert; Tausch
"Tauschhandel"
"Theorie der Preises"

Box 8
Notes on monopoly (prices)
"Freihandel und Schutzzoll," 1908
"Diverses [ad Preislehre]," 1908

"Waare"
"Münze"; "Scheidemünze"; "Urkundengeld"
[Einkommen]: "Die Problemestellung"
"Einkommen"
Einkommen/Wert
"Erwerbswirtschaft und Aufwandswirtschaft"
"Kritik der Smith'schen Einkommens Analyze"
"Capitalseinkommen"
"Capitalbegriffe"
On Capital
"Capital: Erspartes Einkommen"
Misc. notes on etymology of terms, capital, and interest
Notes on exchange, capital, etc. (on back of railway map of Central
    Europe)
On: Vermögen, Capital, Einkommen
On origin of term "capital"; Wert; Vermögen
"Capital: Gegen Böhm"
On Böhm-Bawerk's theories: transcripts by A. Zlabinger
Typescript on capital
On Capital

Box 9
"Capital"
"Böhms Capitalzinstheorie"
Material on Böhm, including a draft obituary notice
Material on "Zinslehre," 1879
Notes on interest
Notes on production and interest
"Theorie des Vermögenertrages," 1901
On property and ownership
"Gemein-Eigentum"
"Besitz-Eigentum"
"Grund Eigentum"
Kritik ad Lotz, ca. 1890s–1910s

Notes on money

"Geld," sections 5–14 translated by A. Zlabinger
Transcripts of manuscripts by A. Zlabinger

Box 10
Miscellaneous notes, 2 folders
"Diverses ad Geld"
Excerpts on money

"Ueber die Natur und die Funktionen des Geldes"
"Ueber die Entwicklung der Geldwirtschaft"
"Geld," 2d ed.
"Geld," revisions to 2d ed.
"Aufgabe der Theorie des Geldes"
"Gangbarkeit"
"Bisherige Lösungsversuche [über die Erscheinung des Geldes]"

Box 11

"Entstehung des Geldes, 3 und 4. Aufl."
"Ob Geld Ware [sei]"
"Juristische Geldlehre," revisions to 2d ed., section 10; 3d ed., section 2
"Entstehung des Edelmetallgeldes"
"Vervollkommnung des Metallgeldes . . ."; "ad Münze"; "Scheidemünze" (2d ed., section 3; 3d ed., section 4)
"Währung" (2d ed., section 4)
"Beeinflussung des Geldwertes durch den Staat"
"Einfluss des Staates"

Box 12

"Funktionen des Geldes" (2d ed., sections 5–7; 3d ed., sections 6–9)
"Preismesser" (2d ed., section 8; 3d ed., section 10)
"Das Geld als Massstab des Tauschwertes," 2 folders (2d ed., section 9; 3d ed., section 11)
"Massstab des Tauschwertes; Entstehung des Irrthums, 1909"
Miscellaneous notes, 1911–15, with transcriptions by A. Zlabinger (concerns Tauschwert)
"Begriff des Geldes" (2d ed., section 10; 3d ed., sections 12–13)

Box 13

"Bedarf an Geld" (2d ed., section 11; 3d ed., section 14)
"Differenzierung des Geldes"
"Wertscalen"
Miscellaneous notes
"Neue Parthien"
Currency reform, 1892
Currency reform, clippings
Currency reform
Currency report notes

Teaching materials

Seminararbeiten über Kapitalbegriff, etc.
Lectures, 1872
Lectures, ca. 1884–94

Notes on methodology

Box 14
  Material on *Irrthümer*
  "Schmoller"
  "Franz. Nationaloekonomie"
  Notes on classical economics
  Untersuchungen, 1 p.
  "Die Frage über die Methode . . ." from *Juridicheski Westnik* no. 12
    (1884):581
  "Methode," 1876
  "Methode Material," 2 folders
  "Diverses ad Methode" pt. 1

Box 15
  "Diverses ad Methode" pt. 2
  Typed transcript of plan for work on method; related notes
  "Ad Methode"
  Miscellaneous notes
  "Grundrichtungen der Forschung"
  "Etymologie/Philosophie"
  "Schema für eine Classification der Wissenschaften überhaupt
  Notes on "Classification der Wissenschaften"
  "Classification der Wirtschaft. Wissenschaften"; includes material
    on "Erkenntnisziele der Forschung" and "die realistische Richtung
    der Forschung"
  "Classification der Wissenschaften," ca. 1892–1904

Box 16
  Printed work on plants, 11 pp., concerned with classification
  Verständnis und Voraussicht
  "Gegen Wundts Auffassung der Wissenschaft," 2 folders
  "Mathematik: Ideele Richtung," ca. 1895
  Erkenntnisziele/Richtungen der Forschung, 2 folders
  Material on directions of research, with special attention to "Deduc-
    tion," 1890s

Box 17
  On induction
  "Induction"
  "Ueber Wesen der Methoden . . ." (Induction/deduction)
  "Empirismus in der deutschen Nationaloekonomie," 2 folders (late
    1890s)
  "1. Empirische Gesetze; 2. Arten"
  "Material ad Unzulänglichkeit des Empirismus"
  "Empirismus, Realismus, Positivismus in deutscher Nat. Oek."

Box 18

"Realistische Richtung . . ."

"Ob exacte realistische Theorien auf Geb. d. Tat. Erscheinungen mogl?" (ca. 1890s)

"Realismus"

"Realistische auch idealistische Richtung der ideologischen Forschung"

"Theorie . . . Realismus . . ."; On Logik, 2 folders

Box 19

"Kritik von Wundts Logik"

"Causalität," ca. 1905–14

"Willensfreiheit; Ethik," ca. 1904–10

Notes on free will; self-consciousness, ca. 1912–14

Notes on role of value judgments in "Wissenschaft"

"Moral im Handel," scattered pp. and notes

Notes on philosophical topics, ca. 1907–13

Notes on philosophical topics, ca. 1910s, 3 folders

Box 20

Notes on philosophical topics, ca. 1910s

Correspondence

Carl Menger, 1863–84

Carl Menger, 1885–88

Carl Menger, 1889–1920 and n.d.

Karl Menger, 1914–85 and n.d.

Anton Menger, 19??

Biographical materials

Box 21

Diary, 1875–94 (with information from 1840)

Diary transcriptions and notes on Carl Menger's life by Karl Menger, 12 pp. and 1 blue notebook

Honors

1. Iron Cross, III class, 1876
2. "Correspondant," Institut de France, 1894; 2 letters of congratulation
3. "Correspondant," La Société de statistique de France, 1897
4. Certificate of Admission, Regia Lynceorum Academia, 1899
5. Honorary president for 1901, Institut international de sociologie, 1900
6. Requests for C. Menger to accept other positions; 1 envelope, 2 sheets

Miscellaneous information, dates, etc.

News clippings, articles in honor of Menger's 60th, 70th, and 75th birthdays, his retirement (1903), and on the occasion of his death

Commemoration of Menger on his 70th birthday by R. Zuckerkandl

Introduction to *Collected works of Carl Menger* (London School of Economics and Political Science), by F. Hayek

Photographs
1. Carl Menger?
2. "Daughter of Dr. Perin," 1911
3. Carl Menger and friend, n.d.

Related family material

Box 22

Unidentified register of railways and financial institutions

Anton Menger: "Sein Leben und Lebenswerk" (K. Grünberg); *Das Recht auf den vollen Arbeitsertrag;* "Neue Sittenlehre"; "Ueber die sozialen Aufgaben der Rechtswissenschaft"

Anton Menger: *Volkspolitik*

Anton Menger: *Neue Staatslehre*

Anton Menger (?): "Rede beim Antritte des Rectorats," 1874

Max Menger: Diary, 1861–70

Max Menger: *Die Reform der directen Steuern in Oesterreich*

Max Menger: Obituaries

Box 23

Karl Menger: "The logic of the laws of return" (reprint)

Karl Menger: articles
1. "Italien . . . Flugmalerei" (R. Vasari)
2. "On equilibrium in Graham's model of world trade . . ." (L. McKenzie)
3. "Pluralist approach to the philosophy of history" (K. Popper)
4. "Educational theatre and Unesco" (H. Schnitzler)
5. "Cowles Commission for Research in Economics"
6. "Derivation of bond pricing formula"

Karl Menger: Recht und Logik (F. Paradies)

Karl Menger: Miscellaneous news clippings

Karl Menger: Miscellaneous recollections, 1 partial page

Miscellaneous

Bill for *Neue Freie Presse,* 1909

Early writings

Writings

Entwurf der Statuten für die Redehalle

Printed description of university life, after 1903

Notes on Prague University student associations
Bibliographical references
Catalog of Carl Menger's library
List of materials in the Vienna University Library not in Menger's
personal library
"Von alten Bücher und Antiquare"
Notes on Austrian politics
Notes on progressive income tax
Miscellaneous notes, Carl Menger and Karl Menger (?)
"Sonnenfels"

Printed Matter

Box 24

News clippings: reviews by Carl Menger
News clippings: articles by Carl Menger
News clippings: reviews of Carl Menger's works
News clipping copies: reviews concerning Menger
News clippings: articles by Carl Menger on universities and their
reform
News clippings: miscellaneous
News clippings: reviews of *Grundsätze,* 2d ed.
Grundsätze, copies 1 and 2 (2 folders)
Grundsätze, unnumbered copy

Box 25

Grundsätze, unnumbered copy
Grundsätze, 2d ed., Handexemplar
Grundsätze, 2d ed., galley proofs for pp. 87–91, 99–101
Untersuchungen with Menger's annotations
Untersuchungen (2 folders)
Untersuchungen, bound in signatures with blank leaves. Used by F.
Hayek in preparing a 2d ed., nos. I–II, 1–10, 12–14.

Box 26

Untersuchungen, bound in signatures with blank leaves. Used by F.
Hayek in preparing a 2d ed., nos. 15–19
Irrthümer des Historismus with revisions by Karl Menger
"Zur Kritik der Politischen Oekonomie," 2 copies
"Zur Theorie des Kapitals," 2 copies in German; 1 translation in
French
"Grundzüge einer Klassifikation der Wissenschaften"
"On the origin of money"
"Ein Gesetz gegen Kartelle"
"Geld," 1900 (2d ed. of *Handwörterbuch*), 3 copies
"Geld," 1909 (3d ed. of *Handwörterbuch*), 6 copies

"Geld," 1909 (3d ed. of *Handwörterbuch*), 5 copies
Articles on currency reform
1. "Beiträge zur Währungsfrage . . ."
2. "Das Goldagio und der heutige Stand der Valutareform"
3. "Der Uebergang zur Goldwährung"
4. "Die Valutaregulierung in Oesterreich-Ungarn" (incomplete)
Miscellaneous works not by Menger
1. *Das Selbstbewusstsein* (T. Lipps), incomplete
2. On "geistige Arbeit," incomplete
Works by colleagues
1. "Zins" (Böhm-Bawerk)
2. "Preis" (Zuckerkandl)
3. "Sostarnyia chasti i metody politicheskoi ekonomii" (A. A. Isaeva)
Articles relating to Carl Menger and the Austrian School
1. Fundamentals of Austrian Economics (T. C. Taylor)
2. "Menger on Ricardo" (K. Yagi)
3. "Böhm-Bawerk's first interest theory" (K. Yagi)
4. Review of *Carl Menger and the Austrian School of Economics* (Jaffé)
Articles by Karl Menger
1. "Austrian marginalism and mathematical economics" (galley proofs; 1 English copy; 1 German copy; 1 German summary)
2. Program from "One hundred years of Carl Menger's *Grundsätze der Volkswirtschaftslehre*," 2 copies

Oversize Material

Printed matter: "Die Schillerzeit" (contribution by Menger, among others, to commemoration of Schiller, 1905)
Printed matter: review of Böhm-Bawerk's "Positive Theorie des Kapitals"
Biographical materials, honors: election to Societas Regia Edinensis, 1895
Biographical materials: application for habilitation, 1871
Miscellaneous: notes on Austrian student rising

I. Origins and economic policy

The influence of German economics on the work of Menger and Marshall

Erich W. Streissler

I

Intellectual history is overgrown with myth. The preconceptions of successive generations, and of generations preceding our own, make it difficult to uncover the truth. We tend to be wary of myths surrounding the interpretation of political or even of social history. As scientists trained in detached objectivity many of us are, however, naively surprised when confronted with distorted interpretations of the history of our own subject. But as intellectual history is often closely linked with political and social history, the same ideological forces which weave and shape myths here may be present there as well.

This paper addresses itself to uncovering three myths. The first is the myth that in its beginning the Austrian School, in particular Carl Menger, elaborated their novel insights quite independently and in actual contrast to German economics of their day. Or, as Joseph A. Schumpeter, one of the main originators of this first myth, put it in 1915: "As if out of another world—unexplainable and uncaused—Menger, Böhm-Bawerk and Wieser surfaced in the social economics of that day."[1]

The second myth is still more fundamental: it is the mental projection backwards in time of the Prussian-dominated imperial, unified Germany of about 1900 and its confusion with the quite different Germany of, say, 1825 or 1850, a country politically diffuse and dominated, at least intellectually, by the many independent, medium-sized German states. This is a backward projection to which the generation which had witnessed the catastrophic impact of the First World War was much too prone. But one has only to name the old and prestigious German universities to realize that they were all situated *outside* Prussia and, at least until the very late nineteenth century, also outside her influence: Heidelberg and

---

1. Schumpeter 1915, 9. In German: "Wie aus einer anderen Welt—unerklärlich, ursachenlos—sind Menger, Böhm-Bawerk und Wieser in der Sozialökonomie von damals aufgetaucht." In this article Schumpeter also gives an astonishing précis of the history of economic thought: there were three periods of intellectual prosperity (*Blütezeiten*) in economics, the first around 1700 (no names), the second 1750–1820 (marked by Quesnay and Ricardo; Smith is not mentioned), the third at the end of the nineteenth century, initiated by Menger!

Freiburg in Baden, Munich in Bavaria, Göttingen in Hanover, Leipzig (with the greatest law school) in Saxony, Tübingen in Württemberg, Marburg, Giessen, Jena, Erlangen, and so on.

True, the most expansionary university in Germany was the University of Berlin in the Prussian capital, founded only in 1810. It had a novel educational program. The Prussian state, which paid and appointed its professors, used this university more and more for the explicit purpose of inculcating national consciousness and even nationalistic sentiments through the manner in which German studies, or history, and also economics were taught there; and it did everything to foster the spread of these "modernized" subjects throughout Germany after the unification in 1871. In terms of the history of economic thought this second myth is thus equivalent to the confusion of Gustav Schmoller and his school (Schmoller became professor in Berlin only in 1882) with the economics dominated by Karl Heinrich Rau (1792–1870) in Heidelberg, Friedrich B. W. Hermann (1795–1868) in Munich, and later by Wilhelm G. F. Roscher (1871–94) in Leipzig. For it is with the work of these older men that Carl Menger linked up.

It is the misfortune of the thriving German tradition in economics around the middle of the nineteenth century that it was repudiated, on the one hand, by the Austrians from the third generation of the school onwards—Schumpeter's and Mises's generation—while on the other hand it was at the same time smothered by the Schmoller school in Germany itself. Add to this a stylistic difference—the dominant academic economists wrote *textbooks instead of monographs*—and we have found sufficient reasons for a third myth: that German economics around 1850 was unimportant. Actually, I think, Roscher was quite correct when he remarked in his monumental history of German-language economic thought for the period 1850 to 1875: "In the present age too, German economics is at least the equal of any economics in foreign countries."[2] German economics specialized in a strong subjective value mood, a protoneoclassical tradition, as one might call it, from which Menger could amply borrow; and he did so, citing mainly German authors in his *Principles of economics* (1871). In his own *Principles of economics*—a standard German title, not the typical English title "Political economy,"[3]—Alfred Marshall too used both the key unifying principle of German economics and many of its fundamental ideas. He

2. Roscher 1874, 1011: "Auch im vorliegenden Menschenalter steht die deutsche Nationalökonomik jeder ausländischen mindestens gleich."

3. Sir James Steuart, Ricardo, Malthus, McCulloch, Senior, Carey, Mill, and Jevons, among the better known, use the two words "political economy" in the titles of their treatises. Beginning with Rau in 1826, German authors have called their treatises, in general, books on *Volkswirtschaftslehre*, "economics." Marshall himself, of course, thought economics "the broad term," political economy "the narrower term."

says[4] that his *Principles* are "similar in some respects, though not in all, to that of volumes on *Foundations* (*Grundlagen*) which Roscher and some other economists have put in the forefront" of their collective volumes.[5]

II

For anyone who has actually read Menger's *Principles* it is quite puzzling how the first myth, that of Menger's intellectual isolation and his and the Austrian School's independence from German economics, could ever have arisen. The book certainly advertises its intense attachment to German economics—almost ad nauseam. The preface ends with the words

> It was a special pleasure to me that the field here treated, comprising the most general principles of our science, is in no small degree so truly the product of recent development in *German* political economy, and that the reform of the most important principles of our science here attempted is therefore built upon a foundation laid by previous work that was produced almost entirely by the industry of *German* scholars. Let this work be regarded therefore as a friendly greeting from a collaborator in Austria, and as a faint echo

4. Preface to the 8th edition; see Marshall 1961, 1:xii.

5. As an example of these three myths in practice I quote one of the most detached members of the third generation of the Austrian School, Karl Pribram (1877–1973) from his (posthumous) *History of economic reasoning:* "When viewed in the light of the intellectual atmosphere in which he developed his ideas, Menger showed perhaps more independence of thinking than Jevons or Walras. . . . Menger developed his conception of economics as an exact science in the course of a dispute with convinced adherents of organismic methods, such as Gustav Schmoller, who at the time exercised a predominant influence on the economic reasoning of Central Europe" (1983, 290).

It is easy to show that very few of the basic ideas of Menger's *Principles* cannot be found foreshadowed in the books of German economics that he knew well. Consequently he was immediately hailed by Roscher, for Roscher, not Schmoller, was the man "who at the time," when Menger's *Principles* were published, "exercised a predominant influence" on German economics. Menger was hailed as a successor to Hermann (as in fact he was, intellectually). And the reference to Schmoller in the last sentence of Pribram very nearly makes us forget that between the publication of Menger's sole book on economic theory, his *Principles* of 1871, and the start of the conflict with Schmoller in 1883–84 twelve whole years were to elapse, years in which the young Menger had already achieved both academic recognition and social distinction as the tutor to the Austrian crown prince. We should not forget that the conflict between Menger, the main professor of economics in the old and now-demoted German capital Vienna, and Schmoller, the main professor of economics (appointed in 1882, three years after Menger's appointment as full professor) in the new German capital Berlin—a conflict on the real issues of which most participants remained very hazy—was also a conflict over social and political influence. It was a signaling device to noneconomists responsible for professorial appointments in economics what a good German economist should look like. As so often happens, those who lost politically—and had to lose, because the Prussian Ministry of Education stood behind Schmoller—by and by turned world opinion in favor of the justice of their cause.

of the scientific suggestions so abundantly lavished on us Austrians by *Germany* through the many outstanding scholars she has sent us and through her excellent publications.[6]

The two mentions of Austria and the Austrians in this passage are, by the way, the only ones in the book, apart from a passing mention of the Austrian currency and the Austrian civil code. On the other hand the *Principles* name "Germany," the "Germans," or "German" contributions no fewer than twenty-three times altogether, and in the key passages at that: "A deeper treatment of the problem of the measure of use value is to be found only among the *German* writers."[7] "Perhaps nothing reveals the *German* tendency toward philosophical penetration of economics and the practical sense of the English better than a comparison of the treatments given the theory of value by *German* and English writers."[8] The next sentences make it clear that this is a nasty dig by Menger against English economists, who (to him) seemed incapable of making fine but essential distinctions. From a mere comparative count of national labels it would appear that "German"—and not, for instance, English—economics seemed to Menger to have comprised about one half of the whole subject.

And what of the authors Menger quotes? Here the preponderance of German economics is confirmed. Roscher, the central German textbook author of Menger's time, to whom the *Principles* are dedicated, is quoted most often: 17 times. He is followed by Hermann, perhaps the most protoneoclassical German author, who was nevertheless two generations older than Menger: 12 times. Adam Smith follows with 11, and J. B. Say with 10 quotes. Albert Schäffle (1831–1905), another German, Menger's immediate predecessor in Vienna and a likely referee of the *Principles* as a thesis,[9] also scores 10 quotes. Karl G. A. Knies (1821–98), another German, soon to be the most important teacher (in Heidelberg) of Böhm-Bawerk and Wieser,[10] nets 9 quotes—as does Aristotle.

6. Menger [1871] 1976, 49.
7. Menger 1976, 297.
8. Menger 1976, 307.
9. Schäffle became full professor (for economic theory) in Vienna in 1868. Menger had to expect that Schäffle would be the main judge on his thesis of habilitation, the *Principles,* published in the first half of 1871. However, Schäffle was appointed minister of trade in February 1871, being the guiding light in the short-lived Hohenwart cabinet (until October 1871). Just when Menger applied for his habilitation, Schäffle had thus moved on and could, as minister, no longer vote in the faculty. According to the then prevalent ideas of social status he also could not return to his professorial position after the termination of ministerial office, a professorship being three to four steps in rank below a minister (eight months of ministerial office earned Schäffle a pension as retired minister for the rest of his long life). Menger eventually succeeded Schäffle in his professorial chair, which had been so unexpectedly vacated. This chance event much facilitated his rise to academic prominence.
10. Old school friends of equal age, Eugen Böhm Ritter von Bawerk (1851–1914) and Friedrich Freiherr von Wieser (1851–1926) took leave of absence from their civil service

They are followed by E. B. de Mably de Condillac (1715–80), Roscher's pet source for notions on utility, who gets 8 quotes, and Rau, the main German textbook author in the generation before Roscher, who gets 7, as does A. R. J. Turgot (1727–81). Thus among the ten authors quoted most often, five are German, three French, one an ancient Greek, and only one, Adam Smith, is British. The Germans themselves—Roscher especially, but also Rau—quote non-German and especially British authors much more frequently than Menger does. Not that Menger does not know the English-language authors: Carey, Lauderdale, McCulloch, Malthus (5 times), John Stuart Mill, and Ricardo (6 times) are all quoted more than three times. But evidently they were not as important to Menger as German economists. We could immediately cap Ricardo's six quotations with the same number for the Germans Johann F. E. Lotz, Hermann Roesler, and Lorenz von Stein; and Malthus's five quotations with the same number for Bruno Hildebrand and Gottlieb Hufeland.

What is even more puzzling is that—apart from Schäffle and Stein in Vienna—Menger also neglects many Austrian-born authors or German-born authors teaching in Austria. He does not quote Josef von Kudler (1786–1853), professor in Vienna and the author of the standard Austrian textbook around 1850. A copy of this textbook, richly annotated by Menger, exists in the Menger library in Tokyo. Kauder thinks that Menger had studied this book as a student.[11] In the absence of pertinent

---

employment from 1875 to 1877 to study economics with (in succession) Karl Knies in Heidelberg, Bruno Hildebrand in Jena, and Wilhelm Roscher in Leipzig. By then both had read the *Principles* of the young associate professor in their hometown Vienna, and they presented marginalist papers in Knies's seminar.

11. See Kudler 1846. Kauder says: "Kudler's text-book was Menger's primer in economics. Menger's copy is well worn and dilapidated, and as a university student Menger underlined vigorously Kudler's theory of comparative value (*der verglichene Werth*). Kudler taught that man compares the different purposes for which commodities can be used. The higher the intensity of a specific need, the higher is the rank of the commodity which satisfies this need" (1965, 84). Of Kudler's textbook he says: "Apparently used by Menger for his state examination, 1860–63" (233).

We can see three misconceptions of Kauder's in these quotations. First, Kauder knows that in the early 1850s Kudler was the obligatory primer in economics; but a little later, this was no longer so, when the newly appointed professors had written their own texts, as Mischler did in 1857. Secondly, Kauder seems to suppose that Menger was examined in economics in his "state examination" (actually there were three). This would have been true in the last decades of the nineteenth century in Austria; but not for Menger, who pursued his juridical studies according to the statute of 1855 (2 October 1855, RBGl. 172/1855), which says: "Wer sich dem Staatsdienste auf Grundlage seiner rechts- und staatswissenschaftlichen Studien widmen will, ohne das Doctorat zu erwerben, hat . . . noch eine zweite und dritte Prüfung . . . zu bestehen." Only the third examination included economics. As Menger intended to take the doctorate and only then become a civil servant, he would not need to pass the examination in economics. And there is no evidence that he did. Thirdly, the topics Kauder assigns to Kudler can be found in many other German textbooks, which Menger certainly read before writing his *Principles*, for instance in Rau and especially in Hermann; and they certainly are treated extensively in

documentary evidence, I think this highly unlikely. No traces of material unique to Kudler can be found in the *Principles,* and Menger in later life disparaged Kudler.[12] I rather think that it was only pointed out to Menger after the publication of the *Principles* in 1871—either during the protracted process of habilitation which lasted more than a year in 1871–72 or when Menger was about to start his own lectures as associate professor in 1873—that he had overlooked a main Austrian textbook, and that Menger's notes in his copy thus postdate the *Principles.* For we have documentary evidence from the University of Cracow that Menger was only examined in "statistics" during his doctoral course, never in economics (for which subject he might have used Kudler's text in preparation).[13] And in his undergraduate days at the University of Prague (1860–63) he would have used (in the winter term of 1862–63) the then recently published textbook of his own professor, Peter Mischler, *Grundsätze der National-Oekonomie* (Vienna, 1857), and not Kudler's book.

For Menger *did* have a teacher in economics—and here another myth

---

the text by Mischler, Menger's actual teacher in Prague.

In another place Kauder says more correctly about Kudler: "Ob Menger das Werk vor oder nach seiner Staatsprüfung studiert hat, kann man heute nicht mehr feststellen" (1962, 12). He thinks Menger took from Kudler "die Unterscheidung zwischen unmittelbarem und mittelbarem Wert." This distinction in itself is common in the German textbook literature, and Menger does *not* use the actual *words* suggested. Basically Kauder thinks that Menger must have used Kudler as a student because he copied out from Kudler the sentence "Die Ursache des Tauschwertes ist die *Arbeit*" (the labor theory of exchange value), a theory which Menger certainly did not endorse as a mature man. But this is much more in conformity with my suggestion that Menger only thumbed through Kudler when he started to *teach* economics. He would then certainly have wished to point out to the students a decided *fallacy* in a textbook so recently used in Vienna. The labor theory of value had not been endorsed by Hufeland or Rau, had been disproved by Hermann (1832), and was anathema to Roscher (from 1854 onwards). Thus when Kudler put it down in 1846 it was already a *deviant* view in German economics. Actually, while Kauder thinks the Menger excerpt on the labor theory of value is proof of the fact that Menger read Kudler before his own "conversion" (presuming such a thing ever took place), I think it argues exactly in the opposite direction that Menger did *not* know Kudler's text before he wrote his *Principles.* For Menger always quoted authors on deviant opinions which he did not endorse—as he quoted Rau on wrongly thinking that only material goods are goods ([1871] 1976, 289 n. 6) and on wrongly assuming that trade is not productive (184).

12. Personalakt Carl Menger, Allgemeines Verwaltungsarchiv, Ministerium für Kultus und Unterricht, Vienna, 19 March 1903—Menger's application to be retired, and basically a brief autobiography of his own achievement—says that "Der verdienstvolle, indess in seinen literarischen Arbeiten unselbständige Professor der Nationaloekonomie an der Wiener Universität J. *Kudler* hatte keinen gelehrten Nachwuchs herangebildet" (14). Menger thus calls Kudler "unoriginal" and chides him with failing in the most important duty of a professor in Vienna: the recruitment of a sufficient number of future academic teachers.

13. Photocopies of the protocol of Menger's three "rigorous" doctoral examinations at the University of Cracow (March 1865 to March 1867) have been kindly provided for the University of Vienna by Dr. Kuninski.

has to go overboard.[14] Mischler (1821–64) was yet another of those German imports to Austria; he became full professor in Prague in 1855 and died only a year after Menger would have studied under him. Menger does not quote Mischler's textbook, but he was in fact considerably influenced by him, to the extent of taking over from him otherwise unexplainable passages nearly verbatim. There may be several reasons for Menger's not citing Mischler. One could be that he quoted from lecture notes without having the actual book at hand (professors then basically read their textbooks during lectures); another that Mischler, a strict Catholic, a conservative, and a protectionist, was politically obnoxious to him.[15]

Nor does Menger cite Julius Kautz's *Theorie und Geschichte der National-Oekonomik* (Vienna, 1858). Kautz (1829–1909) became full professor in Pest in 1862, which was then the next German-language university from Vienna, if you went 150 miles down the Danube. Kautz's book is, as far as I can see, the only economics text in the German language to mention H. H. Gossen;[16] in fact, it was from this book, written by a then "Austrian" (later, of course, Hungarian) professor and published in Vienna, that Jevons learned of the existence of Gossen.[17]

14. Friedrich von Wieser says about Menger and the *Principles:* "jenes Erstlingswerk . . . das er ohne Lehrer, Vorbild, noch Genossen, in stiller Zurückgezogenheit geschaffen hatte" (1923, 84). Like quite a few of Wieser's polite statements, this is more or less true if one knows the truth but misleading if one does not. As Mischler had died in 1864, Menger had no teacher—apart perhaps from Schäffle—while writing the *Principles* (1867–71); but he did have a teacher *before* that. Whether Roscher, to whom the *Principles* are dedicated, should not rank as a *Vorbild* (a model or paragon) is another question. Menger was at least very proud that he (and not for instance Schmoller) had succeeded Roscher as a member in the Académie des sciences morales et politiques (Institut de France) in Paris.

15. Menger did cite, however, the other professor of economics in Prague, Leopold Ritter von Hasner (1860). Hasner would not have taught Menger, because he was away from Prague serving in high political office in Vienna in 1862–63, but it was wise to quote him, as he was minister of education and briefly even prime minister when Menger wrote.

16. Kautz 1858, 9 nn. 1–2: "(1) Eine formelle Theorie und Philosophie des Genusses (und noch dazu auf mathematischer Grundlage!) hat in jüngster Zeit Fr. [*sic*] Gossen in seinem Werke 'Entwicklung der Gesetze des menschlichen Verkehrs' 1854 (S.1 bis 45 und sonst) zu liefern gestrebt. Manches gute, aber freilich auch Breite enthält in dieser Beziehung Mischler's National-Oekonomie I, S.175–184. (2) Gossen bemerkt (o.c. S.2): dass alle Menschen ihren Genuss stets zum höchsten zu bringen streben. . . ." Kautz thus attributes "a formal theory and philosophy of pleasure (and that on a mathematical foundation!)" to Gossen. Note that Menger's teacher Mischler is quoted immediately after Gossen. I owe this reference to Kautz on Gossen to Professor Antál Matyas of the University of Budapest.

17. Professor Antál Matyas has provided me with a photocopy of the German summary of an article published in Hungarian in Budapest in 1930 by Miyoji Hayakava, which says (I translate): "Jevons's attention was called to Gossen by his colleague Robert Adamson, who had found some remarks about this author in Julius Kautz, *Theorie und Geschichte der Nationalökonomie.*" Doubtless it was the phrase about the "mathematical foundation" of Gossen that kindled Jevons's interest. See also Kauder 1965, 81–82.

Gossen was thus nearly within the grasp of Menger from the start, though probably he would have appreciated Gossen's thought just as little in 1869–70 as he did in the 1880s.[18] And in fact he need not have known about him either, because all those ideas of Gossen which the Austrian School actually used were already around in the German literature which Menger read.

Menger thus tried to attach himself closely to German economics, in contrast to English and even to his native Austrian economics. How did the German economists, on whom one might say he fawned so obsequiously, receive him? Here again the myth, which tends to confound Schmoller a decade later with Roscher in the early 1870s, cannot go uncontradicted. Roscher published his monumental history of German economics in 1874, only three years after Menger's *Principles,* two years after Menger passed his habilitation and only one year after he became the most junior associate professor in the German-language area. In a history of thought one does not generally dwell long on the most recent developments. But Roscher gives Menger a full four lines, while many other important younger economists of the day get only half a line (L. Brentano, for instance) or go unmentioned, like Menger's own (by then dead) teacher, Mischler. Roscher notices among "those economists, who are continuing in the road of Hermann . . . finally the Austrian C. Menger with his very abstract, always original and frequently quite fruitful conceptual analysis which is usually founded on a thorough knowledge of the history of thought. For instance, he examines price formation first for the case of isolated exchange, then for monopoly trading and only finally under the influence of competition on both sides."[19] Coming from Roscher, who prided himself on his vast knowledge and his felicitous use of the history of economic thought (and rightly so), the reference to Menger's "thorough knowledge" on this point is high praise by a grand master. And we should not think the remark about Menger's treatment of competition (as only the limiting case) superficial. For Menger is indeed distinguished among the founders of "marginalism" for the theoretical importance he attached to not

18. Kauder 1965, 82: "Menger had bought his copy of Gossen on May 8, 1886 . . . Menger did not approve of Gossen, rejecting his purely hedonistic approach, his emphasis on labor, and the application of mathematics in the realm of psychology."

19. See Roscher 1874, 1040: "Endlich der Oesterreicher C. Menger, mit seiner sehr abstracten, meist auf gründliche Dogmengeschichte gestützten, immer selbständigen und oft recht fruchtbaren Begriffsanalyse, die z.B. die Preisbildung zuerst beim isolirten Tausche, dann beim Monopolhandel und erst schliesslich unter dem Einflusse beiderseitiger Concurrenz erörtert."

That this was considered high praise by contemporaries is shown by the fact that the Vienna faculty quotes this passage in support of Menger's appointment as full professor. See Personalakt, note 12 above: "Roscher selbst, gegenwärtig eine der ersten Autoritäten auf dem Gebiete der Nationalökonomie, spricht in seiner *Geschichte der Volkswirtschaftslehre in Deutschland* von Menger mit besonderer Wertschätzung."

fully competitive situations.[20] The fact that Menger was a subjective-value theorist or used diminishing marginal utility was, as we shall see, only "old hat" for Roscher. It merited no comment but was implied in the statement that Menger continued the road followed by Hermann.

What was even more important, in the twelfth (1875) edition of his own textbook, the *Foundations,* Roscher quotes Menger no fewer than seven times, more than twice as often as Schmoller and about as much as that very senior scholar, Lorenz von Stein.[21] (This edition is, by the way, also the one which acquaints German students with the fact that in the preceding year L. Walras had published his *Eléments:* nothing parochial about Roscher!) Mention by Roscher could make or mar a German-language scholar, as Knies bitterly remarked.[22]

Nor is it true that Menger's *Principles* received unfavorable reviews.[23] If neither the reviews nor Roscher really raved about Menger, this was simply due to the fact that, as we shall see, German economists were already so used to subjective-value economics that they did not grasp the full consequences of Menger's "reform." After all, those were not even fully brought out by Menger himself, but only by three subsequent generations of his school. At least the Vienna faculty could credibly claim when suggesting Menger for appointment as associate professor in 1873 that his *"Foundations [sic!] of Economics* had met with a very favorable reception by the experts."[24] And from 1872 to 1875 Menger was offered a professorship by no fewer than three German-language universities outside Austria: the Technical University of Karlsruhe, the Polytechnical University of Zurich (with a likelihood of simultaneous appointment at the University of Zurich), and finally the University of Basel.[25]

20. Roscher too was especially interested in noncompetitive pricing and may therefore have been particularly appreciative of this aspect of Menger. See Roscher 1875, §§ 101, 112, 113. Menger is promptly quoted in § 101 and twice in § 112.

21. See Roscher 1875, 5, 13, 95, 214, 216, 232, 233.

22. Knies 1882, iv.

23. In the most important review of the *Principles,* in *Jahrbücher für National-ökonomie und Statistik* 18 (1872): 342–45, Menger is favorably compared with Mangoldt (no mean competitor, as we shall see) and a number of laudatory remarks, such as "mit Vergnügen," "angemessene Begriffsuntersuchung," "tüchtiger Ansatz," are heaped on him. What is criticized is his "pretension of writing a textbook on general economics," which for such large fields should be left to older scholars. The surfeit of textbooks is criticized sarcastically. Having myself read about twenty for the period 1825–75 and knowing many more to exist, I cannot think this latter remark is wholly misplaced!

24. Personalakt (see note 12 above), Report of the minister of education to the emperor, 2 September 1873, with appointment of Menger by the emperor, 19 September. Menger's *Grundsätze* are misreported as *Grundzüge,* of which book it is said: "[es] in fachmännischen Kreisen eine sehr günstige Beurtheilung fand."

25. The call to the chair of the old University of Basel, evidently the one vacated in 1873 by F. J. Neumann, is mentioned in the Personalakt (note 12 above). Menger seems proud of it.

Even in later years Menger's close connection with and dependence on German economics was not forgotten by members of the older generation. F. von Wieser stressed this connection in the obituary notice for the Academy of Sciences, though not in his biographical article on Menger for the general public: "It is usually overlooked that M.'s *Principles* had been prepared for in an important way by the older [!] German theory." Wieser then enumerates "the fundamental concepts of the German textbook"—"especially wants, goods, value in use and value in exchange"—and continues: "In general these fundamental concepts were empty boxes, which only an economist of the rank of Hermann could fill with content, but even as mere boxes they had their significance. By positing them one staked out claims, one showed up the questions which had to be elucidated if one was to achieve clear insight. The insights reached were determined by these claims to a not inconsiderable extent."[26]

But the next generation of the Austrian School, dominated by Schumpeter and Mises, no longer wished to see any German connection. Immediately before and after the First World War a liberal political position in Austria was nearly synonymous with an Anglophile mental outlook and opposition to German influence. Schumpeter in particular was vehemently Anglophile and markedly anti-German. He married into the English establishment; he was involved in the highly hazardous maneuvers to get Austria out of the war in 1916 by a separate peace which would have left her German ally isolated;[27] and he fell in 1919 as minister of finance precisely because he had done everything in his power to render impossible an "Anschluss" of Austria towards Germany by facilitating the sale of important Austrian firms to non-German (i.e., Italian) foreign interests.[28] At that time the Austrian socialists and the foreign secretary, Otto Bauer, in particular, stood for the "Anschluss" of Austria to Germany. But Bauer and the socialists in general were the pet aversion of Mises. Is it so very farfetched to assume that the strongly held political views of Schumpeter and Mises also clouded their perception of the history of their subject? But let us stick to published evidence. Schumpeter wrote the article on the history of economic thought in the collective standard textbook of German economics in 1914, an

26. Österreichische Akademie der Wissenschaften, Bericht des Sekretärs der phil.-hist. Klasse, 1922, obituary on Menger by Friedrich Wieser, 214ff. Wieser says: "Es wird meist übersehen, dass M.'s *Grundsätze* durch die ältere deutsche Theorie in besonderer Weise vorbereitet ist" (245). The remaining quotations translated into English are to be found on 245–46. On p. 249 Wieser once again speaks of Menger as "aus dem Boden der älteren deutschen Ökonomie hervorgewachsen."
27. On the numerous and insistent anti-German political activities of Schumpeter during the First World War see Seidl 1984, 201–5.
28. See März 1981.

article of 106 pages.[29] In this, before dealing extensively with the clash of the Austrian with Schmoller's historical school, he achieves the incredible feat of mentioning the older German economists of the first three-quarters of the nineteenth century in a mere two pages (55–56), though the reader is made acquainted in detail with every conceivable minor English-language economic luminary of the pre-Marshall (i.e., pre-1890) period.[30] On the German economists Schumpeter passes one of his characteristic value judgments: "On these little has to be said. Not as if they had written little; not as if not now and then something of value cannot be found in them. But no spirit flows in these books."[31] But even Schumpeter notes that these German economists "form a school, which by and by and especially through Hermann gained characteristic features, particularly in the theory of value."[32]

III

What is it that the marginalist revolution tried to achieve and what did it achieve up to about 1890? It replaced Ricardo's cost-of-production theory of value by a price theory mainly geared towards demand; and in doing so it realized that production costs themselves were demand-dependent. Let us quote the leading author of this new price theory:

> Even if we were willing to leave aside completely the large number of price determinations where we can think of no connection whatsoever with production costs, we would still find that even for those goods which come to market regularly and in any desired quantity the price is in no way determined by cost alone, as Ricardo and his school teach. The first and most important factor determining price is, in fact, in all cases demand, the main roots of which are the value in use and the ability to pay of the purchasers. From demand and from what the demanders are willing to bid for a good we see which amount of goods they are willing to forgo for the sake of the desired good and this determines how high the cost of the least remunerative production can be.[33]

29. Schumpeter 1914.

30. Schumpeter mentions in italics in the main text in chapter 3 on the "classical system" E. West, de Quincey, Sidgwick, A. Hamilton, D. Raymond, Th. Cooper, John Rae, H. Carey, H. George, Gunton, F. A. Walker, Mrs. Marcets, Miss Martineau, Whately, Godwin, Gray, Sadler, Everett, MacLeod, Fosters, Torrens, Th. P. Thompson, M. Longfield, Longe, and Thornton, in that order—apart, of course, from Ricardo, the two Mills, Senior, McCulloch, and Cairnes, who are treated extensively.

31. Ibid., 55–56: "Ueber diese ist wenig zu berichten. Nicht als ob wenig geschrieben worden wäre; nicht als ob darin nicht manches Gute gewesen wäre. Aber es weht kein Geist in diesen Büchern."

32. Ibid., 56.

33. Hermann 1832, 95: "Wollte man auch die grosse Zahl von Preisbestimmungen ganz übergehen, bei denen gar kein Bezug auf Productionskosten denkbar ist, so erhellet doch,

This is not Menger or one of the Austrians; it is Friedrich B. W. Hermann in 1832, fifteen years after the first publication of Ricardo's *Principles*. It is no remark in passing but the summary of thirty pages of analysis in which (for the first time, I think) the demand-dependence of the actual equilibrium cost of production is announced. Hermann treated this question in a whole chapter, "The influence of price changes on cost,"[34] basically generalizing Ricardo's theory of diminishing returns in agriculture to one applicable to all kinds of production (for Hermann there is always an array of firms with different costs). Many Germans are credited with various types of generalizations of Ricardo's theory of rent;[35] such generalization was a permanent concern with them. Notice further that Hermann uses a type of opportunity-cost argument (demand being measured by the amount of goods people are willing to forgo for the desired good). This would be widely used in many varieties in German economics after Hermann—and was even used before him, in fact from Rau's time on—and is thus an invention neither of Menger nor of Wieser, as Wieser himself liked to believe.

But were not the fundamental concepts of the Austrians much more subjectivist than the concepts of the economists preceding them? Was it not their contention that "all goods are only goods by virtue of the mind-picture which one man or several men make themselves of them"; that there is an "absolute sovereignty of opinion in the realm of goods and of wealth"; and that therefore "things that become goods . . . though they are mainly made by labor do not become goods because of that labor"? That, again, is not Menger; it is Gottlieb Hufeland, the constantly quoted first author on subjective economic concepts in German economics, and the date is 1807 (ten years *before* Ricardo).[36] Or if you prefer a source closer in date and also more immediate in importance for

dass auch von den regelmässig und in beliebiger Menge zu Markt kommenden Gütern der Preis keineswegs durch die Kosten allein bestimmt wird, wie Ricardo und seine Schüler lehren. Der erste und wichtigste Factor der Preise ist vielmehr in allen Fällen die Nachfrage, deren Hauptwurzeln der Gebrauchswerth des Guts und die Zahlungsfähigkeit der Käufer sind. Aus der Nachfrage und dem, was die Begehrer für das Gut bieten, ergiebt sich, auf welchen Betrag von Gütern sie um des Verlangten willen zu verzichten gedenken und hieraus, wie hoch die Kosten der wenigst ergiebigen Production sich belaufen dürfen."

34. Hermann 1832, 82ff.: "Einfluss der Preisänderung auf die Kosten."

35. Roscher (1874) names Hufeland, Schäffle, and Mangoldt (661) and Hermann (867). The statement about Hufeland is not without justice, though his "generalization" antedates Ricardo by ten years!

36. "Alle Güter sind nur Güter vermöge der Vorstellung, die Menschen (einer oder mehrere) sich davon machen" (Hufeland 1807, 20); "unumschränkte Herrschaft der Meynungen im Reiche der Güter und des Vermögens" (23); "dass die Dinge, welche Güter werden, . . . zwar grösstentheils durch Arbeit entstehen mögen; dass sie aber durch Arbeit nicht Güter werden, sondern dass dieses nur durch die Vorstellung von ihrem Werth, von ihrer Tauglichkeit als Mittel zu einem Zweck, den man hat und erreichen will, abhängt" (39).

Menger, here is the definition by the man to whom Menger must have presumed he would have to present his thesis of habilitation, his immediate predecessor, Albert E. F. Schäffle: "Value [is] a relationship between all goods in human consciousness . . . [it is] predominantly of a *subjective* nature. It exists in a consciousness of purpose in matters economic (*Zweckbewusstsein*)."[37] Note the insistence on "purpose" or the *causal* relationship of goods, so typical of Menger himself. What is a want to the Austrians? It is "the sense of a deficiency with the endeavor to redress it"—once again Hermann,[38] not Menger! What is a good? "Anything which is known to be useful for the satisfaction of a true human need"; this is Roscher's standard textbook definition, quoted by Menger.[39] For the justification of a part of this definition Roscher himself quotes Mischler, Menger's own teacher. Naturally this definition— since Hufeland and Hermann—also includes services, not only commodities in the narrower sense. Consequently the economy is "the sum of all those activities which are necessary to provide a certain person with goods"[40]—that is Rau's standard definition. Roscher in the next generation is even more subjectivist: "By economy we understand the well-planned activity of man in order to satisfy his needs for external goods," and "Every normal economy tries to achieve the highest personal utility with the lowest expenditure of cost."[41]

These concepts, constantly reiterated by dozens of economists, were not "empty boxes," as Schumpeter tries to make out. By using them one could show, for instance, that exchange generally increases utility (or value in use; the two terms were synonymous, according to Hermann)[42] and that therefore trade is just as productive as material production. Or as Knies, among others, put it in 1855: "Exchange presupposes that for the individuals concerned value in use of the same quantity of goods is of different magnitude. Exchange takes place not because two quantities of two kinds of goods are equal, but because they are on both sides

37. Schäffle 1867, 52: "Der Werth [ist] eine Beziehung aller Güter im menschlichen Bewusstsein . . . [er ist] vorherrschend *subjectiver* Natur. Er existirt im wirthschaftlichen Zweckbewusstsein."
38. Hermann 1870, 5: "dieses Gefühl eines Mangels mit dem Streben ihn zu beseitigen."
39. Roscher 1864, 1: "alles dasjenige, was zur Befriedigung eines wahren menschlichen Bedürfnisses anerkannt brauchbar ist." Menger quotes the definition (1871, 2; 1976, 287–88).
40. Rau 1855, 2: "die sämmtlichen Verrichtungen welche zur Versorgung einer gewissen Person mit [Gütern] bestimmt sind."
41. Roscher 1864, 2: "Unter Wirthschaft verstehen wir die planmässige Thätigkeit des Menschen, um seinen Bedarf an äusseren Gütern zu befriedigen." The 12th ed. (1875) commences § 11 on "Wirthschaft" with the sentence: "Jede normale Wirthschaft ist darauf gerichtet, den höchsten persönlichen Nutzen mit dem geringsten Kostenaufwande zu erzielen" (20).
42. Hermann speaks of "Gebrauchs- oder Nutzwerth" (1832, 4, 68).

in opposite ways esteemed unequal."[43] Rau had already made the same point, only in less pithily quotable words.[44] And after Rau it was also standard to remark that the social product had to be evaluated in terms of utility.[45] Mischler, Menger's teacher, even pointed out that utility was the correct measuring rod for phenomena concerning the economy as a whole; value in exchange, (i.e., prices) only serves as a measuring rod for the individual household![46]

Against the background of those dozens of closely interlinked German economists, mainly between 1825 and 1875, copiously using subjective-value ideas, a young scholar who in 1871 presented another book full of subjective-value notions and anticlassical theses certainly was no maverick. With Solow, Menger might have said: "It was a little like trotting down to the sea, minding your own business like any nice independent rat, and then looking around and suddenly discovering that you are a lemming."[47] Menger, of course, was a "reforming" lemming trying to point the way to a slightly different sea. Nevertheless in the German-language area of his day it was quite difficult *not* to publish a book in the subjective-value vein. The real revolutionary was Schmoller, not Menger! In fact, after about forty years of subjective-value theory, Menger appeared even a little old-fashioned and outdated; young sparks tended to move on to a "fresher" approach.

But was not the essence still missing, the concept of diminishing marginal utility, the equalization of different utilities by the rational consumer, and finally factor price valuation by marginal product? Is not this the key sentence of the marginal utility revolution: "The more the quantity of a useful commodity is increased, the more the utility of each piece diminishes as long as the want has not changed"? That sentence, originally printed in italics, is by Bruno Hildebrand, the date being 1848;[48] and Menger knew it, for he quotes and criticizes the sentences immediately following it.[49] It was in fact familiar to every German-language economist, as Knies had elaborated on this idea in a frequently cited central article on the theory of value[50]—Knies, in whose seminar

43. See Knies 1855, 467: "Schon der Tauschverkehr setzt voraus, dass für die Individuen der Gebrauchswerth derselben Güterquantität ein verschieden grosser ist. Er findet statt, nicht weil man zwei Quantitäten zweier Arten von Gütern gleich, sondern weil man sie in entgegengesetzter Weise auf beiden Seiten ungleich schätzt."
44. Rau 1826, § 163, p. 114.
45. Rau 1826, § 55, p. 40; § 62, p. 44.
46. See Mischler 1857, 222ff. Similar ideas had already been suggested tentatively by Rau (1826, 41ff.).
47. See Solow 1974, 2.
48. Hildebrand 1848, 318: "Je mehr die Quantität eines nutzbaren Gegenstandes vermehrt wird, desto mehr fällt bei unverändertem Bedürfniss der Nutzwerth jedes einzelnen Stückes."
49. Menger 1976, 297: "Hildebrand's treatment gave an incomparable impetus to investigation."
50. See note 43 above.

both Böhm-Bawerk and Wieser presented their marginal utility ideas in 1875–76 (later visiting the seminar of Hildebrand himself). Similar statements implying declining marginal utility can be found in many other German publications.[51] The equimarginal principle of utility in demand was used by Mangoldt in 1863 as a condition of market equilibrium.[52] And Mischler, Menger's teacher, at least came close to stating "Gossen's second law": in a long passage on the rational use of resources he says that "everyone will buy no more of a certain type of good for a given want than he can use from a rational point of view . . . if he has a surplus . . . he will try to use it as a means of exchange for acquiring another good."[53] The use of a factor only up to the point where its cost corresponds to the marginal-value product had already been explained by Rau in a drawn-out quantitative example.[54] The more complicated idea of marginal-product pricing of factors is also frequently suggested, particularly by Hermann;[55] it is most cogently stated by Schüz in 1843 for the case of labor (Schüz uses the same idea for all factors):

The price of a service is determined according to the general rule of price formation. Therefore we have first to look at the value of

51. Certainly in those of Mangoldt (see below), e.g., Mangoldt 1863, 48 (at the bottom). Roscher treated declining marginal utility in his earlier editions in § 6 (e.g., 5th ed., 1864) but dropped it later (e.g., 12th ed., 1875).

52. Mangoldt 1863, 57–58. He says on p. 57: "In dem Falle gegenseitig sich vertretender Güterarten . . . bezeichnet das Verhältniss ihrer Preise dasjenige der ihnen zuerkannten Nutzwerthe" (the relative prices equal the relative utilities). Menger quotes Mangoldt in the *Principles* (1976, 311).

53. Mischler 1857, 231: "Jeder wird nun nicht mehr von einer gewissen Gattung von Gütern für ein bestimmtes Bedürfniss ankaufen, als er eben vernünftiger Weise aufzuwenden hat. . . . Wer nun doch einen Überschuss bei der Verwendung eines Gutes behielt, sucht ihn möglichst zu benützen, und zwar dadurch, dass er ihn als Tauschmittel zur Erwerbung eines anderen Gutes verwendet" (most of this is in italics).

54. Rau 1826, § 219, p. 163. Note that he was writing at the same time as Johann Heinrich von Thünen (1826). Thünen is credited with the first use of marginal productivity theory in German economics. More correctly we should say, the first *extensive* use! Occasional remarks on this point or brief examples were by then already extant in the textbook literature.

55. Hermann says in a truly astounding passage: "For the entrepreneur does not buy labor for consumption purposes, but for the purpose of resale of its product; he acts only as an agent of the consumers of the product. Only what the consumers give for the product, constitutes the true remuneration of the service of the worker . . . labor is in the last resort always meant to serve a want directly and to be paid out of the income of the consumer. The difference between personal services and the so-called productive labor fixed in materials is thus seen to vanish" (1832, 281).

Hermann furthermore suggests numerous directions of *substitutability,* thus introducing a further key notion of neoclassical economics.

His statement on demand-dependent (and evidently rising) marginal cost (in italics) also merits quotation: the lower limit to price is determined by "the cost for that part of the total mass of a product, which is produced by the least productive means of production or under the least favorable circumstances, whose use is made necessary in order just to satisfy existing needs" (1832, 88).

These sentences show that Menger did not have to go to Kudler to learn the idea of immediate and intermediate values (see note 11 above).

labor. But the value of labor is esteemed by him who pays wages according to its result. The more this result answers to his demands and wants, the more valuable the labor is to him and the more is paid for it in the utmost case (maximum price). In any business the wage is thus determined (1) by the degree of productivity of labor and the remunerativeness of the occupation which is carried on with the cooperation of the laborer.[56]

A more succinct nonmathematical formulation of marginal-value product can hardly be found. And it is constantly held before the eyes of the German economist by the standard textbook of the third quarter of the nineteenth century, by Roscher, who says: "In each producing establishment (and also in the economy as a whole!) the additional product which the worker, who is last employed, produces is of decisive importance for the level of wages of his equals."[57]

Thus we see that the basic marginal concepts were all there in German economics for Menger to use. He had only to clarify them and to apply them in a coherent framework.

IV

What were the key notions of German economics between about 1825 and 1875? Did it have any overriding ideas which gave it structure? It certainly did!

First, it tried to *blend the classical theory of growth and production* (in the sense of the creation of the wealth of nations) *with a theory of price* (and distribution!) *governed by individual demand and utility.* In that way it was *neo*classical in the sense of Marshall: half classical, half neo. In other words, it blended the essence of Adam Smith—the division of labor, the importance of saving, the vital role of the factors of production, labor, and capital—with Sir James Steuart's price theory of demand and supply, leavened with the subjective utilitarianism of Condillac. Steuart is repeatedly quoted by Hufeland and later by Hermann,

56. Schüz 1843, 286: "Dieser Preis der Dienste bestimmt sich nach den allgemeinen Regeln der Preis-Bildung. Es ist daher zunächst der *Werth der Arbeit* in Betracht zu ziehen. Der Werth der Arbeit aber wird von dem, der sie belohnt, nach ihrem *Resultate* geschätzt. Je mehr dieses Resultat den Forderungen und Bedürfnissen desselben entspricht, desto werthvoller ist die Arbeit für ihn, desto mehr wird im äussersten Falle für sie bezahlt (Preis-Maximum). Bei allen Erwerbs-Geschäften ist daher der Lohn bedingt (1) *durch den Grad der Productivität der Arbeit und der Einträglichkeit des Gewerbes, das unter Mitwirkung des Arbeiters betrieben wird.*"

57. Roscher 1864, § 165, p. 330: "In jedem Productionsbetriebe* ist daher das Mehrerzeugniss, welches der zuletzt angestellte Arbeiter hervorbringt, das regelmässige Maximum des Lohnes für seines Gleichen." By the 12th ed., he had added (at the asterisk) the reference that this was also true for the economy as a whole—"(auch im Ganzen der Volkswirthschaft!)"—and had changed the words "das regelmässige Maximum des Lohnes" into "von massgebendem Einflusse auf die Lohnhöhe" (1875, 367).

by Roscher, and by Menger. Adam Smith had set out, as he himself put it, to refute every "fallacious principle" in Steuart's book "without once mentioning it"[58]—with the obvious intention of condemning Steuart to oblivion by silence. With respect to the German university tradition, Smith was not successful in that. The Germans continued to read Steuart, and the fact that Steuart saw a much larger agenda for the state than Smith rather recommended him to German authors, coming as they did from an environment of recent and not quite unsuccessful mercantilist experiments.[59]

The German economists between 1825 and 1875 rightly saw that the classicists' theory of wealth generation in no way depended on their theory of value and of price. In other words, Smith went down well with them but not so Ricardo, who tried to fuse wealth creation and distribution. It became standard German practice (from Hermann in 1832 onwards) to refute the labor theory of value: "Purely national is the English notion," said Roscher, "that the equilibrium of prices would depend upon the fact that all goods should have as much value as they had cost in terms of labor," quoting Condillac as his key witness against this "English" peculiarity.[60] To the Germans since Rau prices had depended upon demand *and* supply conditions and, since Hermann, much more on demand—which they always treated first and in utility terms—than on supply. Demand and supply could not be treated superficially: "We examine what are the fundamental aspects on which supply and demand themselves depend," says Roscher.[61]

And here we arrive at the second key notion of German economics, the idea which I call its *protoneoclassical* mood: *all* prices have to be treated in *logically the same* demand and supply framework, in which demand and supply are deduced from their underlying causes. Factor

58. See Adam Smith's letter to William Pulteney, 5 September 1772, quoted in Rae 1965, 253–54.

59. Roscher remarks that it is "eine nationale Eigenthümlichkeit der Deutschen . . . die aus England oder Frankreich eingeführte Regel der *Verkehrsfreiheit* durch zahlreiche Ausnahmen zu Gunsten der Staatseinmischung zu durchbrechen" (1874, 1014–15).

60. Roscher 1864, § 107, p. 200: "Echt national ist die englische Ansicht, als wenn das Gleichgewicht der Preise darauf beruhete, dass alle Güter so viel Werth hätten, wie sie Arbeit gekostet." Condillac is quoted verbatim on p. 201. Menger evidently learned from Roscher the importance of Condillac for his own subjectivism. Roscher's rejection of the labor theory of value infuriated Karl Marx, who was not aware that it only summarized standard German practice, as he seems to know (according to *Das Kapital*) only Roscher among the German textbook authors. See Marx [1867] 1969, 174: "Weil Condillac noch nicht die geringste Ahnung von der Natur des Tauschwerts besitzt, ist er der passende Gewährsmann des Herrn Prof. Wilhelm Roscher für seine eignen Kinderbegriffe." Roscher replied in his 12th ed. (1875), § 47, p. 99: "Wirklich beruhet z.B. das ganze System von K. Marx auf dem ohne Beweisversuch angenommenen Irrthume der Ricardo'schen Schule."

61. Roscher 1864, § 101, p. 191: "Wir untersuchen daher, von welchen tiefer liegenden Verhältnissen Ausgebot und Nachfrage selbst abhängen."

prices are just as much prices as commodity prices: *distribution is therefore part of price theory,* just another side of the theory of *exchange.* This is the basic message of Rau's standard textbook, the book with which Menger started his systematic studies in the autumn of 1867.[62] In a typical German textbook, price theory would therefore be treated *first* and the theory of distribution after that—as had still been the case with Smith, but no longer with Ricardo and Mill.[63]

Rau and Hermann (followed by, among others, Schüz and Roscher) added a final touch to this symmetrical treatment of prices: the utility-determined demand price is the *upper,* the cost-determined supply price is the *lower,* limit to the actual market price, both these limits being treated in an individual reservation-price sense.[64] For beginning with Rau and Hermann, *monopoly pricing* situations—and even isolated exchange—were thoroughly considered (especially by Roscher;[65] note that this is exactly Menger's approach and later that of Böhm-Bawerk). And in these, of course, the reservation prices of consumers and the reservation prices of suppliers are only the upper and the lower bounds to market price; exchange is thus a mutually advantageous division of surplus. In dealing with *aggregate* demand and supply a further standard figure of thought is used: *individuals differ,* demanders as to their wants (Rau) and suppliers as to their costs (Hermann)—again, a basic assumption taken over by the Austrians.

Precisely in order to show that there is no contradiction in using a classical analysis of wealth creation and a utility framework for the treatment of prices and also for the evaluation of national income, the use of the concept of marginal utility was given a paradigmatic place in German economics. The French socialist Proudhon had suggested that the correct evaluation of national income could only be by labor values

62. Kauder says about Menger's copy of Rau: "Menger remarked twice (title page and page 1) that he started his study of Rau in September, October of 1867" (1965, 234)—i.e., half a year after getting his doctorate. Menger used the seventh (1863) edition of Rau: he preferred the well-known old textbook, not the newer Roscher, itself by then in a sixth edition. As I do not think Menger had read Kudler before writing his *Principles,* I think this explicit dating shows that he intended to express by it the *start* of a new phase in his life, the phase of systematic scientific research; and that Rau was thus effectively the *first* economics text he read *thoroughly.* (Menger may in fact never actually have *read* Mischler's textbook but simply have used his lecture notes.) Wieser (1923, 86) says that even for his own generation it was typical to start with Rau.

63. Adam Smith treats price theory in *The wealth of nations* Book 1, chapters 5–7 and only then the theory of distribution in chapters 8–11. Ricardo in his *Principles* treats prices in chapter 4, *in between* rent and wages, and then again in chapter 30, the very last chapter in his first two editions. Mill in his *Principles* calls Book 2 "Distribution" and Book 3 "Exchange," exactly the reverse of the German textbook order. Demand and supply are only introduced in chapter 2 of Book 3.

64. Hermann 1832, 66–96, esp. 67, 74, 94.

65. Roscher 1864, §§ 100 (later 101), 112, 113. See note 20 above.

and not by prices, if one considered the latter as measures of utility. Otherwise an increase in production (more labor value) would appear as a loss of welfare; for as everyone knew, a larger supply entailed lower prices and hence, if one thought that prices measured utility, a fall in utility! To Proudhon, value and price thus moved in opposite directions. Hildebrand countered that the fall in prices only showed that *marginal, not total,* utility had fallen. He thought, clumsily, that for given wants, but varying quantities of supply, total utility for every commodity always remained constant; for this he was taken to task by Menger. But by then the whole question had already been thoroughly analyzed by Knies: even if total utility, taken to be measured by price times quantity, rose if supply were lowered, as would be the case with wheat after a bad harvest, this was only due to the fact that the "intensity" of the want for wheat had increased due to the dearth at the cost of other wants so that total utility (taken over *all goods*) duly would have declined with lower supply of one good only.[66] Knies was quite positive (against Proudhon) that value and price moved in the same direction, "value" being identified by all Germans since Rau with utility.

What is the German "protoneoclassical" mood? A standard German textbook will treat goods first, then wants, then the economy, as Rau already does in 1826; Menger uses the same sequence of subjects though dealing with them at much greater length than Rau.[67] There could be slight variations: Hermann in 1832 starts with a subjectivist clarion call—"Whatever satisfies any want for man, he calls a good"[68]—but then only treats extensively of various types of goods, the economy, value, and national wealth. Roscher uses the series wants, goods, value, wealth, and the economy.[69] These are called "the *fundamental* concepts" in German economics. Evidently they are all of a subjectivist nature; and it was Hermann in 1832 who introduced the standard Austrian terminology that utility provides a "subjective" and cost an "objective" value basis to the theory of price.[70]

After these "fundamental" concepts the standard German textbook (be it the textbook by Rau, or by Schüz, or by Roscher, or by Schäffle,

---

66. Knies 1855, 451–61. "Intensity" is discussed on pp. 456–57, total utility over all goods on p. 460. Knies uses as his term for marginal utility *Quotegebrauchswerth* (451).

67. See Menger 1976: goods are treated in chapter 1, wants (the translation says "needs") in chapter 2, the economy in chapter 2, § 3.

68. Hermann 1832, 1 (first sentence): "Was dem Menschen irgend ein Bedürfniss befriedigt, heisst er ein Gut."

69. Roscher originally treats only goods (1854, § 1) but later (1864, 1875) starts with a discussion of wants before going on to goods: §§ 4–6 are on value, §§ 7–10 are on wealth, § 11 is on the economy.

70. Hermann 1832, 74: "Man kann den Gebrauchswerth und die Zahlungsfähigkeit der Käufer die *subjective* Gränze des Preises für die Käufer nennen, die *objective* bilden die Kosten."

and more or less also by Hermann) will turn to its classical side. It will treat extensively of the "formation of wealth," as Rau said, stressing the factors of production and the division of labor; or in the terminology of Roscher it will consider "the production of goods." This is the part Menger skips; but so had the first subjectivist German author, Hufeland, in 1807, and so had Menger's teacher, Mischler![71] After that we have general price theory and then income distribution, either in one chapter or in two and either together as the "distribution of wealth" (Rau) or separately as "the flow of goods" and "the distribution of goods" (Roscher). The resemblance to Jean Baptiste Say's *Traité d'économie politique* (1803), from which the sequence "distribution"-after-production is obviously taken, is only an outward one. The important point is that this part of the book is unified by its price theory, which is not the case with Say, and is very extensive (relatively much more extensive than in Say): about 150 pages or nearly one-half of the book in the first edition of Rau; about 300 pages and the same proportion in Roscher. In Menger this part of the book takes up 174 pages, immediately following his long treatment of "fundamental concepts" in 76 pages (which, however, is much shorter than the 142 pages Hermann lavishes on "fundamental concepts" in his second edition).[72] The whole will be closed, as in Say, by a chapter on consumption; but this will be short and can easily be left out, as in Menger.

71. Mischler (1857) treats in his second book (the first is on methodology and the history of thought) wants, goods, value, and wealth. The main review on Menger (see note 23 above) expressly thinks it a good idea that Menger proceeded in that way.

72. Hermann had vastly extended the first part of his textbook on the subjective-value "fundamental concepts" from 19 pages (or, if we include the important discussion on the productivity of labor, which distinguishes the economic from the merely technical aspects of production, from 35 pages) in the first edition of 1832 to 142 pages in the posthumous second edition of 1870. This—in many respects tedious (see Hayek 1976)—elaboration had been written by Hermann only in the very last years of his old age. Menger did *not* know the second edition of Hermann before completing his *Principles* in 1871; he always explicitly quotes the first edition. It is thus seriously misleading that the English translation of the *Principles* (1976) makes Menger quote "Hermann 1874," apparently a reprint of Hermann 1870 but unknown to me. For the two editions of Hermann, separated by thirty-eight years, are in many respects two distinct books. The point I wish to make in the text by pointing to Hermann is, however, another: by 1870–71 it had become *fashionable* in German economics to be very longwinded on the basic subjective-value ideas. In this, as in many other things, Menger was *no exception* in German economics.

Menger himself may have been, perhaps, *oversensitive* about the very fine distinctions of his subjective-value notions relative to those of his colleagues. In his eyes it was a deadly sin to use phrases which might suggest wants of man in general and not those of one *particular* man (see for instance 1976, 297–98). In other words: Menger was allergic to the figure of the "representative individual" (cf. note 95 below). The ability of the Austrians to split hairs already thrice split by their German colleagues into nine further parts is demonstrated by Zuckerkandl 1889, a thesis of habilitation written under Menger and therefore probably representative of his own thought. After reading such arid and also often unjust scholasticism, one can sympathize with economists who turned in disgust towards the Historical School!

So let us construct a hypothetical typical "German" textbook, which wishes to stress wants and goods as much as Hermann had done in his later edition (45 pages). Such a book will start with part 1, "Preliminary survey"; will then present part 2, "Some fundamental notions"; will elaborate in part 3 "On wants and their satisfaction," perhaps in 55 pages; will then proceed to the "classical part," which might be called part 4, "The agents of production"; will then turn (as Roscher does in a separate chapter) to general price theory on demand and supply lines, (let us call this part 5, "General relations of demand, supply, and value"); and will finally discuss, in these price-theoretic terms, part 6, "The distribution of national income"—these last two parts taking up more than one-half of the whole text. At least in his way of presentation, our hypothetical textbook author can be no direct disciple of John Stuart Mill. Everybody will realize, of course, that this hypothetical "German" textbook author is none other than Alfred Marshall![73]

V

After discussing the general structure of German economics around 1850, let us turn briefly to some of the subjectivist highlights of the German textbook tradition, as represented by the most important authors. Hufeland in 1807 wrote a book which by its very title introduced the subjectivist German "fundamental notions": goods, value, and wealth. Rau wrote the first German standard textbook, which had the same title as Menger's: *Grundsätze der Volkswirthschaftslehre;* it was first published in 1826 and, until 1869, ran to eight editions.[74] A student as late as Wieser thought Rau would be the first textbook a German scholar would turn to; and it was also, as we know, among the first economics books Marshall read. Rau not only presents the "protoneoclassical" German paradigm, the symmetric treatment of all prices (including factor prices) on demand and supply lines and the theory of price bounds; he also uses opportunity cost ideas, explains the mutual advantageousness of exchange, has clear notions about the falling demand curve, states that the demand curve falls more steeply for less essential commodities, draws a demand and supply schedule diagram with given supply and the equilibrium price at the intersection of the schedules, from the fourth (1841) edition onwards—and from the same edition onwards remarks on the declining marginal utility of general purchasing power ("money") with rising income.

An important innovation by Rau arises from his misunderstanding of

73. See Marshall 1890, 1961.
74. Editions appeared in 1826, 1833, 1837, 1841 (first appearance of demand and supply diagram), 1847, 1855, 1863 (the edition used by Menger), and 1869. For Menger's use of Rau see note 62 above.

Hufeland. The latter had pointed out that in *disequilibrium* situations the entrepreneur receives an income that is different from that of labor, capital, or land. Rau assigns a separate income to the entrepreneur even in equilibrium, treating *entrepreneurial activity* as a *fourth factor* of production. This consists "in the combination of factors, in drawing up a plan for their most advantageous use, and in the supervision of the execution of this plan by his assistants." Furthermore the entrepreneur also has to be recompensed for "the danger of total loss or at least loss of some of the costs" which arises in every enterprise, due particularly to "the greater or lesser difficulty in forecasting the level of future prices."[75] The remuneration necessary to attract entrepreneurs to these activities may vary with the type of enterprise, even for equal amounts of capital supplied. Roscher follows Rau and uses these ideas as a further argument against the labor theory of value: "Evidently the same amount of common labor achieves quite a different result depending upon whether it is well or badly directed."[76] Rau is, I think, altogether one of the most underrated pioneers in the history of economic thought.

Hermann's textbook of 1832 appeared in two editions only (the second published posthumously)[77] due to the fact that the author moved on to higher office. His text is the source book for the most strongly subjectivist notions until Schäffle. Hermann introduced the concept of free goods to economics, made it clear that services are goods (Rau having followed the English classicists in treating only material goods as goods), and introduced the concept of "relationships" as a further type of goods, which are best explained as collections of positive external effects or as information networks. Hermann developed a rich—some might say tedious[78]—taxonomy of goods, faithfully reproduced by Marshall.[79] The one important—and anything but tedious—idea of his which was not taken over by Roscher is that of rising cost curves.

Roscher wrote the standard German textbook for the generation of students following that which was nurtured on Rau. This textbook was first published in 1854 and eventually ran into a nearly unbelievable

75. Rau 1826, 103–5, 179–80. Page 180 says: "Die wesentlichen Geschäfte des Unternehmers sind das Zusammenbringen der Güterquellen, das Entwerfen des Plans für ihre vortheilhafteste Benutzung und die Aufsicht auf die zur Ausführung dieses Planes mitarbeitenden Gehülfen." Before that he had spoken of "[die] mit einer Unternehmung verknüpfte Gefahr des gänzlichen Mislingens oder doch des Verlustes an den Kosten" (179–80).

76. Roscher 1864, § 128, p. 250: "Offenbar hat dieselbe Quantität gemeiner Arbeit sehr verschiedene Erfolge, je nachdem sie gut oder schlecht geleitet wird."

77. See Hermann 1832, 1870; see also note 72 above.

78. Hayek (1976, 17) calls "the time-honoured 'fundamental concepts' of the traditional German text-book . . . a dry enumeration and definition." Blaug (1987, 638) says of Hermann that "the book revelled in endless definitions and classifications."

79. Marshall 1890 and 1961, vol. 1, Book 2, ch. 2.

twenty-six editions until 1922, being translated, among other languages, into English and French.[80] For German economics Roscher is the source of perfect recall of everything which was published in German, but not only in that language. His unrivaled knowledge of the history of thought sometimes made him, interestingly enough, rather more and not less classical than his German predecessors. He had an incredible ability of condensing everything which came to the scientific market into a few sentences, usually hitting the mark, more or less. As any great textbook author would, he had the knack of the felicitous phrase. He must not be considered unoriginal, though, in his youth (in his later years he kept busy turning out those twenty-six editions). But his originality in economic theory lay outside the "protoneoclassical" vein—in location theory, for instance, and in a fantastically insightful long treatise on the economic causes of recessions,[81] i.e., as we would now say, in macro-, not in microeconomics.

Among the many later German textbook authors I shall single out only Schäffle,[82] because he taught in Vienna when Menger was writing his *Principles*. In his strongly subjectivist text of 1867 we find even Wieser foreshadowed: "All goods become comparable in terms of value." As value is synonymous with utility to the Germans, it is thus utility which makes goods comparable, and not labor embodied. "Value [is] the significance of a good in the economic calculation of man. All economic calculation tries to determine the smallest sacrifice necessary to achieve full satisfaction."[83] The strength of the subjective value mood in German economics around 1870 is shown by the fact that Roscher quotes the two most strongly subjectivist authors, Hermann and Schäffle, most often: in the 1875 edition, for instance, each about fifty times.

Not Menger, but Hans K. E. von Mangoldt (1824–68) is the really unjustly treated great author in German economics of the third quarter of the nineteenth century, with his books *Entrepreneurial profit* (1855) and *Elements of economics* (1863).[84] The first touches on many themes with which Schumpeter was later credited (Schumpeter did not like to

80. See Roscher 1854. In later editions the article *Die* is missing. I do not have an English translation at hand; all translations given are my own.
81. See Roscher 1861. This was a republication out of Brockhaus's encyclopedia *Die Gegenwart* (Leipzig, [ca. 1850]), 3:721ff., which Roscher calls a "source not easily available" even in 1861.
82. See Schäffle 1867 and note 9 above.
83. "Im Werthe werden daher alle Güter vergleichbar" (Schäffle 1867, 52, in italics); "Der Werth—die Bedeutung eines ökonomischen Gutes in der wirthschaftlichen Berechnung" [a caption]. "Alle wirthschaftliche Berechnung geht auf mindeste Opfer bei vollste Befriedigung" (51).
On Wieser's penchant for thinking of economics as the art of correct calculation see Streissler 1986.
84. See Mangoldt 1855, 1863.

quote Mangoldt): It is the role of the entrepreneur to produce new products better suitable to demand and awaken latent wants. Any first use of new methods of production is risky, for it is especially difficult to forecast prices.[85] Mangoldt had a clear theory of monopoly rent, which others saw as an elaboration of Ricardian rent theory. Most important, he gives a clear and fully understood theory of risk aversion, presented in somewhat clumsy mathematical terms. As the average entrepreneur is risk-averse, he must on average receive profits.[86] Mangoldt even draws the conclusion that as workers are on average more risk-averse than entrepreneurs, profit-sharing schemes imposed by law are not to their advantage; they are better off with a fixed wage.[87] It is remarkable that the Austrians did not realize that the concave utility function under uncertainty assumed by Mangoldt is exactly the same idea as declining marginal utility with rising quantity under certainty: Menger found fault with Mangoldt's logic, as losses and profits have to wash out (he thus implies risk neutrality as a matter of course);[88] this non-argument was repeated by Wieser;[89] and as late as 1950 Schumpeter probably still thought along the same lines.[90] Böhm-Bawerk too, in his seminal intro-

---

85. Mangoldt 1855, 51ff. On p. 58 he says: "Die Einführung neuer Productions-methoden pflegt mit einem Risico verbunden zu sein." He summarizes his theory of profits in his textbook (Mangoldt 1863, 103–10).

86. Mangoldt 1855, 80ff. He expresses the cost of a risky venture in a mathematical formula (faithfully rendered in Roscher 1864, § 106, but no longer present in Roscher 1875): he multiplies the cost per venture by the total number of ventures and divides this by the number of successful ventures. This would correspond to the mathematical expectation of cost. But he then weights this by a further factor which is the disutility of the (average) loss divided by the utility of the (average) gain. He thus gets (more or less) the Neumann-Morgenstern expected utility of cost for a risk-averse entrepreneur: "Der Ertrag muss umso höher sein, je schmerzlicher man etwaige Verluste empfindet, je weniger man Empfänglichkeit für die Freude des Gewinnes hat, und umgekehrt" (90). He expressly states (95) that it is therefore not enough for profits to wash out on average. All this is again repeated in the summary (162ff.).

87. Mangoldt 1855, 173.

88. Menger gives as the reason why risk is no source of profit, that "the chance of loss is counterbalanced by the chance of profit" (1976, 161).

89. Wieser 1914, 251.

90. Schumpeter mentions Mangoldt as "still worth reading" (1914, 56) but does not tell us why. In his *History of economic analysis* he mentions Rau's textbook and comments: "But from this level and far above it rose the performances of two men of remarkable talent and force, Hermann and Mangoldt" ([1954] 1972, 503). (By this date Schumpeter was doing a little more justice to the Germans of the nineteenth century, whom he had nearly totally neglected in 1914.) On the same page he calls Mangoldt "among the century's most significant figures in our field." He mentions Mangoldt's "rent of ability" explanation for the wages of management (1972, 646 and again on 679, 935). Mangoldt is then repeatedly mentioned in the section on "enterprise" (893–94), without telling us about his risk theory; he also reappears under the heading "partial analysis" (990–91). This proves that Schumpeter was devoid of any understanding of decision theory under risk on Neumann-Morgenstern lines—after all an offshoot of the Austrian economic tradition—and only appreciated Mangoldt for his mathematical demand and supply analysis on (imperfect) Marshallian lines.

duction of what was later called Neumann-Morgenstern utility, assumed only risk neutrality.[91]

Mangoldt repeated his arguments about risk aversion and entrepreneurial profit in his textbook, which is of the standard German type: fundamental concepts, production, exchange, distribution. What is interesting is Mangoldt's price theory, full of demand and supply diagrams, diminishing marginal utility as a reason for the falling demand curve, substitution and complementarity of commodities, and even a discussion of the question whether market equilibrium will be unique.[92] Mangoldt was the only German economist who really tried to derive demand functions from the underlying utilities for the case of variable quantities, and he was the only one before Menger who tried—though quite differently from the latter—to tackle the "interrelationship of prices." But to the detriment of his reputation, Mangoldt died at the early age of forty-four, and a self-declared friend even republished his textbook posthumously, carefully purged of all of Mangoldt's original ideas![93]

In general, however, German economists, though making utility-analytical noises, were relatively soon satisfied that they had found sufficient causes behind demand and supply. They did not delve very deep. And they always treated *one price at a time*. German economics was—already in the period 1825 to 1875—*partial equilibrium analysis of demand and supply* par excellence.

VI

It was partial equilibrium analysis par excellence. But is not that the essence of the economics of Marshall? Just so! Marshall used exactly the structural framework German economists had developed in the two middle quarters of the nineteenth century. But he also supplied its theoretical underpinnings. He likewise used, as we have seen, the very sequence of topics used by the German textbook. (The structural framework and the sequence of topics logically correspond to each other.) In supplying the theoretical underpinnings Marshall used two simplifying notions: competitive markets, a very English notion well suited to the most highly developed economy, whereby he avoided the indeterminacy of those German price bounds, within which, according to Roscher and Menger, "price conflict"[94] raged; and the representative individual,

91. Böhm-Bawerk [1881] 1924, 74–76, renders the evaluation of expected utility by a lottery on Neumann-Morgenstern lines.

92. Mangoldt 1863, ch. 3, 45ff. The question of the uniqueness of market equilibrium is treated in a separate paragraph (§ 68, p. 63).

93. See Mangoldt n.d., dated to June 1868 from the foreword (by "Ein Freund und Fachgenosse des Verfassers"). This vapid and longwinded text is practically worthless.

94. Roscher 1864, § 100, p. 188 (in later eds. § 101); Menger 1976, 195 ("price duel"). Similar notions can already be found in Hermann 1832, 67, and elsewhere.

more specifically the representative firm, which allowed him to sidestep the tough problem of aggregation, but against which, when used by a minor "German" economist by the name of Friedländer, Menger, in true German fashion, had fulminated.[95]

We have Marshall's own words (written in 1900) on how he started to learn economics: "My acquaintance with economics commenced with reading Mill, while I was still earning my living by teaching Mathematics at Cambridge; and translating his doctrines into differential equations as far as they would go. . . . That was chiefly in 1867–68. I fancy I read Cournot in 1868. I know I did not read von Thünen then, probably in 1869 or 70: for I did not know enough German."[96] Other German economists also came to his early notice. We know from Keynes's biographical article on Marshall that he stayed in Dresden in 1868 and again in Berlin in the winter of 1870–71 expressly to learn German (originally in order to read German texts on philosophy). Keynes says, "He also came in contact with the German economists, particularly Roscher."[97] The ninth (variorum) edition of Marshall's *Principles* renders a pencil note by Marshall on a page of the third edition of the *Principles:* "Fleeming Jenkin's curves are of a peculiar shape, unlike any with which I am acquainted except those which Rau appended to the earlier editions of his *Volkswirtschaftslehre* [*sic*]. Neither Rau nor Jenkin refers to any predecessor. I saw Rau's work before I saw Jenkin's paper in the Recess Studies published in 1870; but even before that I had learnt from Cournot and Thünen."[98] If Marshall's memory was right, this, together with the first quotation, gives 1869–70 for his reading of Rau (after Thünen but before a paper read in 1870).

The "peculiar curve" is Rau's demand curve, which is published in his *later* (not earlier) editions—to be more precise, from the fourth edition of 1841 onwards.[99] Cournot had presented the first demand curve in the

---

95. Menger (1976, 299) chides Friedländer for "a complete misunderstanding of the subjective character of value if an average man with average needs is posited. For the use value of one and the same good is usually very different for two different individuals, since it depends upon the requirements of and quantities available to each of them." (Here his reasoning is faulty: correct averaging would take account of the facts named. That such a theoretically correct averaging may not be feasible in practice is another matter.) "The 'determination of the use value to the average man' does not, therefore, really solve the problem, since we are interested in a measure of the use value of goods that can be observed in real cases and with respect to specific persons." (Are we generally? Is not market demand the typical center of economic interest?) "Friedländer therefore arrives merely at a definition of a measure of the *objective value* of different goods . . . although a measure of this sort does not, in reality, exist." See also note 72 above.

96. Marshall 1961, 2:8–9 ("Editorial introduction").

97. Keynes 1924, 320.

98. Marshall 1961, 2:574.

99. Blaug (1985, 309) misquotes Rau for the year 1844. See note 74 above for correct dates.

history of economics in 1838; Rau's was the second, only three years later. But while Cournot posits his curve without explanation, i.e., quasi-axiomatically, Rau presents a derivation of it, the typical German derivation: individuals differ in their preferences or, more precisely, in their willingness *and* ability to pay.[100] (His curve assumes each individual buying one unit of a commodity, the typical case for reservation price analysis and thus for "price bounds.") But what is more interesting in relation to Marshall: Rau's demand curve alone is drawn exactly like Marshall's, with price on the *vertical* axis; Cournot's (or Mangoldt's) demand curves are drawn the other way round with prices measured horizontally.

A roll call of German authors in Marshall's quotations shows the importance he attaches to German authorities. Let us take the ninth (variorum) edition by Guillebaud as our guide. True, his *Principles* are "neoclassical": Ricardo with some hundred references and Adam Smith and John Stuart Mill with more than fifty each outdistance all other economists. But Thünen (24 references) and Roscher (22) come close to Malthus (29), to Marshall's beloved Cournot (28) and his contemporary Edgeworth (27), and just outdistance Böhm-Bawerk (21); Knies (14) and Menger (14) rival Senior (14) and outdistance Carey (13) and Bentham (12); and Hermann (10) is to Marshall still of equal importance as Walras or Wieser (10 each) and nearly as important as J. B. Clark, Schmoller, and Herbert Spencer (11 each). But the main Germans by far outdistance minor classical authors like McCulloch (5) or James Mill (4). Earlier editions of the *Principles* show the influence of German economists even better. In the first edition four authors (Smith, Ricardo, Jevons, and Mill) stand out as those quoted most. But in the next group of twelve authors, quoted from 5 to 10 times, four are German: Hermann, Knies, Roscher, and Thünen.

Some of Marshall's "German" economists were the authors of the Historical School, as in Book 1, chapter 2 or in the main in his Appendix B. But some were still of the "protoneoclassical" tradition, as in Book 2, chapter 2. In fact, anyone well-versed in "protoneoclassical" German textbooks will recognize that that chapter, on wealth, is evidently taken over nearly completely from them and depends heavily on Hermann, as Marshall says. The same is partly true of Book 3, chapter 3, "Wants in relation to activities" (inserted as such only from the second edition onwards).

It would be tedious to enumerate all the passages where Marshall shows German influence from the (by his time) already older tradition

100. Rau gives as a reason for the falling demand curve that "Von denen, die ein Gut z.B. um einen Preis von 10 fl. kaufen wollen, ist nur ein Theil geneigt, bis auf 18 fl., und ein noch kleinerer Theil, bis 24 oder 30 fl. hinaufzugehen" (1841, 525).

analyzed here. And it would not be so very important, either. As I pointed out, it is much rather the structural framework (the partial equilibrium supply and demand analysis) which evidently stimulated him. But there is one theory, new in Marshall, which he most certainly owes to the Germans: his theory of entrepreneurial "organization" as a fourth agent of production in Book 4. The very term "organization" comes from a phrase used by Roscher (but originating with Riedel)[101] that entrepreneurial income is due to "Organisation, Speculation und Inspection." The underlying theory, of course, is that of Rau mentioned above. The first paragraph of Book 4, chapter 12, § 2 follows the treatment by Rau sentence by sentence. That its source is German can be seen from the use of the word "undertake" by Marshall, which by his time was highly antiquated English but was the literal translation of the German term *Unternehmer* for "entrepreneur." In the same chapter, § 5 leans heavily on Roscher and his melodramatics. When Marshall says that the employer "must be a natural leader of *men,*" the reader of Roscher is immediately reminded that the German compares the entrepreneur to a leader of armies, like Wallenstein![102] And in Marshall's Book 6, chapter 7, "the rarity of the natural abilities" as the main source of managerial wages is evidently the "Seltenheit der . . . erforderlichen *persönlichen Eigenschaften*" of Roscher.[103] What is more, Marshall thinks with Roscher—but against Rau—that in the course of economic development "rising competition among entrepreneurs"[104] will whittle away true profits.

VII

While Marshall took above all the structural framework of analysis from the standard German textbook, Menger borrowed many of its basic concepts and much of what one might call its scientific *Weltanschauung.* But he used a *different* framework of thought: he tried to treat the *interaction of markets,* to analyze *more than one price simultaneously.* This is exactly the innovation Roscher quotes him for.[105] And perhaps

101. Roscher 1864, § 195, p. 401; Riedel 1839, 2:9–13.

102. Marshall 1961, 1:292; Rau 1826, § 239, pp. 179–80 (see part V of this paper); Marshall 1961, 1:297; Roscher 1864, 402.

103. Marshall 1961, 1:608; Roscher 1864, § 196, p. 402.

104. Marshall 1961, 1:601–2, 605ff.; Roscher 1864, § 196, pp. 403–4: "Auf den höherern Wirthschaftsstufen hat der Unternehmerlohn ebenso gut eine Neigung zu sinken, wie der Zinsfuss. Diess Sinken ist . . . hervorgerufen durch die wachsende Concurrenz der Unternehmer."

105. Roscher 1875, § 102, p. 216: "Menger [*Grundsätze* 1:92ff.] sucht den Gebrauchswerth verschiedener Güter aus dem Gesichtspunkte mit einander zu vergleichen, dass Befriedigungsmittel eines weniger dringenden Bedürfnisses, wenn die jeweilig dringenderen Bedürfnisse schon voll befriedigt sind, den Mitteln zur Übersättigung der letzteren vorgezogen werden." Roscher thus tries to render Gossen's "second law" in Menger. None of the references to Menger's *Principles* are changed by Roscher after the *Methodenstreit.* See, e.g., Roscher 1886.

Roscher was not as unperceptive as he is made out to be: marginal utility (which he had already quoted in the case of Hildebrand) was not all that important, either to him or to Menger. What Menger attempted one might be inclined to call a general equilibrium analysis if this term were not already preempted by the Walras variant of the marginalist revolution and if Menger had not been so reluctant to use equilibrium concepts. As is well known, Menger stressed all those aspects which make attainment of point equilibria unlikely: lack of information, stochastic shocks, imperfect or lacking competition, delayed adjustment. So perhaps we should say: Menger tried to present the theory of a *general interactive price system*. I think—against Hollander[106]—that the great classical authors, Smith, Ricardo, and Mill, tried to present a general equilibrium system of economic *activity;* but *not* a "general equilibrium analysis," which is a theory of simultaneous *price* equilibrium. For prices still played only a minor role with the classicists. The analysis of a simultaneous price equilibrium had to wait until the marginalist revolution and was its peculiar achievement. Though Jevons, Menger, and Walras should be "dehomogenized," Menger was not the odd man out.[107] He is the odd man out only if we use perfect information competitive price equilibrium as the sole measuring rod of decisive achievement. In searching for equilibrium, Jevons and Walras resemble each other. But in searching for a *"general"* system, a system of the interconnection of two or even more prices, Walras and Menger have to be paired.

Against the background of the German "protoneoclassical" tradition Menger's achievement can be seen not so much as the "invention" of marginal utility or marginal productivity but much rather as the *formulation of marginal productivity in marginal utility terms and its application to all factor remunerations in exactly the same manner.* This is what Roscher did not understand and where he does *not* quote Menger. Production to Menger is nothing technical, but a purely economic process of the creation of values or of income. If we take Böhm-Bawerk as our guide, early Austrian economics was practically nothing but a *theory of distribution.*[108] For Menger—in contrast to Jevons and even to Walras—marginalist concepts as such were not new. They had already been frequently used in his own scientific tradition, though not to much effect. Menger's lack of excitement about them can be gauged from the fact that in the *Principles* marginal utility is only introduced around page

---

106. Hollander 1987; see also Hollander 1973, 1979.
107. See Jaffé 1976. To my mind Blaug goes a bit too far when he remarks that "Menger is in any case the odd man out" (1985, 306). There are also similarities between Menger and Walras and Jevons.
108. See Böhm-Bawerk 1890. On the untechnical nature of capital according to Menger see Menger 1888.

90 and Menger's variant of marginal value productivity only around page 140 of this slim volume of 285 pages. And as to the creation of subjective value theory by Menger, the whole "protoneoclassical" strain of German economics had been a subjective value theory. Menger's achievement is that he presented a new *variant* of subjective value theory, a variant founded on methodological individualism.

What is important and what is new in Menger is what comes first in chapter 1, § 2 and chapter 1, § 4. It is, on the one hand, the *vertical order of goods,* which is the key to Menger's general interactive price system. It is the explanation of the interaction of prices over the whole array of the intertemporal production structure. This is Austrian "capital theory," which so puzzled and fascinated English economists around 1930. This capital theory has no precursors whatsoever in German economics. And it is, on the other hand, the "time-error" paradigm, the paucity of economic information due to the time-consuming nature of the satisfaction of wants, which is the key to the peculiar variant of Austrian subjective value theory. This idea too had briefly and occasionally been touched upon by German authors (Rau, or Roscher, or Mangoldt, for instance) but had never been systematically pursued.

Menger's unique contribution jumps out at the reader who examines what it was that Menger in the *Principles* took from his teacher Mischler. For Menger did borrow extensively from Mischler without ever quoting him, especially repeatedly on ten pages within the first thirty-five pages of the *Principles,* i.e., the first chapter and the beginning of the second.[109] If we call the first forty pages (approximately) in Menger's *Principles* the Mischler layers, we can note first that we find embedded in them all of Menger's *deviations* from methodological individualism in the evaluation of wants. For Mischler was both a subjectivist and an objective moralist: man had to understand and to learn to

___

109. Menger's page 3 (1871; 1976, 52) is nearly identical with Mischler's page 203 (1857); Mischler speaks of value, not goods, but the two are nearly interchangeable in German economics. Aristotle is quoted (in effect against the unnamed Mischler) on page 4, exactly where Menger *deviates* from Mischler's *different* notion of "imaginary" wants. After an excursion on pages 5 and following, into Hermann's terminology (taken up by the prospective judge of Menger's thesis, Schäffle), pages 7 and following lean again on Mischler, this time on his page 194. Pages 26 and following of Menger closely parallel pages 181–82 in Mischler, and finally Menger's 32–35 (the beginning of chapter 2) in parts strongly resemble Mischler's 164–68. On page 167 Mischler says: "Wants . . . are the unchangeable foundation of all economic endeavor . . . it is wants which develop the forces lying somnolent in man"—a basic idea of Menger's ("Die Bedürfnisse . . . bilden . . . die unwandelbaren Grundfesten aller wirthschaftlichen Bemühungen . . . die Bedürfnisse sind es . . . , *welche die im Menschen schlummernden Kräfte zur Entwicklung bringen,*" emphasis his). And Mischler (and Schäffle, who also evidently influenced Menger) harps on "Zweck," the purpose or the causal relationship, as does Menger. On page 38 (1871; 1976, 83) Menger speaks of "the capacity of human needs for infinite growth," while Mischler on page 166 speaks of the "immeasurable extendibility of wants" and on 181 repeats: "the development of wants has no limit." (I prefer "wants" as the translation of the German *Bedürfnisse,* which both authors use.)

conform to the objective values of creation. And secondly we find embedded in them, but sharply delineated, the ore seams of Menger's *original* thought: "the vertical order of goods" and "time-error."

Mischler, the teacher, and Menger, the pupil, shared a further concern: Mischler was extraordinarily interested in methodology. "How is a science of wealth possible?" he asks, and devotes about eighty pages in his slim textbook to methodology.[110] How far Mischler actually influenced Menger on questions of methodology I leave to the experts to judge. Menger shared two distinctive further concerns with "old" German economics in general: both were highly interested in monetary theory[111] and in the theory of economic crisis,[112] i.e., in what we would now call business-cycle theory. Menger bequeathed this "German" interest to his school.

Apart from this it is exactly Menger's and the early Austrians' (Böhm-Bawerk's and Wieser's) "neoclassical" side proper that stems from German economics. Possibly even more "neoclassical" than Menger was the forgotten Mangoldt. It may come as a relief, however, for many "neo-Austrians" to know that what they think of as peculiarly Austrian economics as distinct from and in contrast to *standard* neoclassical theory—the process-analytic approach, the "time-error" paradigm, capital theory, the strict methodological individualism—has *no* recognizable forebears in German economics, apart perhaps from some faint suggestions of a process-analytic approach, again in Mischler and in Menger's elder Viennese colleague and the actual judge of his thesis, Lorenz von Stein.

VIII

Why is it that the "protoneoclassical" tradition in German economics has been so little noticed? And how did it emerge in the first place? These two final questions appear to be linked.

110. See Mischler 1857, 86–158. The caption of § 37 reads: "Ist überhaupt eine Wohlstandswissenschaft möglich?" (92).
111. Roscher, Knies, Schäffle, and Mangoldt were particularly interested in the theory of money and credit. It is significant for the position of Menger as the "last of the older German economists" that by 1892 it was he who was asked to write the article "Money" for the standard German professional dictionary, the *Handwörterbuch der Staatswissenschaften,* and continued to do so up to its third edition, being succeeded by Wieser in the fourth.
112. Hardly less so than monetary theory, business-cycle theory appeared by the twentieth century as an "Austrian" speciality. But chapters on "crises" are not rare in German textbooks. Roscher was particularly interested in the topic and wrote perhaps his most original monograph on it (Roscher 1861). The two German economists who became professors in Vienna, Lorenz von Stein and Schäffle, were both much interested in the theory of "crises." Schäffle devotes chapter 16 of his book (1867, 214–19) to "Volkswirthschaftliche Krisen" and explains cycles by lack of information and variations in interest rates, both typical ideas of the later Austrians. Stein also devotes a five-page chapter, "Störungen des wirthschaftlichen Lebens" (1858, 225–30), to crises. There the

Long before England or the United States had developed a full-scale academic establishment or established professional academic teaching in economics, economics had become an academic profession in Germany. There the first chairs in economics were established in the middle two quarters of the eighteenth century. In the early nineteenth century the German-speaking world had already at least thirty full professorships in economics in more than twenty-five universities; and by 1875, at least forty chairs. The time when Menger studied was the period with the widest geographical spread of German-language universities: Prague in Czechoslovakia, Pest in Hungary, Cracow in Poland, and even Dorpat in Russia were entirely "German."

Many of these universities were not small: Vienna, the largest, had about 3,000 students in the 1860s and 6,714 in 1894–95. Berlin, smaller than Vienna and falling behind in numbers, seems to have had about 2,400 students in the 1860s and 4,356 in 1892. Prague, the third largest, had 1,500 students in the 1860s and 3,797 (in the by then linguistically divided university) in 1893, followed closely by Munich (Hermann's university) with about 1,200 to 1,300 in the 1860s and 3,754 in 1895. Leipzig (Roscher's university) was next with about 1,100 to 1,200 students in the 1860s and 2,957 in 1895. Heidelberg (the university of Rau and Knies), of which Americans may think sentimentally, was much smaller, with 768 students, one-quarter the number of Vienna, in 1861–62 and 1,028 students, less than one-sixth of Vienna's, in 1894–95. At the latter date Heidelberg was smaller than the university of Graz in Austria, with 1,543 students in 1893, and in summer (though not in winter) smaller than the neighboring university of Freiburg (Mangoldt's university) with 1,477 students in 1894. (With a view to summer amenities one moved to Freiburg in that season.)

Considering the size of these universities, a professorship in a top-ranking subject like economics could be highly lucrative. Apart from his salary, the professor received substantial lecture fees as well as stiff examination fees. In Austria professors received 2 Gulden per student per semester lecture hour (= 4 Kronen from the late 1890s onwards); in Germany fees were similar. For Menger's prescribed ten semester hours a year (five on economic theory, five on public finance) this amounted to 20 Gulden or 40 Kronen per student in 1895, about $8 of that date and probably about $200 (per student!) at present purchasing power. And Menger had at least some 400 students a year at that date, some possibly at reduced or waived fees because of poverty. Anyhow, Menger, when retiring, gave his university income as some 20,000 Kronen in 1903

---

astonished reader is already presented with the so-called Austrian Theory of the Business Cycle, the expansion and contraction of credit, at considerable length (227–28)!

(saying it had been reduced lately because of a ceiling on lecture fees recently introduced). This is some $4,000 of that date or about £840 of 1903. And he received a pension of 12,000 Kronen a year,[113] i.e., $2,400. Convert this to a present-day purchasing power of perhaps $100,000 on active duty and $60,000 in retirement; and remember that the level of income was then much lower. So think of the first-named sum as perhaps $500,000 dollars in relative income terms—and that with hardly any taxes to pay! Professorial chairs thus were not only among the very highly honored but also among the best-paid positions of the establishment in the German-speaking world, which explains why it was worth so much to fight over them.

Economic rationality drove professors to try to be interesting lecturers and thus attract students migrating from one university to the other. (Remember those summer students of Freiburg!) Menger was a lecturer of great reknown.[114] Furthermore, at the medium-sized universities, you tried to increase your "market" by writing your own textbook for those hordes of students. As an academic you wrote monographs only as a very young man in order to start your career. At the largest universities, particularly Vienna, you hardly *could* write anything after establishing yourself as a full professor: you were busy examining those four or five hundred students a year, devoting one half-hour examination time to each. But then you did not need to write, either: your lecture and examination fees made you affluent.

Monographs were written by nonacademic outsiders: by Thünen, who was noticed by the German establishment and also outside Germany, or by Gossen, who remained unnoticed by either (until Jevons in

113. See Menger's application for retirement (Personalakt, note 12 above). This application also gives the number of students he taught each year as "about 400."

Menger tends to gild the lily a bit in financial matters. Documents dealing with his appointment as associate professor in 1873, evidently inspired by him, point out his disinterested desire to serve science, proven by his willingness to work at a much *lower salary* (2,300 fl. instead of 3,000 fl. per year) at the university than he had had at the prime minister's office. Apart from the fact that one finds out later that he actually received not 2,300 fl. but 3,800 fl. as salary up to January 1875 (because he was until then continued part-time in the prime minister's office, so that he actually started his university career at an *increased total salary*), Menger "forgets" to mention the lecture fees (for perhaps some 200 students in 1873), which were his by legal right. His total income must therefore have about doubled by his move to the university, a move which only a great economist can thus make appear wholly disinterested. Secondly, in a document signed by him, Menger explicitly claims that it was very "loyal" of him not to ask for a higher salary, when, as still an associate professor in Vienna, he declined the offer of a full professorship in Basel. Actually it was financially out of the question to accept Basel anyway, even if one was only an associate professor in Vienna—once again because of the lecture fees: Basel was a tiny university, and Vienna was the largest. Thus Menger made a merit out of not trying to bargain with his ministry when actually his bargaining position was nil.

114. Wieser's obituary of Menger for the Academy of Sciences (see note 26 above) says that Menger had "einen Vortrag von seltener Klarheit und Eindringlichkeit" (246). The same is attested in an outside opinion by Seager (1892–93, 255).

1878).[115] But it was and still is difficult to evaluate a mere textbook literature—which has been our main focus here on purpose.[116] Text-books are ponderous, often pedantic. At first they all look alike. It is very difficult to find the new ideas in them, for the author will not tell you where they are. It was thus difficult for men like Marshall and Menger to assign priority when quoting from textbooks. In fact it was unusual to quote textbooks at all, and therefore they did not do it. Today you basically have to read all those textbooks together. The interesting thing is the common pattern and, of course, the actual deviations of one textbook from another, which can only be found by close comparison.

The German "protoneoclassical" textbook literature is, I think, much underrated today for the reasons named above; and it became under-rated for the ideological reasons I gave in the first section of this paper. But why did it develop subjectivist "protoneoclassical" views in the first place—an economics centered on prices, on goods, on wants, on utility, on economizing? Why did *a* subjective-value school arise in German academe long before *the* subjective-value school? The best explanation is, I think, given by George J. Stigler. He characterizes the transition from classical to neoclassical economics as follows: "Previously it was a science conducted by nonacademicians whose main interest was in the policy implications of the science; thereafter it was conducted by pro-fessors who accepted the ruling values and incentives of scholarly activity." From the angle of England or the United States, Stigler places this transition at the *end* of the nineteenth century: "Economics became primarily an academic discipline in the last decade of the nineteenth century."[117] In the German-speaking university, though, economics be-came primarily an academic discipline in the *first decades* of the nine-teenth century—in consequence of the revival of academic life after the Napoleonic wars! Some of the professional journals still extant go back to the period around 1850 and earlier (e.g., *Zeitschrift für die gesamte Staatswissenschaft* since 1844 or *Jahrbücher für Nationalökonomie und Statistik* since 1863). And it was precisely in this period that the "protoneoclassical" tradition established itself.

Neoclassical economics is a dialogue between academic teachers and students. But why is the dialogue one on goods, on wants, on subjective notions? Perhaps Bukharin is not that far off the mark after all when he thinks it is the economics of the rentier.[118] The German academic youth hardly ever came from families with a mercantile background and prac-tically never from manufacturing families. They were the sons of profes-

---

115. See Gossen 1854 and note 17 above. See Thünen 1826 and note 54 above.
116. This paper has centered on the question of what suggestions Menger could—and did—get when reading the "normal science" around him.
117. Stigler 1972, 580, 576.
118. See Bukharin [1919] 1968.

sionals and of civil servants. And these classes traditionally supplemented their earnings by inherited rentier income. This was especially true for the law schools, where economics was mainly taught at that time: the law schools were socially a cut above the rest. On the other hand, the German upper class was poor, especially right after the Napoleonic wars. To economize was something the students would understand. Economy, as Rau said on his very first page, was "the sum of all those activities which are necesary to provide a certain person with goods."[119] To the German student the "protoneoclassical" tradition evidently spoke of his own interests, his own person: he *was* the "certain person."

But there is also a further reason why academic economics became neoclassical economics. The classroom needs a *simple paradigm,* lucidly applicable to many cases. German "protoneoclassical" economics had such a paradigm: utility-dependent demand and cost-dependent supply as the perfectly symmetrical explanation of all prices. This was a much simpler theory than the dozen or so different price determinations found in Mill. Today, demand and supply is still our bread-and-butter economics, the idea that distinguishes, according to Sir Alec Cairncross, economists from other professionals.[120] In his quest for a "unified theory of price"[121]—in a sense a curious quest, as German economics *did* already have a unified theory of price, in contrast to classical economics—*Menger provided an even simpler paradigm:* in the last resort (as Hermann had already glimpsed "as through a glass but darkly"), costs themselves depended on utilities, on demand, only once-removed.

But this simpler paradigm of Menger's rests on more complicated theoretical underpinnings; and in fact it is wrong, precisely on Menger's terms of incomplete information and individual bargaining. Even if German economics had not turned away from its own roots and pursued the will-o'-the-wisp of a nationalist historical identity, it is still not at all clear what paradigm would have prevailed eventually. But if German academic economics had continued in the traditions of the 1850s and 1860s, this fight could have been waged on the shared ground of basic subjective-value notions. The result might quite possibly have been something closer to Marshall's *Principles,* something therefore closer to the parent protoneoclassical tradition than to Menger. Had Menger persevered, on the other hand, we might have gone immediately to the imperfect information disequilibria and the bargaining and auction theories of today.

119. Rau 1855, 2.
120. Cairncross 1985, 3.
121. In the preface of the *Principles* Menger gives as one of his main aims "establishing a price theory . . . placing all price phenomena . . . together under one unified point of view" (1976, 49).

References

Blaug, Marc. [1962] 1985. *Economic theory in retrospect*. 4th ed. Cambridge.
———. 1987. Hermann, Friedrich Benedict Wilhelm von. In *The new Palgrave: a dictionary of economics*, edited by John Eatwell, Murray Milgate, and Peter Newman, 2:637–38. London.
Böhm-Bawerk, Eugen von. [1881] 1924. *Rechte und Verhältnisse vom Standpunkte der Volkswirthschaftlichen Güterlehre*. Innsbruck. Reprinted in *Gesammelte Schriften von Eugen von Böhm-Bawerk*, ed. Franz X. Weiss. Leipzig.
———. 1890. The Austrian economists. *Annals of the American Academy of Political and Social Science* 1.
Bukharin, Nikolai. [1919] 1968. *The economic theory of the leisure class*. New York.
Cairncross, Alec. 1985. Economics in theory and practice. *American Economic Review*, Papers and Proceedings, 75.
Gossen, Hermann Heinrich. 1854. *Entwicklung des menschlichen Verkehrs und der daraus fliessenden Regeln des menschlichen Handelns*. Braunschweig.
Hasner, Leopold Ritter von. 1860. *System der politischen Oekonomie*. Vol. 1. Prague.
Hayek, F. A. 1976. Introduction. In Menger 1976.
Hermann, Friedrich B. W. 1832. *Staatswirthschaftliche Untersuchungen*. Munich.
———. 1870. *Staatswirthschaftliche Untersuchungen*. 2d ed. Munich.
Hildebrand, Bruno. 1848. *Die Nationalökonomie der Gegenwart und Zukunft*. Frankfurt am Main.
Hollander, Samuel. 1973. *The economics of Adam Smith*. London.
———. 1979. *The economics of David Ricardo*. Toronto.
———. 1987. *Classical economics*. Oxford.
Hufeland, Gottlieb. 1807. *Neue Grundlegung der Staatswirthschaftskunst, durch Prüfung und Berichtigung ihrer Hauptbegriffe von Gut, Werth, Preis, Geld und Volksvermögen mit ununterbrochener Rücksicht auf die bisherigen Systeme*. Giessen and Wetzlar.
Jaffé, William, 1976. Menger, Jevons and Walras de-homogenized. *Economic Inquiry* 14.
Kauder, Emil. 1962. Aus Mengers nachgelassenen Papieren. *Weltwirtschaftliches Archiv* 89.
———. 1965. *A history of marginal utility*. Princeton.
Kautz, Julius. 1858. *Theorie und Geschichte der National-Oekonomik*. Vienna.
Keynes, J. M. 1924. Alfred Marshall, 1842–1924. *Economic Journal* 34:311–72.
Knies, Karl. 1855. Die nationalökonomische Lehre vom Werth. *Zeitschrift für die gesamte Staatswissenschaft* 11.
———. 1882. *Die politische Oekonomie vom geschichtlichen Standpuncte*. Braunschweig. (Neue Auflage der "Politischen Oekonomie vom Standpuncte der geschichtlichen Methode.")
Kudler, Joseph. 1846. *Die Grundlehren der Volkswirtschaft*. Vienna.
Mangoldt, H. von. 1855. *Die Lehre vom Unternehmergewinn*. Leipzig.
———. 1863. *Grundriss der Volkwirthschaftslehre*. Stuttgart.
———. n.d. [1868]. *Volkswirthschaftslehre*. Stuttgart.
Marshall, W. E. 1890. *Principles of economics*. London. 8th ed., 1920.
———. 1961. *Principles of economics*. 9th (variorum) ed. Edited by C. W. Guillebaud. 2 vols. London.

Marx, Karl. [1867] 1969. *Das Kapital—Kritik der politischen Ökonomie*. Ed. MEG, vol. 23. East Berlin.

März, Eduard. 1981. Joseph A. Schumpeter as Minister of Finance of the First Republic of Austria, March 1919–October 1919. In *Schumpeterian economics*, ed. Helmut Frisch. Eastbourne and New York.

Menger, Carl. [1871] 1976. *Grundsätze der Volkswirthschaftslehre*. Vienna. Translated as *Principles of economics* by J. Dingwall and B. Hoselitz. New York and London.

————. 1888. Zur Theorie des Kapitals. *Jahrbücher für Nationalökonomie und Statistik* 17:1–49.

Mischler, Peter. 1857. *Grundsätze der National-Oekonomie*. Vienna.

Pribram, Karl. 1983. *History of economic reasoning*. Baltimore and London.

Rae, John. 1965. *Life of Adam Smith*. Reprinted with an introduction by Jacob Viner. New York.

Rau, Karl H. 1826. *Grundsätze der Volkswirthschaftslehre*. Heidelberg.

————. 1841. *Grundsätze der Volkswirthschaftslehre*. 4th ed. Heidelberg.

————. 1855. *Grundsätze der Volkswirthschaftslehre*. 6th ed. Heidelberg.

————. 1863. *Grundsätze der Volkswirthschaftslehre*. 7th ed. Heidelberg.

Riedel, A. F. 1839. *Nationalöconomie oder Volkswirthschaft*. Vol. 2. Berlin.

Roscher, Wilhelm. 1854. *Die Grundlagen der Nationalökonomie: Ein Hand- und Lesebuch für Geschäftsmänner und Studierende*. Stuttgart.

————. 1861. Zur Lehre von den Absatzkrisen. In *Ansichten der Volkswirthschaft aus dem geschichtlichen Standpunkte*, section 6:279–398. Leipzig and Heidelberg.

————. 1864. *Grundlagen der Nationalökonomie*. 5th ed. Stuttgart.

————. 1874. *Geschichte der National-Oekonomik in Deutschland*. Munich.

————. 1875. *Grundlagen der Nationalökonomie*. 12th ed. Stuttgart.

————. 1886. *Grundlagen der Nationalökonomie*. 18th ed. Stuttgart.

Schäffle, Albert E. F. 1867. *Das gesellschaftliche System der menschlichen Wirthschaft*. Tübingen.

Schumpeter, Josef. 1914. Epochen der Dogmen- und Methodengeschichte. *Grundriss der Sozialökonomik* 1.1:19–124. Tübingen. 2d ed., 1924.

————. 1915. Zum 75. Geburtstage Karl Mengers. *Neue freie Presse* (Vienna), 23 February.

————. [1954] 1972. *History of economic analysis*. London.

Schüz, Carl W. Ch. 1843. *Grundsätze der National-Oeconomie*. Tübingen.

Seager, H. R. 1892–93. Economics at Berlin and Vienna. *Journal of Political Economy* 1.

Seidl, Christian. 1984. Joseph Alois Schumpeter: character, life and particulars of his Graz period. In *Lectures on Schumpeterian economics*, ed. Christian Seidl. Berlin.

Solow, Robert M. 1974. The economics of resources or the resources of economics. *American Economic Review*, Papers and Proceedings, 64.

Stein, Lorenz von. 1858. *Lehrbuch der Volkswirthschaft*. Vienna.

Stigler, George J. 1972. The adoption of the marginal utility theory. *HOPE* 4.

Streissler, Erich. 1986. Arma virumque cano—Friedrich von Wieser, the bard as economist. In *Die Wiener Schule de Nationalökonomie*, edited by Norbert Leser. Vienna.

Thünen, Johann Heinrich von. 1826. *Der isolierte Staat in Beziehung auf Land- wirthschaft und Nationalökonomie*. Vol. 1: *Untersuchungen über den Ein- fluss, den die Getreidepreise, der Reichtum des Bodens und die Abgaben auf den Ackerbau ausüben*. Hamburg.

Wieser, Friedrich von. 1914. Theorie der gesellschaftlichen Wirtschaft. In *Grundriss der Sozialökonomik,* 1.2. Tübingen. 2d ed., 1924.
————. 1923. Karl Menger. *Neue österreichische Biographie.* Vienna.
Zuckerkandl, Robert. 1889. *Zur Theorie des Preises mit besonderer Berücksichtigung der geschichtlichen Entwicklung der Lehre.* Leipzig.

The cameralistic roots
of Menger's achievement

Paul Silverman

The origins of the Austrian school of economics in the history of Austrian economic thought has until very recently never been a topic of serious historical inquiry, not even in Austria itself.[1] The reasons for this are largely bound up with the well-known influence the present continually has on our perceptions of the past. In the case at hand, the belief that the contributions of the Austrian School had been integrated into an internationally recognized body of valid economic doctrine produced the corresponding belief that the prehistory of the Austrian School was simply the general history of economic thought, a general history which in the first half of the nineteenth century was dominated by English classical economics. This accounts for the treatment of the Austrians usually found in textbooks of the history of economic thought. Here Menger appears simply as one of the pioneers who attempted to resolve important difficulties within classical economics and to reconstruct economic theory as a unitary and comprehensive body of doctrine rooted in a single set of logically sound principles. As the exposition unfolds, the reader is led to assume that all Menger needed to carry out his task was classical economics, a fertile mind, and an adequate supply of intellectual elbow grease.

1. See the brief sketches in Wilhelm Weber, "Wirtschaftswissenschaft und Wirtschaftspolitik in Österreich 1848 bis 1948," in *Hundert Jahre österreichischen Wirtschaftsentwicklung 1848–1948,* ed. Hans Mayer (Vienna: Springer, 1949), 625–33, and Alois Brusatti, "Die Entwicklung der Wirtschaftswissenschaften und der Wirtschaftsgeschichte," in *Die Habsburgermonarchie 1848–1918,* ed. Adam Wandruszka and Peter Urbanitsch (Vienna: Österreichische Akademie der Wissenschaften, 1973), 605–11. Professor Streissler's very important contribution to the present volume is, to my knowledge, the first serious attempt to relate Menger's thought to earlier Austrian writers. He, of course, stresses the importance of the German textbook literature and minimizes the contribution of Austrian writers. I do not wish to contest his conclusions but rather hope to show that the German textbook literature of the first half of the nineteenth century itself had important eighteenth-century antecedents which were heavily Viennese in provenance. That this latter body of writings survived well into the nineteenth century in Austria is well known. In what follows I certainly do not wish to suggest that Menger was heavily dependent upon the Austrian cameralists and their most important nineteenth-century Austrian successor when working out the details of his economic theory. These writers were important for the development of the Austrian School on account of the way they framed economic questions, not on account of the answers they provided. These questions created the academic ethos in which Menger grew to intellectual maturity.

Conversely, variegation within current doctrine ought to produce sensitivity to variety in the past, and this has indeed been so with respect to the Austrian School. However, to date attempts to reevaluate the prehistory of the Austrian School in light of its newly appreciated distinctiveness have strangely failed to contain any significant discussion of economic thought in Austria prior to Menger's appearance. Thus far those who have sought to explain what is unique about the Austrian School through reference to Austrian history have focused largely on matters other than economic thought itself—in the main, the history of Austrian philosophy and, beyond that, Austrian literary, social, and political culture in general.

This practice of beginning the search for the Austrian roots of the Austrian School in these areas has been a mistake. While the Austrian School does indeed manifest many of the characteristic features of the Austrian mind, at least as we understand it today,[2] attempts to explain it in terms of those features have often been extremely speculative and have produced, as we shall see presently, some highly improbable results. While the genius of Austrian culture certainly left its mark on the Austrian school of economics, that school's specifically Austrian roots lie squarely in the branch of Austrian intellectual history that the casual observer would consider to be the most plausible one, the history of Austrian economic thought.

In order to prove my thesis it will be necessary to consider briefly wherein the distinctiveness of the Austrian School lies. For the purposes of the present inquiry, the most useful way to do this is to concentrate on the general approach to economic problems taken by Menger and his followers, the causal-genetic method. This method eschews the search for definite recurring relationships among economic magnitudes in favor of an exploration of how various typical *patterns* of economic activity arise and pass away and how changes in knowledge, tastes, the availability of resources, and governmental policies affect these patterns. It begins with a rational, introspective examination of everyday experience, and it seeks to identify within that experience the basic necessary elements of all economic activity, or the ultimate "causes" to which all economic phenomena can be traced. These "most original factors of human economy," as identified by Menger, consist of "needs, the goods offered directly to humans by nature (both the consumption goods and the means of production concerned) and the desire for the most complete satisfaction of needs possible (for the most complete covering of material needs possible)."[3] The patterns of economic ac-

2. This is no minor qualification. Research in Austrian intellectual history lags far behind that in its English, German, and French counterparts.
3. Carl Menger, *Problems of economics and sociology,* trans. Francis J. Nock (Urbana: University of Illinois Press, 1963), 63.

tivity that these causes engender consist of interrelated, purposeful human actions in which individuals attempt to exchange lesser for more preferred circumstances. These patterns form institutions whose functioning the economist seeks to understand. Causal-genetic analysis is thus introspective, rationalistic, methodologically individualistic, and interpretive, i.e., it seeks not to measure but to interpret or "understand" (*verstehen*) economic phenomena more or less in the sense that Max Weber used the term. In addition, because the causal-genetic method seeks to discover relations of cause and effect, relations that are sequential rather than functional, it seeks to explain change and development through time rather than interdependencies existing within static states of affairs. It must be stressed, as it was stressed by Menger and most of his followers, that the central and ever-present categories of economic analysis are "goods" (*Güter*) and "needs" (*Bedürfnisse*). These are the key terms of causal-genetic analysis, and they are also the key terms of the Austrian prehistory of the Austrian school of economics.

The causal-genetic method clearly does not involve an attempt to produce the economic equivalent of Newtonian mechanics, as has so much of modern academic economics. It is here that those who have attempted to explain the distinctiveness of the Austrian School by examining Austrian history have usually begun. For them the aims of the Austrian economists have appeared to be premodern in their scientific implications. The concern with definitions as well as with first and final causes, the teleology inherent within the patterns the economist explores, and the secondary concern given to relationships among economic magnitudes all seem to suggest that Austrian economic theory has affinities with an Aristotelian approach to the world, a suggestion made plausible by the importance that Aristotle has had for Austrian philosophical thought. The individual most responsible for popularizing the view that it is not simply plausible to discuss causal-genetic analysis in Aristotelian terms but that the early members of the Austrian School wrote under the direct influence of Aristotle himself is Emil Kauder.[4] His arguments have gained considerable credence,[5] but despite their popularity they fail to bear the weight of even modest critical inquiry.

Kauder maintained that Menger and his immediate followers rooted the causal-genetic method in Aristotelian metaphysics. This must be stressed. He did not claim that the Austrians relied upon Aristotle's

4. Emil Kauder, "Intellectual and political roots of the older Austrian School," *Zeitschrift für Nationalökonomie* 17 (1957): 411–425.

5. Lawrence H. White, *Methodology of the Austrian School* (New York: Center for Libertarian Studies, 1977), 3–4; Samuel Bostaph, "The methodological debate between Carl Menger and the German historicists," *Atlantic Economic Journal* 6.3 (September 1978): 11–15. Bostaph notes that he reached this conclusion independently of Kauder.

practical philosophy, as one might assume given the close connection between it and economic questions in general. Kauder contended that the Austrians were Aristotelian in their approach to the most basic questions of being. They were "social ontologists" whose search for the "exact laws" that controlled economic phenomena was really a search for a deeper reality hidden behind outward appearances.[6] Ultimately what the Austrians hoped to find was a "general plan of reality" that gave all social phenomena their meaning,[7] a general plan that encompassed a timeless system of economic "essences." Kauder viewed these essences as composites of the physical world and a rational structure determined by human nature or the human mind, and he seems to have understood them as being subject to Aristotelian fourfold causation.[8]

To support his contention that the various parallels and congruencies between Aristotelian metaphysics and Austrian economic theory were not merely fortuitous but instead reflected concrete historical influence,[9] Kauder presented evidence that falls into two classes. First of all he attempted to demonstrate that "Menger wrote his epistemology as a student of Aristotelian metaphysics." Menger supposedly repeated "time and again" that Aristotle was one of "the authors who . . . helped to create his philosophy of science."[10] Kauder made much of the fact that in debating the general nature of economic science with Léon Walras, Menger argued that economics was not simply a study of relationships among magnitudes but rather a study of what he referred to as *das Wesen* of such things as value, rent, entrepreneurial profit, and so forth.[11] Kauder translated *das Wesen* as "the essence" and concluded that Menger must have been speaking of Aristotelian essences. Secondly, Kauder contended that what he saw as the pervasive role of Aristotelianism in Austrian culture made itself felt in the work of the Austrian economists. He noted (but did not substantiate)[12] the fact that well into the twentieth century, young boys at Vienna's elite Schottengymnasium read Aristotle's *Metaphysics* as part of their Greek lessons. Since both Wieser and Böhm-Bawerk attended this school, two of the most important early members of the Austrian School absorbed the

6. Kauder, "Intellectual and political roots," 417.

7. Ibid.

8. Ibid., 418.

9. This distinction must be stressed, for failing to recognize it can lead to great confusion. Kauder postulated the existence of historical influence, not simply parallel patterns of thought.

10. Kauder, "Intellectual and political roots," 414 n. 12.

11. Ibid., 412–13.

12. According to William Johnston, *The Austrian mind* (Berkeley and Los Angeles: University of California Press, 1972), 68, "in the better gymnasien like the Schottengymnasium, the Greek course culminated in the reading of Aristotle." He does not indicate which portions of Aristotle were actually read.

foundations of Aristotelianism at a young and thus impressionable age.[13] Beyond details such as this, Kauder claimed that Austrian culture as a whole bore the stamp of such great men as the "realists and ontologists" Aristotle, Aquinas, Leibniz, and Bolzano, as well as a wide range of politicians and writers, such as Joseph II, Metternich, Grillparzer, Stifter, and Anzengruber, who reinforced, developed, and applied the ideas of the philosophers in ways too complex to recount here.[14] The culture these men created manifested numerous attitudes and patterns of thought that Kauder felt he could also identify in the Austrian economists, and he viewed the many parallels he found as evidence that, consciously or unconsciously, these economists were typical creatures of their surroundings.

All of these arguments are flawed, and some of them are catastrophically erroneous. First of all, Menger makes no statements that even remotely imply that Aristotle "helped to create his philosophy of science." Menger refers to Aristotle seven times in his *Untersuchungen*. None of these references involves Aristotle's metaphysics, and only two involve epistemological questions. To be specific, Menger used Aristotle's denial of "the strictly scientific character of induction" and his view that in the realm of "ethical phenomena" it is valid to focus on a single dimension of experience, to support similar views of his own.[15] Any follower of Karl Popper would accept the former position, and most economists regardless of their philosophical proclivities would accept the latter. There are, in other words, simply no grounds for concluding that Menger's agreement with Aristotle on such points demonstrates his acceptance and use of Aristotelian metaphysics. The other mentions Menger makes of Aristotle note such things as that Aristotle held that "other factors contributed to the formation of states besides the impulse for socializing or for community"; that he did not accept the view often ascribed to him to the effect "that the state is something 'original,' that it is something given with the existence of man itself"; that he held that "money came about through *agreement,* not by nature, but by *law*," a

13. Kauder, "Intellectual and political roots," 420.

14. Ibid., 419–24. It is worth noting that Kauder's account has also been loosely associated with the important postwar discoveries of the importance of late medieval and early modern Aristotelian scholasticism in establishing a tradition of subjective theories of value in continental European economic thought. See Murray N. Rothbard, "New light on the prehistory of the Austrian School," in *The foundations of modern Austrian economics,* ed. Edwin G. Dolan (Kansas City: Sheed & Ward, 1976), 52–74. While these discoveries may be helpful in explaining the origins of Menger's theory of value, they do little to reinforce Kauder's case. The tradition of subjective value theories that stretches from Aquinas and Henry of Langenstein through the Spanish scholastics to Galiani, Turgot, and Condillac need not lead to acceptance of the causal-genetic method, and this is the heart of the matter.

15. Menger, *Problems of economics and sociology,* 57, 87.

view profoundly at odds with Menger's own; and that he "emphasize[d] . . . the relativity of political institutions," a fact Menger referred to to make the polemical point that "the basic notions of the
historical school of German economists have long been known in political science."[16] None of this supports Kauder, and in fact, when one
combines these references with the uses that Menger made of Aristotle
in his *Grundsätze* (and when one also recalls Menger's citation of an
extraordinarily wide range of ancient and modern authors), it becomes
clear that the entire enterprise was simply a product of his deep commitment to understanding the historical origins of contemporary doctrines,
a commitment that is impressive but hardly unusual in nineteenth-
century Germanic scholarship.[17]

Beyond this, there can be little doubt that Kauder subjected Menger's

16. Ibid., 88, 149 n. 52, 163, 166.
17. To demonstrate this point it is worth noting the instances where Menger refers to
Aristotle in his *Grundsätze*. Seven of these references are at the opening of historical
appendices, where Menger simply presents Aristotle as the first thinker to express an
opinion on a particular matter. Except for a single reference to *De anima*, all materials are
drawn either from the *Nicomachean ethics* or the *Politics*. (1) "Aristotle (*De anima*
iii.10.433ª 25–38) already distinguished between true and imaginary goods according to
whether the needs arise from rational deliberation or are irrational" (*Principles of economics*, trans. James Dingwall and Bert F. Hoselitz [Glencoe: Free Press, 1950], 53 n. 5).
(2) "Aristotle already observed that money serves as a measure in the trade of men (*Ethica
Nicomachea* v.5.1133ᵇ, 16; and ix.1.1164ª, 1)" (277 n. 24). (3) "Aristotle (*Politics* i.4.1253ᵇ,
23–25) calls the means of life and well-being of men 'goods'" (286). (4) "As early as
Aristotle we find an attempt to discover a measure of the use value of goods and to represent use value as foundation of exchange value. In the *Ethica Nicomachea* (v.5.1133ª, 26–
1133ᵇ, 10) he says that 'there must be something that can be the measure of all goods. . . .
This measure is, in reality, nothing other than need, which compares all goods. For if men
desire nothing or if they desire all goods in the same way, there would be no trade in goods"
(295–96). (5) "The error of regarding the quantities of goods in an exchange as equivalents
was made as early as Aristotle, who says: 'To have more than one's own is called gaining
and to have less than one's original share is called losing, e.g., in buying and selling . . .
but when they get neither more nor less but just what belongs to themselves, they say that
they have their own and that they neither lose nor gain.' (*Ethica Nicomachea* v.5.1132ᵇ,
13–18.) Continuing, he says: 'If, then, first there is proportionate equality of goods, and
then reciprocal action takes place, the result we mention will be effected. . . . And this
proportion will not be effected unless the goods are somehow equal (*Ethica Ibid* v.5.1133ª,
10–26)" (305). (6) "Theodor Bernhardi . . . says that it has frequently been noted in recent
times that Aristotle had already mentioned the difference between use value and exchange
value in his *Politics* (i.6.), and that Adam Smith distinguished between the two concepts
independently of the Greek philosopher" (306). (7) "Aristotle, in a much quoted passage,
says that money originated by convention, not by nature but by law (*Ethica Nicomachea*
v.5.1133ª, 29–32). He expresses this view even more distinctly in his *Politics*, where he
says that 'men agreed to employ in their dealings with each other something . . . for
example iron, silver, and the like,' and offers this as his explanation of the origin of money
(i.9.1257ª, 36–40)" (315). (8) "Aristotle points to the ease with which [precious metals] can
be handled and transported (*Politics* i.9.1257ª, 39–41) and in another place to their relative
stability of price (*Ethica Nicomachea* v.5.1132ᵇ, 13–15.)" (316). (9) "In this context [the
problem of coinage], several authors also take the opportunity of discussing the problem
of the origin of money, which they solve on the basis of the findings of the writers of
antiquity, with regular reference to Aristotle" (317).

use of the term "essence" to extraordinary overinterpretation. In fact it is not even entirely clear whether "essence" is the most appropriate rendering of *das Wesen* in this particular context. *Das Wesen* can indeed mean "essence" or "substance," but it can also mean the "state," "condition," "nature," or "character" of a thing. In any event, even if "essence" were the best translation, this hardly permits one to conclude that in his confrontation with Walras, Menger was resorting to Aristotelian metaphysics. On the contrary, in such situations one ought to take seriously Menger's own claim that his method accorded with the dictates of the modern natural sciences,[18] disciplines that he surely understood arose out a centuries-long development propelled in part by criticism of Aristotelian scholasticism.

Kauder's discussion of the influence of Austrian culture upon the Austrian School is also questionable. Even if the curriculum at the Schottengymnasium included Aristotle's *Metaphysics*, what the adolescent Wieser and Böhm-Bawerk were able to glean from their Greek lessons is something we shall never be able to gauge.[19] More importantly, Menger, who wrote considerably more on method than either Wieser or Böhm-Bawerk, did not attend the Schottengymnasium, and unless his personal papers contain some information on this point, it is probable that we shall never be sure which Greek texts he became familiar with as a boy.

Finally there are Kauder's comments on Austrian culture and the way that the Austrian School might be an expression of it. Here it is clear that he was indulging largely in speculation. It is speculation that occasionally has a certain plausibility, but to verify one of its typical products in one lifetime—such as the hypothesis that Wieser's love of order had something to do with Metternich's[20]—would require monographic resources that we are unlikely to have anytime soon.

But even if Kauder failed at almost every turn to support his case with adequate evidence, one nonetheless comes away with the feeling that he did put his finger on something. While Menger, the man of nineteenth-century liberal and scientific culture, might have blanched at the suggestion that his method was associated with ideas that dominated the Middle Ages, causal-genetic analysis surely in some sense involves a search for a timeless set of categories that can comprehend outward appearances. The means-ends relationships that are fundamental to all Austrian theoretical discussions clearly touch on issues closely related

18. See, e.g., Menger, *Problems of economics and sociology*, 54–65.
19. The accounts we have of students' experiences in the Austrian classical *Gymnasien* ought to make us somewhat skeptical of the ability of these schools to make deep impressions upon young minds. See Stefan Zweig, *The world of yesterday* (Lincoln: University of Nebraska Press, 1964), 28–59.
20. Kauder, "Intellectual and political roots," 421.

to Aristotelian fourfold causation. Not mentioned by Kauder, but more significant than most of the parallels he draws, is the close relation between Menger's depiction of rational economic man as an uncertain creature who only gradually and haltingly gains the knowledge and resources necessary to reach his true ends and Aristotle's depiction of the emergence of the man of excellence or *arete*—that mature, rational citizen of the *polis* capable of making the decisions that lead to the good life—as a gradual educational process in which the individual becomes aware through experience of the possibilities and limitations created by his own nature and that of the world around him.

Kauder's failure to support his plausible conclusion about the historical origins of the Austrian School stems largely from his failure to examine what for many would seem to be the most important historical evidence, namely, the writings of the economists in Austria who preceded Menger and who helped shape the economics curriculum in the Austrian legal faculties where he received his formal education in the subject. Surely if there is something Aristotelian about his approach, the history of economic thought in Austria prior to the 1860s could have something to do with it. It is, of course, my contention that this is so. But I also want to argue that the Aristotelianism one finds in these earlier writers had been assimilated into a philosophical system that Kauder and his followers have ignored and, moreover, that in one respect the Aristotelian heritage of the Austrian School burdened its development as much as it aided it.

The specifically Austrian prehistory of the Austrian school of economics begins with the Austrian cameralists of the seventeenth and eighteenth centuries. Cameralism encompassed much more than economics. It was a comprehensive theory of state administration closely tied to administrative practice, and it was extremely broad in scope, largely because the cameralists made no clear distinction between state and society.[21] Since the cameralists did not assume a strictly economic point of view and since their treatment of economic questions was weak in theory and largely concerned with empirical descriptions of contemporary practice, their importance for the later development of economic thought in Austria has little to do with the specifics of their positions on this or that economic issue. It lies rather in their general approach to society, their understanding of society's origins, purpose, and development.

In one sense the emergence of cameralism represented a sharp break from established Aristotelian traditions. In the universities of medieval Germany and Austria, Aristotelian scholasticism shaped most discus-

21. For a general review with useful bibliographic information see Keith Tribe, "Cameralism and the science of government," *Journal of Modern History* 56 (1984): 263–84.

sions of politics and society, and it did so in the form of ethical and theological discourse on the good life and its conditions that had little to do with the empirical realities of the early modern state. It was by breaking with this tradition and posing independent technical questions about state building that ambitious absolutist princes wanted answered that cameralism evolved as an independent discipline.[22] Indeed the cameralists of the seventeenth century wrote largely independent of any comprehensive system of thought, concentrating upon recording practical maxims without much regard to the principles that might underlie them.

Such a hodgepodge created both pedagogical problems and uncertainty in the formation of policy. The response was, of course, systematization, and it was with the imposition of system in the middle of the eighteenth century that a certain Aristotelian element reappeared in Central European treatments of state and society. However, this reappearance resulted not from a return to Aristotelian scholasticism but rather from the adoption of a philosophical system that had integrated some Aristotelian and scholastic features into a very different framework. This was the rationalism of Christian Wolff that had come to dominate the German universities at the time.[23]

While Wolff's philosophy was largely a systematization and popularization of that of Leibniz, in some respects it also reflected his schooling in traditional Aristotelian scholasticism, this being reinforced by certain Aristotelian themes evident in Leibniz's writings. Wolff followed Leibniz in dividing all knowledge into two classes, truths of reason and truths of fact. The former were self-evident statements whose opposites could not be asserted without contradiction, and the latter were contingent truths, also subject to the principle of noncontradiction but ordained by God's free decision to be part of this best of all possible worlds rather than simply logically unobjectionable possibilities.[24] The two fundamental principles of Wolffian philosophy thus became those of noncontradiction and sufficient reason, with sufficient reason being the free decree of God that establishes contingent truths.

Philosophy for Wolff was "the science of the possibles insofar as they can be."[25] One encountered the possible through experience of this

22. Hans Erich Bödeker, "Das staatswissenschaftliche Fächersystem im 18. Jahrhundert," in *Wissenschaften im Zeitalter der Aufklärung,* ed. Rudolf Vierhaus (Göttingen: Vandenhoeck & Ruprecht, 1985), 145–48.

23. On the introduction of Wolffian rationalism into Austrian universities see Werner Sauer, *Österreichische Philosophie zwischen Aufklärung und Restauration* (Amsterdam: Rodopi, 1982), 17.

24. Christian Wolff, *Preliminary discourse on philosophy in general,* trans. Richard J. Blackwell (Indianapolis: Bobbs-Merrill, 1963), 3–6.

25. Ibid., 17.

world. The philosopher's task was to comprehend it through clear and distinct ideas. These he combined into definitions, which through the use of syllogism eventually brought him back to the empirical starting point. The philosopher understood the world as composed of substances, each of which represented an essence. Through knowing these essences it was possible to deduce the necessary truths that one could understand with rational certainty, the order of possibility irrespective of God's choice. What could not be known with rational certainty was, of course, a matter of faith, and the sum was a comprehensive view of a world both rational and benevolent.

The rational order of the possible thus represented a system of essences with links to the old Aristotelian scholasticism. Wolff's philosophy also had a significant teleological feature that resulted from Leibniz's reliance upon Aristotelian ideas. This became extremely important in the fields of ethics and social thought, for when Wolff wrote on them he followed Leibniz in assuming that this world had been created by God as the best of all possible worlds and that humanity had a preestablished goal within it, the attainment of perfection through action. Perfection was defined metaphysically as the perfect harmony and interconnection of all the essential attributes of a thing that flowed from its intrinsic nature. Acting man thus developed toward the goal of achieving his true nature, another Aristotelian theme that Leibniz had drawn into his system.[26]

From these conceptions emerged an approach to politics and society that accorded with the established pattern of German absolutist thought by combining the natural rights of individuals with broad powers of the state to intervene in the lives of these same individuals. Wolff squared this circle by advancing a concept of the "public good" whose custodianship rested exclusively with "he who exercises the civil power" and which gave the ruler the irresistible "right to establish everything that appears to him to serve [it]." The sovereign had not only to secure individual rights but to promote the full perfection of life, and for this reason the individual's rights were transformed into duties. His freedom became the freedom "to advance the common good as much as he can" and to abide by his duty "to do what tends to the perfection of himself and his condition."[27]

These conceptions provided the cameralists with a framework in which to systematize their great masses of empirical materials. The goal

26. See in particular Lewis White Beck, *Early German philosophy: Kant and his predecessors* (Cambridge, Mass.: Belknap Press, 1969), 263–75.

27. Christian Wolff, *Institutions du droit de la nature et des gens,* 6 vols. (Lyden: Luzac, 1772), 1:20–25, 2:141, 165–68, 181, as quoted by Leonard Krieger in *The German idea of freedom* (Chicago: University of Chicago Press, 1972), 66–68.

of "perfection" united the physical and the moral realms into a single teleological structure controlled by the duties and liberties of the sovereign. As a result all administrative questions began to revolve around a means-ends distinction in which the ends, in good Aristotelian fashion, represented fairly specific conditions of the good life. The individual was to strive toward the end of perfection, and the state was responsible for providing the requisite means, with state power increasing in tandem with increasing recognition of individual rights. The cameralists' practical maxims were to be evaluated and ordered according to their suitability as aids in the realization of the preestablished harmony of this best of all possible worlds.[28]

These ideas were to become the official philosophy of Austrian enlightened absolutism when they were appropriated virtually without alteration by Karl Anton von Martini as a foundation for his system of natural law. The fact that Martini was a jurist, theorist of natural law, and leader in the movement for the codification of Austrian law rather than a cameralist does not diminish his importance for this discussion. On the contrary his system of natural law became the foundation for most academic thinking on questions of state and society in Austria during the second half of the eighteenth century.

Martini enthusiastically accepted Wolff's "mathematical" method of establishing "necessary truths" by locating certain "fundamental truths" and then "deriving from these, in proper order, necessary conclusions."[29] Natural law had its "sufficient reason in the nature of man and things." Its subject was action in relation to the "all perfect" nature of God.[30] As one would expect, Martini integrated these principles of method into a larger teleological framework, a framework which became fundamental for much of the thinking of the cameralists.

At the heart of Martini's system stood the categories of means and ends. According to him, things existed on account of some "final goal," and whatever led to this goal could be designated as "means." The ends of human action were intimately bound up with divine purposes, although Martini was not one to slight the good life on this earth. Accordingly, the "highest final goal of creation" was the "spreading of divine glory" through "the worship of God, the love of oneself, and sociability." All actions were to be judged in the light of this goal.[31] This meant that the fundamental principle of natural law was the "imitation" of "divine perfection," or the perfection of oneself and the world in an

28. Krieger, *German idea of freedom*, 69–70.
29. Karl Anton Freiherr von Martini, *Lehrbegriff des Natur- Staats- und Völkerrechts*, 4 vols. (Vienna: Sonnleithner, 1783–84), 1:112.
30. Ibid., 1:39, 43.
31. Ibid., 1:17–19, 36.

effort to come as close as possible to the "highest good." The individual had a range of duties, all of which were tied to the goal of individual perfection. Among other things, he had to maintain his health, to perfect his soul through the proper exercise of the will and the understanding, and to increase his abilities through exercise and art.[32]

This much applied to the isolated individual. Upon entering society, the individual found that his duties were compounded. Society had emerged to serve a higher common end, the "general" or "common benefit." This end became the principle from which "societal laws and obligations were recognized" and derived,[33] and it thus became the fundamental principle of government. It is worth noting that in Martini's hands this principle took on something of a liberal cast. The individual was to perfect himself; the task of the ruler was to maintain security and make the cooperative move toward collective welfare possible.[34]

These conceptions were seized upon by the two most important Austrian cameralists in the second half of the eighteenth century, Johann Heinrich Gottlob von Justi (1720–71) and Joseph von Sonnenfels (1732–1817), although it should be noted that they displayed less interest in Wolff's metaphysics than did Martini.[35] They saw their role as that of systematizers of cameralistic doctrine, a point stressed by Justi with respect to his own work when he claimed that "we at last perceive that the great housekeeping of the state, in all its economic, police, and cameral institutions, rests upon coherent principles, which are derived from the nature of republics."[36] This view was seconded by Sonnenfels, who spoke of his predecessor Justi as "the first who traced political science with all of its subordinate sciences to a general principle."[37] But

32. Ibid., 2:6, 17, 18–19.
33. Ibid., 2:168–71.
34. In general Martini lays great emphasis on the collection of knowledge by the ruler and has great confidence in the ability of the monarch to attain a comprehensive overview of society. See, e.g., ibid., 3:51, 123–25. Clearly, changing attitudes toward this problem must be one of the most important themes of any attempt to follow up on the general point of this essay. This attitude toward knowledge played an enormous role in the thinking of the cameralists and led to the development of cameralism's sister discipline, *Statistik,* an undertaking devoted to the collection of great masses of empirical information. See Karl Přibram, "Die Statistik als Wissenschaft in Österreich im 19. Jahrhundert," *Statistische Monatschrift,* n.s. 18 (1913): 665–72.
35. See Louise Sommer, *Die österreichischen Kameralisten,* 2 vols. (Vienna: Konegen, 1920–25), 2:210–15. Sommer argues that Justi was dependent upon Wolff merely in matters of external form. For a treatment of Justi and Sonnenfels which is particularly enlightening from the standpoint of the themes treated in this essay see Leonard Krieger, *An essay on the theory of enlightened despotism* (Chicago: University of Chicago Press, 1975), 49–56. For biographical data on Justi see Albion W. Small, *The cameralists* (Chicago: University of Chicago Press, 1909), 285–92. On Sonnenfels see Robert A. Kann, *A study in Austrian intellectual history* (New York: Praeger, 1960), 146–56.
36. Johann Heinrich Gottlob von Justi, *Staatswirthschaft,* 2 vols. (Leipzig: Breitkopf, 1758), 1:xxvi.
37. Joseph von Sonnenfels, *Grundsätze der Policey, Handlung und Finanzwissenschaft* (Munich: Strobel, 1787), 21.

while they pursued this program of systematization with considerable energy, the general principle they had inherited from Wolffian rationalism severely limited their progress. While the ideal of individual perfection, and its corollary, the perfection of society or the general welfare, might have been able to induce in Justi, Sonnenfels, and several generations of law students exposed to their ideas an agreeable vision of the good life in the prosperous state, it offered virtually nothing in the way of principled guidance to that end. It provided neither a means for identifying interdependencies among empirical phenomena nor standards that would allow one to evaluate critically the rationality and internal consistency of plans. In the end both Justi and Sonnenfels were reduced to asserting that everything that leads to the betterment of society should be encouraged, and everything that leads society's decline should be discouraged. Their rational principles, in turn, became little more than categories for classifying the various administrative measures that they and previous authors had identified as salutary.[38] But this is not to say that their work was fruitless. On the contrary, Wolffian rationalism did allow them to develop a basic framework which later authors could bring to life once an adequate "general principle" had been found. It is this basic framework that I would like to consider here.

For Justi, the "ultimate purpose" which the state existed to serve was the "happiness" of its members.[39] Thus the "first and universal principle" of political science read: "all the governmental activities of a state must be so ordered that through them the happiness of the state may be promoted."[40] This made the "final goal" of cameralism "the communal happiness." In explaining how this goal was to be reached, Justi followed the Wolffian strategy of integrating the powers of the individual into the supreme power of the state and assuming for the ruler the ability to determine the best use of both and to direct them to it. This meant that the "means and powers of the state" included not only "all sorts of goods both fixed and movable" but also "all the talents and abilities of the persons who reside in the country." The "supreme power" of the state was "the reasonable use of all things . . . and the prerogative of such use." The welfare of the ruler and the happiness of the subjects were one and the same and could be reduced to "freedom, assured property, and flourishing industry."[41]

For Justi this meant that the sovereign had two fundamental activities, "securing and increasing the 'means' of the state" and "the reasonable

---

38. See Joseph A. Schumpeter, *History of economic analysis* (New York: Oxford University Press), 173.

39. Justi, *Staatswirthschaft*, 1:35.

40. Johann Heinrich Gottlob von Justi, "Kurzer systematischer Grundriss aller Oeconomischen und Cameralwissenschaften," in his *Gesammelte Politische und Finanzschriften*, 3 vols. (Copenhagen: Rothen, 1761), 1:506.

41. Justi, *Staatswirthschaft*, 1:47–48, 66.

and wise use of the 'means,' "[42] activities which were the respective subject matters of two sciences, cameralism and its cousin *Polizeiwissenschaft*.[43] The latter of these dealt with "the preservation and increase of the total 'means' of the state through good internal institutions" and the creation of "all sorts of internal power and strength for the republic" through such things as cultivation, improvement in the condition of the laboring class, and the maintenance of "good discipline and order in the community."[44] Cameralism itself dealt with the "reasonable and wise use of the 'means.' "[45] Both sciences were concerned largely with planning for the use of the means available to individuals and the state.

But Justi's weaknesses become painfully obvious when he moved from such programmatic statements to their implementation. For example, in applying his deductive method to *Polizeiwissenschaft,* he established as its "fundamental principle" that "one must arrange the inner constitution of the commonwealth so that the general means available to the state are maintained and increased and the common welfare is continually promoted." According to Justi, "the correctness and the universality of this principle is best revealed by proving how all other fundamental principles and doctrines are derived from it." The proof that Justi then provided amounted simply to an enumeration of the various classes of "the general means of the state"—namely, "unmovable, movable," and "the skills and abilities of all who belong to the commonwealth"—and an assertion that the state must maintain and increase them. He followed this up with three platitudinous propositions that should guide state action in connection with each of these classes: (1) "one must above all cultivate and build up the lands of the republic in every possible way"; (2) "one must seek to promote in every possible way the gaining of products from the land and raising of the standard of living"; and (3) "one must provide that the subjects possess such abilities and characteristics and are maintained in such decorum and order as required by the goal of communal happiness."[46]

What followed was a discussion divided into three parts, each corre-

42. Ibid., 2:3.

43. The term is virtually untranslatable but means roughly "science of internal order," internal order being understood as including all the conditions that go to make up the good life. *Polizeiwissenschaft* was concerned with promoting these and thus went far beyond the problems of internal security covered by the modern conception of "police." See Marc Raeff, *The well-ordered police state* (New Haven: Yale University Press, 1983); Franz-Ludwig Knemeyer, "Polizei," *Economy and Society* 9 (1980): 172–96.

44. Johann Heinrich Gottlob von Justi, *Grundsätze der Policeywissenschaft* (Göttingen: Vandenhoek, 1782). See Justi's unpaginated preface to the first edition included in this volume.

45. Ibid., 7–8.

46. Ibid., 9–14.

sponding to one of these three basic rules and each containing a wealth of recommendations for their implementation. What Justi did not do was provide any sense of how these recommendations were related to each other or what sorts of priorities they might impose. He simply asserted that one must pursue every desirable goal as far as possible and avoid every undesirable situation equally assiduously. When one found an appropriate mean, then one must strike it. Indeed Justi virtually admitted that his general principles had no connection with any general and constant interdependencies among phenomena when he stated that the "means" available for reaching the ends of states are "randomly and infinitely differentiated from each other depending upon the nature of the lands, the times, and the customs" of the state in question. Correspondingly the rules for the application of these means were "simply random and allow infinite differentiation." There were no rational criteria for choosing among alternatives; the best one could hope for was simply a practical "astuteness" which could aid one in selecting the best.[47] In the end Justi was unable to blend his rational method with empirical reality, and the gap between the two left him with an elaborate system of classification but little in the way of scientific comprehension.

Justi's successor Sonnenfels recognized the problem but made only minimal progress in overcoming it. Sonnenfels has been described as more empirical in his method, having been influenced by writers such as Hume and Ferguson.[48] However his empiricism was restricted largely to a hostility to the contract theories of society that had had some influence upon Justi. In his approach to cameralism as both science and administrative practice he did manifest a certain empiricist caution, but the ultimate goal remained rational system. He insisted that "the measures through which the general welfare is managed" be derived "from a fundamental principle and set forth according to their agreement with the final goal" of the state.[49]

Sonnenfels differed with Justi by rejecting the "promotion of general happiness" as the fundamental principle of cameralism. He did this because, while this aim was "indeed the cause of the rise of states and their perpetual final goal," as stated it offered no useful criteria for gauging the value of measures purported to accord with it. To overcome this difficulty Sonnenfels chose to confer primacy upon a principle that many previous cameralists, in particular Justi himself, had stressed heavily, the principle of population.[50] According to Sonnenfels, "the

47. Ibid., 334.
48. Sommer, *Die österreichischen Kameralisten*, 2:323–24.
49. Sonnenfels, *Grundsätze*, 20.
50. Indeed most of the earlier Austrian cameralists had to one degree or another been populationists, and the issue became an obsession of Austrian policy makers in the middle

expansion of society encompasses within itself . . . all of the subordinate means which taken together promote the general welfare." Increases in population were important because by combining with others individuals increased their ability to maximize their own welfare; the greater the size of a society, "the greater becomes the force that it can bring to bear in particular situations." Moreover, "the more numerous society is, the more numerous become its needs and the easier it becomes to provide for both these needs and society's comforts." Increases in population increased human needs and also increased the means necessary for fulfilling them. As society grew, life became more secure, more variegated, and more prosperous. Sonnenfels thus judged all governmental actions according to their implications for population growth, or in his own words: "we take the expansion of civil society through the promotion of population as the fundamental communal principle of political science and the sciences which it encompasses."[51]

Starting from this fundamental principle, Sonnenfels proceeded to carry out a tripartite reorganization of cameralism that centered on what he took to be three distinct classes of means relevant to the growth of population.[52] There were means relevant to security, the subject matter of politics and *Polizeiwissenschaft,* which dealt respectively with threats to external and to internal security; means relevant to individual welfare, the subject matter of *Handlungswissenschaft,* or the science of internal wealth-creating activity of all sorts; and means relevant to general welfare, the subject matter of public finance. In each case Sonnenfels applied the principle of population to obtain a fundamental maxim that would guide the application of the relevant means. The fundamental principle of politics was "the more populous the people, the greater is the degree of resistance upon which its security rests." In the case of *Polizei,* the greater the size of the population "upon whose ready assistance one can depend, the less one has to fear from within."[53] In the case of the *Handlungswissenschaften,* the more individuals there were, "the more needs, the more diverse the domestic means of subsistence" (an expression of concern for variety as an indicator of welfare that would be

eighteenth century. See John Fred Bell, *A history of economic thought,* 2d ed. (Malabar: Krieger, 1967), 90, 96; Gerhard Stavenhagen, *Geschichte der Wirtschaftstheorie,* 4th ed. (Göttingen: Vandenhoeck & Ruprecht, 1969), 24; Schumpeter, *History of economic analysis,* 251–53; Joachim Moerchel, *Die Wirtschaftspolitik Maria Theresias und Josephs II. in der Zeit von 1740 bis 1780* (Munich: Minerva, 1979), 36–40, and literature cited there. It is interesting to note that population growth and decline is still a measure of welfare for some Austrian economists, especially Hayek.

51. Sonnenfels, *Grundsätze,* 21–22.

52. Karl-Heinz Osterloh, *Joseph von Sonnenfels und die österreichische Reformbewegung im Zeitalter des aufgeklärten Absolutismus* (Lübeck: Matthiesen, 1970), 43.

53. Sonnenfels, *Grundsätze,* 22.

much on Menger's mind),[54] and "the more hands, the more copious the products of agriculture and industry." In the case of public finance, Sonnenfels, apparently assuming that public expenditures need not rise with population growth, claimed that increases in the number of tax-payers would reduce the size of individual contributions without decreasing public revenues.[55]

Beyond this Sonnenfels made little progress in his search for system. His works, like Justi's, became for the most part catalogues of practical administrative maxims. He did believe in a stable set of interdependencies that controlled the correct relationship between society's means and its various ends, and he held that if men were allowed to pursue their purposes, these interdependencies would actualize themselves. Indeed of all the Austrian cameralists he was the one who most clearly anticipated a liberal outlook, emphasizing as he did the role of the state as the preserver of security rather than creator of order.[56] But while he believed in a system of preestablished social harmony which the state was to watch over and protect, he remained largely silent about the principles that regulated this system.

In the end the cameralists proved incapable of developing some principle or method of analysis that would allow them to move beyond categorizing means and ends to a real understanding of the various interdependencies that existed among them. The impasse was broken through the reception of English classical political economy in the German-speaking world, an event that produced a somewhat peculiar hybrid doctrine that Schumpeter labeled "Smithian cameralism."[57] Smithian cameralism was important for two fundamental reasons. First, it established the skeptical and critical attitude toward economic theory that would be characteristic of much German economic thought in the nineteenth and twentieth centuries. But, secondly and somewhat paradoxically, it also established the basis for the creative and innovative use of economic theory that would be found in some quarters of the German-speaking world during this period. What produced both of these developments was the persistence of the teleological means-ends patterns of thought that Wolffian rationalism had imparted to mature eighteenth-century cameralism and the statism that accompanied it. On the critical side, this engendered the typically German opposition to the

54. See esp. Erich Streissler, "To what extent was the Austrian School marginalist?" in *The marginal revolution in economics,* ed. R. D. Collison Black, A. W. Coats, and Craufurd D. W. Goodwin (Durham, N.C.: Duke University Press, 1973), 161.

55. Sonnenfels, *Grundsätze,* 22–23.

56. Although this theme is already apparent in Justi (see Schumpeter, *History of economic analysis,* 171–72), Sonnenfels generally is identified as the central figure in the transition to liberalism.

57. Schumpeter, *History of economic analysis,* 501.

individualism of Adam Smith as well as the strong tendency to treat economic phenomena from an ethical point of view. On the theoretical side, the teleological approach helped to produce two of the most important concepts in German economic science during the nineteenth century: the concepts of the economic good and objective use value.[58] It is this latter development that deserves attention here, for since the concepts of the economic good and objective use value eventually became the "goods" and "needs" that form the foundation of the causal-genetic method, it is this development that ties the matters discussed to this point to the eventual emergence of the Austrian School.

To some extent the reception of classical political economy by cameralist writers took place under the influence of Kantian philosophy, and this helped to inject an idealist cast into German economics. However, for the most part it was the established patterns of cameralist thinking that were decisive. They can be seen in the early phase of the development of the concept of the economic good in the work of Gottlieb Hufeland. In dealing with the economic good, he followed the lead of the older literature and chose to define it as a means to an end.[59] But the idealist strand in his thought caused him to take a significant subjective turn when drawing up his definition. Nothing was a good in and of itself but only "by virtue of the ideas" or conceptions that individuals had of it. Such ideas were based upon ends and the way the things in question could serve as means to them. The basic economic phenomena of value and price were not determined by real relationships, but rather by the opinions that people form of these relations.[60] Labor was not the cause of value. Things had value rather as a result of ideas and "their suitability as means to an end that one wishes to reach."[61]

The theory of objective use value was a concern of most of the major Smithian cameralists. Their general strategy in approaching the topic was to attempt to discover categories of needs (*Bedürfnissgattungen*), which, true to the convictions of the cameralists, were understood ethically and politically as general conditions of the good life. The correct ordering of these needs would reveal the objective use values of the goods which could satisfy them, and these values and the relationships among them were seen as a key to explaining and promoting economic development. To this end, the Smithian cameralists searched for a concrete average need unit and held that one of the main goals of

58. Particularly helpful on this entire episode is Stavenhagen, *Geschichte der Wirtschaftstheorie,* 102–6.
59. Gottlieb Hufeland, *Neue Grundlegung der Staatswirtschaft,* 2 vols. (Vienna: Baüer, 1815), 1:15.
60. Ibid., 1:17–24; Stavenhagen, *Geschichte der Wirtschaftstheorie,* 103.
61. Hufeland, *Neue Grundlegung,* 1:36–37.

political economy was to instruct people about their true needs. The entire question of the processes by which goods were ordered so that needs could be satisfied clearly contains within it the starting point of Menger's project, and the inability of the Smithian cameralists to move beyond discussions of the relationships among general classes of goods is highly suggestive of both the debt he owed to them and the point at which he departed from them.[62]

While most of the representatives of Smithian cameralism were Germans, there was one significant Austrian among them. This was Joseph Kudler (1786–1853), a writer whose importance stems less from his originality than from the fact that his work on economics became the prescribed text in Austrian universities during the 1850s and 1860s. Although he is usually passed over in discussions of Austrian social thought during the *Vormärz* in favor of conservatives like Adam Müller and Friedrich Gentz—whom historians tend to identify as more representative of the time—Kudler was in fact one of the most significant figures of the period, combining vast legal and cameralistic learning with a staunchly liberal outlook and an interest in classical economics.[63] It is the way that he represented a stage in the general development of economic thinking in Austria rather than the specific ideas that Menger might or might not have drawn from him that makes Kudler of interest here.

Kudler's role as a liberal found ample expression in his major work on economic theory and policy, *Die Grundlehren der Volkswirtschaft*, published in 1846.[64] Until this time Sonnenfels's *Grundsätze der Policey, Handlung und Finanzwissenschaft* had remained the prescribed economics text in Austrian universities, and Kudler, at least in part at the instigation of the liberal Archduke Wilhelm Franz Karl, whose tutor he had been, hoped to help bring the teaching of economics in Austria up to date.[65] But like other authors in the tradition of Smithian cameralism, he remained highly dependent upon the past. Indeed while he was hostile to much of the restrictive system that had become associated with the cameralists, he, like other Smithian cameralists, still posed economic questions in terms of the categories that Justi and Sonnenfels had used.

Kudler's system thus became a peculiar hybrid. It contained a large dose of the teleological thinking of the cameralists, and it combined with this a set of theoretical propositions meant to point out and explain the

---

62. Stavenhagen, *Geschichte der Wirtschaftstheorie,* 104.

63. On Kudler see Kurt Ebert, *Die Grazer Juristenfakultät im Vormärz* (Graz: Leykam, 1969), 88–92, and sources cited there.

64. Joseph Kudler, *Die Grundlehren der Volkswirtschaft,* 2 vols., 2d ed. (Vienna: Gerold, 1856). This second edition does not vary from the first.

65. Ibid., 1:vii–viii.

interdependencies that existed among the elements of purposeful social institutions. These theoretical propositions were, of course, drawn from classical economics, but when absorbed into the patterns of thought established by the cameralists, their meaning and function began to change.

True to cameralist thinking, Kudler made means and ends, goods and needs, the central focus of economic theory. He understood the economy to be "that activity which is concerned with the procurement and administration of goods," and he held its goal to be "the enduring satisfaction of needs through appropriate income."[66] Correspondingly, economic theory became the "totality of *rules* related to the acquisition, maintenance, and utilization of means."[67] In other words, in the spirit of cameralist tradition, economic theory involved principles of administration, principles that directed purposeful action. Kudler recognized that the category "goods" could be very broad. Thus he held that "everything which is suitable for the satisfaction of a human need is termed a good in the broader sense of the term." Economics was concerned only with "goods in the narrower sense," i.e., material things. But despite the basic materialism of his approach to economics, Kudler's teleological thinking introduced a strong subjective element into his definition of goods. He held that nothing was a good in and of itself. A thing becomes a good when its connection with needs is recognized, and value depends upon this recognition. It is opinion that brings goods into being, not reality itself.[68] Moreover, Kudler's teleological approach led him to conceive of goods as arranged within a hierarchical structure. There were two main classes in this hierarchy, goods of higher orders and consumption goods, the former being termed goods of mediate value and the latter termed goods of immediate value.[69] In turn Kudler treated needs as natural desires "for that which spares us discomfort or which gives pleasure or satisfaction."[70] Needs impel man to action, to seek out goods, to collect them, and produce them. Needs will increase as the economic process develops, the eventual result of the process being a well-ordered set of economic institutions.[71]

This much was a product of the cameralist heritage. That heritage clearly impelled Kudler to treat economic value as a subjective phenomenon and to see goods as the product of perceptions of the suitability of things to serve human needs. A thing had value, or what Kudler termed

66. Ibid., 1:2; see also 1:43–66.
67. Ibid., 1:2, emphasis added.
68. Ibid., 1:46, 47, 51.
69. Ibid., 1:48.
70. Ibid., 1:43.
71. Ibid., 1:1.

"positive" value, if it was deemed useful for some purpose. For a thing to have value, a need must exist, the thing must have qualities necessary to satisfy that need, and these qualities must be recognized. "Comparative" or relative value referred to the place that a good occupied within a collection of goods. According to Kudler, this was not determined "arbitrarily," but rather "according to ideas that one has of the importance of goals and the ability of a thing to reach them." The actual magnitude of such value was dependent on "the view we have of the importance and urgency of a certain end," "on the degree of suitability of the object for reaching an end," and on "the fact that a thing serves to reach several ends."[72]

It is a very short step from this to Menger's treatment of goods and value. However, Kudler's use of classical economics injected a competing element into his system that he was able to reconcile only loosely with his subjectivism. When he moved beyond "positive" and "comparative" to "exchange" value, he took an objective turn and made labor both its cause and its measure. He integrated this objective theory of value into a system of "cost prices," or theory of production and distribution, that became something of a confusion of subjective and objective factors. Labor was the measure of exchange value, but things exchanged on the basis of the "conceptions" that people have of them. There was an equality in exchange based on equality of costs, but there was also inequality in exchange, since people will only engage in exchange if what they receive is more valuable than what they give up. In the end Kudler's "cost prices" simply placed certain basic constraints on the economy, in that they formed centers of gravity around which market prices revolved.[73]

Kudler thus represented something of an uneasy compromise between the teleological thinking of the cameralists that centered on the categories of goods and needs and the new classical economics that seemed to prove a set of criteria that placed constraints on the administration of goods. The compromise was an unstable one, with subjective perceptions and objective factors competing as the ultimate causes of economic phenomena. His accomplishments hardly qualified him as a leading figure in the history of economic thought, but his fall into historical oblivion has nonetheless been unfortunate. That Kudler's "vision" adumbrates Menger's in much of its broad outline hardly needs emphasizing, and, returning to the main point of this essay, it is not difficult to picture the young Menger being introduced to the basic elements of what has come to be seen as his "essentialistic" and "Aristo-

72. Ibid., 1:47.
73. See ibid., 1:73–74, 80–81, 89–91, 104, 115, 119–20.

telian" approach to economics during the course of the first few lectures on economics that he heard at the university, lectures which doubtless dealt with goods and needs and which on these points probably followed Kudler closely.

Finally, what does all of this tell us about the current understanding of the prehistory of the Austrian School, and what suggestions regarding the future course of research on the topic can be drawn from it? First of all, it should be clear that Kauder's evidence does not support his thesis and that further attempts to find direct influence of the writings of Aristotle on the early members of the Austrian School are unlikely to bear much fruit. To the degree that the causal-genetic method of the Austrian School does exhibit "Aristotelian" features, these have their roots in the Wolffian rationalism that became the basis of the systematizing efforts of the late Austrian cameralists, Justi and Sonnenfels. But as I indicated briefly at the outset, while this heritage played an important role in shaping the distinctive approach of the Austrian School, it also impeded the development of that school in important ways, and it was by way of breaking free from a number of its central elements that later Austrians made many of their most important contributions.

What Kauder and his followers have tended to forget about Aristotelianism in general is the specificity of the ends attached to the essences of all entities. Man for Aristotle was not simply an actor who pursued ends, he was a creature who realized his true being when he achieved a rather specific set of ends, those that defined the good life. Aristotle's entire practical philosophy was devoted to discussing this issue, and there can be no truly Aristotelian inquiry into action and society apart from a discussion of the conditions of the good life. This much of Aristotle was clearly absorbed by Leibniz and Wolff, and it was one of the reasons that the cameralists found their ideas so appealing. The Smithian cameralists continued in this tradition; that is what their concern with objective use value was all about.

Menger too devoted considerable attention to this issue. Indeed one might say that he was obsessed with it. While many authors have duly noted the way Menger depicted the movement of rational economic man toward equilibrium as a slow and painstaking process, what has usually been overlooked is the fact that he attributed to rational economic man's final goal a fairly specific content. Menger defined economics as the science which inquires into the laws of cause and effect which control the processes through which goods satisfy human needs. These laws were for him not simply abstract rules of economic rationality. They also dealt with the *content* of needs and the suitability of particular goods to serve them. This is why Menger stressed that there are both real and imagined needs and real and imagined goods.[74] Fully rational economic man was for him an enlightened creature who understood his real needs, and the movement toward equilibrium was more than simply a slow and uncertain process; it was the entire movement of human history as nineteenth-century European liberals, echoing Condorcet, had visualized it. The goal of the market process for Menger was the emergence of the enlightened individual who realized his true being through the powers of science, natural and economic. While they might have been somewhat disturbed by his secularism, there can be little doubt that Leibniz, Wolff, Martini, Justi, Sonnenfels, and Kudler would have recognized their understanding of the ultimate ends of man and society in Menger's approach to economic development.

In other words, the weight of the past placed serious limits on both Menger's ability and his willingness to pursue subjectivism with the consistency that later Austrians aspired to. Indeed we know that he spent much of his later life searching for the biological foundations of human needs,[75] the key to the integration of economics with material reality. Whether that search led to frustrations and new beginnings is one of the most important questions those examining his late notebooks must try to answer. However, for the time being one thing is certain: Menger's dependence upon the past did lead to frustrations and searches for new beginnings among younger members of the Austrian School. Indeed one can see the early methodological writings of Ludwig von Mises as an attempt to cut the ties with the past that Menger held on to. Mises's claim that "through its subjectivism, modern theory becomes objective science,"[76] meant, among other things, that only by ceasing to differentiate between an actor's real and imagined needs could one begin to understand the implications of his actions from the standpoint of what is, rather than what ought to be. All needs that determine what ought to be are imagined, and the "essences" that control what is, are simply the logical rules discovered by "the science of the possibles insofar as they can be."[77]

74. Menger, *Principles of economics,* 53–54.

75. This aspect of Menger's later development is briefly described by his son, Karl Menger, in his introduction to the second edition of the *Grundsätze* (Vienna: Hölder-Pichler-Tempsky, 1923), viii–x.

76. Ludwig Mises, *Grundprobleme der Nationalökonomie* (Jena: Gustav Fischer, 1933), 164.

77. See note 25 above.

Menger, classical liberalism, and the Austrian school of economics

Israel M. Kirzner

A series of valuable recent papers has reflected increasing current interest in the political and ideological stance of the founding economists of the Austrian School. What is particularly intriguing about this literature is that it offers what appears, at least superficially, to be a set of sharply differing readings and assessments of this politico-ideological stance. Especially in regard to Carl Menger, we are offered apparently contradictory assessments. He was a champion of laissez faire; he favored substantial state economic intervention; he had no clearly defined and articulated political position at all—each of these views of Menger and the early Austrians is to be found expressed somewhere in the literature. Each of these views is supported by citations from the early Austrians. The purpose of the present paper is to reconcile the apparent inconsistencies presented in these earlier papers.

Our conclusions will be: (1) that the early Austrians, especially Menger, occupied a position which recognized both the efficacy of markets and scope for useful governmental economic intervention; (2) that this half-full, half-empty position was not articulated in any deliberate, integrated fashion, so that individual remarks can be cited that might suggest more extreme positions than the one in fact occupied; (3) that this half-full, half-empty position nonetheless expressed an understanding of markets which, *taken by itself,* strongly suggested a more radical appreciation for free markets than the early Austrians themselves in fact displayed. It is this latter circumstance, we surmise, which explains how, when later Austrians arrived at even more consistently laissez-faire positions, they were seen by historians of thought as somehow simply pursuing an Austrian tradition that can be traced back to the founders.

As must be apparent, the development of this thesis, while at first glance in conflict with the various contributions to the current literature on this topic, in fact differs from them only in matters of emphasis. Indeed the present paper contains very little that is new: it draws most of its ideas from the existing literature, merely weaving these ideas into what makes up, we wish to maintain, a more acceptable, integrated story. Writers have pointed out that the cup was not full; writers have pointed out that the cup was not empty; writers have even pointed out that the cup was half-full, and half-empty. We will not merely confirm the half-full, half-empty reading but help explain, perhaps, why the cup could seem quite full to some observers while appearing quite empty to others.

Menger, the Austrians, and laissez faire: some paradoxes

Stephan Boehm has drawn our attention to one strand of the conventional wisdom in regard to the Austrian School from the time of Menger onwards, namely the identification of the Austrians as "rigorous defenders of laissez-faire and outspoken apologists of the capitalist system."[1] Against this traditional view of the Austrians Boehm marshals powerful evidence from Menger's own writings: "Menger presents a list of five legitimate tasks ascribed to the state, respectively 'improvement of the situation of the working class, just distribution of income, encouragement of individual ability, thrift and entrepreneurial initiative.' "[2] If this (ambitious!) list of governmental responsibilities were not sufficiently impressive, Boehm cites both Menger and Böhm-Bawerk as emphatically, even vehemently, rejecting charges that they followed a laissez-faire, "Manchester" approach to social policy. Menger, Boehm cites, maintained explicitly that "nothing could be more opposed to his school than to vindicate the capitalist system. In fact, the only thing that he appreciated in Schmoller was his passionate concern for the poor and weak."[3]

Yet the view that the Austrian economists were indeed uncompromising advocates of laissez faire—and certainly the view that they were *perceived* as such—cannot be summarily dismissed. Erich Streissler has, particularly in his recent work, drawn our attention to newly available material supporting this view of Menger. As is well known, Menger spent several years as tutor to Crown Prince Rudolph of Austria. Ru-

---

1. Stephan Boehm, "The political economy of the Austrian School," in *Gli economisti e la politica economica,* ed. Piero Roggi (Naples: Edizioni Scientifiche Italiane, 1985), 249.

2. Boehm, "Political economy," 250, citing Carl Menger, "Die Social-Theorien der classischen National-Oekonomie und die moderne Wirtschaftspolitik" (1891), reprinted in Menger's *Gesammelte Werke,* 3:245.

3. Boehm, "Political economy," 251, citing Carl Menger, *Die Irrthümer des Historismus in der deutschen Nationalökonomie* (1884), reprinted in *Gesammelte Werke,* 3:93. Boehm could also have emphasized the interventionist flavor of Friedrich von Wieser's later work; see especially his *Social economics,* translated from the German edition of 1914 by A. F. Hinrichs (New York: Adelphi, 1927), 408–16. See also Professor Streissler's remark that "Wieser was by instinct at least an unabashed paternalistic interventionist, if not to say finally a fascist" ("The intellectual and political impact of the Austrian school of economics," *History of European Ideas* 9.2 [1988]: 200). Recently Carl G. Uhr has referred to Menger as a "moderate social-minded liberal" who was "no uncritical defender of laissez faire" (in a book review, *HOPE* 21.1 [Spring 1989]: 152).

dolph was required to prepare essays setting forth the lectures he had heard from Menger. These lecture notes, with corrections by Menger, have recently been rediscovered by Brigitte Hamann, who provided typewritten copies to Streissler. From these essays Streissler has concluded that Menger taught Rudolph "a liberalism possibly even more rigorous than that of Adam Smith. In 'normal' cases economic action of the state is always harmful: it is only to be allowed in 'abnormal' cases."[4]

Perhaps even more persuasive, in regard to the perception of the Austrian School as champions of noninterventionism, are the personal reminiscences of Ludwig Mises. Mises studied at the University of Vienna in the very early years of this century, and he became one of Böhm-Bawerk's best-known disciples. His name is invariably cited as a prominent participant in Böhm-Bawerk's famous seminar at the university. There can be little doubt that Mises was thoroughly familiar with the political stance of the members of the Austrian School. Although he did not study under Menger, he could not but have been aware of what Menger's political views were understood to be. For Mises there seems to have been not a shadow of doubt that the Austrians saw themselves (and were seen by their contemporaries) as vindicating not merely an abstract science of economics (against historicist challenges), but also at the same time the effectiveness of the market economy (against its socialist and statist detractors).

In a chapter entitled "The political aspects of the *Methodenstreit*" Mises describes the alliance between Schmoller and his Historical School, and the Bismarckian policies in Prussia which "began to inaugurate its Sozialpolitik, the system of interventionist measures such as labor legislation, social security, pro-union attitudes, progressive taxation, protective tariffs, cartels, and dumping."[5] It is true that Mises recognized that when "Menger, Böhm-Bawerk and Wieser began their scientific careers, they were not concerned with the problems of economic policies and with the rejection of interventionism by Classical economics. They considered it as their vocation to put economic theory on a sound basis and they were ready to dedicate themselves entirely to this cause."[6] But this passage is followed by the flat assertion that "Menger heartily disapproved of the interventionist policies that the Austrian Government . . . had adopted."[7] A skeptic might be tempted to wonder if Mises (writing in 1969) was not perhaps independently

4. Streissler, "Intellectual and political impact," 201; see also his n. 2 for further details on the Menger-Rudolph lecture-essays.
5. Ludwig von Mises, *The historical setting of the Austrian school of economics* (New Rochelle, N.Y.: Arlington House, 1969), 30.
6. Mises, *Historical setting*, 18.
7. Ibid.

reading into his teachers' attitudes the laissez-faire stance which he himself came to adopt in his own career. But a fair-minded reader of Mises's many references to the political implications of the *Methodenstreit* will find it difficult to avoid concluding that Mises is simply expressing the generally held perception of the Austrians as being strongly opposed to the statist intervention espoused by the Historical School.

And yet, as cited by Boehm,[8] we find Gunnar Myrdal describing the Austrians as being the rare nineteenth-century economists who did not inject political motives into their economics: "In Austria, economics has never had direct political aims."[9] Apparently Myrdal's reading of Austrian economics found it neither tendentiously interventionist nor seeking to promote laissez faire.

To round out our sketch of perceptions of the Austrian School's political stance (or lack of such) we must refer to a most explicit statement by Nikolai Bukharin, the eminent Marxist theorist and economic scholar, who spent time as a participant in Böhm-Bawerk's seminar and wrote a book-length, trenchantly Marxist critique of Austrian economic theory. In his preface to the Russian edition of this book Bukharin refers to his having chosen to attack the Austrian School (rather than other schools of modern economics): "Our selection of an opponent for our criticism probably does not require discussion, for it is well known that the most powerful opponent of Marxism is the Austrian School."[10] Of course, to be a powerful opponent of Marxism is not yet to be a champion of laissez faire. Yet it seems clear that the Austrians were seen as providing a strong intellectual defense of capitalism.[11] Nothing in their writings, it appears, could suggest any principled reasons for doubting the effectiveness of capitalist institutions in promoting human economic welfare.

This, then, is the situation in which we find ourselves. Evidence apparently exists to support the view that the Austrians were propo-

---

8. Boehm, "Political economy," 248.

9. Gunnar Myrdal, *The political element in the development of economic theory* (Cambridge: Harvard University Press, 1953), 128.

10. Nikolai Bukharin, *Economic theory of the leisure class,* reprint of first (1927) U.S. edition (New York and London: Monthly Review Press, 1972), 9.

11. This Marxist perception of the Austrians as spearheading the bourgeois counter-revolutionary intellectual campaign has persisted, sometimes in bizarre fashion, into our own time. Thus Maurice Dobb has misread Schumpeter's reference to Böhm-Bawerk as "the bourgeois Marx" (*History of economic analysis* [Oxford: Oxford University Press, 1954], 846) to mean that Schumpeter saw Böhm-Bawerk primarily as leader of the "conscious *apologists* of the existing system" (Dobb, *Theories of value and distribution since Adam Smith,* [Cambridge: Cambridge University Press, 1973], 193). Schumpeter, of course, meant nothing of the kind by this way of describing Böhm-Bawerk. Rather he wished to draw attention to Bawerk's comprehensive, system-embracing theoretical perspective on capitalism—one which matched Marx's own view in grandeur of scope. Nonetheless Dobb's remark confirms the point made here in the text.

nents of laissez faire, the view that they were sympathetic to interventionism, and the view that they were unconcerned with the political implications of their doctrines. Let us consider independently, quite apart from any of the cited evidence, what one might *expect* to conclude, in terms of political implications, from the economic theory of the Austrian School, especially in its initial, Mengerian incarnation.

Menger and the marginal utility revolution

A certain ambiguity has come to surround the question of the degree to which Menger's *Grundsätze* represented a revolutionary, pioneering contribution to the economics of his time. The traditional view among historians of thought has seen Menger's work as one of the three basic contributions to the "marginal utility revolution" (besides being a manifesto upholding the theoretical method in economics, in opposition to the historical method that had become entrenched in German economics). From this traditional reading of Menger, his book was a frontal, pioneering, revolutionary attack on classical orthodoxy. Yet at the same time Menger's book, and especially its preface, freely acknowledged profound indebtedness to earlier writers, particularly to the "foundation laid by previous work that was produced almost entirely by the industry of German scholars."[12] Indeed Streissler has in recent work drawn attention to a mid-nineteenth-century German "protoneoclassical" tradition in which Menger's work should be recognized as a contribution offering continuity of forward development, rather than providing any revolutionary departure.[13] Although Menger emphasized themes central to the marginal utility revolution, Streissler argues, Menger saw himself as a reformer rather than a revolutionary.

Yet this ambiguity concerning possible links between Menger's *Principles* and this German "protoneoclassical" tradition must surely relate strictly to specific features of Menger's system, especially his subjective theory of value. There seems little doubt concerning Menger's awareness that he was, in his *Principles,* offering *a perspective on the economic system* which was entirely new. Menger's emphasis, in his preface, on the need to balance "careful attention to past work in all the fields of our science thus far explored" against criticism, "with full independence of judgment, [of] the opinions of our predecessors, and even [of] doctrines until now considered definitive attainments of our science,"[14] suggests his very clear sense of breaking sharply with the

12. Carl Menger, *Principles of economics,* translated from the original German edition (1871) by B. F. Hoselitz, 1950 (reprinted New York: New York University Press, 1981), 49.

13. E. Streissler, "Menger, Böhm-Bawerk, and Wieser: the origins of the Austrian School," in *Neoclassical economic theory, 1870 to 1900,* ed. K. Hennings and W. J. Samuels (Boston: Kluwer, 1990).

14. Menger, *Principles,* 46.

past. Hayek has told us that Menger is said to have "remarked that he wrote the *Grundsätze* in a state of morbid excitement."[15] It seems reasonable to attribute this excitement to Menger's conviction that he was writing a pathbreaking book.

Menger's acknowledgment of debt to German scholars and his dedication of his book to Wilhelm Roscher, the famous leader of the (older) German Historical School, should not be misunderstood. These references are surely to be understood, not as reflecting any failure to perceive the novelty of his own work, but as expressing his meticulous sense of propriety towards earlier scholars whose contributions he valued (as well as being prudent strategic policy in seeking to ally himself with the most influential scholars of his time, in his effort to dislodge the classical orthodoxy). This interpretation is entirely consistent with the measured criticism which Menger accorded the work of Roscher himself a dozen years after the *Grundsätze*.[16] The difference in tone (in regard to Roscher and the other pre-Schmoller German economists) that separates Menger's *Untersuchungen* from the *Grundsätze* need not be attributed to a change of heart, or of opinion, on these matters (to be explained perhaps by the coolness with which the *Grundsätze* was received in Germany). Menger still warmly acknowledged (in 1883 as in 1871) the "virtues of the scientific personality of the learned Leipzig scholar; his outstanding merits and his advancement of the historical understanding of a number of important economic phenomena; the incomparable stimulation which his studies in the literature of our science have given to all younger colleagues."[17] The criticisms of Roscher in 1883 may rather be understood as expressing Menger's recent realization that his own success in fashioning his new understanding of the economic system depended crucially on his own theoretical orientation, with which the now-dominant German approach must be sharply contrasted. (Moreover, the cool reception accorded to the *Grundsätze* in Germany may have convinced Menger that no strategic alliance with the German economists could now realistically be anticipated.)

So Menger's work in 1871 is surely to be read as quite deliberately offering an entirely fresh perspective on the economic system as a whole. It is true that important elements (concerning subjectivism, utility, and so on) were drawn from earlier German writers, as Streissler

15. Hayek, "Introduction" to Menger, *Principles*, 16.
16. Carl Menger, *Investigations into the method of the social sciences with special reference to economics*, translated from the original German edition (1883) by F. J. Nock (New York and London: New York University Press, 1985), a reprint of *Problems of economics and sociology* (Urbana: University of Illinois, 1963), 185–89.
17. Menger, *Investigations*, 189.

(and Hayek)[18] have pointed out. Yet the overall vision of the economy as a system driven entirely and independently by the choices and valuations of consumers—with these valuations transmitted "upwards" through the system to "goods of higher order," determining how these scarce higher-order goods are allocated among industries and how they are valued and remunerated as part of a single consumer-driven process—was one which Menger surely (and correctly) sensed as being wholly new.

And if this, rather than any technical innovations in marginal utility theory, is to be seen as Menger's self-recognized original contribution, then it seems reasonable to understand Menger as perceiving a correspondingly original implication of his vision for normative economics. This assertion calls for brief elaboration.

Menger and the efficiency of the market economy

Menger's vision of the economic system as one controlled entirely by consumer preferences, valuations, and choices has significant welfare implications. Against a given background of scarce resources (potential goods of higher order) consumer preferences and choices set in motion an ever-widening ripple series of entrepreneurial productive activities which result in market valuations of factor services, and corresponding allocations of them among industries. From this vision there emerges a clear sense of *consumer sovereignty*—a concept with obviously important normative implications.

This vision of consumer sovereignty offers a normative criterion which differs sharply from the classical basis for laissez faire. Classical economists saw the free market economy producing (under the incentives afforded by the invisible hand) the *greatest possible volume of material wealth*. Menger's view of the market pointed, not so much to a maximization of aggregate output, as to a pattern of *economic governance exercised by consumer preferences*. This aspect of Menger's vision suggests an appreciation for the outcomes of free markets that differs subtly from more standard neoclassical welfare theorems concerning the social optimality of laissez faire. For Marshall and Pigou the sense in which free markets can be argued (in the absence of externalities) to be economically optimal is one which focuses on the *maximization of aggregate welfare*. For Walras and other continental neoclassical welfare economists, markets achieve welfare ideals by achieving *an optimal allocation of resources* (equivalent, in a world of interpersonal utility comparisons, to maximization of aggregate welfare). It is true

18. Hayek, "Introduction" to Menger, *Principles*, 13–14, 17.

that such optimality is predicated upon the welfare primacy accorded to the need to respect consumer preferences; but this still-standard mainstream perspective of welfare economics does not focus on the effective control exercised by consumer choices. For mainstream welfare theory what is important is the pattern of allocation achieved by the market (measured against the yardstick of the structure of consumer preferences). But from Menger's vision of the economy appears the insight that it is *in fact* solely the series of choices taken by consumers which create the market values and determine the entrepreneurial valuations which control the actual allocation of resources.

It is difficult to avoid the conjecture that Menger's appreciation for the achievements of the free market economy (as expressed, let us say, in Rudolph's essays) is to be attributed in large measure to this novel Mengerian insight concerning consumer sovereignty. It seems plausible in the extreme that it was in this insight, thoroughly absorbed into the economics of Menger's younger colleagues and followers, Böhm-Bawerk and Wieser, that Marxists saw their principal conflict with Austrian economics. For Bukharin, steeped in the Marxian perception of the capitalist economy as a system of exploitation, the claim that the pure capitalist economy is one in which consumer preferences dictate all, in which the capitalist assignment of income shares is that pattern "required" and imposed by consumers, must have appeared dangerous indeed. No wonder that he saw Austrian economics as the most powerful opponent of Marxism. And there can be no doubt that it was this tenet of consumer sovereignty, so central to Austrian economics, which subsequently inspired Mises's critique of socialism. As Mises was to emphasize throughout his career, the key to economic literacy is the understanding that entrepreneurial decision making is grounded entirely in the incentive to anticipate consumer preferences: "By themselves the producers, as such, are quite unable to order the direction of production. This is as true of the entrepreneur as of the worker; both must bow ultimately to the consumers' wishes. And it could not well be otherwise. People produce, not for the sake of production, but for the goods that may be consumed."[19] It was this thoroughly Mengerian insight which nourished Mises's lifelong polemic against socialist and interventionist misunderstandings of the market economy.

Yet, as we shall see, this insight of Menger's, his pioneering perception of the role of consumer sovereignty, was not by itself sufficient to require him unambiguously to subscribe to a policy of pure laissez faire. Certainly the appreciation for consumer sovereignty carries normative implications. But for a mind as careful, as sensitive to subtle distinc-

19. L. Mises, *Socialism* (London: Jonathan Cape, 1936), 443.

tions, and as thorough as Menger's, his understanding of the paramountcy of consumer valuations in the structure of an economic system can hardly have guaranteed unqualified endorsement of pure laissez faire. Menger's own economic theory left a number of openings for conceivable arguments, economic or social, in favor of specific interventions. Let us see how this must have been the case.

Menger, consumer sovereignty, and scope for government intervention

We wish to identify three circumstances which rendered Menger's vision of the consumer-driven market economy an insufficient basis for *Manchestertum,* for a policy insisting on unblemished laissez faire. There is every reason to assume Menger was alive to these circumstances (and for us to explain the various conflicting strands of evidence concerning his position by reference to these circumstances and the extent to which he articulated the social implications of these circumstances). Streissler has emphasized externalities as a basis for Menger's concessions to interventionism.[20] We wish to suggest three other circumstances that are likely to have been at the basis of Menger's list (cited above from Stephan Boehm's discussion) of legitimate tasks for the state.

First, we have every reason to believe Menger recognized that his vision *assumed* a *given* structure of property rights and property law. When Menger discussed the scarcity-based reasons for the institution of private property, he referred to the arbitrariness of such an institution. A "new social order," he explained, "could indeed ensure that the available quantities of economic goods would be used for the satisfaction of the needs of different persons than at present." But such redistribution would never eliminate scarcity; it would not avoid the need for the institution of property itself. Any "plans of social reform can reasonably be directed only toward an appropriate distribution of economic goods but never to the abolition of the institution of property itself."[21] Nothing in Menger's theory suggested that the status quo, in regard to the distribution of resource ownership, is socially optimal. It seems highly plausible to understand much of Menger's sympathy for "Schmoller's passionate concern for the poor and weak"[22] as reflecting this extraeconomic dissatisfaction with the status quo. Menger's vision of consumer sovereignty was, logically speaking, entirely consistent with a social conscience which preferred a different set of effective consumers to be in control.

20. Streissler, "Intellectual and political impact," 201.
21. Menger, *Principles,* 97–98.
22. See above, note 3.

Second, although Menger emphasized the role of consumer preferences, he was certainly of the opinion that consumers may be "mistaken" as to what is in fact in their own best interest. Menger dwelt explicitly on the possibility that consumers may erroneously assign value to primitive medicines, love potions, and the like.[23] He noticed the weakness which people display for "overestimating the importance of satisfactions that give intense momentary pleasure but contribute only fleetingly to their well-being,"[24] and so on. This paternalistic attitude on his part might easily suggest state policies to correct consumer errors in valuation. It is plausible to read Menger's reference to the need for state action to encourage thrift[25] as expressing his paternalistic urge to counteract the circumstance that "men often esteem passing, intense enjoyments more highly than their permanent welfare, and sometimes even more than their lives."[26]

Third, we must emphasize that Menger distinguished sharply between the "economic prices" explained by his theory of exchange (based, in turn, on marginal utility foundations for consumer valuation and demand) and real-world prices. The former are the prices which would prevail in the absence of error, if economizing individuals acted in their own best mutual interests without the hindrance of incomplete information.[27] In the real world, error clouds human decision making, considerations of goodwill toward others affect the economic character of transactions, and other causes complicate the outcomes: "A definite economic situation brings to light precisely *economic* prices of goods only in the rarest cases. *Real* prices are, rather more or less different from economic."[28] The sense in which Menger's overall view of the economic system saw it as governed entirely by consumer valuations is confined to the model in which the effects of error and similar complications are ignored. Only if economic prices—prices which "correctly" reflect the underlying realities of "correct" consumer valuations—were to prevail, would it be true that resource allocation indeed expresses, faithfully and efficiently, the wishes of the sovereign consumers. I have elsewhere[29] expressed bafflement at the absence, in Menger, of any *analysis* of a market process through which, possibly, errors on the part of market participants might be systematically eliminated. Be this as it

23. Menger, *Principles,* 53.
24. Ibid., 148.
25. See above, note 2.
26. Menger, *Principles,* 148.
27. On this point see Israel M. Kirzner, "The entrepreneurial role in Menger's system," *Atlantic Economic Journal* (September 1978), reprinted in Kirzner, *Perception, opportunity and profit* (Chicago: University of Chicago Press, 1979), 62–69.
28. Menger, *Investigations,* 69.
29. See above, note 27.

may, it can confidently be asserted that while Menger did indeed apparently assume that markets will, sooner or later, tend toward an array of economic prices, he certainly did not claim that at all times such an array can be assumed to be already in place. It is plausible to read his reference to the need for state action to encourage entrepreneurial initiative[30] as expressing a fear that circumstances may arise where entrepreneurial error or otherwise-founded lack of initiative will lead to pathologically uneconomic prices (and allocations of resources) unless state action to spur corrective entrepreneurial initiatives is introduced.

The Mengerian revolution and the case for laissez faire: summary assessment

We are now in a position to sum up discussion thus far. Menger had introduced a revolutionary view of the operation of a market system, in which he saw consumer valuations governing the entire structure of production and rigorously determining the allocation of resources and the corresponding market remunerations of scarce resource services. This perception of consumer sovereignty certainly carried with it important implications for the social assessment of the efficiency of the capitalist system.

There can be little doubt that (as we have seen to be the case for Mises) acceptance of the Mengerian vision carries with it a powerful defense of capitalist results. These results can be seen as rigorously necessary and desirable, *if* we indeed wish to respect the wishes of consumers as they themselves express them, and *if* we wish to treat existing property and other rights and endowments as given and not subject to challenge. What we have seen, however, is that for Menger himself it was not necessarily the case that the expressed wishes of consumers are to be seen as requiring respect; nor was it the case that any given initial pattern of property endowment be invested with title to moral approbation. More to the point, we have seen that Menger's insight into the nature of consumer sovereignty was circumscribed by his awareness that entrepreneurial errors and other aberrations may easily serve as a wedge separating the real-world economy from Menger's consumer-governed "economic" model of that reality.

What we wish now to submit is that these considerations serve adequately to account for the conflicting strands of evidence (concerning Menger's attitude towards state intervention in the market economy) cited at the outset of this paper. We should not be at all surprised to find passages in Menger consistent with pure laissez faire; we should not be surprised to find passages in Menger consistent with thoroughgoing

30. See above, note 2.

interventionism; we should not be surprised to find passages in Menger consistent (as Gunnar Myrdal read them) with a complete detachment from policy issues. And we should certainly not be surprised to find Marxist writers such as Bukharin perceiving in Mengerian economics a powerful enemy of any exploitation theory of capitalism.

Reconciling the conflicting evidence

There can surely be no mystery concerning the widespread perception (cited by Boehm) of the early Austrians as stout defenders of the free market system. As we have seen, Menger's basic vision of the market economy, a vision never totally lost sight of in the subsequent Austrian tradition, certainly does have to it a strong classical-liberal ring. It shows how, absent error and aberration, markets may faithfully express consumer sovereignty rather than entrepreneurial control. Markets are not only not seen as chaotically discoordinated, they are seen as systematic, efficient servants of the consuming public. It is easy to see how the centrality of this vision could lead subsequent historians of thought (as well as subsequent Austrians themselves) to conclude—without reference to the Mengerian fine print[31]—that Austrian economics vindicates the free market as a requirement for the achievement of consumer sovereignty.

But as we have seen, the Mengerian fine print is indeed there to be read and taken account of. When we move from the realm of economic theory to that of social policy, the apparently clear message arising out of the Mengerian view becomes cloudy, complex, and ambiguous. Not only may one harbor doubts as to the applicability of the theory to the real world (since in the real world the array of "economic" prices is likely to be absent—with an inefficient, erroneous, array of "noneconomic prices" in place instead); in addition the social policy maker may legitimately question the moral acceptability of the pattern of resource ownership which the economic theory had simply taken for granted. Moreover, once one moves from the value-free desk of the economic theorist to the paternalistic podium of the policy maker, it becomes necessary to consider the extent to which freely made consumer choices may appear mistaken and wrong, not consistent with the "true" wellbeing of the consumers. All these considerations are amply sufficient to account for the statements adduced by Boehm and others testifying to Menger's willingness to assign important interventionist responsibilities to the state.

31. As we shall argue, this conclusion was, to a significant degree, a justified one. It was legitimate to accept the central Mengerian message while rejecting or ignoring the fine print. Even Menger himself, in lecturing to Rudolph, felt that the importance of the central message required that the fine print be almost entirely set aside, at least for introductory purposes.

And, again, an observer such as Gunnar Myrdal could legitimately cite the Austrians as having no political or ideological axes to grind. Menger's exposition of his central vision of the market did not attempt to articulate any laissez-faire policy implications—and, as we have seen, did not in fact preclude adoption of a moderately interventionist program. So while Bukharin quite correctly read the Austrian theory as a powerful threat to the Marxist vision of the capitalist economy, Myrdal could equally correctly commend the Austrians for pursuing a program of scientific research untainted by any political agenda. A number of further observations need to be made in order to complete our story, reconciling the apparently conflicting strands of evidence concerning Menger and the early Austrians.

Concluding considerations

Our reconciliation of the conflicting strands of evidence has depended upon being able to distinguish sharply between Menger's central vision of the economic system on the one hand, and complicating considerations regarding error and property rights on the other. It is because the context in which Menger articulated his central vision was one into which these latter complicating considerations did not have to be explicitly introduced, that apparently conflicting conclusions concerning Menger's views on economic policy could come to be drawn. Certain additional circumstances combined to create this somewhat confusing situation.

Streissler has pointed out that the tradition in German and Austrian universities was for there to be "two chairs of economics in each university: a chair of economic theory and a chair of economic policy."[32] Menger and the early Austrian economists held chairs of theory; they were not responsible for the teaching of economic policy. Their research and their books dealt almost exclusively with positive theory. This circumstance must have encouraged followers of the early Austrians, as well as historians of thought, to draw their own conclusions concerning the policy direction to which Austrian theory was pointing. This tendency can only have been strengthened by the fact that the centrality of Menger's new vision of the economic system was given so much emphasis in his theoretical work, while the "fine print" acknowledging the legitimacy of state intervention found its way into the more peripheral, even journalistic, contributions of the Austrian founders. It is plausible that Menger himself may have seen his "fine print" as having distinctly less impact on practical policy considerations. This would explain his being able to lecture to Rudolph along lines which, at a first approxima-

---

32. Streissler, "Intellectual and political impact," 200.

tion, so to speak, permitted him to avoid emphasis on his own "fine print."

As Boehm has reminded us,[33] the principal frontier of ideological and political conflict in late nineteenth-century Austria was not that which separated proponents of pure laissez faire from those of aggressive state intervention. Rather it was between the champions of the older, entrenched privileges of the clergy, aristocracy, army, and bureaucracy and the exponents of "*Josephinismus,* the Austrian version of enlightened absolutism." The Austrian economists endorsed a "liberalism . . . deeply rooted in Josephinic traditions, whose primary [purpose] was to do away with feudal privileges and guilds."[34] Menger's scientific work did not need to address these concerns. His openness towards state interventionism could quite easily be relegated to the fine print. When, in the course of decades, the frontier shifted, so that the principal policy issues among economists revolved around the degree of desirable state intervention, it became easy to focus almost exclusively on Menger's central, consumer-sovereignty vision of the economic system and to draw one's own conclusions.

Moreover, as Austrian economics entered its second and third generations, the focus of public policy inquiry shifted towards the feasibility of socialism. Here Mises was, as noticed above, able to draw on both the Böhm-Bawerkian and Mengerian roots of Austrian economics to restate the case for the free market with a new sharpness of focus. It is not surprising, therefore, that in light of this twentieth-century concern of the Austrians their tradition has come, in the view of historians of thought, to be identified with a consistent support for the free-market economy.

Our conclusions are, therefore, that each of the positions cited at the outset of this paper can be defended but that an understanding of the complexities surrounding the policy positions of the early Austrians permits us to see how this involves no necessary inconsistencies, either in regard to what the Austrians themselves maintained or in regard to what they were perceived to have maintained.

33. Boehm, "Political economy," 256–57.
34. Ibid.

Carl Menger on economic policy: the lectures to Crown Prince Rudolf

Erich W. Streissler

I

Up to now we have known practically nothing about Menger's ideas on the principles which should guide economic policies. This has the following institutional reason. In the later nineteenth century larger universities in the German language area generally had two professorial chairs for the subject matter of economics: one for economic theory and one for applied economics. To be more precise, from the very start of academic economics in the then Holy Roman Empire of the German Nation,[1] economics was considered to be a threefold subject: economic theory, economic policy (originally called "police," i.e., administrative law in matters economic), and public finance (originally called the subject matter "of the chamberlain's office," i.e., the treasury). This tripartition soon characterized the German textbooks as well: that of Sonnenfels of 1765–67[2] and later the very successful textbook of Karl Heinrich Rau, first published in the 1820s[3]—a textbook which is generally considered to have established the typical German tripartition,[4] though this is basically a century older. When the tradition of having two chairs in economics was established early in the second half of the nineteenth century it was not clear which of the two professors would teach public finance; but unquestionably one of them would be concerned with the basic principles of economics and the other with the

---

1. See Roscher 1874, 357, 371, 431. The first German chairs in economics were founded in the law faculties of the Prussian universities of Halle an der Saale and of Frankfort on the Oder by Frederick William I in 1727. The one in Halle, for Simon Peter Gasser, was termed a chair of "Oeconomie, Policey und Cammer-Sachen," a similar one being created for Justus Christof Dithmar in Frankfort. A corresponding chair was instituted in 1763 in the law faculty of the university in the imperial capital, Vienna, for Joseph Sonnenfels and was called a chair of "Polizei- und Kammeralwissenschaften."

2. Sonnenfels 1765–67, which ran altogether to eight editions (until 1819). Note that in his title Sonnenfels calls economic theory *Handlung,* i.e., "trade," the standard English term before Sir James Steuart, probably the original title of Cantillon's *Essay.* Roscher 1874, 431, notes that Dithmar was the first to use the German tripartition in a textbook.

3. See Rau 1826–37.

4. Roscher (1874, 855), who aptly calls Rau (1792–1870) *the* economist of the well-governed German "Mittelstaaten" from 1815 to 1848, also notes (348) that Rau had merely "returned" to the former standard practice of the tripartite division of economics, giving the constituent subjects somewhat modernized names.

institutional framework shaping economic policy. Certainly this was standard practice at the university of Vienna.

Menger held the chair of economic theory in Vienna (the chair founded for Sonnenfels in 1763). He held this chair provisionally from 1873 as associate professor, and from 1879 as full professor until his retirement in 1903. Thus economic policy was none of his academic "business." Rather, it was the concern of his senior colleague, Lorenz von Stein, and later of Stein's successors. So it is not surprising that we have practically no published accounts by him of what he thought about the principles that should guide economic policy. In fact, Menger scrupulously avoided any political activity whatsoever—in contrast to his elder brother, Max, who was a liberal member of parliament, and his younger brother, Anton, who, although a professor, was a concerned socialist writer. It is commonly stated in biographical notes on Carl Menger that he liked to listen to political discussions but never took part in them;[5] and the police report on the occasion of his appointment as associate professor commends his detachment from any political party.[6]

What is a little more surprising is that we also have no published opinions whatsoever of his on questions of public finance. For according to the particular division of the subject matter in Vienna, the sole responsibility for teaching this subject fell to him (and to his next three successors, including his immediate successor, Friedrich von Wieser). But even on the topic of public finance Menger remained silent, unless we include in this subject his pronouncements on the reform of the Austrian currency, i.e., the introduction of the gold standard in Austria in the nineties of the last century. Even his pronouncements on the currency reform do not enlighten us on his convictions on matters of economic policy, for they are basically of a very practical nature, concerned merely with the details of the best possible rate of conversion of the old currency into the new.

II

The question of what Menger really thought on matters of economic policy would be of little historical interest were it not for the fact that the neo-Austrian School now thriving in the United States and in Great

5. Rosenberg (1921, 33–34) even says: "Menger selbst hat sich ängstlich von der Politik ferngehalten." His passive participation in discussion is attested by Hayek (1976).

6. We can read in Menger's "Personalakt" in the Allgemeine Verwaltungsarchiv, Beilagen zu dem allerunterthänigsten Vortrage des treugehorsamsten Ministers für Cultus und Unterricht Carl von Stremayr, 2 September 1873, that the Polizeidirektion of Lower Austria reported on Menger as follows: "dass Dr. Karl v. Menger . . . sich bisher, soviel der Polizeidirektion bekannt ist, jeder Theilnahme an politischen Fragen und Parteien ferngehalten hat und sich nur den Wissenschaften widmet. Das Vorleben . . . ist makellos, wie auch seine staatsbürgerliche Haltung stets korrekt gewesen ist."

Britain has a notable and commonly recognized policy bias, and that the last generation of the Austrian School proper, especially F. A. von Hayek, G. von Haberler, and F. Machlup, are (or were) classical economic liberals of the strictest kind and are (or were) very much concerned with the fundamental principles of economic policy. Is this all due to Ludwig von Mises, who, as he did not become a full-time academic, was no longer bound by the academic divisions of the subject and could therefore freely (and, of course, magisterially) discourse on matters of economic policy? And who, not without truth, though certainly with little charity, might also be called the arch-lobbyist for entrepreneurial concerns in interwar Austria?

Upon reading Menger's sole pronouncement on the fundamental principles of economic policy, his article in the main Austrian newspaper on the occasion of the centenary of the death of Adam Smith (1891),[7] one might be tempted to conclude that Menger in his time stood far to the "left" of Mises, that Menger had been, in fact, a very socially minded "liberal" or a liberal socialist. Evidently the subject of the economic policy of the classical school touched Menger deeply: he made Richard Schüller write the last thesis of habilitation completed under his supervision on this topic.[8] His newspaper article is in a sense one on economic theory, being merely an inquisition into the history of economic thought, but of course with a political impact. It points out what the classicists and Adam Smith had actually said on questions of social policy and how much they were being wrongfully slandered in contemporary (late nineteenth-century) German and Austrian political discourse. Menger's orotund phrases in this essay in persuasion may give the impression that he himself was fully in sympathy with all types of legislative measures in favor of the "working man," including massive interference with free enterprise and numerous redistributive measures. This is what one might gather in hindsight, reading his text after another century of social (and socialist) policies.[9] Actually, however, in this article Menger does not even mention the Austrian social security system (a medicaid and old-age pension scheme with heavy redistributional subsidization by the state), which had been introduced a few years earlier. What he actually says is simply that Adam Smith did not

7. See Menger [1891] 1970.
8. See Schüller 1895.
9. Menger uses florid terminology, for instance when he says: "A. Smith stellt sich in allen Fällen des Interessen-Conflictes zwischen den Armen und Reichen, zwischen den Starken und den Schwachen *ausnahmslos* auf die Seite der Letzteren" (1970, 223). Or: "Die staatliche Einmischung *zu Gunsten* der Armen und Schwachen weist er [i.e., Smith] so wenig zurück, dass er sie vielmehr in allen Fällen billigt, in welchen er von der Einmischung des Staates eine *Begünstigung* . . . der besitzlosen Volksclassen erwartet" (224).

consider justice always to be on the side of the employers in all their conflicts with and all their demands against their workers (obviously true!); and that Smith was not against all types of state actions in all cases (again obviously true). In fact in similar endeavors Jacob Viner, Lionel Robbins, and George Stigler (to take them in historical order) distilled a far more copious agenda for economic policy out of Adam Smith[10] than Menger dwells upon—though admittedly they were writing on economic policy of the classicists in general, and not only on social policy.

All this has changed. Now we have one highly important unpublished source from which to ascertain Menger's fundamental views on questions of economic policy: the lecture notebooks of Crown Prince Rudolf of Austria, unearthed by the historian Brigitte Hamann. In 1876 Menger was appointed tutor in economics to the crown prince. The crown prince had to follow the teacher's lectures without taking notes; he had to write them out afterwards from memory and present them to the teacher, who corrected them in his own handwriting whenever he considered them not in conformity with what had been taught. In 1876 the crown prince was turning eighteen; according to general opinion he was a highly intelligent young man, though emotionally somewhat unbalanced. In view of the fact that Menger corrected the notebooks, we must therefore consider them as representative in substance (though not in style) of Menger's and, despite Rudolf's intelligence, not of the adolescent crown prince's thought. These notebooks—about 80 pages in print or 123 pages of typescript—are mainly on economic policy; for the crown prince was obviously not to be taught abstract scientific principles but much rather problems likely to be of practical import during his—presumable—future rule.

The notebooks of the crown prince show Menger to have been a classical liberal of the purest water with a much smaller agenda for the state in mind than even Adam Smith. (And when carefully rereading Menger's 1891 article on Smith and the classicists one can see that—in spite of the orotund verbiage which might be misconstrued—he had not changed his mind.) In the centenary year of the publication of *The wealth of nations* the Austrian crown prince was in effect taught pure Adam Smith—and Smith pared down, at that. No mention whatsoever is made of Smith's antimonopolist strictures or his condemnation of actions in restraint of trade. (One recalls that the Austrian School as a whole was never much in favor of active antimonopoly legislation.) What is even more astonishing: no mention is made that national security might ever be a legitimate reason for regulative or protective

10. See Viner 1927; Robbins 1952; Stigler 1972.

action—and that despite the fact that Rudolf was trained as a member of the Austrian armed forces!

At this point the reader should be warned: this paper takes the lecture notes of Crown Prince Rudolf as an accurate mirror of Menger's own opinions on questions of economic policy. This can never be fully proved now. Other interpretations are possible; many were suggested to me by discussants. The reader will therefore have to make up his own mind.

The first alternative interpretation is that Menger, who had only half a year for teaching the crown prince, though it was half a year of intensive studies, gave the crown prince merely the traditional and standard "crash course" for undergraduates. To my mind the main thrust of this argument does not hold water; it is, I think, the weakest of all alternative interpretations. First of all it was not Menger's own crash course: he did not teach economic policy. And secondly a classically liberal course was not at all traditional or standard for the Austria of the 1870s. Adam Smith had been taken up early in Austria, in the 1780s and 1790s, but since the era of Metternich liberal thought had been anathema for a long while; and the Austrian state was traditionally highly paternalistic and interventionist. In fact Menger was the rediscoverer of Adam Smith in Austria—and he communicated this rediscovery to the crown prince.

A second alternative interpretation is that Menger was set the task to teach Adam Smith to the crown prince by those responsible for his education, by Count Joseph Latour, for instance, or even by the Empress Elisabeth, well-known to have been of a liberal persuasion. Here again, nothing absolutely conclusive can be proved, as no instructions to Menger survive. This interpretation is a little more plausible, for a top-ranking aristocrat or even royalty might have heard the name of Adam Smith and suggested Smith as a source. But then again, noneconomists like generals or empresses with little formal education would not be able to determine the line of argument of an extensive lecture course very closely. It is evident from the lectures that Menger had fully absorbed Smith's line of thought, which argues that he had studied Smith closely long before he gave the lectures at short notice to the crown prince. And from possible (vague) instructions we can construct no argument for Menger's rendering an even more classically liberal version of Adam Smith with fewer exceptions in favor of state action, instead of giving a more toned-down version. At least Smith must have been in full conformity with Menger's own predilections.

The kernel of truth in these first two alternative interpretations is that Menger shows an evident penchant for using as his sources old and renowned texts: in 1876 Smith's *Wealth of nations,* which was exactly one hundred years old; and Rau's textbook, which was exactly fifty years old. But to my mind this again only argues that Menger thought that the (classically liberal) ancients had much more of importance to say on questions of economic policy than the moderns. It is not at all typical that a teacher tries to be consciously old-fashioned and to teach ideas he thinks are outdated to a budding statesman.

A third alternative interpretation would be that the thirty-six-year-old Menger had, for the purpose of teaching the crown prince, made up his mind on policy issues for the first time and then later changed it—in other words that the lecture notes reflect Menger on economic policy, but an immature Menger. This appears to me again implausible. Menger is known never to have changed the opinions of his youth, in fact to have stuck to them pertinaciously. Furthermore, there is not a shred of evidence in his writing that he did change his position towards a more muted liberalism. His *general* pronouncements just appear more in favor of social policy; but he never gives *concrete* examples in conflict with the lecture notes. To my mind the generalities of his later pronouncements have much rather to be reinterpreted in the light of the lecture notes.

A fourth alternative interpretation would address itself only to the issue that Menger gives even fewer exceptions to a classical liberal noninterventionism than Smith. This argument runs as follows: in giving a first undergraduate course to an eighteen-year-old student you simplify; you present only the main argument without the exceptions. To this I reply that you leave out the exceptions only if you do not think them vital; and this was not only the first, but also, as Menger knew, the last course to be taught to the crown prince. To my mind, leaving out even the caveats Smith himself gave at least argues that Menger fully endorsed Smith.

So if we take the lecture notes as fully reflective of Menger's considered views on economic policy, as I have argued, we can conclude: Menger had very clear-cut ideas of the proper subject matter for economic policy. These are best explained in the terminology of R. Musgrave: there certainly was to be *no distributive division* to state activity. Not that such an activity was unthought of at the time; we should remember that in 1872 the Verein für Socialpolitik had been founded,[11] the society of those German economists who made the propagation of income redistribution their main concern. Secondly, there certainly was to be *no stabilization division* to economic policy. Again, such activity was not at all unheard of then. Wilhelm Roscher (the foremost living German economist and the man to whom Menger had dedicated his own *Principles*) in his magisterial long essay on market crises had examined

---

11. The Verein für Socialpolitik was founded in October 1872 in Eisenach. See Roscher 1874, 1045ff.

practically all Keynesian and also all monetarist measures to cope with economic recessions and their consequences;[12] and in that depression period of the 1870s the emperor, the crown prince's father, had just pleaded in parliament (the Reichstag) for more "labor for good and loyal hands."[13] What Menger admitted was *only an allocative division* to state activity, and that only on a narrow basis.

The crown prince was taught Adam Smith as received and interpreted by German economists in the 1820s and 1830s (i.e., forty to fifty years earlier). The notebooks also throw some light on this original German restatement of Adam Smith as seen with the eyes of Menger. Smith had already hinted at a duty to erect such "public works . . . which it can never be for the interest of any individual, or small number of individuals, to erect or maintain."[14] His ideas on this point were much enlarged upon by Karl Heinrich Rau and especially Friedrich B. W. Hermann. From their remarks Menger distills a pervasive principle: *the principle of external effects.* The mitigation of negative external effects and the provision of public goods with positive external effects is the *sole agenda* conceded to the state. For Menger, the allocative division of state action is not to be a consequence of all types of "market failures" but only of those due to external effects. (This will be shown in detail in part III, below.)

There is a further point where Menger goes beyond Smith: he is much concerned with *incentives.* With Smith, "private people" are mature and knowledgeable economic agents; with Menger in his lectures to the crown prince, "private people" are seen as still somewhat immature and in the course of learning. This concept of man would rather favor paternalistic state action, state action meant to "protect" the individual against the harsh blasts of competition. But with Menger the argument runs exactly in the opposite direction: all state activity has *disincentive effects* in the future; it makes economic agents unlearn self-reliance. Thus state activity is not only statically "wasteful" in the classical sense; it is above all *dynamically wasteful,* wasting the skills acquired in order to achieve a developed market economy.

III

Right at the outset of the lectures, i.e., in the second paragraph of the first notebook, the crown prince writes: "Heads of states must pay

12. See Roscher 1861.
13. This frequently quoted reference—"Arbeit für brave Hände"—is not exactly traceable. Both the emperor and his prime minister made, however, statements in the Reichsrat in 1873–74 which implied the "need" for quasi-Keynesian employment-creating policies. See "Thronrede Kaiser Franz Josef I.," 5 November 1873, and "Kaiserliches Handschreiben" to Fürst Auersperg, 8 February 1874.
14. Smith [1776] 1976, Book 4, ch. 4, 51. (Cited below as, e.g., *WN* 4.4:51.)

particular attention to [the importance of satisfying needs] and through welfare and contentment make their country powerful by successfully promoting the citizens' economic efforts. But there has to be a limit to such interference on the part of the state. It is better for the general welfare of society if the individual has the responsibility of caring for his own and his family's livelihood. Such responsibility constantly drives him to an unceasing activity that fosters the well-being of all mankind. Without being patronized, however, the individual citizen should understand that the state is prepared to take measures to promote such efforts or to protect and support him if his own willpower is insufficient to overcome obstacles in his way."[15] This paragraph seems to start out in a decidedly mercantilist vain. Pretty soon it will become clear, though, how very narrowly drawn that "limit" to state action has to be, according to Menger. The constant concern of the notebooks is that the individual should not feel "patronized" by the state. In fact Rudolf uses a much stronger German term: the individual must not feel *bevormundet*, he must not feel in the position of a minor in tutelage with the state as the guardian (*Vormund*) in the legal sense. It is typical for Menger's subjectivism that he seems to stress insufficient "willpower" rather than insufficient means as the cause of external effects. But possibly the crown prince here renders Menger incompletely, who might have given "insufficient means and willpower of the individual" as motives for state action. Anyhow, when the crown prince takes up this point once more in the two lectures specifically devoted to state action, he says that the state should lend "support only in cases where an individual's strength is insufficient."[16]

Of the seventeen notebooks extant (many of which deal with case studies), two whole notebooks (6 and 7) deal solely with the principles which should govern economic policy. In notebook 6 these general principles are summarized as follows:

> Nevertheless, there are instances in the life of a state when the economic performance of individuals or of groups of citizens runs up against obstacles that require the government's powers to remove them, since individual resources would not possibly be enough.

> We deal with abnormal situations here, since only these justify government interference. In everyday economic life we shall always have to denounce such action as harmful.

15. Archduke Rudolf, Crown Prince of Austria, Politische Ökonomie, Hefte, January–August 1876, mostly written in his own hand, Österreichisches Staatsarchiv. I have used the typescript translation by Monika Streissler and David F. Good and quote by the number of the notebook and the page (in continuous numbering) of their typescript. The citation here is 1:2.
16. Rudolf, 6:49.

For the most part, these abnormal situations concern such powerful phenomena that they either require special laws, which, of course, only the state can pass, or involve such high costs—because of the size of the obstacle—that government support becomes indispensable. If, under such circumstances, the principle of individual responsibility and self-reliance of citizens in economic matters were to be carried to its extreme, it would be most harmful to them and thereby to the state. The very art of government consists in realizing the precise moment when the greatest diligence and most valiant sacrifice of citizens may yield to impending disaster. In such cases, government interference must not be seen as an obstructive patronizing of the citizens' personal interests, but rather as their necessary rescue.[17]

This is probably one of the most extreme statements ever put to paper of the principles of laissez faire in the academic literature of economics, in contrast to the polemical pamphlets of lobbyists. There is just cause for economic action of the state only in *abnormal* circumstances. Only when "disaster" is impending should the state step in. In this sense only, the benevolent inactivity of the state should not "be carried to its extreme." And the two possible types of state action are neatly classified as follows: nearly always "special laws" are required, as we shall see, merely to ward off negative external effects; and state projects are permissible only where (as public goods) they yield sizable positive external effects, i.e., where "government support becomes *indispensable*" because "such high costs" are involved. For in reality, it is not so much the economies of scale argument ("such high costs") but the lack of private provision of certain services because of strong positive external effects which lies at the root of Menger's cases.

Notebook 6 deals with the first type of economic policy actions, those warding off negative external effects. Altogether, only four cases are named, which Menger evidently already thinks quite a lot, as the crown prince summarizes: "Such instances make one realize most clearly the wide and welcome latitude within which government can interfere with individual economic efforts and not become guilty of having patronized the individual or infringed upon his freedom."[18] This way Menger has of putting the case for state action makes his statements so liable to misconstruction: habitually he calls the tiniest mite of state action already a vast mountain.

The four cases named by Rudolf are: "The individual farmer or forest owner, e.g., can do nothing to prevent a cattle plague from being

17. Rudolf, 6:52.
18. Rudolf, 6:53.

brought into the country or to stop phylloxera or the bark beetle from spreading. The state, on the other hand, can easily take measures to contain a cattle plague, by ordering a quarantine, or it can prohibit the import of vines from abroad. It can also fight the bark beetle on a large scale by ordering sizable tracts of infested forest to be cut down and refunding the owners for the damage. All such measures can never be adopted by an individual, as they usually extend over more than one private property and therefore can only be ordered by the community, by government. In trade relations with foreign countries . . . the individual citizen cannot possibly gain access to a foreign country for his goods. . . . Commercial treaties" have to be signed, "which promote individual trade interests and thereby cause a state to prosper in one of the most essential areas."

The first three cases are clearly ones of negative external effects; the fourth might be called a creation of a positive external effect in the sense of providing a pure public good, a commercial treaty. Note that Menger introduces commercial treaties merely as measures to make exports possible, i.e., as measures furthering free trade, and not as measures to limit imports. That it may ever be sensible to limit imports is not even touched upon anywhere in the lectures, though even Adam Smith had thought some import duties not totally amiss.[19]

At the end of notebook 7 the same topic is taken up once more, and three further cases of state regulation to prevent negative or to create positive external effects are enumerated, making a total count of seven for the lectures as a whole. The fifth and sixth cases have to do with labor legislation:

> If and when the egoism and greed of a few become an obstacle to the interests of the many, then the time has come for the state to defend the equal rights of all and, for the benefit of society, intervene forcibly with the activities of an individual and to put his egoism in its legally defined place. . . . The damage that an individual can do by selfishly pursuing his economic interests at other people's expense is enormous and—over and above the concerns of the moment—may often have long-term detrimental effects. Factory owners, e.g., have the opportunity to do evil in this manner; therefore government must protect their workers from being treated too badly and injuriously. . . . The factory owners may influence decisively even the physical development of the working class. For this very reason, the state must pay close attention to life in the factories in order to prevent workers from physically degenerating as a result of being overworked. Therefore, factory owners

19. Smith, *WN* 5.2k:31, 32.

are not allowed to let their workers labor more than a certain maximum (fifteen hours), even if workers were willing to submit to such ruinous treatment, pressed either by necessity or induced by a higher wage. The government prohibits a fifteen-hour day in factories since the worker's physical strength and health suffer if he spends that number of hours daily at hard labor. It completely blunts his mental faculties and sinks him to the state of a machine.

Children and minors!

An even more dreadful feature of factory life is the employment of young children, which impairs the physical and intellectual development of whole generations of workers. Hard labor at a tender age permanently undermines a person's health and impedes vigorous growth. In addition, regularly attending school becomes impossible and, apart from the lack of formal education, continued association with often depraved older workers also leads to utter corruption.

It is the task of the state to act in the interest of the polity as a whole by intervening strongly on behalf of such an important and populous class.

Although it is important to have many wealthy factory owners, as a source of general development and prosperity, the state should interfere with their economic activities in such cases. It should prevent additional profits from accruing to those factory owners if it is in the greater, general interest of society to protect the *vital interests* of a whole class of the population from being harmed, since the existence of industry rests on its shoulders, too.[20]

The actual suggestions made by Menger after many sentences of social rhetoric—much shortened here—are thus very modest: the work day should be limited to—or slightly less than—fifteen hours, and child labor should be prohibited. Safety regulations at the workplace, by then well known in many countries, are never mentioned; neither is the need for continuous control, by factory inspectors, of compliance with the laws. The prohibition of the payment of workers in kind, which Smith had thought justified, goes unmentioned.[21] The argument from external effects, on the other hand, becomes quite clear. Otherwise Menger sticks close to Smith. Smith had noted numerous cases where "excess of avarice" and similar motives cause negative external effects;[22] and Smith in his passage on piecework also uses exactly the same reasoning,

20. Rudolf, 7:58–60.
21. Smith, *WN* 1.10c:61.
22. Viner 1927, 215.

evidently taken over by Menger, that voluntary agreement by workers is no safeguard against their overworking themselves: "Workmen . . . are very apt to over-work themselves, and to ruin their health and constitution in a few years . . . mutual emulation and the desire of greater gain, frequently prompted them to over-work themselves, and to hurt their health by excessive labour."[23]

The seventh and final instance of regulation to ward off negative external effects given by Menger and copied out by the crown prince may properly be assigned to defective willpower. The pursuit of "momentary benefit" by individuals may harm many. Basically the problem here is that the individual time discount rate of many agents in an economy with capital markets that are working far from perfectly might be much above the social rate of time discount. The example given is the classic one of prohibitions against deforestation, limited, interestingly enough, to high-lying mountain forests:

> Quite often a forest-owner in the mountains who is temporarily short of money will want to clear out his high-lying forests. This can *easily* cause irreparable damage, since the rainfall will then run off in torrents and wash out the humus layer. Floods in springtime, droughts in summer, and other kinds of damage in agriculture in the plains result from such deforestation of the mountainsides and tend to worsen over time. The Southern Tyrol, Istria, Dalmatia are sad object lessons of the blind greed of individuals and thoughtless negligence of former governments. Protecting forests is among the major duties of the state that, by virtue of their importance, justify interference with individual economic activity.[24]

This is the last example. Lest we look for more, we are immediately afterwards warned: "The state may interfere with the citizens' economic activities only in the manner described in the above examples."

In these seven cases the state acts only by regulation and international treaties and not by spending—apart from, possibly, the "refunding [of] damages." In the first half of notebook 7, however, public works are named which entail government expenditure. They are characterized by positive external effects. Once again the list is extremely short, only five being named. Let us first turn to the general principle characterizing them: "Government has to interfere in economic life for the benefit of all not only to redress grievances but also to establish enterprises that promote economic efforts, but because of their size are beyond the means of individuals and even private corporations."[25] Smith, we have seen, used precisely the same argument.

23. Smith, *WN* 1.8:45.
24. Rudolf, 7:61–62.
25. Rudolf, 7:55.

Rudolf (or Menger) then mentions three examples from infrastructural investment in transportation: "Important roads, railroads and canals that improve the general well-being by improving traffic and communications are major prerequisites for the prosperity of a modern state."[26] This is very close to Smith again. Interestingly enough, the postal service, which Smith had thought "perhaps the only mercantile project which has been successfully managed by, I believe, every sort of government,"[27] is not even touched upon; much less any other of the numerous services of the Austrian state.

Rudolf continues and gives the following fourth example: "The building of schools, too, is a suitable field for government to prove its concern with the success of its citizens' economic efforts."[28] It is significant that Rudolf speaks only of *building* schools, not of *running* them, though free public education had long been a major concern of the Austrian state. Apparently Menger echoes Smith's opinion that the "publick" should on the whole limit itself to "establishing" schools, "the master being partly, but not wholly paid by the publick; because if he was wholly, or even principally paid by it, he would soon learn to neglect his business"[29]—an idea so wholly at variance with Austrian practice that Menger does not enlarge upon it.

Very much in the spirit of Smith the crown prince continues: "It is of the greatest possible benefit to [the individual citizen] if the state establishes agricultural or vocational training institutions and relieves him of worries that often weigh hardest on him, but about which he can do nothing."[30] In the subsequent passage the positive external effect of this on economic development is stressed.

The final example concerns subsidies:

> The state may equally well *support* the various sectors of the national economy by actual subsidies, of course only when it would be useful to the citizens but surpasses their individual means. Strictly speaking, such subsidies are intended to become a useful public good, owned by the community as a whole. This will occur, e.g., if the state wants to promote agriculture and especially cattle breeding by purchasing prime-quality breeding animals whose price exceeds most people's means. By making them public property, the animals best serve their purpose—to serve all alike.[31]

Happy indeed the state whose most important subsidies go to the pur-

26. Ibid.
27. Smith, *WN* 5.2a:5.
28. Rudolf, 7:55.
29. Smith, *WN* 5.1f:55.
30. Rudolf, 7:56.
31. Rudolf, 7:57.

chase of breeding bulls! The twelve examples show that Menger's state is indeed minimal in its economic activity.

How minimal, may again be seen in notebook 13, which presents a *famine* as a case study in economics. Once more we read: "It is one of the most sacred obligations of the state and each of its individuals to do their utmost to help alleviate the lot of the poorer classes in cases of famine."[32] Apart from "large purchases abroad," where it remains unclear what is to be done with them (whether they are to be given away, e.g., at reduced price), not much actually can be done, for "during famines the government, which cannot interfere much in economic matters anyway, will also run into difficulties that thwart and considerably constrain its efforts."[33] But government effort is not even needed, because a famine is one of the best examples of the beneficent working of the price system: exports will stop, becoming too expensive, imports will be sucked in, the distilleries of corn will cease to work, fodder will be saved, and the poor will economize of their own accord. At the most, the court and the nobility should set a good example in frugality.

On the other hand, attempts to lower prices would be ineffective and prohibitions of exports useless. Once again Menger closely parallels Smith in his "Digression concerning the corn trade and corn laws," though Smith, in contrast to Menger, adds several caveats, admitting, e.g., that the merchant exporter sometimes finds it to his interest, when dearth prevails both at home and abroad, "very much [to] aggravate the calamities of dearth" at home by exporting corn.[34]

In arguing against the provision of economic services by the state, Rudolf—or rather, of course, Menger—in fact introduces what I believe to be a new reason against their advantages, a reason which is typical of Austrian thought. A key idea of Austrian subjectivism was the notion that different individuals have different preference functions—an idea at variance, e.g., with the predilection of the Cambridge tradition of arguing in terms of the "representative" individual. This leads naturally to the conclusion that the fundamental diversity of individuals can never be served well by state provision, which of necessity has to be stereotyped:

> A government cannot possibly know the interests of all citizens. In order to help them it would have to take account of the diverse activities of everybody. . . . However carefully designed and well-

---

32. Rudolf, "On the measures that government should take in case of famine (on the theory of price)," 13:98.

33. Ibid.

34. Viner 1927, 215; see Smith, *WN* 4.5b:38. It is interesting that Menger himself added similar doubts in handwriting to his own copy of his *Principles* but did not teach them to the crown prince (see Kauder 1962, 11).

intentioned institutions may be, they never will suit everybody. Only the individual himself knows exactly his interests and the means to promote them. . . . The variety of work performed follows from the variety of individuals and, by its many-sidedness, promotes progress in every way. It would be altogether lost with *comprehensive* bureaucratic controls. Even the most devoted civil servant is but a blind *tool* within a big machine who treats all problems in a stereotyped manner with regulations and instructions. He can cope neither with the requirements of contemporary progress nor with the diversity of practical life. Therefore it may seem impossible that all economic activities be treated in a stereotyped way, following one and the same rule with utter disregard for individual interests.[35]

What can be worse in the eyes of a liberal than drab uniformity?

IV

In the picture that Adam Smith paints of man it is exactly the "statesman" who is shown up as an "insidious and crafty animal," as full of "folly and presumption" as "the greatest spendthrifts in the society," the source of "publick prodigality and misconduct," whereas "private people" not only know much better what is useful to them but are also characterized by "application and industry."[36] Menger, as seen from Rudolf's notebooks, is not so sure on the latter point. To him "private people" are not necessarily the vessels of the economic virtues of "application and industry." Much rather, they are constantly in need of a good example and of positive incentives.

For this reason one of the major tasks of government is to promote thrift and industry, thereby setting a good example itself . . . the state can greatly harm the citizens' interest by interfering too much. . . . Being responsible and caring for the well-being of one's self and family is a powerful incentive for work and industry. The discharge of these duties becomes the purest joy and truest pride of the free citizen. Now, if the state seizes some of these responsibilities, the individual will feel patronized and not free, even in such matters as pertain to his most personal interests. The pride he takes in providing for his family on his own without anybody's help and the knowledge that he is able, on his own, to master the great struggle for existence are the most precious goods of an educated citizen.[37]

35. Rudolf, 6:50–51.
36. Smith, *WN* 4.2:39, 9; 2.3:36, 30; 4.2:42.
37. Rudolf, 6:49.

The welfare state thus degrades man; it destroys the most precious goods in society!

Quite near the beginning of the lectures, immediately after explaining the division of labor, Menger introduces this motive under the subheading "Incentives to work": "In addition to the division of labor, intensity of work contributes importantly to increasing the quantity and thereby the cheapness of products. Thus any incentive which makes the workers work harder may be regarded as gain to the economy. The most effective inducement for the workers lies in their recognizing that their reward depends on their own diligence."[38] This passage is strictly correct only if Menger thinks labor to entail no disutility, to be without psychic cost and perhaps even to award positive pleasure. In consequence he—in contrast to Smith—mainly sees advantages in piece-rate remuneration: "Another *incentive* mechanism is the *piece-rate* system . . . [the worker's] activity is not forced or even controlled, but is left to his own judgment"; though as a drawback he thinks that piece-rate remuneration will lower product quality, as the workers will tend to work more carelessly. Smith, on the other hand, had seen no need for an extra goad to workers' industry, apart from a "liberal reward," but quite to the contrary had feared that with piece-rate remuneration "workmen . . . are very apt to over-work themselves, and to ruin their health and constitution in a few years."[39] Similarly, Menger defends inheritance of property in incentive terms: "The institution of inheritance laws provides the most important incentives to human industry, self-restraint and thrift."[40]

Only if the citizens are aware "that government is represented and headed by wise and enlightened men will [it] lead them to develop the true civic virtues of thrift and honesty and consequently of learning . . . a modern state in the noblest sense of the word will develop as the arena of the unfettered activities of a genuine citizenry."[41] Debasement of the coinage is therefore harmful above all because it spoils the necessary and always highly precarious economic virtues: "In addition to undermining all moral sense of right and wrong, such action destroys confidence in the government at home and abroad, thus impeding trade and leading to poverty. The monarch who has recourse to such methods undermines his own position and sinks to the level of a common swindler."[42] Here Menger may have echoed the prevalent notion that the particularly heavy inflation in Austria during the Napoleonic wars had

38. Rudolf, 1:8.
39. Rudolf 1:8, 9; Smith, *WN* 1.8:44.
40. Rudolf, 2:13.
41. Rudolf, 7:62.
42. Rudolf, 5:44.

led to the "fried chicken dinner period" of the "Biedermeier," a supposed wave of heedless consumption and a lack of saving, which was
seen as the reason why Austria fell behind German states in economic
development during the 1820s and 1830s. Menger certainly strongly
condemns an issue of paper currency, where the government makes its
"acceptance obligatory": "This is an act of considerable arbitrariness
and even compulsion against the citizens, since they are forced to accept
like specie bank notes they would otherwise not accept."[43] Moreover:
"An orderly and reliable monetary system is the prerequisite for prosperity and steady economic development. Insecurity, on the other hand,
deters the individual, prevents him from making reliable calculations,
and makes him worry about the most vital interests. A disorderly monetary system is as injurious for the state as for the individual. It deprives
the state of all possibilities for reliably calculating its own big budget.
For the sake of temporary relief, the state is tempted to adopt measures
that will eventually get it into ever greater difficulties."[44] Wieser's great
obsession with the need for exact economic calculation is already foreshadowed here. On the other hand, any distinction between an exactly
foreseen and an unforeseen inflation still lies well in the future. In fact
this is a distinction the Austrians never made.

The notebooks of crown prince Rudolf are wholly imbued with the
mid-nineteenth century's unlimited confidence in progress, especially
the economic progress of mankind. Therefore "public squandering . . .
is an inexcusable crime against all members of society and an offense
against mankind and its progress."[45] But "progress" also entails structural economic change, and it is quite significant what Menger thought
about the role of economic policy in the face of structural change.
Consonant with the general opinion of his time—though, as it proved,
historically quite wrongly—Menger thought that "on the whole, *small
business* may be considered an obsolete institution." However, "it is
always sad when an entire class or guild is doomed. . . . It should be
maintained for as long as possible, especially if it would be an advantage
to the community." But appropriate measures can "be for a period of
transition only."[46] What then are the measures suggested in order to
facilitate transition? We may be tempted to expect restrictive practices
or even protective tariffs. Far from it! Menger only offers "government
advice"; apparently the small businessmen are intellectually at a loss
how to help themselves: "The state should therefore strive to induce the

43. Rudolf, "On the state of paper money in Austria–Hungary and the means to reform
it, part 1," 8:65.
44. Rudolf, 8:66.
45. Rudolf, 3:25.
46. Rudolf, 4:34–35.

small tradesmen to combine and by joining their efforts to take on the character of large-scale enterprises."[47] Menger thinks of the organization of cooperatives by the state, so that, as is explicitly noted, machines can be used jointly and the price of the raw materials purchased can be reduced if they are bought at wholesale prices. It is not quite clear whether he thinks it appropriate that the state should extend credit for this purpose.

In spite of the pure doctrine of economic liberalism he propounds—a doctrine much purer and with fewer exceptions than that of Smith—Menger, the reputedly archetypical protagonist of methodological individualism, does not prove an outright methodological individualist in the notebooks of Crown Prince Rudolf. True, "the state is but the sum total of its citizens"; but this sentence goes on: "considered as a whole, [it] is like a person."[48] In common with Rau and the liberal German economists of the early nineteenth century—and of course, also in common with Smith—Rudolf writes: "In political life there may arise a conflict between the interests of those responsible for the public sector and the interests of the national economy as a whole. In this case, public interest must take precedence over private interest."[49] We know that Menger had learned this idea from Rau, whose textbook was the first he studied systematically. Evidently "the state" as a "person" seems to have preferences of its own which differ from those of the sum of the individuals constituting it. In most of Menger's policy prescriptions such a conflict does not really manifest itself; for if there are external effects, markets cannot correctly reflect individual preferences in their choice between limited means. But there are some slight echoes of the idea of "merit" goods, even in Menger, e.g., when the state furthers vocational over general education, or when it limits the working day, even where the workers would actually want to work longer. And as a faint echo of Smith's productive and unproductive labor, Menger thinks that some "services are of greater use to the state" than others (Rudolf uses the typically German word "state" for "the general public"), e.g., "various types of construction work" and the manufacture "of objects important to the national economy."[50] Menger in the *Principles* had similarly thought some preferences misguided.

V

Menger taught the crown prince a type of economic policy which by 1876 appeared a little outmoded. It was liberal economic thought, as

47. Rudolf, 4:35.
48. Rudolf, 6:46.
49. Rudolf, 1:6. Menger had studied Rau's *Grundsätze* (1826–37, in its 7th ed. of 1863) since October 1867 (Kauder 1962, 2) and had annotated a similar passage in Rau (Kauder 1962, 10).
50. Rudolf, 3:24. Kauder points out that Menger "hated the unproductive consumers of luxuries" (1962, 12), again a typically Smithian notion.

represented in German economics by Rau and Hermann in the 1820s and 1830s; it was the credo of the "generation of 1848," the men represented in the abortive constitutional diet of Frankfort in 1848–49 and the corresponding constitutional diets in Austria. It was Adam Smith only very slightly adapted to German thought. Peter Rosner has recently analyzed this type of theoretical framework for deriving a "correct" economic policy of "the state" as represented by Karl Heinrich Rau's influential textbook on economic policy of 1828.[51]

The topic of this paper is Menger's ideas about economic policy, but we cannot ignore the fact that he was above all one of the three originators of the marginalist revolution in economics and the founder of the Subjective Value or Austrian School of economics. All the ideas of the Austrian tradition are at least foreshadowed or presented in a nutshell in his *Grundsätze der Volkswirthschaftslehre* (Vienna, 1871), published five years before the lectures to crown prince Rudolf. What can we learn about those new economic concepts of the reputed "revolutionary" Carl Menger, those concepts which he considered most important, those concepts which were closest to his heart, from the notebooks?

The answer is absolutely astounding. If the notebooks of Crown Prince Rudolf were the only work from Menger that had come down to us, we could never have guessed that Menger had had anything new to say on the subject matter or the methodology of economics. Not a single one of his own important new ideas was taught to the crown prince. From the lectures to Rudolf we must conclude that Menger evidently thought his innovations unimportant frills on the great edifice of classical economics erected by Adam Smith.

Not only in matters of economic policy, but also in matters of theory, in matters of the foundations of economics, the crown prince was taught—let us stress it once more: in the centenary year of the first publication of *The wealth of nations*—nearly undiluted Adam Smith (in the German version of Rau and Hermann of the 1820s and 1830s). True, in what I have called the German protoneoclassical vein of the latter two, the crown prince was at the very outset introduced to "the importance of satisfying needs for man" and to the division of goods into economic and noneconomic goods (the classification of Hermann)— goods, of course, including (since Hermann's work of 1832)[52] also "labor services" and "relationships." But that was standard German economics, by then more than forty years old. The "basic principles according to which men economize" were taken from Rau and Hermann,[53] since whom it had become typical practice to stress how impor-

51. See Rosner 1988.
52. See Hermann 1832.
53. Rau (1826–37 and later; vol. 1) stressed in all editions in § 7 (close to the beginning of the book) the subjective economizing of the individual and valued goods by an opportunity-cost calculus; Hermann (1832, 68) stressed the different degrees of impor-

tant it was "to satisfy the more important needs before the less important ones." "The ability to rank needs and disregard less important,
though often pleasurable, things characterizes the economizing person,
while uneconomic man typically satisfies less important needs at the
expense of the more important ones. This is true of the individual as well
as the state."[54]

But from these brief first passages onwards Adam Smith rules supreme. With the "second principle of economy" (we are not told what
the first is) we come to Smith's division of labor, followed by the theory
of incentives already remarked upon, a basically classical theory, as it is
supply-oriented. We then proceed to the factors of production, the
concept of income, of wealth, and of capital. Here the crown prince was
instructed, very much in the Smithian vein, that "for many people . . .
their labour potential is their capital"[55]—surely reminiscent of Smith's
pronouncement that "the property which every man has in his own
labour, as it is the original foundation of all other property, so it is the
most sacred and inviolable."[56] Menger goes on to explain the importance of thrift and saving, no topic being more Smithian; then he comes
to the theory of value, here treated (in contrast to Smith) in the German
protoneoclassical vein, and concludes the theoretical survey by explaining the importance of money, a topic likewise touched upon, as is well
known, by Adam Smith in the fourth chapter of his first book. This brief
survey of economic theory fills the first five notebooks. Notebooks 6 and
7, on the proper role of the state, have already been dealt with extensively here. The succeeding notebooks deal with case studies, mainly
taken from Adam Smith, as that on famines. The notebooks conclude
with two lectures on the subject that concludes *The wealth of nations:*
taxation.

That the theory of value is treated somewhat differently from Smith
must not surprise us. The labor theory of value was rejected by the
German tradition from Rau and Hermann onwards and was characterized by Wilhelm Roscher, the senior German textbook author of Menger's day, as a "mere English aberration."[57] In the pre-Smithian way
(but well known to Smith and referred to by him)[58] Menger distinguishes
"value in use" and "value in exchange." He suggests two definitions of
value: "Value is the importance that a good acquires for the individual
because it can satisfy his needs"; and "Value is the importance that a

---

tance of wants and thus the degrees of necessities of goods and used this idea to describe
optimal consumption (341ff., esp. 343).
   54. Rudolf, 1:1–6.
   55. Rudolf, 3:22.
   56. Smith, *WN* 1.10c:12.
   57. See Streissler 1990a (this issue).
   58. Smith, *WN* 1.4:13.

specific good acquires for us once we recognize that one of our needs could be less fully satisfied if we had no command over the good."[59] Again, however, these had been standard German textbook definitions long before Menger. Among the very few authors mentioned in the notebooks, Menger here expressly gives the eighteenth-century French writer Condillac as his source—Condillac being the source typically quoted by Roscher on this point, so typically that Karl Marx attacked Roscher for having taken his value theory from Condillac.[60] The only sentence where we may scent a whiff of Menger's own thought is the following: "The standard of measurement [of value] is quite relative and depends upon the most varied influences of the taste, character, and customs of individuals and whole peoples." This sentence, though, is immediately negated in a phrase which we might have thought quite untypical of the originator of subjective value theory: "But to render communication possible, items of trade must be assigned more or less definitive values that are fixed according to civilized people's long-standing experience and needs."[61]

Nowhere in the notebooks can we find even a hint at marginal valuation, despite the fact that Hermann had already come very close to it in 1832.[62] Nowhere, of course, is the concept of marginal utility—or even of utility itself—even broached. The crown prince merely renders the very muddled statement: "For some objects value is determined by their scarcity, for others by the importance of the need satisfied, and for still others by the quantity of the object available."[63] Nowhere is the equilibrium valuation of two goods simultaneously suggested, the cornerstone of the new subjective value theory. Nowhere, above all, are factor prices introduced as derived utilities depending on their productive contribution to final satisfaction. If H. R. Seager could say of the lectures of Menger in 1892–93 that "here in Vienna the marginal-utility theory of value is anything but an 'academic plaything.' It is through the application of this theory to the general problem of distribution" that answers are "expected," he certainly cannot have gotten the slightest inkling of this scientific program from the notebooks of the crown prince.[64]

Quite the contrary, in fact. The crown prince was taught pure classical

59. Rudolf, 3:27.
60. See Marx [1867] 1987, 157.
61. Rudolf, 3:28.
62. See Hermann 1832, both in his long discussion about the productivity of various employments ("In the eyes of the consumer that service will appear as productive, which, when the product is exchanged, entails no higher subjective cost than would be necessary when an alternative method is used," 32) and on optimal consumption.
63. Rudolf, 4:30.
64. See Seager 1892–93, 260.

wage theory, explicitly the "iron law of wages," as F. Lasalle had termed this theory memorably for German speakers.[65] "The simplest sort of labour," Rudolf recorded, "for which no training at all is required, will be paid just enough to provide the means of subsistence for working-class families. The more advanced, highly skilled types of labor require previous training and will be paid more, in proportion to the cost of necessary training."[66] Wage theory in general is, however, only noticed in passing in this tenth notebook. Its main concern is the appropriate remuneration of civil servants. What principle should guide us here? "It is [the state's] foremost duty to see to it that those devoted to the common good, to the state, are paid wages in proportion to their training and their sphere of activity."[67] Smith, as is well known, was the originator of the theory of human capital. This is nothing but a brief statement of his opportunity-cost-of-investment-in-education argument for the determination of wage differentials for the highly skilled.[68] It is just this argument, particularly in its application to the learned professions, which the whole marginalist school, and Menger especially, had set out to refute.[69]

Taking some superficial critical remarks at face value, it has evidently become a general tendency in the history of economic thought to underestimate by far the influence of Adam Smith on German economic thought. The impact of Smith was the more lasting and all the stronger because David Ricardo simply did not come across in German academic economics[70] and was constantly attacked for his labor theory of value by economists as early as Rau and Hermann.[71] J. S. Mill, on the other hand, was considered, at least by Menger, hardly better than a socialist.[72] As Ricardo and Mill were just not "there" to obscure Smith, Smith

65. In German: "das eherne Lohngesetz." Ferdinand Lasalle (1825–64) was a German socialist and nationalist. The term is used in Lasalle 1863a and 1863b.

66. Rudolf 10:76.

67. Rudolf, 10:78.

68. See Smith, *WN* 1.10b:6: "When any expensive machine is erected, the extraordinary work to be performed by it before it is worn out, it must be expected, will replace the capital laid out upon it, with at least the ordinary profits. A man educated at the expense of much labour and time to any of those employments which require extraordinary dexterity and skill, may be compared to one of those expensive machines."

69. I give this as one of the main ideas in Streissler 1988.

70. It is thus at the same time true and untrue when Hayek says: "Nowhere, however, had the decline of the classical school of economics been more rapid and complete than in Germany . . . the classical doctrines . . . had never taken very firm root in that part of the world" (1976, 13). This is wrong if we consider Adam Smith the focus and pivot of classical economics. For nowhere was Smith's influence greater and nowhere was he taught longer. The statement is, however, correct if by classical economics we understand Ricardo and Mill; their influence was indeed minimal and ephemeral.

71. See Streissler 1990a, 1990b.

72. Seager says about Menger's lectures in the winter of 1892–93: "Especially interesting to the foreign student is his characterization of the historical school and of *Kathedersozialismus,* the forerunners of which last he finds in Simonde de Sismondi and J. S. Mill" (1892–93, 256).

could continue to rule supreme. It was the theoretically highly conservative Menger, in a sense more backward-looking than forward-looking, who continued this admiration for Smith among mid-nineteenth-century German economists and bequeathed it to his school. It is thus no coincidence that the admirers of Smith in the first half of the twentieth century came largely from the Austrian School—Mises and Hayek spring immediately to mind—or that they were at least in close contact with the Austrians, as was George Stigler.

The notebooks of Crown Prince Rudolf present us Carl Menger, both politically and also theoretically, as a very neoclassical economist—in fact hardly "neo" at all, but nearly a *pure* classicist. Politically his disclaimer of not being a "Manchester liberal" and of not being opposed to all reforms in the matter of economic policy appears somewhat forced, or at least liable to be misconstrued.[73] Menger certainly was a minimalist as regards state action. Theoretically, as is well known, in his *Principles* he presented himself not as a scientific revolutionary but rather as a mere reformer—or should we even say as a reviver of a well-established train of thought? The notebooks of Crown Prince Rudolf reinforce this impression. Thus if there was one man who took extremely long to realize fully Carl Menger's revolutionary impact on economics, it was Carl Menger himself!

References

Hayek, F. A. 1976. Introduction. In Carl Menger, *Principles of economics*. Translated by James Dingwall and Bert F. Hoselitz. New York.

Hermann, Friedrich B. W. 1832. *Staatswirthschaftliche Untersuchungen*. Munich.

Kauder, Emil. 1962. Aus Mengers nachgelassenen Papieren. *Weltwirtschaftliches Archiv* 89.

Lasalle, Ferdinand. 1863a. *Offenes Antwortschreiben an das Zentralkomitee zur Berufung eines allgemeinen deutschen Arbeiterkongresses zu Leipzig*. Zurich.

———. 1863b. *Zur Arbeiterfrage*. Leipzig.

Marx, Karl. [1867] 1987. *Capital*. Vol. 1. International Publishers Edition. New York.

Menger, Carl. 1884. *Die Irrthümer des Historismus in der deutschen Nationalökonomie*. Vienna.

———. [1891] 1970. Die Social-Theorien der classischen National-Oekonomie und die moderne Wirthschaftspolitik. *Neue Freie Presse*, 6 and 8 January. In *Gesammelte Werke*, edited by F. A. Hayek, 3:219ff. Tübingen.

73. Menger 1884, 83. Menger denies as "frivolous" the charge that he is a member of the "Manchesterpartei," points out that it is impossible to deduce such a thing from his writings on economic theory, asserts that it would be altogether honorable to see in the free play of private self-interest the main source of the common economic good, and finally remarks that his caution that in designing reforms one should take into account what has already been achieved, does not mean that he is always against reform. Again the oblique phraseology makes Menger appear by far more interventionist than he actually was.

Rau, Karl Heinrich. 1826–37. *Lehrbuch der politischen Ökonomie.* Vol. 1, *Grundsätze der Volkswirthschaftslehre.* Heidelberg, 1826. Vol. 2, *Grundsätze der Volkswirthschaftspflege.* Heidelberg, 1828. Vol. 3 (in two parts), *Grundsätze der Finanzwissenschaft.* Heidelberg, 1832, 1837.

Robbins, Lionel. 1952. *The theory of economic policy in English classical political economy.* London. 2d ed., London, 1965.

Roscher, Wilhelm. 1861. Zur Lehre von den Absatzkrisen. In *Ansichten der Volkswirthschaft aus dem geschichtlichen Standpunkte,* ch. 6, pp. 279–398. Leipzig and Heidelberg.

————. 1874. *Geschichte der National-Oekonomik in Deutschland.* Munich.

Rosenberg, Wilhelm. 1921. Karl Menger. *Juristische Blätter* 1:33–34.

Rosner, Peter. 1988. Wirtschaftsliberalismus und Staatseingriffe bei Karl Heinrich Rau. Working Paper no. 8803, July. Department of Economics, University of Vienna.

Schüller, Richard. 1895. *Die klassische Nationalökonomie und ihre Gegner.* Berlin.

Seager, H. R. 1892–93. Economics at Berlin and Vienna. *Journal of Political Economy* 1:236–62.

Smith, Adam. [1776] 1976. *An inquiry into the nature and causes of the wealth of nations.* Glasgow edition by R. H. Campbell and A. S. Skinner. Oxford.

Sonnenfels, Joseph von. 1765–67. *Grundsätze der Polizei, Handlung und Finanz.* Vienna.

Stigler, George J. 1972. Smith's travels on the ship of state. *HOPE* 4:265–77.

Streissler, Erich. 1988. The intellectual and political impact of the Austrian school of economics. *History of European Ideas* 9:191–204.

————. 1990a. The influence of German economics on the work of Menger and Marshall. *HOPE,* this issue.

————. 1990b. Menger, Böhm-Bawerk, and Wieser: the origins of the Austrian School. In *Neoclassical economic theory, 1870–1930,* edited by K. Hennings and W. J. Samuels, 150–89. Boston.

Viner, Jacob. 1927. Adam Smith and laissez faire. *Journal of Political Economy* 35:198–232.

II. Successors

Austrian capital theory: the early controversies

Roger W. Garrison

I. *The Austrian vision*

Austrian economics owes its uniqueness, in large part, to its attention to the economy's capital structure. Theorizing about the value of capital, about the time element in the structure of production, and about market mechanisms that facilitate intertemporal adjustments to the capital structure has constituted a significant part of the research agenda for the early as well as the modern Austrian School. Yet fundamental differences emerged during the earliest developments of Austrian capital theory—differences which even today are not fully resolved.

Menger's harsh assessment of Böhm-Bawerk's contribution is well reported in modern literature: "the time will come when people will realize that Böhm-Bawerk's theory is one of the greatest errors ever committed" (Schumpeter 1954, 847 n. 8). Although the context in which the statement was made remains a matter for conjecture, a prevalent—and plausible—interpretation is that Böhm-Bawerk strayed too far from the subjective value theory outlined by Menger (Endres 1987, 291 and passim; Kirzner 1976, 54–58; Mises 1966, 479ff.; Streissler and Weber 1973, 232). This essay considers Menger's judgment as it applies to the treatment of the time element in the structure of capital. It is argued that the subsequent development of capital theory along formalistic lines (e.g., by Wicksell) rather than along subjectivist lines (e.g., by Mises) provides some justification for Menger's use of the superlative: "one of the greatest errors."

Capital theory is beset with many perplexities and ambiguities. Most of the theoretical difficulties stem from the fact that capital has no natural unit of account corresponding to worker-hours of labor and acres of land. The "quantity of capital," then, has no clear meaning. If capital is reckoned in physical terms, gauging the total quantity of it involves an insurmountable aggregation problem; if it is reckoned in value terms, the quantity of capital becomes dependent upon its own price. Similar difficulties are associated with the notion of production time or the degree of roundaboutness of production processes. If two processes are compared strictly in terms of their respective blueprints, it may be unclear which of the two is the more roundabout; if capital values are used in gauging the comparative degrees of roundaboutness, the comparison will depend in a critical way on the rate of interest used to calculate the capital values. Attempts to spell out the precise relationship between the rate of interest and the degree of roundaboutness are bound to run afoul of these difficulties—as was roundly demonstrated during the controversies of the 1960s over "technique reswitching" and "capital reversing."[1]

Such perplexities and ambiguities, however, are largely if not wholly irrelevant to the early development of capital theory. What is important about the theoretical developments over the final thirty years of the nineteenth century is the new vision of capital and of a capital-using economy. Essential to this new vision were the ideas that using capital takes time, that time, in fact, is one of the dimensions of the economy's capital structure. Production time, or the degree of roundaboutness, was recognized—and highlighted—as an object of choice to be dealt with by economic theory.

Some treatment of the time element can be found in British economics, particularly in Ricardo's discourse on machinery, and even in early French writing such as that of Turgot. But the Austrian ideas about capital and time constitute a significant break from classical doctrine and from the corresponding vision of capital. Dominated as it was by agricultural production, classical economics treated the time element in production as a technological datum. The very nature of agriculture dictated that the production period, the period for which wages had to be "advanced" from the capitalists to the laborers, was one year. Formal economic theory was required to take the time constraint into account, but it was not required to account for the time constraint itself. The new vision required the treatment of time as an endogenous variable in any theory of a capital-using economy. Characterizing it further requires that we speak of visions and recognize the differences between the early visionaries, particularly between Menger and Böhm-Bawerk.

Menger's and Böhm-Bawerk's contributions can be assessed in the light of the distinction made by Ludwig Lachmann (1969, 89–103; 1978, 8ff. and passim) between two antithetical methods of analysis: subjectivism and formalism. For subjectivists, economic phenomena can be made intelligible only in terms of the intentions and plans of market participants; for formalists, economic magnitudes, such as inputs, outputs, and production time, can be related to one another without specific reference to the plans and actions of individuals.

There are several related, but not perfectly synonymous methodolog-

---

1. For a treatment of this controversy from a subjectivist point of view, see Garrison 1985, 181–84.

ical contrasts: causal-genetic analysis and simultaneous determinacy; market-process analysis and equilibrium theory; microeconomic analysis and macroeconomic modeling. Lachmann's distinction, however, seems appropriate for understanding the early developments in Austrian capital theory. Menger was a thoroughgoing subjectivist. Böhm-Bawerk straddled the fence between subjectivism and formalism: his formalism underlies what Menger saw as one of the greatest errors; his subjectivism allows for an interpretation thoroughly consistent with Menger's own work.

II. *The Mengerian formulation*

Menger (1950, 152) presented his vision of a capital-using production process in terms of consumers' goods, or goods of the first order, and capital goods, or goods of the second order, third order, and higher orders. The time element of the production process was represented as a sequence of orders. Higher-order (capital) goods are transformed sequentially into goods of lower and lower order until ultimately they emerge as consumers' goods. The time element in the production process was built right into the concept of capital. The relationship between the quantity of (future) consumption and the time spent transforming goods through the several orders was made clear:

> The transformation of goods of higher order into goods of lower order takes place, as does every other process of change, in time. The times at which men will obtain command of goods of first order from goods of higher order in their present possession will be more distant the higher the order of these goods. While it is true . . . that the more extensive employment of goods of higher order for the satisfaction of human needs brings about a continuous expansion in the quantities of available consumption goods, this extension is only possible if the provident activities of men are extended to more distant time periods. (1950, 152–53)

Menger summarizes this relationship by stating that "economizing men can . . . increase the consumption of goods available to them . . . but only on condition that they lengthen the periods of time over which their provident activity is to extend" (153). This statement not only captures the fundamental notion that underlies Menger's conception of capital but anticipates much of the work that was to be done in subsequent years by Böhm-Bawerk.

In light of modern capital controversies it might be objected that the relationship between future consumption and the required production time holds only for some types of changes in the production process but not for others. It holds, that is, for capital "deepening" but not for capital "widening." Alternatively, it could be objected that for Menger's claims to be true, time periods cannot be reckoned in pure time units. An increase in the number of transformations that are undertaken simultaneously must be seen as involving more "time." The simple time dimension in Menger's formulation may have to be replaced with Böhm-Bawerk's more complex dimension of roundaboutness or, equivalently, with Cassel's concept of "waiting" (1903, 54), whose units measure both value and time. While these objections call for a clarification of the notion of production time in Menger's vision of capital, they do not constitute a wholesale condemnation of the vision. At this early stage in the development of Austrian capital theory, addressing such ambiguities was far less important than understanding the basis for the vision and the issues that the vision helped resolve.

The reasoning that underlay Menger's concept of capital is no mystery. Nature, on its own, yields up some goods that can be consumed by man. The quantity and characteristics of these goods, however, are independent of the "wishes and needs" of the consumers. But man can, to some extent, take charge of the natural process before the consumers' goods emerge. He can exert some influence on these processes with the result that the eventual product is no longer independent of his wishes and needs. Instead production will be determined, at least in part, by "human purposes" (Menger 1950, 73–74). Clearly, the earlier in the process that man takes charge, the greater are his opportunities for influencing the final product. The earliest point at which man begins to influence the course of nature, earliest with respect to the wishes and needs he is attempting to accommodate, marks the highest order of the production process. It marks the earliest point for which there is an *economic* relationship between man's purposes and the resulting quantities and characteristics of the goods of the first order which are to serve those purposes.

Carefully formulated in terms of purposes and "wishes and needs" (rather than in terms of physically defined inputs and outputs), Menger's arguments were exempt from the sort of criticism that was aimed at subsequent formulations. The idea, that constructing, say, a hydroelectric power station may involve less production time than building a redwood fence—owing to the many years required for the redwood tree to grow—is seen immediately to be foreign to Menger's formulation. The age of the redwood tree has no bearing whatever on the issue. Production time is meaningfully discussed only in terms of man's designs on the redwood relative to the satisfaction of his desire for a redwood fence.[2] A second sort of criticism to which Menger's concep-

2. The primacy of human purposes is often overlooked. One longtime critic of Austrian capital theory (Rolph 1980, 502) called the concept of roundaboutness into question

tion is immune stems from the fact that physically defined inputs may continue to be used almost indefinitely. Iron mined in Roman times may be present in a modern pocket knife (Schumpeter 1954, 908). But unless it is argued that the Roman miners were motivated, at least in part, by the present-day demand for pocket knives, this physical continuum is an economic irrelevancy (see Kirzner 1966, 88).

The prehistory of production processes was excluded by Böhm-Bawerk as well as by Menger, although the grounds for exclusion were fundamentally different. Böhm-Bawerk (1959, 2:86) simply argued that production activities of the remote past are so heavily discounted that they can be safely neglected. Higher powers of the discount rate are sufficiently close to zero that for practical purposes they are equal to zero. But according to Menger, unless the earlier activities can be linked to the later production processes in terms of "human purposes," they should be ignored on principle. That is, in the absence of a teleological connection, even those early inputs that are not mathematically insignificant are still economically irrelevant.

Menger's vision of the capital-using production process is important in its own right and for the understanding of subsequent developments. Two closely related aspects of his value theory, however, can be singled out as having special significance. They constitute a sharp break from the classical cost-of-production theories and a high-water mark in the development of Austrian capital theory not to be surpassed for another two generations. First, the direction of value imputation was reversed by Menger. A consumption good is not valued on the basis of the labor and other means of production that were used to produce it. Rather the means of production are valued on the basis of the prospective value of the consumption good. Menger expresses this relationship in terms of goods of different orders: "The value of goods of higher order is always and without exception determined by the prospective value of goods of lower order in whose production they serve" (1950, 150).

Modern theorists may lament Menger's choice of terminology. Higher-order goods can be easily misinterpreted as "highly finished goods," a term used by Alfred Marshall. The terminology can clash with diagrammatic representations that show goods-in-process *ascending* through time from higher to lower orders. It can also clash with the fact that higher-order goods are discounted with respect to lower-order goods: higher order means lower value. But to lament Menger's terminology is, more than likely, to overlook one of his most important insights. Consumption goods are lower, or more basic, in the logical structure of his value theory. His terminology captures the insight that

---

by remarking that "not infrequently, a squirrel must be given credit for planting the proverbial acorn."

the value of higher-order goods is logically dependent upon (rests upon the foundation of) the value of lower-order goods.

The second aspect of Menger's value theory which deserves emphasis concerns the treatment of entrepreneurial expectations. The notion of various orders of goods requires that time be taken into account, but Menger was careful not to introduce the time element in an overly restrictive way. His theory dealt with the valuation of higher-order goods at a point in time when the corresponding consumers' goods still lay in the future. That is, his was a forward-looking theory. In Menger's own words, "The principle that the value of goods of higher order is governed, not by the value of corresponding goods of lower order of the present, but rather by the prospective value of the product, is the universally valid principle of the determination of the value of goods of higher order" (1950, 151).

Consistently taking a prospective view rather than a retrospective view is not just a matter of style. It is a means of focusing the analysis on expectations and hence on the role of the entrepreneur. Significantly, Menger excluded from his formulation any particular, or determinate, expectational scheme:

> The prospective value of goods of lower order is often—and this must be carefully observed—very different from the value that similar goods have in the present. For this reason, the value of the goods of higher order by means of which we shall have command of goods of the lower order at some future time is by no means measured by the current value of similar goods of lower order, but rather by the prospective value of the goods of lower order in whose production they serve. (1950, 152)

Menger avoided the assumption of static expectation (prospective value in his formulation is different from present value) and of any other particular type of expectations (he did not specify just what the difference is). The use of any particular or determinate expectational scheme would have had the effect, as modern theorists have recognized (e.g., Hicks 1976), of virtually eliminating the time element from the theory. If, for instance, it is specified that expectations are static (or that they are elastic or inelastic to some specified degree), then the past, the present, and the future become analytically indistinguishable. The vision of a capital-using process becomes one of a constant flow of inputs and outputs (Clarkian synchronization), or it becomes one in which changes are always anticipated and reacted to in predictable ways (equilibrium growth). In such "metastatic" visions the choice between taking a prospective view and taking a retrospective view *is* just a matter of style. But by giving free play to expectations, Menger maintained a meaningful distinction between the present and the future. His treatment of the time element cast the entrepreneur in a key role. The "correctness" of the valuations of higher-order goods depends critically on entrepreneurial abilities.

III. *Böhm-Bawerk's reformulation*

Böhm-Bawerk's contribution to the theory of capital must be viewed with ambivalence in many respects. His lengthy and often tedious formulations, particularly his treatment of production time, give great scope for selective reading and are subject to diverse interpretations. The concept of "period of production" was seen by John B. Clark (and later by Frank Knight) to make no sense at all. It was seen by Wicksell to make a good deal of sense, but primarily from a technological point of view. For Keynes, the concept was logically sound but referred to an utterly trivial aspect of the production process. And for Mises, it was the vital concept in capital theory but had meaning only when given a thoroughly subjectivist interpretation.

Assessing the detail of Böhm-Bawerk's reformulation must be consistent with the more general assessment of his work. Is his *Positive theory* a precise and definitive statement of the economic relationships that constitute capital theory, or is it a crude and skeletal outline of these relationships? Assessments can be found to support either view:

> Böhm-Bawerk's scientific work forms a uniform whole. As in a good play each line furthers the plot, so with Böhm-Bawerk every sentence is a cell in a living organism, written with a clearly outlined goal in mind. . . . And this integrated plan was carried out in full. Complete and perfect his lifework lies before us. There cannot be any doubt about the nature of his message.

Alternatively:

> Böhm-Bawerk's work [was not] permitted to mature: it is essentially (not formally) a first draft whose growth into something much more perfect was arrested and never resumed. Moreover, it is doubtful whether Böhm-Bawerk's primitive technique and particularly his lack of mathematical training could have ever allowed him to attain perfection. Thus, the work, besides being very difficult to understand, bristles with inadequacies that invite criticism—for instance, as he puts it, the "production period" is next to being nonsense—and impedes the reader's progress to the core of his thought.

These two passages provide a remarkable contrast, all the more remarkable when it is realized that both were written by one and the same

Joseph A. Schumpeter.[3] A study of Böhm-Bawerk's text itself, together with a survey of the critical and interpretive work of others, suggests that the second quoted passage is closer to the truth. It will be argued, though, that it was not his lack of mathematical training that stood in the way of perfection; rather it was his failure to adhere to Menger's subjectivism.

To treat Böhm-Bawerk's work as a valuable but rough diamond is to suggest that a detailed treatment of his argumentation may be unproductive. To focus on the simple calculations of the average period of production, or to question why the arithmetic average rather than, say, the geometric average was used is to overlook the more fundamental and more important message: capital theory must be concerned with the time dimension in the economy's structure of production.

Abstracting from details, Böhm-Bawerk's vision of a capital-using economy is very similar to Menger's. He depicts the essentials of a production process with a number of concentric circles (Böhm-Bawerk 1959, 2:106). Time is seen as progressing radially outward from the center of the circles. The center, then, represents the production process in its incipiency, and the outermost ring represents the ultimate fruition of the process. Menger's first, second, and higher orders become Böhm-Bawerk's first, second, and higher "maturity classes." The new terminology, like the old, is subject to misinterpretation: the least mature capital is in the highest maturity class. (Was Böhm-Bawerk in his choice of terminology attempting to retain Menger's fundamentally subjectivist insights?)

For the special case of the stationary state, the concentric rings have two interpretations: (1) the areas of the different rings can represent the amount of different kinds (maturity classes) of capital that exist at a given point in time, or (2) the initial inputs of the production process can be seen as radiating outward through the several maturity classes until they finally emerge at the outermost ring as consumers' goods.

Depicting the stationary state, however, was of very little interest to Böhm-Bawerk. He briefly considers the question (1959, 2:109): "What is the procedure if we wish just to preserve the amount of capital in its previous magnitude?" This issue is disposed of in short order. His answer serves primarily as a stepping stone to the more important question of "What must be done, if there is to be an increase in capital?" The answer to this second question involves some sort of a change in the configuration of the concentric rings. Several types of changes are suggested, each involving the idea that real saving is achieved at the expense of the lower maturity classes (a thinning of the outer rings) and

---

3. See (1) Schumpeter 1951, 847, written on the occasion of Böhm-Bawerk's death; and (2) Schumpeter 1954, 847.

that the saving makes possible the expansion of the higher maturity classes (a padding of the inner rings) and the creation of higher maturity classes than had previously existed. Böhm-Bawerk (2:112) even hints that in a market economy, it is the entrepreneurs who bring such structural changes about and that their action is guided by changes in relative prices of capital in the various maturity classes. The most fundamental message in his discussion is clear: an increase in capital is not to be viewed as a simultaneous and equiproportional increase in each of the maturity classes; it is to be viewed as a change in the relationship between the maturity classes.

This formulation is unobjectionable on Mengerian grounds, and it is compatible with the developments by subsequent capital theorists in the Austrian School. What is to be lamented—even by Böhm-Bawerk's followers—is that he tried to capture this important insight into the relationship between the maturity classes with a single number, the average period of production. The attempt to stipulate just how such an average period could be calculated led Böhm-Bawerk away from Menger's forward-looking vision in which (subjective) values are to be gauged by entrepreneurs. Calculating the average period of production required that the production process be formulated in terms of physically defined inputs, physically defined outputs, and the span of calendar time between them. Examples of production processes which allowed for the calculation of the average period of production required the assumption of a steady state, which virtually robbed the production period of its economic relevance. Böhm-Bawerk opened the door to criticisms of the type made by Clark (and later by Knight). It will be argued below that his vision of a capital-using economy can be defended against Clark's objections only by returning to the Mengerian subjectivist formulation—or, what amounts to the same thing, resorting to a subsequent reformulation, such as that of Mises.

IV. *Clark as counterpoint*

The period of production appears to be calculable only when the production process is described in a very stylized manner, preferably a continuous repetition of overlapping point-input/point-output processes. The archetypal case is the forest in which a fixed number of trees is cut each year, and simultaneously the same number of seedlings is planted. If the forest is characterized by a linear maturity structure, then it can be maintained in an unchanged state year after year while production and consumption (planting and cutting) proceed simultaneously. This will be recognized as Clark's most celebrated example (1924, 313–14) of the synchronization of production and consumption.

In Clark's example the forest consists of twenty acres. Each year the trees on one of the twenty acres are ready for cutting. Technologically speaking, there is a time dimension to the production of wood, which can be expressed precisely and unambiguously. It takes twenty years, in his example, for a tree to mature. Clark's point, of course, is that the time element—undeniably twenty years—is totally irrelevant. The forest should simply be viewed as a perpetual source of wood. Because both planting and cutting take place each year, the inputs and outputs of the process are seen as being simultaneous. The economically relevant period of production, according to Clark, is not twenty years, but zero years. This is the synchronization view of the production process: production and consumption are simultaneous.

When Clark collapsed the time element out of the capital-using economy, he hedged his description of the production process: "The planting and cutting are, *in a way,* simultaneous" (1924, 313, emphasis added). In other similar statements he used the phrases "so to speak," "as it were," "in a sense," "virtually," etc.[4] The aspects of the production process which these phrases served to mask are the very aspects that are important in the Austrian visions of capital. Production and consumption would appear to be simultaneous only to an outside observer who had no inkling about the "wishes and needs" and the "purposes" of the individuals engaged in the production process. While Menger had grounded his theory squarely on these subjective concepts, Clark had deliberately abstracted from them.

Böhm-Bawerk was not always careful to stress the subjective element in his capital theory, and he often departed from the subjectivist view in order to mathematize his reasoning. But his vision of a capital-using economy makes sense only when interpreted in strict Mengerian terms. To return to the overworked example, the economic significance of the planting of a seedling can be understood only in terms of present "human purposes" and future "wishes and needs." If the essential role of these subjective factors is recognized, then the time element cannot be eliminated from the theory of a capital-using economy without undermining the very basis of the analysis.

The Mengerian view and the Clarkian view are comparable only for the special case in which future "wishes and needs" are identical with present "wishes and needs," but even then the two views themselves are not identical. One is an explanation of the production activity (individuals plant now in order to be able to cut twenty years from now), while the other, by coincidence of the identity of the present and the future subjective factors, is descriptive (individuals are planting and cutting simultaneously). At points in his discussion Clark suggests a

---

4. I am indebted to Gerald P. O'Driscoll, Jr. for calling my attention to Clark's systematic hedging.

causal connection between the simultaneous planting and cutting: "[Today's cutting] is made *practicable* by today's planting. The tree that is just set is, then, an *enabling cause* of the consuming of the one that is twenty years old" (1924, 313, emphasis added). Knight was to go a step further and claim that it is today's planting that *produces* today's twenty-year-old tree. This is the concept of production that Hayek (1936, 214 n. 25) referred to as an "absurd use of words."

In the context of the Mengerian vision Clark's formulation must be rejected. Either his causal connection, like Knight's, is absurd, or it simply obscures the time element by assuming that the subjective factors remain fixed through time. Clearly, Stigler (1941, 308–15) adopts the Clarkian vision as his basis for assessing the debate between Clark and Böhm-Bawerk over the synchronization of production and consumption. He approvingly details the activities of a stationary economy in terms of a slowly maturing forest—this time one in which the trees reach maturity in fifty years. Maintaining the forest is a technological detail; capital is permanent; it yields a perpetual income; production and consumption are simultaneous. Böhm-Bawerk's entire analysis is dismissed with the statement "We can say that any one row [of trees] takes fifty years to mature, but since there is a constant output of timber forever, there is simply no point in saying it" (313).

But if, as Menger believed, capital theory is to establish causal relationships, Stigler's statement should be turned on its head. It is the anticipation of future wants and needs that causes individuals to plant trees now. Simply to state that "there is a constant rate of output of timber forever" is to build into the theory a specific and rigid constellation of future wants and needs, anticipations, and production decisions in the guise of a technological datum. It is true, of course, that if this specific constellation materializes, then the Clarkian view will be descriptive of the associated production and consumption activities. In this particular—but, according to Böhm-Bawerk, not particularly interesting—case, we can say that individuals are producing and consuming simultaneously, but there is simply no point in saying it!

The purpose of contrasting the Böhm-Bawerkian and the Clarkian visions of a capital-using economy is not simply to defend Böhm-Bawerk against his critics. Rather it is to call attention to the difference between formalism (Clark) and subjectivism (Menger) in the development of capital theory. The assumption of stationary state has a different significance for each. For Clark's theory of capital, it is a technologically defined benchmark essential for theorizing about the stocks and flows that characterize a capital-using economy; for Böhm-Bawerk's theory, interpreted Mengerianly, it is an uninteresting special case. This contrast is nowhere more obvious than in the Clark–Böhm-Bawerk debate, but it is no less relevant in the assessment of Böhm-Bawerkian capital theory as formalized by Knut Wicksell.

V. *Wicksell and the formalization of Böhm-Bawerk's theory*

A full assessment of Wicksell's contribution to capital theory would reveal much commonality between Austrian and Swedish theorizing. Discussions in Wicksell's *Lectures* (1934, 1:158–66), for instance, bear a close relation to Hayek's treatment of the structure of production. The issues relevant here, however, require attention to Wicksell's formalism as it affected the Austrian-Swedish transformation of the concept of capital.

Aspects of Böhm-Bawerk's contributions that drew criticism from Menger were, at the same time, an inspiration to Wicksell. The direction of the Swedish development can be identified in terms of Schumpeter's critical evaluation of Böhm-Bawerk's contribution cited earlier. Two claims were made in that evaluation, one that "it is doubtful whether Böhm-Bawerk's . . . lack of mathematical training would have allowed him to attain perfection," the other that the concept of the "period of production" is inadequately developed and "impedes the reader's progress to the core of his thought." Schumpeter appears to be of two minds here—unless he is making the implausible judgment that the use of more sophisticated mathematical techniques would hasten the reader's progress to the core of Böhm-Bawerk's thought.

The evaluation suggests two separate directions for development. The first claim suggests that Böhm-Bawerk's work is to be perfected by replacing the crude arithmetic examples with more sophisticated mathematics—presumably, a system of simultaneous equations. These equations would constitute a formal statement of the equilibrium relationships implied by Böhm-Bawerk's arithmetic. The second claim suggests that the essential concepts in his theory, such as the period of production and the degree of roundaboutness, could be made more intelligible by relating them to the purposes and choices of market participants. This would constitute the subjectivization of the relationships postulated by Böhm-Bawerk.

Wicksell undertook to incorporate Böhm-Bawerk's ideas about capital-using production processes into a general equilibrium framework consistent with that of Walras. This formalization of the theory, however, caused the essential concepts to lose economic relevance and intelligibility. If the relationship between the time element in the production process and the economic choices of individuals had become tenuous in Böhm-Bawerk's reformulation of Menger's theory, it became even more so in Wicksell's formalization of Böhm-Bawerk's. The assessment of Böhm-Bawerk's work applies a fortiori to Wicksell's. The relationships among the economic magnitudes—particularly those relationships involving the time element—make sense only when given a Mengerian interpretation.

Not surprisingly, Stigler finds the Swedish development to be nonsense. Wicksell's entire theoretical framework is judged invalid because it contains that erroneous Austrian time element. Stigler (1941, 278) considers Wicksell's theory in detail only after denying, in effect, that it has any economic relevance: "his technical analysis . . . deserves praise on the score of elegance, but it becomes primarily a display of technique."

VI. *The Austrian-Swedish transformation*

Wicksell indicated a fundamental agreement with what he saw as the central thesis of the *Positive theory of capital:* "Böhm-Bawerk's main formula of the explanation of interest—that interest is an agio or a premium which arises from the exchange between present and future goods—is quite correct and appropriate" (1970, 21). But judging Böhm-Bawerk's presentation to be "rather clumsy" and his theory incomplete, Wicksell set about rectifying these problems by recasting the theory in a more sophisticated language. His mathematical reformulation constituted a gain in his view in terms of "simplicity and perspicuity." Wicksell also incorporated an additional variable to represent land and what he calls "rent goods." Although he considered this extension to be "pretty obvious," it was essential for achieving a "generalization" of his theory. With the additional variable he could set down five equations that would state "exactly" and "for the first time . . . the relationship between the main economic factors, labour, land and capital" (21). There are further differences between the theories of Böhm-Bawerk and Wicksell which are of particular relevance to the issues of subjectivism versus formalism. Unearthing these differences requires that we go beneath the simultaneous equations and arithmetic examples and examine the respective concepts of capital that the theories employ.

Böhm-Bawerk's lengthy discussion of alternative capital concepts (1959, 2:10–101) constitutes a taxonomy of capital in which he identifies such categories and (overlapping) subcategories as national capital, social or productive capital, and private or acquisitive capital. For his own theoretical purposes, he was interested in a concept of capital that suited his vision of a capital-using economy. His vision makes his definitions understandable.

Two defining statements can be found in the opening pages of Böhm-Bawerk's *Positive theory.* "Capital is nothing but the sum total of intermediate products which come into existence at the individual stages of

the round-about course of production" (1959, 2:14). And what amounts
to the same thing, "We may define social capital as an aggregate of
products which serve as the means of the acquisition of economic goods
by society" (2:32). Capital in its relationship to the multistage process of
production is what Böhm-Bawerk called social or productive capital.
"Private capital" includes uninvested resources, "national capital" includes capital loaned abroad; but these categories were not so closely
related to his theory and hence were not of primary interest to him.

By contrast, Wicksell's definition of capital has little or no relationship to the actual process of production. Capital in his formulation is
taken to be "all interest bearing (material) goods" (1970, 105). His
definition is meant to include all durable consumer goods as well as all
means of subsistence. No attempt is made to sort out capital goods that
are used in the multistage production process from those that are not.
Durability is the only basis for defining subcategories. "Capital in the
wider sense" includes both producers' durable goods and consumers'
durable goods; "capital in the narrow sense" excludes both. "Highly
durable goods" are identified as "rent goods" and are treated as equivalent to land.

Stigler (1941, 272) sees Böhm-Bawerk's formulation as a "complex
and artificial classification of types of capital." He sees Wicksell's formulation as incorporating a "vastly improved capital concept." This
assessment reflects the rejection of the Austrian vision of a capital-using
economy and the adoption of the Clark-Knight vision. But in the context
of Böhm-Bawerk's vision, interpreted Mengerianly, Stigler's assessment is largely unjustified. Three separate but related issues, involving
the subsistence fund, the treatment of durable goods, and the relationship between social classes and their functions, will be considered in
some detail. Only on the third issue, it will be argued, does Wicksell's
formulation constitute an improvement over Böhm-Bawerk's.

(1) One alleged improvement of Wicksell's formulation over Böhm-
Bawerk's involves the treatment of the subsistence fund. Stigler contrasts the Swedish with the Austrian version by saying that the former
includes the "means of subsistence of laborers, even when these means
are owned by entrepreneurs" (1941, 272). Contrary to the implications
of Stigler's wording, Böhm-Bawerk excluded all means of subsistence
from his concept of social or productive capital. These means consist of
consumption goods, and Böhm-Bawerk (1959, 2:71) insisted that "the
concept 'means of production' is thought of as an antithesis of the
concept 'consumption goods' and is intended to be just that." Restating
for emphasis (2:72), "The goods with which the working members of
the community feed, warm and clothe themselves are goods of direct
consumption use; they are not means of production." Again, Böhm-

Bawerk's concept of capital is tailored to fit his vision of the production process. The relevant distinction is that between goods used directly by consumers and goods used in the multistage production process.

Wicksell's treatment of the subsistence fund is not as clear as Stigler's discussion suggests. Wicksell (1970, 104) offers two different criteria for identifying means of subsistence as capital. According to one, the means of subsistence "should be thought of all the time as capital until the moment when they find themselves in the possession of the consumers concerned." Clearly, Stigler's "even" should be changed to "only": Wicksell included the means of subsistence *only* when these means are owned by entrepreneurs. This criterion, which is completely consistent with Böhm-Bawerk's concept of private, or acquisitive, capital, could hardly be an improvement in Stigler's judgment. It commits the "classical error . . . [of] making ownership a criterion of capital, when in fact this aspect is completely irrelevant" (Stigler 1941, 197).

According to the alternative criterion, the subsistence fund maintains the status of capital "up to the moment of consumption" (Wicksell 1970, 104). Undoubtedly it was this criterion that won Stigler's approval. It has that distinct Clark-Knight flavor. But from an Austrian perspective this reformulation is a decided change for the worse. The category of capital goods is now so broad that it leaves no room at all for the category of consumption goods. Wicksell's formalistic approach led him to abstract from the process of production that was so emphasized by Böhm-Bawerk and to adopt a concept of capital that was more compatible with his system of equations than with the underlying economic realities. Wicksell was only a short step from rejecting altogether the distinction between capital goods and consumer goods and adopting in its place the dimensional distinction between stocks and flows. A thorough reformulation on this basis would represent a complete victory of form over substance—the ultimate consequence of the formalistic approach.

(2) A second alleged shortcoming of Böhm-Bawerk's capital concept that was overcome by Wicksell involved the treatment of durable consumer goods. Their exclusion, according to Stigler (1941, 197), constitutes a "major omission in Böhm-Bawerk's capital concept." Durable consumer goods, of course, can be considered as capital in some sense of the term, as has been recognized by theorists writing in the Austrian tradition from Menger to the present. Menger's view of capital, for instance, focuses on the good's "usefulness" and can be taken, as Stigler acknowledges, to include consumer durables. But capital in this very broad sense involves a distinction that is completely arbitrary if the line between capital goods and consumer goods is to be drawn short of the stock-flow distinction.

More importantly, such a distinction is unrelated to the theoretical problems with which Böhm-Bawerk was dealing. To call a dining-room table a capital good yielding a stream of services and a table cloth a consumer good is to play word games. To call both the table and the cloth capital goods yielding streams of services is to nullify the concept of consumer goods. More to the point, neither manner of classifying table and cloth is particularly helpful in the analysis of the economy's multistage production processes.

The problem of distinguishing between consumer goods and capital goods outside the context of a production process is not strictly related to the durability of the good. Mises (1966, 94) calls attention to the inherent element of arbitrariness in such distinctions:

> It is . . . superfluous to enter into pedantic discussions of whether a concrete good has to be called a good of the lowest order or should rather be attributed to one of the higher orders. Whether raw coffee beans or roast coffee beans or ground coffee or coffee prepared for drinking or only coffee prepared and mixed with cream and sugar are to be called a consumers' good ready for consumption is of no importance.

For a distinction between capital goods and consumer goods to be meaningful, it must have some relationship to the theory in which it is employed. Böhm-Bawerk's theory dealt with the process of production conceived as a sequence of maturity classes or stages of production. He was concerned with the allocation of resources among these stages and with the economic process by which resources are shifted from one stage to another. The relationship between the various stages of production can best be analyzed with a capital concept that excludes goods in the hands of their ultimate consumers—whether or not those goods are durable.

The Austrian concept of capital was not derived from the "classical error of making ownership the criterion of capital." Rather it was designed to reflect the one-way passage of goods from the lowest stage of production (retailing) into the hands of consumers. The general lack of effective markets for secondhand consumer goods creates a relevant boundary between capital goods and consumer goods. A consumer *can* resell a consumers' good, say, an overcoat, but only at a great loss. To adopt this interpretation of Böhm-Bawerk's capital theory is to suggest that the criterion is not ownership or even durability per se but remarketability. Goods that cannot be readily resold by consumers are not to be considered as part of the economy's capital structure.[5] Goods such

---

5. The issue of remarketability is only implicit in Böhm-Bawerk's formulation. Rothbard (1970, 1:320) explicitly takes account of the fact that "consumers' goods, once sold, do not ordinarily re-enter the exchange nexus."

as houses and (less so) automobiles, for which there are effective secondary markets, should be considered capital goods even from an Austrian point of view. Such remarketable goods can be shifted back into business inventories (the lowest maturity class) in response to changing supply and demand conditions. They may eventually be absorbed into even higher maturity classes, as in the case of a dwelling that is converted to a business use. For most other goods in the hands of consumers, however, the potential for such absorption into higher maturity classes is negligible.

Replacing the criterion of durability with the criterion of remarketability refocuses our thinking about capital goods in the hands of consumers. It does not cause a great change in the goods normally thought of as capital goods. Durability, after all, is one of the characteristics that makes a good remarketable. But durability is not a sufficient characteristic. An automobile and an overcoat, for instance, may be equally durable, but the former is more plausibly categorized as a capital good than is the latter—which is to say that remarketability better describes the distinction that is typically made. There are, of course, borderline cases in distinguishing capital goods and consumer goods. There is no black-and-white distinction between goods that are remarketable and goods that are not, but the distinction does have relevance. It serves to tailor-fit the concept of capital to Austrian capital theory.

All this is foreign to Wicksell's formulation. The need for any such distinction between capital goods and consumer goods is obscured by the formalization of the theory and the homogenization of the capital concept. A mathematical formulation is, by its very nature, ill-suited to incorporate distinctions that are based on such things as the purposes for which the good is to be used or on the notion of remarketability. It is much better suited to distinguish between dimensionally different magnitudes such as the stocks and flows of the Clark-Knight vision.

The nature of mathematical or formalistic analysis was clearly recognized by Böhm-Bawerk in his treatment of Alfred Marshall. His critical remarks focused on Marshall's well-known discussion of whether such goods as furniture and clothing are to be considered as productive capital.

It would, to be sure, be possible and conceivable to count as income the benefits derived from the utilization of [furniture and clothing]. And it is also true that such a reckoning might appear admissible in the strictly mathematical treatment of the entire distribution problem. (1959, 2:30)

Böhm-Bawerk clearly saw the formalistic relationship between capital and income, but he was concerned that a strictly mathematical treatment would divert attention from the capital-using production process and the markets for the goods that are associated with the various maturity classes. The potential danger of formalism was emphasized when Böhm-Bawerk criticized the ideas of one theorist who

> could at times strangely distort [his ideas] into shapes that failed entirely to coincide with the lines of the foundation on which they were reared. I cite as an example [the] extension of the concept of social capital to include all sorts of *personal* traits, talents and skills. These certainly present an odd appearance, decked out as component elements of a "stock" and they were destined, like the spirits unwisely exorcised, to bedevil capital theory for many a long year. (2:22)

These critical remarks about the notion of "human capital" were directed not at Wicksell nor even at Clark; they were directed at Adam Smith. Clearly, Böhm-Bawerk's opposition to formalism is not at all explained by his lack of mathematical training. He objected to the purely dimensional distinction whatever the mode of expression. But in defending his own formulation against the classical view, he managed to rescue substance from form only to have it relinquished once again by Wicksell.

In sum, Böhm-Bawerk did exclude from his definition of social capital durable goods in the hands of their ultimate consumers. This definition did not involve a gross oversight, nor was it adopted and defended in ignorance of the mathematical relationship between stocks and flows. Its purpose was to direct attention to the economic relationships between the various stages of the multistage production process. While Wicksell's reformulation may have achieved greater "generality, simplicity, and perspicuity," it directed attention away from the production process.

(3) The third issue to be considered stems from Böhm-Bawerk's peculiar treatment of the category of private capital and Wicksell's corresponding generalization. It is here that Stigler's charge of artificiality has merit. But much lies behind this issue. The significance of the peculiar way in which private capital is treated derives from Böhm-Bawerk's theory of interest—or more accurately, from his particular formulation of that theory.

Well known are his "three main grounds" for the existence of a positive rate of interest (1959, 2:265–89). The first two grounds, having to do with individuals' estimates of their future incomes and with their present evaluation of future utilities, were explicitly introduced as subjective factors. Böhm-Bawerk referred to these as "the factors of provision and perspective." The third ground involves subjective considerations as well insofar as it accounts for value differences as opposed to physical differences between present goods and future goods, but it is offered as a technological factor. Because of the increased productivity of roundabout production processes, present goods are preferred to future goods.

Less well known is the differential way in which Böhm-Bawerk, adopting in this regard a very classical viewpoint, applied the above reasoning to the social classes with which his theory dealt—the entrepreneur, or capitalist, and the worker. The productivity of roundabout processes is the concern of the capitalist alone. More significantly, the workers alone are affected by the factors of provision and perspective, the factors that make up the first and second grounds. That the capitalists are not themselves imbued with time preferences on the basis of the first two grounds is repeatedly asserted: "in his subjective circumstances the capitalist as a rule places the same valuation on a sum of present goods as on an equal sum of future goods" (2:353). The subjective circumstances of the workers and the capitalists are vividly described in the following passage.

> The workers are in urgent need of present goods and there is little or no possibility of their accomplishing anything by working for their own account. To the last man they will prefer to sell their labor cheaply rather than not at all. But a similar situation obtains with respect to the capitalists. As far as conditions go with respect to their particular wants and the satisfaction of them, their present goods (which they would in any event save up for future use) are worth no more to them than an equal quantity of future goods. They will therefore prefer to make any purchase of labor that affords them any agio at all, even if only a small one, rather than allow their capital to lie idle. (2:354)

Thus, after describing at great length the subjective factors that determine the rate of interest and hence the allocation of resources among the various maturity classes of the production process, Böhm-Bawerk built into his theory a particular set of subjective evaluations, in which workers and capitalists were represented by opposite extremes. There was no relevant margin at which these evaluations could guide the process of production; the factors of provision and perspective became, instead, a part of the setting. In modern terms, the supply of labor is perfectly inelastic, and thus the level of employment is supply-determined; the wage rate is indeterminate given the similarly inelastic demand conditions. The artificiality about which Stigler complained is seen to be rooted in Böhm-Bawerk's specifying, without justification, the particular evaluations and hence the particular intentions of capitalists and workers.

Given these specifications, however, Böhm-Bawerk's treatment of private capital as distinct from social capital is understandable. Social capital includes all capital that is invested in the process of production. This excludes the (uninvested) means of subsistence whether in the hands of capitalists or workers. The means of subsistence in the hands of capitalists *are* private capital, nonetheless, by virtue of the capitalists' intention to invest. They cease to be capital, however, when transferred to the worker by virtue of his urgent need for present goods. True to the subjectivist perspective of Menger and the Austrian School, the means of subsistence are given or denied the status of capital on the basis of the purpose for which they are to be used. Unfortunately, the subjective factors were set in (classical) concrete by Böhm-Bawerk's characterization of the capitalists and workers.

The much-needed generalization of Böhm-Bawerk's formulation which Wicksell achieved in this respect can be seen clearly by comparing their respective discussions of the loan market. According to Böhm-Bawerk (1959, 2:20), "all the sellers [of credit] estimate present and future goods as just about equal in value, and all the buyers estimate the value of present goods as higher than that of future goods." In modern terms, the supply of credit is perfectly interest-inelastic, and thus the volume of credit is completely supply-determined. In contrast, Wicksell gives free play to subjective valuations on both sides of the market:

> the interest on the loan, just like exchange value in the case of ordinary exchange, will depend on *two proportions of market utility;* that is to say, it will depend first on the proportion between the marginal utility of present and that of future goods *for the creditor,* and secondly on the proportion between the analogous marginal utilities for the debtor. . . . The interest which must really be paid will then fall somewhere between these two different valuations. (1970, 107–8, emphasis his)

This generalized formulation had the potential of keeping the subjective factors alive. But when Wicksell turned his attention from the theory of interest to the theory of capital, these factors were all but lost. Böhm-Bawerk's third ground for explaining the rate of interest, which was accepted as a purely technological consideration, became the *only* ground for Wicksell. It was this domination of the technological relationship in his formal theory which allowed him to dispense with Böhm-Bawerk's "complex and artificial classification of types of capital" and to adopt a "single capital concept." If the Swedish transformation appears to be a gain, it is because the subjective factors that lay behind Böhm-Bawerk's classification had been impounded by classical prescriptions that fixed the valuations and hence the behavior of both capitalists and workers.

Menger's concern with intentions and "wishes and needs" had already been eliminated.

VII. *One of the greatest errors?*

Even before the turn of the century, capital theory was being developed in the direction of formalism and away from subjectivism. Böhm-Bawerk's reformulation of Menger's capital theory and Wicksell's formalization of Böhm-Bawerk's put formalism and subjectivism in direct conflict. An assessment of Wicksell's contribution from a Mengerian perspective would be the precise opposite to Stigler's. The indeterminacy of wages resulting from the dramatically differing valuations by capitalists as compared to laborers could not have troubled Menger, whose own theory of prices involved a fundamental element of indeterminacy. But Wicksell's treatment of the subsistence fund and of durable goods would have troubled Menger for reasons already suggested. The formal stock-flow distinction diverts attention from the subjective relationship between the lower-order and higher-order goods that make up the production process.

Modern economists who prefer to theorize in terms of the dimensionally distinct stocks and flows will not see the "greatest error" as an error at all. But those who applaud the recent Austrian resurgence, who prefer subjectivism to formalism, and who believe that the time element in the economy's multistage structure of production is trivialized by the "average period," are likely to agree with Menger and to see Böhm-Bawerk's error as "one of the greatest."

Comments on earlier drafts by Gerald P. O'Driscoll, Jr. (Federal Reserve Bank of Dallas), Parth Shah (Auburn University), and an anonymous referee are gratefully acknowledged. The author thanks the Ludwig von Mises Institute for financing his participation at the Menger conference.

References

Böhm-Bawerk, Eugen. [1889] 1959. *Capital and interest*. Vol. 2. South Holland, Ill.: Libertarian Press.

Cassel, Gustav. 1903. *The nature and necessity of interest*. London: Macmillan.

Clark, John Bates, 1924. *The distribution of wealth*. New York: Macmillan.

Endres, A. M. 1987. The origins of Böhm-Bawerk's "greatest error": theoretical points of separation from Menger. *Journal of Institutional and Theoretical Economics* 143:291–309.

Garrison, Roger W. 1985. A subjectivist theory of a capital-using economy. In *The economics of time and ignorance*, edited by Gerald P. O'Driscoll, Jr. and Mario J. Rizzo. Oxford.

Hayek, Friedrich A. 1936. The mythology of capital. *Quarterly Journal of Economics* 50 (February): 199–228.

Hicks, John R. 1976. Some questions of time in economics. In *Evaluation, welfare and time in economics,* edited by Anthony M. Lang et al., 135–51. Lexington, Mass.: D. C. Heath.

Kirzner, Israel M. 1966. *An essay on capital.* New York: Augustus M. Kelley.

———. 1976. Ludwig von Mises and the theory of capital and interest. In *The economics of Ludwig von Mises,* edited by Laurance S. Moss. Kansas City: Sheed & Ward.

Lachmann, Ludwig M. 1969. Methodological individualism and the market process. In *Roads to freedom,* edited by Erich Streissler et al., 89–103. London: Routledge & Kegan Paul.

———. [1973] 1978. *Macro-economic thinking and the market economy.* Studies in Economics, no. 6. Menlo Park, Cal.: Institute for Humane Studies.

Menger, Carl. [1871] 1950. *Principles of economics.* New York: The Free Press.

Mises, Ludwig von. 1966. *Human action.* 3rd rev. ed. Chicago: Henry Regnery.

Rolph, Earl R. 1980. On Austrian capital theory. *Economic Inquiry* 18 (July): 501–3.

Rothbard, Murray N. [1963] 1970. *Man, economy, and state.* 2 vols. Los Angeles: Nash.

Schumpeter, Joseph A. 1951. Eugen von Böhm-Bawerk: 1851–1914. In *Ten great economists,* 143–90. Oxford: Oxford University Press.

———. 1954. *History of economic analysis.* Oxford: Oxford University Press.

Stigler, George J. 1941. *Production and distribution theories.* New York: Macmillan.

Streissler, Erich, and Wilhelm Weber. 1973. The Menger tradition. In *Carl Menger and the Austrian school of economics,* edited by John R. Hicks and Wilhelm Weber, 226–32. Oxford: Oxford University Press.

Wicksell, Knut. [1893] 1970. *Value, capital and rent.* New York: Augustus M. Kelley.

———. [1934] 1977. *Lectures in political economy.* 2 vols. New York: Augustus M. Kelley.

Lionel Robbins and the Austrian connection

D. P. O'Brien

I. *Introduction*

Lionel Robbins was a major figure in English economics for more than fifty years and a prominent figure in public controversy, particularly during the 1930s. During the controversies of the 1930s it was widely held that the basis of positions advanced by the critics of Cambridge, including Robbins, lay in Austrian economics. (Indeed, in the macro-economic controversies, the Cambridge side seems to have regarded the London School of Economics as "a suburb of Vienna.") But Robbins lived for a very long time; and he was active as a writer on economics long after the controversies of the 1930s had receded into the middle distance (O'Brien 1988a, 1988b). As they so receded, the question of the extent of the Austrian base for Robbins's thought also receded, although it was revived at the end of his life in connection with his important writings on methodology (Addleson 1984).

This paper attempts to evaluate the strength of Robbins's Austrian connection and to indicate how far he can honestly be called an Austrian economist. As will become clear, the task of disentangling the roots of his *micro*economic views can never be completely solved, because in this area his primary source was undoubtedly Wicksteed's *Common sense*, while he drew from the Austrians precisely those elements which coincided most directly with what he had drawn from Wicksteed. The task in dealing with his *macro*economics is more straightforward, both because he rejected much of aggregated macroeconomics on straight-forwardly Austrian grounds (there could, he held, be no useful concept of production in the aggregate) and because his adoption of the Mises-Hayek theory of economic fluctuations was explicit and clear-cut, at least in the 1930s. However, even here we shall find that, partly because of the very roots of the work of Mises and Hayek themselves, the filiation is not absolutely straightforward.

This is not really surprising. Robbins was an eclectic, seeking to assemble the common strands in a wide range of different sources in economics so as to weld together, to present to the public, and to use in controversy, a common body of developed, received, and professionally attested economic theory. This in itself was connected with his pride in the intellectual content of a subject which had proved a revelation to him when he first became an undergraduate.[1] Seeing the compatibility of the analyses originating in different countries, from the pens of different writers, at different historical times, he felt considerable satisfaction at the progress which economics had made. Indeed students and contemporaries of Robbins have stressed the almost messianic quality of his lectures on economic theory. The message was made very clear. This stuff was important. A corpus of theory had emerged and it had to be grappled with, absorbed, and used.[2]

Robbins's drive to "open up" British economics must be seen in this light. He was not motivated merely by a desire to weaken what he saw as the predominance—at times amounting almost to an intellectual monopoly—possessed by Cambridge, although this was undoubtedly a motive, especially during the 1930s. Rather, he was concerned to draw together the different threads of what he regarded as being not only a valid body of theory but also an outstanding intellectual achievement. This in turn reinforced the authority possessed by the subject and the persuasive strength of its conclusions.

It was not that he was blind to the differences in the work of different authors. But drawing on what Wicksteed had made of Jevons's approach (especially the replacement by Wicksteed in his *Common sense* of utility by ranking) and on the material in the Austrian writers, he pulled together what he felt to be the corpus of *modern* economic theory (circa 1930) and was then critical of those developments—partial equilibrium analysis of costs, for instance—which were at variance with this corpus of analysis (1934c, 465; 1933a, xv n.; 1934a, 6–11). In particular, he criticized Marshall's Representative Firm from the (somewhat irrelevant) standpoint of Austrian general equilibrium (Robbins 1928).

This concern with authority also led Robbins to read into earlier, and indubitably great, authors, a rather Austrian view of the world. In particular, he was prone in the 1930s to view *The wealth of nations* more in terms of general equilibrium than as an essay in economic development (1935a, 50, 68–69).

In drawing together this corpus of modern theory, the two most important sources, at least in the initial stages of Robbins's development as an economist, after his graduation, were Wicksteed and Wicksell. He

---

1. "For me, at least, this was an entry to a new world. Here was really first-rate intellect. Here was free discussion of the great problems of man in society. Here, without abatement of personal convictions, was integrity and a search after truth" (1971a, 74–75).

2. On Robbins's delight in economics see 1930a, 194; 1930b, 16, 24; 1934a, 1; 1935a, 2–3. See also Hutchison 1979 and (on Robbins as a young lecturer at Oxford) Meade 1984. Various people who were students of Robbins in the postwar years have also confirmed this picture. On this, as on many other aspects of Robbins's personality, Phelps Brown (1988) is a valuable source.

was thus initially exposed to Austrian economics at one remove; Wicksteed essentially reinterpreted his Jevonian origins in a way which *mirrored* Austrian economics (though the *stimulus* for this seems to have come, ironically, from Lausanne rather than Vienna, through the influence of Pareto), while Wicksell ranks as the most important expositor and developer of Austrian economics outside the ranks of the Austrians. Having, so to speak, imbibed this initial message, Robbins then explored the Austrian literature; and he strengthened his assimilation of principles which he had derived from Wicksteed and Wicksell to the point where he felt able to contrast favorably the composite tradition which he had absorbed with that of Cambridge.

As will become particularly clear when we turn attention to the macroeconomic aspects of Robbins's work, he regarded Wicksell as a very important economist (1935b; 1970, 223–28; 1958c, q. 10219). Indeed Wicksell's work had the advantage that it incorporated (and indisputably improved) not only much Austrian theory but also much that was valuable in the classical treatment of capital (1935b, xiii–xiv), thus yet again enabling Robbins to point with pride to the achievements of economists in producing a coherent body of theory over a long period.

Nonetheless, despite these complications it should prove possible to give some indication of the weight to be attached to Austrian sources for Robbins's thought. There is no doubt that he regarded Austrian economics as a whole as being of very considerable importance, as is shown by the links which he established with Vienna in the 1930s (1934a, 1; 1971a, 127, 132, 143). Moreover, while he suggested that the study of economics could begin with Wicksteed's *Common sense,* followed by Wicksell's *Lectures* in the second year of study (1935b, xi n., xviii, xix), the London School of Economics was prominent in making Austrian works available to a wider audience—in particular there were translations of two of Mises's major works, *Money* and *Socialism* (Mises 1934, 1936), and a reprint of the works of Menger (1933–36).

II. *Microeconomics*

1. *Analytical structure: content*

Robbins sought a microeconomics which was capable of including both nonmaterial aims and activities and also destructive (rather than constructive) activities, such as war, which nonetheless used resources, as well as the more obvious categories of economic activity (1971a, 146; 1935a, 129; 1929b, 249). He also sought a system which would allow him to separate economics and ethics (1927a; 1935a, 91, 147–48, 151; see also Weber 1949, 11). He was anxious to place outside the domain of "scientific" economics both value judgments and the scientific pretensions of Pigovian welfare economics.[3] He thus wanted a demarcation criterion to exclude such forms of analysis from scientific economics proper. Value judgments were indispensable for the application of analysis to particular policy situations; but they did not themselves enjoy scientific status (1938a).

Robbins found what he was looking for in the distinction between positive and normative economics.[4] Only the former was economics proper; the latter required extrascientific value judgments. Positive economics involved the employment of a maximization model (though without perfect consistency of rankings).[5] Thus economics was essentially to be about choice models. Rational behavior, which amounted to acting consistently in accordance with the ranking of different possibilities, lay behind demand, which was the ultimate force in economics.[6] The supply curve was merely the sellers' own demand curve (1933a, xx; Wicksteed 1910, 510, 785). In the perfect form of this model the chooser has, in effect, perfect information. Factor allocation thus falls into place as the reflection of the communal rankings of the outcome of the employment of factor services, expressed through the market (1934c; 1935a, 32–38, 65; Wicksteed 1910, 358–98). *All* ends, which involved scarce resources, and which were thus subject to choice, came within the purview of this analysis—there was no special category of economic ends (1935a, 24–32; 1971a, 147).

We thus have microeconomic analysis as essentially an a priori analysis of the implications of choice for the allocation of scarce resources. The focus of the analysis was upon equilibrium—*general* and not *partial* equilibrium.[7] This led in turn to an approach to cost theory which was in terms of opportunity cost—which could *only* be analyzed in a general equilibrium framework (1934a). Throughout, the emphasis is upon a high degree of subjectivism. This enabled Robbins to adopt an extremely agnostic attitude towards index numbers. In particular he was able to cite in his support the argument put forward by Haberler in his book on index numbers that it was impossible to say which of two incomes was the larger, on any objective basis. Such a question could only be answered by each individual income recipient (1935a, 63; Haberler 1927, 83).[8]

3. See in particular 1938c, 635–38; 1934c, 464–65; 1971a, 147–48; 1935a, 87; 1939a, 164; 1959, 45; 1932c, 173–74; 1953, 107–8.
4. 1935a, 88–90, 106; 1981, xviii; 1963, 6–7, 19; 1938c, 639; 1927a; 1971a, 147–48; 1964, 18–19; see also Weber 1949, 52; Menger 1963, 46; Kirzner 1976, 137.
5. Robbins 1932a, 92–94. Such a view is to be found alike in Mises (1949, 103) and Wicksteed (1910, 32–34).
6. 1935a, 7, 12, 14, 16, 30, 87–88, 152–53; 1930b, 24; 1954, 201–25; 1934c, 465; 1971a, 147. See also Menger 1871, 52–53; 1950, 94–95.
7. 1935a, 55, 67–68; 1933a, xvi; 1934a, 11, 14–15; 1934c, 465; 1930. See also Wicksteed 1910, 212–400.
8. He was still stressing this point in his postwar lectures at LSE.

Building upon premises which were either obviously true empirically or derived from introspection (1935a, 73–75, 78, 104–6; 1938a, 347–49; 1971a, 149), the individual subjective maximization model resulted in theorems which were necessarily true. Quantification work was not required to test them. "*Verification,*" however—checking whether the assumed initial conditions were actually fulfilled—was a proper form of quantitative analysis.[9] But the emphasis throughout Robbins's work is upon a very substantial degree of apriorism.

2. *Analytical structure: sources*

This approach was founded upon a fusion of English- and German-language sources. The German-language sources were entirely Austrian, with the exception of Weber. The general methodology came from strands in English classical economics, especially the work of J. S. Mill and Cairnes, but the most important English source by far was Wicksteed. From Weber came the distinction between positive and normative economics and the idea of the necessity of a *Wertfrei* character for economics (1935a, xii, 90, 148; see also Weber 1949, 1–47, 52; Hutchison 1979). But Wicksteed and the Austrians—and Robbins typically couples these two sources together in acknowledgment—provided the vast majority of the intellectual apparatus. From Wicksteed came the emphasis upon equilibrium, upon ranking, upon the primacy of demand, even upon the lack of perfect consistency in ranking (1910, 32–34). Though ranking is to be found throughout the work of the Austrians and is clearly involved in Menger's work (Hayek 1934, xiv–xv), it is Wicksteed's *Common sense* which provides Robbins's main source.

But here we encounter a major problem in the intellectual history we are considering. Wicksteed's treatment of ranking seems to derive from the influence upon his own Jevonian thought of his reading of Pareto (Steadman 1987). It is difficult to find Wicksteed drawing *directly* from the Austrians, even though Robbins, time and time again, while recognizing the significance of Pareto (1933a, xix), makes a direct connection between Wicksteed and the Austrians and indeed refers to Wicksteed as illustrating Wieser's "Law of Cost" brilliantly (1933a, xviii)—even though Wicksteed makes no reference to Wieser at all and even though the very phrase "Law of Cost" comes not from Wieser himself but from Pantaleoni (1898, 183–84, 250–51; Robbins 1934a, 2).

The influence of Pantaleoni, whose book dated from 1889 (and from 1898 in English), on Robbins seems to have been peripheral. He stated clearly the proposition that the marginal utility of a productive instrument will be determined by the marginal utility of the least significant

9. 1935a, 116–19; 1937a; 1934c, 465; 1971b, 188–89; 1938a, 352; 1938b, 161; O'Brien 1988a, 34–39; 1988b. The best discussion of "verification" is in Blaug 1980.

final product that it produces, and that its services will be spread across products to equalize the marginal utility of these services in producing different products. But the whole approach, based very firmly on marginal utility, not mere ranking, went much further than Robbins in the direction of cardinalism. In the treatment of this issue, indeed, it is Robbins's eclecticism which is most apparent. In introducing Wicksteed he refers to Wicksteed's exposition of the work of one economist (Wieser) using a term which he had got from another (or others—apart from Pantaleoni it is also in Mayer 1925, 638), although in the Wicksteedian exposition, which uses ranking rather than marginal utility for the most part, there is no reference to these other sources.

A number of Austrian economists writing in the 1920s have attracted relatively little attention from later commentators. But in this story they may be important. The particular form in which they couched their analysis made it easy for Robbins to couple Wicksteed's name with a general reference to the Austrians. Having come across the work of Schönfeld (1924)—possibly through Hayek ([1925] 1984)—Robbins was then enabled to cite Schönfeld and couple his name with that of Wicksteed in a most illuminating way.

> It does not require much knowledge of modern economic analysis to realise that the foundation of the theory of value is the assumption that the different things that the individual wants to do have a different importance to him, and can be arranged therefore in a certain order. This notion can be expressed in various ways and with varying degrees of precision from the simple wants system of Menger and the early Austrians to the more refined scales of relative valuations of Wicksteed and Schönfeld and the indifference systems of Pareto and Messrs. Hicks and Allen. (1935a, 75, replacing 75–76 of 1932a)

So we have the presentation of a corpus of theory now extending from Menger to Hicks and Allen, an extension which is facilitated by the replacement of material referring to *marginal utility* in the first edition of Robbins's *Essay* with this material from the second edition centered around *ranking*.

There seems no doubt that the microeconomic work of Austrian writers in the 1920s enabled Robbins to come to appreciate, progressively and over quite a long period, that Wicksteed's work involved ranking and was not dependent upon cardinalism. This enabled Robbins to continue to utilize his assimilations from Wicksteed, to whose work he attached particular importance—"A failure to sit through the *Common Sense* is a pretty sure sign of intellectual smallness," he informed his readers (1933a, xiv).

Nonetheless it should be emphasized that there are significant points of difference between Robbins's own approach and that of Wicksteed at various junctures; again, Robbins's eclecticism in building up a corpus of theory is in evidence. Although Robbins was slow to shed the residues of the marginal utility treatment which Wicksteed had carried over from his *Alphabet* to his *Common sense* (1910, 412), residues which are in evidence in Wicksteed's 1914 *Economic Journal* article (1910, 772–96), he quickly shed most of the elements of cardinalism (1910, 457) and he certainly did not make the exalted claims which Wicksteed made for marginalist ranking as the development of a general psychological principle to be used in explaining all human action (1910, 403–4, 776, 780, 800, 816). Indeed Wicksteed's emphasis on the psychological—and his denial of the existence of economic laws (1910, 780)—went far beyond Robbins's own position, while his references to psychological literature, and his interpretation of Pareto as providing psychological interpretation of human action, are much stronger than anything to be found in Robbins's own work (1934b).

In other respects too Wicksteed's work was not entirely satisfactory from what one can see was Robbins's own point of view. On the one hand there was his lack of acknowledgments of the work of others, whether he was drawing upon them or criticizing them;[10] on the other, the discussions of macroeconomics and trade in the *Common sense* are distinctly weak,[11] and Robbins would have had to look elsewhere in building up a body of accepted theory.

But much else in Wicksteed clearly struck a deep responsive chord in Robbins. The impossibility of having simultaneously valid partial equilibrium curves (1910, 528, 536, 545), the refusal to accept the commonly drawn supply curve on the same diagram as a demand curve, the classification of the supply curve itself as not a cost curve (which is what Wicksteed meant by the common variety) but as the sellers' own demand curve (499–500, 542, 785–87), the emphasis upon competing valuations for productive resources as dictating both their valuation and their allocation (517, 545, 788), the all-pervasive emphasis on choice (772–96), the sweeping dismantling of English classical rent theory to

10. See Wicksteed 1910, 479, where Marshall's "tea and coffee" example in discussing interdependence in consumer surplus is used without acknowledgment; see also the (Giffen) case (490) and the criticism of (Marshall's) conflation of increasing and diminishing returns (528).

11. Wicksteed 1910, 664–66, 670–71, 701. The discussion of trade is particularly weak, presenting a conception based upon specialization on the basis of absolute advantage—indeed at one point Wicksteed commits himself to the statement that "there is, properly speaking, no economic theory of foreign trade as distinct from home trade" (666). The discussion of tariffs displays no inkling of the "Cuba case" and is much inferior to Marshall.

show that the choice of which factor to hold fixed was arbitrary (552, 562, 574, 788–89; Robbins 1933a, x–xi; O'Brien 1988a, 209–11)—an achievement which Robbins would have found satisfyingly destructive of the Shove–Joan Robinson "exploitation" approach to distribution (1910, 571, 792): all these clearly appealed to Robbins and underlay his work.

But these elements were fused with what Robbins obtained elsewhere in building up a corpus of theory.

He read German fluently (1932a, 119; 1935a, 108; see also 1927b, 1931c, 1936c, 1937d), and he read the works of a wide range of German-language writers, in particular those of Mises and of Mayer (1934a, 1932a, 1935a). In reading these works he found a close coincidence between the intellectual apparatus which he had already gathered from Wicksteed himself and the content of the Austrians. His reception of the Austrian works as an additional source may have been assisted by the fact that after embracing economics as preferable to socialism, he would have had little sympathy for Wicksteed's own Fabian associations and found the more neutral attitude of the Austrians more immediately acceptable. But in this connection it is important to make the point that no simple ideological lesson can be learned here. As Hutchinson has observed (1981, 207), Wieser, an Austrian economist of whom Robbins was particularly fond, was highly critical of free market institutions. Robbins did not accept this line of criticism any more than he accepted Wicksteed's Fabianism, so that any attempt to see his Austrian borrowings as purely ideological—"political economy"—is bound to be misleading (O'Brien 1989).

Despite Robbins's fondness for referring to Wieser, it was, in the microeconomics sphere, Mises and Mayer who among the Austrians seem to have had the greatest influence on Robbins. The influence of Mises is particularly important in the first edition of Robbins's *Essay on the nature and significance of economic science,* for several of the citations disappear in the second edition. Robbins in fact acknowledged a particular debt to Mises, with whom he had personal contact (1935a, 16, 18, 39, 54, 77, 78, 83, 89; 1971a, 107, 143). The apriorism of Mises would also have appealed to Robbins, preconditioned as he was by the work of Cairnes, Mill, and Wicksteed. The rejection of interpersonal comparisons, by Jevons and Wicksteed, was in turn echoed by Mises in his emphasis upon the idea that we could only scale (i.e., rank) preferences (1932, 93; Robbins 1932a, 56; 1935a, 93; 1953, 102–4).

Robbins's methodological position on a number of issues, whether in his famous *Essay* or in lesser-known publications (1938b), was very much in tune with the Austrian position, especially as put forward by Hayek. Hayek not only regarded introspection as a valid source of information (1933, 27–38, 232; Robbins 1935a, 105) but also held—in contrast to Menger himself—that there was not a parallel between natural and social science (Hutchison 1981, 213–14). Moreover, Hayek was critical of the extensive use of statistical material, holding that this had only the limited role of "verification" noted above (1931a, 133). Indeed in this he was a great deal more purist than Robbins himself was in practice (at least in his *Great Depression*) if not in precept (in his *Essay*).

Mayer seems to have been most important to Robbins in his interpretation of Wieser. For Mayer's work (1925) set Wieser's concept of opportunity cost clearly in the concept of general equilibrium, precisely as Wicksteed had done. As already noted, Wicksteed's own general equilibrium approach, like his replacement of marginal utility by ranking, seems to have had Lausanne sources. But the way in which Mayer spelled out the implications of Wieser's analysis enabled Robbins to interpret Wicksteed in Austrian terms and indeed to classify him together with the Austrians (Robbins 1933a, 1934a, 1935a).

Mayer's account of Wieser's work is remarkable. He shows, with far greater clarity than Wieser himself, the way in which Wieser's theoretical contributions can be used to illuminate the unity of economic phenomena, building on Menger's initial insights. For Mayer, it was Wieser who really built up Austrian economics. It seems clear that this view influenced Robbins greatly; not only did this perception of the unity of economic phenomena form a key element in Robbins's own view of the evolved body of economic theory to which he attached such importance, but it also significantly affected his view of the relative importance of different Austrian economists. Indeed it seems clear that Mayer, Strigl, Hayek, and Mises greatly influenced Robbins, not only with respect to their ideas but also with respect to his perception of the nature of the Austrian School and the contribution of the earlier Austrian economists.

These later writers made very clear, in the 1920s and early 1930s, a general equilibrium view of the economic system. Such a view was to form a fundamental part of Robbins's approach to economics and to be employed by him in both a micro and a macro context. Precisely how far this was genuinely Austrian in origin is, however, a question which is insoluble because of the influence of Wicksteed. The Austrians essentially sharpened Robbins's appreciation of the general equilibrium elements in Wicksteed. Perhaps this is most of all true of Hayek, who until 1937 was very much a general equilibrium theorist (Hutchison 1981, 210–19; McCloughry 1984; Caldwell 1988) and whose elegant expositions would have strengthened Robbins in his search for, and his utilization of, the body of evolved and established theory.

3. The basic micro model applied

It is thus clear that while Wicksteed and the Austrians together constituted, for Robbins in the 1930s, the *modern* representation of a long, evolving corpus of valid microeconomic theory, disentangling the precise Austrian input is a matter of some difficulty. However, if we examine the uses to which Robbins put the basic model which he had assimilated, the issue becomes a little clearer if not wholly clear.

Allocation. Robbins considered allocation in two particular contexts: wartime and the problems of a socialist economy. Coupling together the general equilibrium framework of choice and the ends/means distinction, Robbins was able to analyze the operation of a wartime economy. Although wartime conditions ultimately meant that all other ends had to be subordinated to that of victory, there were still problems of the allocation of resources to achieve subgoals which themselves were conducive to victory. Here Robbins employed the marginal analysis so as to produce optimal allocation at the margin of different factors which could be substituted within and between uses. As far as possible this allocation should be achieved by the market, since the capacity of the state to allocate resources efficiently was extremely limited—primarily because state knowledge was extremely limited (1947, 5, 7, 8, 22, 41–42, 44–46, 50, 53–54; 1954, 201–25; 1935a, 16; 1971a, 146).

This question of knowledge arises again in Robbins's treatment of the problems of allocation within a socialist economy, and it is particularly interesting because otherwise his basic approach, as already indicated, neglected the problem of the generation of knowledge, in its concentration on choice. It is also interesting because where Robbins recognizes the problem of knowledge, as in dealing with wartime and socialist allocation, the source is unambiguously Austrian: the work of Mises.

Socialism involved both allocative and adaptive failures. Because consumer preferences could not be known and because there were no objective engineering data on costs, there was no possibility of efficient allocation, in accordance with consumer rankings, without a market system to register those rankings. Adaptive failure arose both because of the bureaucratic nature of socialism and also because of the lack of knowledge not only of changes in preferences but also of changes in technological opportunities.[12]

All this was based squarely upon Mises's classic critique (1932, 86–138)—and it contrasts both with Robbins's own tendency to neglect

---

12. Mises 1932, 86–138. See Robbins 1934d, 146–56; 1935a, 17–18; 1935c, 92; 1937b, 130–34, 141–54, 194–218; 1939a, 27–28, 85–87, 189, 192, 194–202; 1940, 95–96; 1947, 22–23, 77–80; 1963, 38, 40, 104; 1966, 28–29; 1971a, 55–56, 61–62, 64, 67, 191–92; 1976, 29–31, 142–50.

knowledge-generation elsewhere and to focus on choice, and also with Wicksteed's own Fabian sympathies (though these were not entirely without recognition of some of the problems of socialism). It is, however, interesting that with some weakening of the Austrian influence on Robbins, after World War II, there was also some distancing from the Austrian position on the role of the state in allocation. Robbins certainly did not completely dissociate himself from the analysis. Indeed he reaffirmed its importance in his *Autobiography* of 1971. But he did seem to distance himself from Hayek's position (though without mentioning Hayek by name) as set out in *The road to serfdom,* in which Hayek had viewed nationalization as the thin end of a totalitarian wedge (Robbins 1976, 137–38). It is evident too in Robbins's treatment of education during the 1960s and in his treatment of state patronage of the arts, in both of which the careful general equilibrium analysis of the wartime years played little if any part (Robbins 1963, 53–72; O'Brien 1988b, ch. 6).

Costs and markets. Three key elements derived from the basic model provided, for Robbins, a unified and internally consistent treatment of costs and markets. The first was the insistence upon the general equilibrium context of any market problem. Coupled with this was an emphasis upon the importance of asking *general* equilibrium questions about the "sensitivity" of partial equilibrium conclusions to general equilibrium considerations (1933a, xv n.; 1934a, 10). The second, derived from the general equilibrium approach, was the insistence that cost meant *opportunity* cost, so that it was impossible to have given and fixed cost schedules (1933a, x; 1934a, 2–3; Wieser 1889, 171–73, 176; Wicksteed 1910, book 1, ch. 9 and p. 732). Thirdly, factor supplies, having alternative uses, *including* own consumption, could never be taken as fixed (1930a, 208; 1934a, 3; Wicksteed 1910, book 1, ch. 9; O'Brien 1988b, ch. 7). The analysis of costs and markets, therefore, started from the concept of general equilibrium and analyzed adjustments in terms of disturbances from, and returns to, equilibrium, with the focus of attention upon the equilibrium points themselves rather than upon the intermediate process of adjustment and the knowledge-generation thereby involved (1928, 395–97; 1930, 194; cf. Addleson 1984, 508).

The approach was thus opposed both to aggregation—there was no sense in talking about production in the aggregate, and the study of production was essentially a study of factor allocation (1934c)—and to partial equilibrium analysis which neglected the wider complications (1934a, 8–9; 1933a, xv n.). Robbins criticized Marshall's fishing industry example, a partial equilibrium paradigm, both because it neglected the source of the demand shift (and the implied effect on cost curves if resources were freed from elsewhere) and also—more surprisingly—

for its neglect of expectations (1934a, 16). It was the former criticism which, however, seems to have carried most weight with him. Increasing and diminishing returns to scale could not be discussed in a partial equilibrium context; he insisted that the cost controversies of the 1930s were simply working along the wrong lines (1933a, xv n.). Factor supply variations reflected demand changes. Factor valuation reflected the valuation of the next most highly valued alternative use of the services of any factor (1934a, 6; 1930a, 207–8).

In insisting on a general equilibrium, opportunity cost approach to costs, Robbins made the most of his insistence on the existence of a generally received corpus of sophisticated theory coalescing from a variety of eras and sources. In an article on costs he cited Wieser, Wicksteed, Davenport, Knight, Henderson, Pantaleoni, Wicksell, and Mayer (Robbins 1934a). The work of these authors was all held to lead to the analysis which Robbins was expounding, with costs determined by the *values* of the "goods of first order" displaced.

In the context of costs Robbins placed particular emphasis on Mayer's interpretation of Wieser. This is important because, in contrast to Robbins's writings on socialism, we have in this analysis a fixed range of opportunities between which consumers choose without having to search for information. There clearly *is* an Austrian input here; ultimately, though, it is impossible to separate the message which Robbins took from Wieser (as interpreted by Mayer) from the influence of Wicksteed. For Wicksteed had variable factor supplies seen as a result of demand changes within a given technical environment; Wicksteed drew a parallel between factor allocation and the optimization of personal expenditure, with balancing and substitution at the margin and factor costs determined by the anticipated value of the product (1910, 370–98, 506, 540, 545); Wicksteed was himself quoted by Robbins as showing the true nature of the supply curve (i.e., the sellers' own demand curve), thus demonstrating the irrelevance of the cost controversy around 1930 (1933a, xv); and Wicksteed it was who emphasized the all-pervasive importance of choice.

Nonetheless it does seem reasonable to argue, particularly given the rather prolix nature of Wicksteed's exposition and his fondness for what Hutchison has nicely called "wayside sermons" (1953, 99), that as Robbins found the parallels with Wicksteed's work in that of Austrian writers, the Austrian sources sharpened and deepened Robbins's own perception and influenced him in the discussion of those particular aspects of Wicksteed's treatment of costs upon which he chose to lay key emphasis.

Production. As already indicated, Robbins considered production—most notably in an encyclopaedia article of 1934—to be merely one aspect of allocation theory. He treated it in explicitly Austrian terms. Production was activity, involving goods of higher order, directed to increasing the number of scarce economic goods of the first order. The business of the theory of production was not the summation of technologies but the study of the system of relations within the price system (1934c). Approached in this way, the Austrian approach fundamentally undermined what Robbins regarded as a persistent tendency among economists to confuse the technical and the economic.[13] It also fundamentally undermined, as already noted, the idea of production in the aggregate; and Robbins, in the encyclopaedia article referred to, rejected this concept completely. Production could not be measured in the aggregate without valuations; but the valuations, if not arbitrary, must change with the very composition of output (1934c, 464–65; 1935a, 67–68).

Distribution. Robbins's distribution theory illustrates some interesting aspects of his intellectual capital. At the highest level of generality, the approach was Austrian, based upon Austrian capital theory received via Wicksell, although received by a mind already preconditioned by exposure to the classical wage fund approach, a mind moreover which was able to find important points of contact between the Austrian and wage fund elements. But a key role was given to variations in factor supplies, so that (to use Wicksteed's phrase) they had a "reserve price." Indeed on this basis Robbins was able to oppose one particular branch of the Austrian tradition, albeit a heterodox one: that embodied in the work of Schumpeter (Robbins 1930a).

The treatment of capital was thus along these lines. Because capital was demanded and was limited in supply by time preference, its services enjoyed a price. Interest was a necessary reward—a fundamental tenet of Austrian economics. But given the point about own-consumption of factors and their services, Robbins went further. The very existence of a stock of capital required people to be prepared not to consume that capital, by failing to provide for depreciation. Thus it was necessary, even in a stationary state in which the capital stock did not grow, that capital should receive a reward. (This also reflected an argument of John Stuart Mill; see Robbins 1930a, 211–14; see also O'Brien 1975, 120.)

But as we move away from capital, the treatment becomes much more English and much less Austrian. The treatment of rent bears classical scars, although it was undoubtedly affected by Wicksteed's discussion which stressed the parallel between rent and other factor rewards. It thus avoided the standard pitfall of neglecting transfer earnings. But

---

13. 1934c; 1935a, 35. See also Weber 1947, 147, 201, 207; 1949, 34–35. Cf. Kirzner 1976, 127, 131.

there was nothing uniquely Austrian about this, and Robbins's own treatment seems to have stemmed from an attempt to work out the puzzles which he experienced on reading Marshall's careful, but ultimately rather ambiguous, treatment (1930a, 209–11).

The discussion of labor, in which Robbins did some of his most distinguished microeconomic work in the 1930s, is neither English classical nor Wicksteedian, nor Austrian—it is Marshallian. He used the elasticity of demand for labor as a key concept on the demand side, when examining the effects of variations in labor hours (1929a); and in examining labor supply he used his famous concept (borrowed from Dalton) of the elasticity of demand for income in terms of effort (1930c).

In fact it seems that Robbins, in his detailed treatment of distribution, tended to depart from the highest level of generality as espoused by Menger, Wieser, and Wicksteed and move towards the tripartite English classical division of factors into land, labor, and capital. There was nothing that was particularly Austrian in this. He accepted the high-level generalizations of Wicksteed and the Austrians. But in applying the theory the eclecticism of his approach allowed him to draw on much more traditional analyses. Faced with particular problems, indeed, he frequently seemed to owe more to Marshall than to either the Austrians or Wicksteed, although the point should be made that much of his distribution theory was written before he had come as completely under the influence of Austrian economics as he was to show himself in his 1934 "production" article.

III. *Macroeconomics*

1. *Prewar macroeconomics: content*

Robbins's prewar writings on macroeconomics are to be found chiefly in an article on the trade cycle (1932b) and in *The Great Depression* (1934d), a book which enjoyed considerable success in its time, together with more miscellaneous writings including articles in *Lloyds Bank Review* (1935d, 1937c, 1938d; see also 1936a, 1936b).

Robbins approached macroeconomic fluctuation from the direction of trade cycle theory. Such an approach was in accordance with his general desire, noted already, to perceive the existence of a long-accumulated and well-established body of theory. However, he concentrated on a monetary approach to the trade cycle rather than a "real" approach, whether of the "overinvestment" or other kind. This in itself is interesting in relation to the origins of his thought. In contrast to English classical economics—or at least to the currency school (O'Brien 1971, 63)—Robbins did not start from the idea that there was an endogenous trade cycle which could be magnified or damped by inappropriate or appropriate monetary policy. Rather, he treated the trade cycle as being *in itself* a monetary phenomenon. Thus the origins of his theory, at least in the form in which, finally evolved, he presented it to the world, lie outside English classical roots.

The basic model worked liked this. An exogenous increase in the money supply resulted in a lowering of the rate of interest. This caused investment to increase because marginal investment was now more profitable. This in turn raised demand for investment goods. The relative price of investment goods increased—relative prices of consumption and investment goods are important in this analysis—and resources were bid away from consumption goods industries. Forced saving ensued. The supply curves in the consumption goods industries shifted to the left, resulting in higher prices for consumption goods, reduced consumption of these goods, and the freeing of resources for the investment goods industries. This is critical, because the essence of a monetarily induced boom in this vision is increased investment without increased *voluntary* saving—and this mismatch between voluntary saving and investment is disequilibrating.

As resources, principally labor, are bid away into the investment goods industries, they receive higher wages. The spending of these higher wages shifts the demand schedules for consumption goods. Consumption goods outputs recover their old level. Consumption goods price levels are now higher than before the disturbance, as output has expanded along the new higher supply schedule. Consumption goods are thus able to compete for resources. Wages rise throughout the economy. The *relative* prices of consumption goods and investment goods have been restored to the old ratio, although at a new higher general price level. Forced saving has, for the moment, ceased. In order to continue with investment projects to which they are committed, entrepreneurs seek yet more credit in order to capture resources. This involves bidding up resource prices further and reimposes forced saving. However, this has the effect of raising the rate of interest as the entrepreneurs compete for credit, and thus the boom is choked off (1932b, 424–29; 1934d, 30–37).

The key propositions in all this are, firstly, that monetary expansion, through a lowering of the rate of interest, is the key to the trade cycle; secondly, that investment is very sensitive to the rate of interest. The latter was an argument which Keynes used in his Wicksellian *Treatise,* although his particular employment of it was very effectively criticized by Hawtrey (Davis 1981).

Monetarily induced booms were always faulty. By contrast, a non-monetary boom could occur as a result of an upward shift in the demand for investment goods, accompanied by a leftward shift in the *demand* curve for consumption goods. This involved more *voluntary* saving, and the relative price of consumption goods and investment goods would really represent people's preferences. It is highly significant that Robbins, like Mises and Hayek but unlike the long line of overinvestment theorists (some of whose work was criticized in Robbins's 1932 trade cycle article), believed that there was no harm in this kind of general *equilibrium* adjustment. By contrast, a monetarily induced boom involved a leftward shift in the *supply curve* for consumption goods, so that there was *forced* saving rather than an increase in voluntary saving. The change in the relative price of consumption goods and investment goods did not, in the forced saving case, represent people's true preferences, and thus a *disequilibrium* was created.

Unemployment was, in a sense, incidental to the whole theory. As investment goods industries shrank again, after the rise in the rate of interest, unemployment emerged as essentially an adjustment problem in an economy which tended to a general equilibrium set of relative prices, appropriate to full employment in the long run. Sticky wages might prolong labor market disequilibrium—hence Robbins's approval of wage cuts (an approval of which he was later so very ashamed) and his reservations about trade unions and unemployment insurance (1931a, 51–52; 1931b, 100; 1932b, 429–30; 1934d, 69–71, 82–83, 107, 117–18, 185–89).

Thus it was essential to "sweat out" the unemployment produced by the monetary disequilibrium—monetary expansion to counter unemployment merely reproduced the problem which had caused unemployment in the first place. Arguments that the price level should be raised by monetary expansion, as put forward in particular by the *Economist,* were in Robbins's view wholly mistaken—indeed there were conclusive reasons within Austrian macroeconomic theory for allowing the price level to *fall* if the trend of productivity was upwards. For as we shall see, in Wicksell's model the price level could be *stabilized* by allowing an increase in the money supply in line with productivity increases; but in the Mises-Hayek development of Wicksell's work, the distortion in *relative* prices caused by even this degree of monetary expansion was fundamentally disequilibrating and thus undesirable (1932b, 418; 1932d, 1932e, 1932f, 1932g; 1934d, 73–75).

As a model this has a number of fairly obvious drawbacks. It is not really clear why entrepreneurs should seek further funds when their expansion of investments is initially checked (1934d, 39); the implication is that unless they can obtain further funds they will lose all that they have already invested, because the project will be incomplete. This is not spelled out, although there are scattered references to incomplete investment projects in Central Europe. Moreover, Robbins argued that *proportionately more* funds would be required at the second round of borrowing—again this is not explained, although the implication is that it is due to the need to outweigh the newly enhanced flow of consumption good demand following the initial expansion (cf. Hayek 1931b, 132–35). But the model as a whole is weak on the secondary phases of the cycle, and it does not spell out exactly what it is in the monetary regime that stops banks from creating yet more credit—an issue which indeed Wicksell had explored in his concept of the pure credit economy, although treading, as Hicks has noted, on the borderline between stability and hyperinflation (Hicks 1939, 251–54; 1982; cf. Robbins 1934d, 38–41; Hayek 1931b).

The question of what happens to the *general* price level, given an increase in the money supply, also involves a significant ambiguity in the Austrian model. The Austrians were critical of Fisher for envisaging a general proportionate rise in prices; and Hayek insisted that the key issue was *relative* prices. He emphasized this element in the work of Mises and contrasted it with the attention which Wicksell had focused on the general price level (Hayek 1933, 16, 103–4, 118–19). Yet in fact the general price level *must* change in this model. Firstly we have a rise in the relative price of investment goods caused by an increase in the demand for investment goods; then we have an upward shift in the supply curves for consumption goods; then we have an upwards shift in the demand curves for consumption goods to restore parity of relative prices at a higher general price level. Robbins himself was vague on this issue, although chapter 3 of *The Great Depression* does envisage general price level variations. He rejected the quantity theory in its most direct form, but he avoided the issue of effects on the general price level produced by successive changes in relative prices (1932b, 424). On the one hand it is difficult to argue that he anticipated the neoclassical synthesis, at least in the form in which this involves an exogenous price level; on the other hand his ambiguity over the question of the general price level enabled him to revert to the Wicksellian framework after World War II.

Nonetheless, despite these problems the model satisfied Robbins's desire for continuity in economic thought and for a body of analysis which could be presented as embodying accumulated economic wisdom—indeed, quite apart from the main sources for this approach, to be discussed below, there are also points of contact with Marshall's discussion of monetary transmission in *Official papers* and with Keynes's Wicksell-like model in his *Treatise*.

The approach had the attraction that it could be couched in terms of the disaggregated general equilibrium to which both the Austrians and Robbins attached such importance at that date. In terms of that general equilibrium approach the role of the rate of interest in checking excessive investment, in the absence of monetary disturbance, could be clearly spelled out. Hayek in particular explained the general "intertemporal" equilibrium concept involved. Changes in the money supply then violated this intertemporal general equilibrium by producing demand changes for which there were not corresponding initial supply changes, thus disequilibrating savings and investment (1933, 74–75, 93, 102). Robbins was able to draw upon this general equilibrium framework in criticizing J. A. Hobson and arguing that the price and cost information, and the rate of interest, facing entrepreneurs would prevent the overinvestment envisaged by Hobson. A rise in *voluntary* saving was a general equilibrium adjustment and simply reflected a change in society's preference for present and future goods (1932b, 420–27).

All this was strongly influenced by, in particular, Hayek (1931a, 150; [1928] 1984); and it is perhaps ironic that Hayek should have changed his mind so firmly, in 1937, over the fundamental importance of employing a general equilibrium framework (Hutchison 1981, 210–19; McCloughry 1984; Caldwell 1988).

This whole approach to macroeconomic problems came under very considerable attack. Robbins, in its defense, produced *The Great Depression* with a mass of statistical material to buttress his contention that, in the world of the 1920s and 1930s, this model had significant explanatory power. He argued, as Hayek had done (1984, 124–25), that the United States had provided the motor of world monetary expansion (1934d, 22–29, 44–54). What was needed to counter this kind of thing was a tight gold standard regime, not the bogus post-1925 gold standard in which domestic monetary expansion and contraction had not followed gold movements. A "managed money supply" of which Keynes was an advocate (and attacked over this, though rather obliquely, by Robbins in 1925 in his very first publication) was exactly what was *not* required (Robbins 1925; see also 1929c, 412).

As already indicated, monetary expansion in the face of unemployment was another dose of what, in this model, had already created the unemployment in the first place. (This fundamental belief was also coupled with a fear, stemming in particular from the 1923 German hyperinflation, of inflation itself as a socially destructive force which was to produce the rise of the Nazis in Germany; see Robbins 1936b, 415; cf. 1937a; 1939a, 272–74; 1972, 20.)

There is a bit more to Robbins's prewar macroeconomics than all this. By 1939 he had retreated a little from the position of *The Great Depression,* in which he had held that public expenditure diverted voluntary saving, which was required for investment, and thus aggravated disequilibrium. In the model of this book, a shortage of voluntary saving is of central importance. At the time of its writing Robbins was very critical of the National Recovery Administration's policies in the United States and hostile towards the idea of government as the pacemaker of the economy.[14] But by 1939, in his *Economic basis of class conflict,* he recognized that in the presence of unemployed resources a vital part of the model was no longer relevant. It was no longer true that resources were captured from consumer goods industries, which previously employed them, by expanding investment goods industries. Since Robbins was methodologically a "verificationist," to whom the appropriateness of assumptions was of key importance, the change of position in the face of *sustained* unemployment was perfectly understandable. (The approach in his earlier writings had been that the unemployment then being experienced was a temporary disequilibrium phenomenon which would not last, given correct monetary policies, and which would not have existed in the first place but for ill-advised monetary expansion.) In the late 1930s he repudiated the "Treasury view" of crowding out, and he explored—in *Lloyds Bank Review* of 1938—the conditions for successful deficit finance (1937c, 239–41, 1939a, 217–22, 224–25, 256–57; see also 1941, 24–25; 1976, 26).

Nonetheless Robbins hedged all this around with qualifications, and it is only slightly misleading to represent his prewar macroeconomic thought by the kind of model already described (1937c, 239–41; 1939a, 217–30, 256–77).

2. *Prewar macroeconomics: sources*

In essence, the origins of this model lie in three sources. From English classical economics Robbins took a concern with the money supply and the basic presupposition that causality ran from the money supply to the price level. From Wicksell he took a concern with the implications of changes in that money supply for the rate of interest and the subsequent effect on demand in the economy. From Mises and Hayek he took a concern with the *way* the rate of interest affected aggregate demand and, in particular, the way it altered *relative* prices so as to impose forced saving on the community. The result was classified by Haberler as Austrian trade-cycle theory (1937, 30, 31, 44n., 54n., 56, 57n., 76), and there is no doubt that in fitting Robbins into this group Haberler was doing no violence to the evidence. Despite the other authors referred to, Robbins's principal sources seem to have been the second edition of Mises's *Money* ([1924] 1934) and his 1928 book on monetary stabilization and economic policy; Hayek's essays on intertemporal equilibrium

14. 1934d, 58, 63–64, 91–92, 125, 130–31, 135–36, 141, 144, 190, 192–94, 197; 1937b, 261–62; see also Hutchison 1978, 185.

([1928] 1984) and the paradox of saving (1931a) and his *Monetary theory and the trade cycle* ([1929] 1933); and an article by Strigl on the effects of monetary expansion (1928). To these should be added Hayek's lectures at the London School of Economics, which were published as *Prices and production* (1931b). All the items apart from this were read by Robbins in the original German; indeed neither Mises's 1928 book nor the article by Strigl have ever appeared in English, and Hayek's piece on intertemporal equilibrium only appeared in English in the year of Robbins's death, 1984.

There are undoubtedly some points at which the Austrian affiliation is less than complete. In particular Robbins's treatment of the rate of interest poses something of a problem. Robbins had imbibed Austrian capital theory both directly from Austrian authors and also indirectly from Cassel, Fetter, and Wicksell (1932b, 422, 427; cf. Cassel 1923, 2:537–47; Haberler 1937, 68–70). But he never clearly spelled out the concept of a period of production, unlike Hayek, for whom this was a central concept in the inner mechanics of the trade cycle model ([1927] 1984; 1931b, ch. 2).

But Robbins's analysis was Austrian for all that. Indeed he was writing his 1932 article on the trade cycle at about the time that Hayek was actually lecturing at the London School of Economics, expounding the theory which was to appear in *Prices and production*. Moreover, the latter part of Robbins's trade cycle article is a straightforward exposition of Hayek's theory, with Strigl cited in support. The work of the Austrians would in any case have particular appeal for Robbins, with his desire to obtain a corpus of accepted theory, because their approach was scholarly and involved extensive citation from the work of predecessors. Thus Mises referred to the work of the currency school; and while he did not accept their concept of an endogenous cycle, there was considerable agreement over the fundamentally fallacious nature of the banking (passive money supply) principle, which Mises emphatically rejected in his 1928 book (58, 63–66). Mises too was very conscious of the value of Wicksell's work; and he forms the essential bridge between the work of the Swedish economist and that of Hayek, who was indeed in the habit of referring to the Wicksell-Mises theory (1933, 47, 111, 116–19).

Hayek's work built on that of Mises, as Hayek himself acknowledged, but laid particular emphasis on three factors. Firstly, there was the importance of forced saving (1933, 93, 214–26; 1931b, 54–60). This became central to Robbins's own approach (1932b, 423–27). Secondly, Hayek paid some attention to the structure of interest rates (1933, 200–202, 226–30)—this, as Wesley Mitchell was to note in reviewing *The Great Depression,* seems to have made rather less impression on Robbins (Mitchell 1935). Thirdly, Hayek emphasized expectations ([1928] 1984). This particular message was very firmly accepted by Robbins (1935a, 62), who stressed in his 1934 book that a recovery of business confidence was vital if the economy was to come out of depression (160–61; cf. 1939a, 242–44).

Of all Hayek's works the volume *Geldtheorie und Konjunkturtheorie* of 1928, which appeared in English in 1933 as *Monetary theory and the trade cycle,* was undoubtedly the most influential on Robbins. In introducing the English translation Robbins wrote:

> The criteria of scientific validity take no account of origins, and the economist who refused to avail himself of a particular set of propositions because they were foreign would be acting no less unscientifically than the chemist or physicist who acted on similar principles. It has been well said that there are only two kinds of Economics—good Economics and bad Economics. All other classifications are misleading.
>
> Unfortunately, the economist, far more than the practitioner of the natural sciences, is victim to the curse of Babel. The chemist and the physicist . . . can converse in what to all intents and purposes is an international language. . . . In Economics this is not so. The complicated social relationships which are its chief preoccupation lend themselves much less to merely symbolic analysis. . . . Small wonder too that, in consequence of these conditions, there is probably more overlapping and wasteful duplication of effort in Economics than in any other branch of scientific knowledge. I know of no natural science in which it would be possible for a man to devote years to the discovery of propositions which are already commonplace in language areas other than his own. It is notorious that in Economics this frequently happens. (1933b, 5–7)

To put the matter crudely: here was a well-developed and refined body of macroeconomic thought which people in Cambridge had been rediscovering with a futile waste of effort. They should read Hayek's work.

But in one important respect Robbins was closer to Mises than to Hayek. Robbins typically treated monetary disturbances as exogenous—the result of foolish behavior by central bankers. This was also Mises's position. But Hayek argued that increases in the money supply were endogenous (1933, 150–79), resulting from the operation of the deposit multiplier in the commercial banking system, and that the initiating cause need not even be monetary at all (182).

However, Robbins and Hayek were very much in agreement with the idea that credit expansion would simply make macroeconomic problems worse. Robbins's opposition to such expansion has already been noted. Hayek argued that counter-cyclical monetary policy, even if directed towards consumption goods, would raise the price of production goods in a search for means to increase output of consumption goods (1933, 18–19; 1931a, 150).

Hayek was also one of the sources for Robbins's view that depression in Austria itself had been accompanied by capital shortage (1932b, 430; 1934d, 91), a finding which was exactly as predicted by the Austrian model, in which forced saving plays a transient role in providing extra resources for investment and is ultimately overcome. Hayek had argued that the problem lay partly in public investment, which exacerbated the problems facing firms in a disequilibrium situation by crowding out the available funds (1931c). Another source cited by Robbins was Morgenstern, who argued that the whole capital base of Austrian industry had become eroded through the disequilibrium resulting from monetary expansion (1931, 255). The case of Kaldor, who was also cited by Robbins, is particularly interesting in this context. Kaldor's basic thesis was that rising costs were making business unprofitable but that Austrian firms were investing more. He explained this by the institutional fact of banks' equity participation in firms in Austria. They were thus reluctant to close down firms which they at least partly owned, while they kept receiving savings which they could invest in the firms as long as confidence in the banks remained (1932, 27–29). But in the last part of the article Kaldor retreated from this institutional explanation and for the first time related the argument to forced saving and disproportionality along Austrian trade cycle theory lines (34–35).

One important matter, which had exercised economists since Wicksell's day, concerned the correct monetary policy to be pursued in an economy with secularly rising productivity. As had emerged from an earlier controversy—of which the Austrians themselves apparently remained long unaware (Hayek 1932, 115)—it was necessary to keep the money rate of interest below the real rate of interest in order to achieve a stable price level, because the secularly rising level of output would require an increasing money supply for price stability (see also Hayek 1933, 119–20). But the purity of the Austrian position required that such increases in the money supply should not occur, because they would distort *relative* prices in the economy and thus cause disequilibrium along the lines of the Austrian trade cycle theory. The logical conclusion of this position was that secularly rising productivity should be accompanied by a secularly falling price level. This conclusion was in fact explored and defended as a position by Haberler in 1927 (112–17) and by Mises in 1928 (30–34). It was possible to argue, in terms of the Austrian apparatus, that there was an asymmetry between monetary deflation (which increased the weight of fixed burdens) and a price fall due to rising productivity. This reflected costs *falling* for producers, while fixed income receivers would share in the generally increased prosperity. This was also the position taken by Hayek in his 1929 book ([1929] 1933, 111–16) and the position defended by Robbins in his trade cycle article (1932b, 418). Robbins was able to call in his aid, in a passage which in its reference to "sadistic deflationists" reflected wounded sensitivity, Marshall, Edgeworth, Pigou, Robertson, and Taussig. But the source for his position was Austrian, at least primarily.

In fact there are extra problems here—the celebrated "machinery question" raised by Barton and Ricardo is involved. Both Haberler (1927, 114–15) and Hayek (1931a, 150) explored this aspect of the problem, but Robbins avoided it.

Nonetheless there is no doubt that he had read, digested, and thought a great deal about the Austrian writings. They were certainly the immediate sources for the microeconomic positions which he expounded in the early 1930s. They also had the advantage that they fitted in as *further developments* of the general corpus of evolved theory, to the existence of which Robbins attached such importance in all aspects of economics, whether macroeconomics or microeconomics. Such a corpus of theory could, so to speak, be brandished at Cambridge to show the Cambridge crowd the error of their ways and the subjective nature of their own originality. Robbins attached great importance to "the authority of competent economists," and this was not merely, though it certainly was also, a polemical device. It reflected his "conversion" to economics from socialism.

3. *Postwar macroeconomics*

Robbins went out of his way, at least in his later postwar writings, to stress his repudiation of the precise Mises-Hayek model and its implications for policy. As he wrote in his *Autobiography:* "I had become the slave of theoretical constructions which, if not intrinsically invalid as regards logical consistency, were inappropriate to the total situation which had then developed and which therefore misled my judgement" (1971a, 117).

Robbins now accepted that government should act counter-cyclically (1971a, 188–89). But he had not become a Keynesian; and the underlying model which informed his judgment on macroeconomic matters was not all that different from what had gone before. He certainly did not accept the whole of the analytical apparatus in *The general theory*. As he was later to write: "It would not be true to say that then [during war service], or at any subsequent period, I had become a Keynesian in the sense of accepting au pied de la lettre all the analytical propositions of the *General Theory*" (1971a, 188). He was publicly skeptical about the fundamental importance of *The general theory* when he reviewed Harrod's biography of Keynes (Robbins 1951; 1970, 244), and he was some considerable distance both from Beveridge, with the latter's concept of permanent excess demand in the labor market (Robbins 1954, 18–40; 1978, 10), and from what Keynes's associates in the so-called Circus believed to be macroeconomic truth.

The Radcliffe Report attracted Robbins's particular criticism, and he published, no fewer than three times, a closely reasoned critique in which he argued that in replacing the money supply with liquidity the committee had been guilty of a fallacy of composition—the money supply determined how far liquidity could be *realized*. He also thought the committee's view that there was no upper limit to velocity of circulation "highly implausible." He certainly did not accept—and here we go back to the currency and banking controversy—that the money supply depended on the price level, as the later self-styled Keynesians tended to believe (1963, 204–10; 1971a, 235; 1971b, 7–9; 1979, ix).

Robbins's position in the postwar world was basically this. He held that macroeconomic disturbances originated in excess monetary aggregate demand. In this view changes in the money supply were critical. The money supply could be controlled either through the use of interest rates or through operation directly on monetary aggregates (1971a, 233). In practice he believed it was better to control the money supply directly than to operate on the rate of interest (though bank rate was a valuable supplementary weapon), and the monetary aggregate that he had in mind was sterling M_3.[15] Control of aggregate demand was important, both because of the economically destructive and disruptive effects of inflation and because of its social injustice.

But there are two fundamental characteristics of this later work which mean that it is, for the most part at least, no longer Austrian. Firstly, the whole emphasis on *relative* prices of consumption and investment goods, and the importance of forced saving and of the dislocation produced by monetary expansion, is played down. Although Robbins approached the matter primarily from the monetary side, he did so essentially in terms of the Keynesian aggregates, for the most part. (His prewar opposition to the concept of aggregation as a whole had disappeared; but in any case the Mises-Hayek model itself implied a significant degree of at least sectoral aggregation in practice, so this change may not be important.) Robbins's attention had now switched from relative prices to the general price level as a whole, something strongly

---

15. 1949, 21; 1954, 76–80; 1958a, 12–14; 1958b, 217–19; 1963, 210–21; 1971b, 9; 1976, 98; 1979, 19, 36–37, 58, 66, 76, 96.

opposed by Hayek in *Monetary theory and the trade cycle* (1933, 111–12). Secondly, the approach was no longer *exclusively* monetary. Robbins now held that fiscal policy had a fundamental role to play in controlling aggregate demand. It had to operate in conjunction with monetary policy, but it could not be ignored: "I do not believe in tying one arm behind my back when coping either with inflation or deflation" (1979, 80).

So what were the Austrian residues in Robbins's postwar macroeconomics? Firstly, there are traces—but only traces—of an Austrian general equilibrium approach to the economy in some of his writings. Secondly, Wicksell, on whose work Mises and Hayek had built, still clearly exercised an influence on Robbins, an influence which could all the more easily be exercised now that Robbins had switched his attention from relative prices to the general price level. Indeed Robbins referred to Wicksell in his dealings with the Radcliffe Committee (1958c, q. 10219). He thus still attached importance to the expansion of bank credit. Thirdly, some of the discussions of the harmful effects of inflation have an Austrian ring—especially the argument that inflation produces a cumulative shortage of working capital, which was one that had been put forward by Hayek in *Prices and production* (1931b, 151–52). Fourthly, although it does not occupy the central position which it had enjoyed in Robbins's prewar writings, the forced saving argument pops up from time to time, particularly in the 1970s, when he expressed concern about credit creation unmatched by saving, a rate of interest lower than the going rate of profit, and the operation of adaptive expectations in preventing forced saving from filling the gap between voluntary saving and investment demand (1958a, 24; 1958b, 21; 1958c, q. 10190; 1971b, 12–14; 1979, 28–29).

IV. *Conclusion*

The Austrian connection in Robbins's work is thus important, but it is not exclusive of other influences or completely overwhelming. Separating the influence of the Austrians from that of Wicksteed in Robbins's microeconomic writings is virtually impossible, partly because Wicksteed gave so very few clues as to the nature of the development of his own thought. But if it is in fact true that Wicksteed relied little on the Austrians and evolved his own body of thought by developing the work of Jevons and then coming into contact with the work of Pareto, then the influence of the Austrians on Robbins in the area of microeconomics is limited. But if limited, it is nonetheless important. Quite clearly it significantly affected Robbins's own view of *writers other than the Austrians*. It was an Austrian perspective which he adopted in synthesizing, in the interwar period, that corpus of economic theory to which he attached such importance. As he read the Austrians' works, he found in them not only elements which coincided with what he had already learned from Wicksteed but also insights which enabled him to see what was essential to Wicksteed and what could be dispensed with in the building up of an authoritative treatment of microeconomics.

In the area of macroeconomics, on the other hand, the story is very much clearer. Beginning from a base in English classical economics and in the work of Wicksell, Robbins became an articulate and influential expositor of the monetary trade cycle theory developed on a Wicksellian base, but in the light of the English classical monetary literature, by Mises and Hayek. At the height of the influence of Mises and Hayek in the 1930s, not only on Robbins but on economics generally, Robbins could be classified without difficulty as, in macroeconomic matters, a disciple of the Austrian economists. But the last part of the 1930s saw some fairly subtle shifts of position on his part; and in the postwar years, after wartime association with Keynes and, perhaps more importantly, with "Keynesians," Robbins no longer put forward the Mises-Hayek model. Nonetheless he certainly did not become a Keynesian; and many of the concerns of the Mises-Hayek approach continued to influence his attitude towards macroeconomic theory and policy, even though he now recognized the value of fiscal policy and accorded it significant weight in macroeconomic management.

But throughout all the shifts of emphasis, and even of position, one thing stands out very clearly. Without the literature of Austrian economics, and Robbins's own capacity to read it in the original German, the positions on theory and policy adopted by one of the most influential British economists of the twentieth century would have been significantly different.

I am most grateful to Bob Black, John Creedy, Sir Henry Phelps Brown, and Jack Wiseman for comments.

References

Addleson, M. 1984. Robbins's essay in retrospect: on subjectivism and on "economics of choice." *Rivista internazionale di scienze economiche e commerciali* 31:506–23.

Blaug, M. 1980. *The methodology of economics.* Cambridge.

Caldwell, B. 1988. Hayek's transformation. *HOPE* 20:513–41.

Cassel, G. 1923. *The theory of social economy.* Translated by J. McCabe. London.

Davis, E. G. 1981. R. G. Hawtrey, 1879–1975. In *Pioneers of modern economics in Britain,* edited by D. P. O'Brien and J. R. Presley, 203–33. London.

Haberler, G. von. 1927. *Der Sinn der Indexzahlen.* Tübingen.

——. 1937. *Prosperity and depression.* Geneva.

Hawtrey, R. 1938. *A century of bank rate.* London.
Hayek, F. von. [1925] 1984. Review of L. Schönfeld, *Grenznutzen und Wirtschaftsrechnung.* Reprinted in *Money, capital and fluctuations.* London.
———. [1927] 1984. On the problem of the theory of interest. Reprinted in *Money, capital and fluctuations.* London.
———. [1928] 1984. Intertemporal price equilibrium and movements in the value of money. Reprinted in *Money, capital and fluctuations.* London.
———. [1929] 1933. *Monetary theory and the trade cycle.* Translated by N. Kaldor and H. Croome. London.
———. 1931a. The "paradox" of saving. Translated by N. Kaldor and G. Tugendhat. *Economica* 11:125–69.
———. 1931b. *Prices and production.* London.
———. 1931c. Wirkungen des Mietzinsbeschranküngen. *Schriften des Vereins für Sozialpolitik* 182:253–70.
———. [1932] 1984. The fate of the gold standard. Reprinted in *Money, capital and fluctuations.* London.
———. 1934. Carl Menger. In Menger 1933–36, v–xxxviii.
Hicks, J. 1939. *Value and capital.* 2d ed. 1946. Oxford.
———. 1982. LSE and the Robbins Circle. In *Collected essays in economic theory*, vol. 3, *Money, interest and wages.* Oxford.
Hutchison, T. W. 1953. *A review of economic doctrines 1870–1929.* Oxford.
———. 1964. *Positive economics and policy objectives.* London.
———. 1978. *On revolutions and progress in economic knowledge.* Cambridge.
———. 1979. Robbins, Lionel. *International encyclopaedia of the social sciences*, edited by D. L. Sills, vol. 18, *Biographical supplement:* 660–63. New York.
———. 1981. *The politics and philosophy of economics.* Oxford.
Kaldor, N. 1932. The economic situation of Austria. *Harvard Business Review* 11:23–34.
Kirzner, I. 1976. *The economic point of view.* 2d ed. Kansas City.
McCloughry, R. 1984. Introduction to Hayek, *Money, capital and fluctuations.* London.
Mayer, H. 1925. Friedrich Wieser zum Gedächtnis' *Zeitschrift für Volkswirtschaft und Sozialpolitik*, n.s. 5:633–45.
Meade, J. E. 1984. In *Tributes in memory of Lord Robbins*, 5–7. London (LSE).
Menger, C. 1871. *Grundsätze der Volkswirthschaftslehre.* Vienna.
———. [1871] 1950. *Principles of economics.* Translated by J. Dingwall and B. Hoselitz. Glencoe, Ill.
———. [1883] 1963. *Problems of economics and sociology.* Translated by F. J. Nock. Urbana, Ill.
———. 1933–36. *Collected works.* With an introduction by F. von Hayek. Reprints of Scarce Tracts in Economic and Political Science, nos. 17–20 (LSE). London.
Mill, J. S. 1844. *Essays on some unsettled questions of political economy.* Reprinted in *Essays on economics and society*, edited by J. M. Robson. Toronto, 1967.
Mises, L. von. [1924] 1934. *The theory of money and credit.* 2d (1924) ed. translated by H. E. Batson. London.
———. 1928. *Geldwertstabilisierung und Konjunkturpolitik.* Jena.
———. 1932. *Die Gemeinwirtschaft.* 2d ed. Jena.
———. [1932] 1936. *Socialism.* 2d (1932) ed. translated by J. Kahane. London.
———. 1949. *Human action.* 3d ed. Chicago, 1966.

Mitchell, W. C. 1935. Review of L. Robbins, *The Great Depression. Quarterly Journal of Economics* 49:503–7.

Morgenstern, O. 1931. Kapital—und Kurswertänderungen der an der Wiener Börse notierten österreichischen Aktiengesellschaften 1913 bis 1930. *Zeitschrift für Nationalökonomie* 3.2 (December): 251–55.

O'Brien, D. P. 1971. *The correspondence of Lord Overstone.* Cambridge.

——. 1975. *The classical economists.* Oxford.

——. 1988a. Lionel Charles Robbins, 1898–1984. *Economic Journal* 98:104–25.

——. 1988b. *Lionel Robbins.* London.

——. 1989. Robbins as a political economist. *Economic Journal* 99:479–80.

Pantaleoni, M. [1889] 1898. *Pure economics.* Translated by T. Bruce. Reprinted. New York, 1957.

Phelps Brown, H. 1988. Lionel Charles Robbins, 1898–1984. *Proceedings of the British Academy* 1987 [publ. 1988] 73:601–29.

Robbins, L. 1925. Review of T. E. Gregory, *The present position of banking in America. Economica* 5:358–59.

——. 1927a. Mr. Hawtrey on the scope of economics. *Economica* 7:172–78.

——. 1927b. Review of M. J. Bonn, *Das Schicksal des Deutschen Kapitalismus. Economic Journal* 37:613–16.

——. 1928. The representative firm. *Economic Journal* 38:387–404.

——. 1929a. The economic effects of variations of hours of labour. *Economic Journal* 39:25–40.

——. 1929b. Review of Sir J. Stamp, *Some economic factors in modern life. Economic Journal* 39:248–50.

——. 1929c. Review of E. Cannan, *A review of economic theory. Economic Journal* 39:409–14.

——. 1930a. On a certain ambiguity in the conception of stationary equilibrium. *Economic Journal* 40:194–214.

——. 1930b. The present position of economic science. *Economica* 10:14–24.

——. 1930c. On the elasticity of demand for income in terms of effort. *Economica* 10:123–29.

——. 1931a. Economic notes on some arguments for protection. *Economica* 11:45–62.

——. 1931b. A reply to Mr. Keynes. *New Statesman and Nation,* 14 March, 98–100.

——. 1931c. Review of M. S. Braun, *Theorie der Staatlichen Wirtschaftspolitik. Economica* 11:469–72.

——. 1931d. Review of F. Machlup, *Borsenkredit, Industriekredit und Kapitalbildung. Economica* 11:472–75.

——. 1932a. *An essay on the nature and significance of economic science.* London.

——. 1932b. Consumption and the trade cycle. *Economica* 12:413–30.

——. 1932c. Tariffs for revenue. In *Tariffs: the case examined,* edited by Sir W. Beveridge et al., 170–84. London.

——. 1932d. Letter to the *Economist,* 14 May, 1081.

——. 1932e. Letter to the *Economist,* 28 May, 1118–19.

——. 1932f. Letter to the *Economist,* 11 June, 1295.

——. 1932. The Ottawa resolutions on finance and the future of monetary policy. *Lloyds Bank Review,* n.s. 3, no. 32 (October): 422–38.

——. 1933a. Introduction. In *Philip H. Wicksteed: the common sense of political economy* [1910]. London.

————. 1933b. Introduction to F. von Hayek, *Monetary theory and the trade cycle*. London.

————. 1934b. Remarks upon certain aspects of the theory of costs. *Economic Journal* 44:1–18.

————. 1934b. Remarks on the relationship between economics and psychology. *Manchester School* 5:89–101.

————. 1934c. Production. *Encyclopaedia of the social sciences*, edited by E. R. A. Seligman, 12:462–67. New York.

————. 1934d. *The Great Depression*. London.

————. 1934e. Introduction. In Mises, *The theory of money and credit*. 2d ed., translated by H. E. Batson, 11–13. London.

————. 1935a. *An essay on the nature and significance of economic science*. 2d ed. London.

————. 1935b. Introduction. In K. Wicksell, *Lectures on political economy*, translated by E. Classen. London.

————. 1935c. The planning of British agriculture—a rejoinder. *Lloyds Bank Review*, n.s. 6:89–92.

————. 1935d. The problem of stabilisation. *Lloyds Bank Review*, n.s. 6:207–18.

————. 1936a. The consequences of economic nationalism. *Lloyds Bank Review*, n.s. 7:226–39.

————. 1936b. Economic nationalism and monetary policy. *Banker* 38:192–97.

————. 1936c. Review of R. Nurkse, *Internationale Kapitalbewegungen*. *Economica*, n.s. 3:108–9.

————. 1937a. Foreword. In C. Bresciani-Turroni, *The economics of inflation* [1931], translated by M. E. Sayers. London.

————. 1937b. *Economic planning and international order*. London.

————. 1937c. How to mitigate the next slump. *Lloyds Bank Review*, n.s. 8:234–44.

————. 1937d. Review of G. Haberler, *Der internationale Handel* and of *The theory of international trade*, translated by A. Stonier and F. Benham. *Economica*, n.s. 4:102–5.

————. 1938a. Live and dead issues in the methodology of economics. *Economica*, n.s. 5:342–52.

————. 1938b. Les méthodes d'observation économique et les problèmes de la prévision en matière économique [delivered 1934]. In L. Robbins et al., *Cinq conferences sur la méthode dans les recherches économiques*. Paris. Translated in O'Brien 1988b.

————. 1938c. Interpersonal comparisons of utility: a comment. *Economic Journal* 48:635–41.

————. 1938d. The long-term budget problem. *Lloyds Bank Review*, n.s. 9:158–67.

————. 1939a. *The economic basis of class conflict*. London.

————. 1939b. The export problem. *Lloyds Bank Review*, n.s. 10:214–27.

————. 1940. Review of B. Souvarine, *Stalin: a critical survey of Bolshevism*. *Economica*, n.s. 7:94–96.

————. 1941. *Economic aspects of federation*. London.

————. 1947. *The economic problem in peace and war*. London.

————. 1949. The sterling problem. *Lloyds Bank Review* 14 (October): 1–31.

————. 1951. Review of R. F. Harrod, *The life of John Maynard Keynes*. *The Times*, 26 January, 7f–g. Reprinted in Robbins 1970.

————. 1953. Robertson on utility and scope. *Economica*, n.s. 20:99–111.

————. 1954. *The economist in the twentieth century and other lectures in political economy*. London.

————. 1958a. Thoughts on the crisis. *Lloyds Bank Review,* 48 (April): 1–26.

————. 1958b. *The aims of monetary policy and the means of achieving them*. Memorandum to the Committee on the Working of the Monetary System (Radcliffe Committee). London, 1960.

————. 1958c. Evidence to the Committee on the Working of the Monetary System (Radcliffe Committee), 24 July, pp. 673–78, qq. 10190–254. London: HMSO, 1960.

————. 1959. The present position of economics. *Rivista di politica economica*. Reprinted in *Guest lectures in economics,* edited by E. Henderson and L. Spaventa, 31–46. Milan, 1962.

————. 1963. *Politics and economics*. London.

————. 1966. An economist looks at business. In Institute of Economic Affairs, *Economics, business and government,* 25–31. London.

————. 1970. *The evolution of modern economic theory*. London.

————. 1971a. *Autobiography of an economist*. London.

————. 1971b. *Money, trade and international relations*. London.

————. 1972. Inflation: an international problem. Concluding observations. Both in *Inflation as a global problem,* edited by R. Hinshaw. Baltimore.

————. 1976. *Political economy past and present*. London.

————. 1978. Economists and trade unions, 1776–1977. In Institute of Economic Affairs, *Trade unions: public goods or public "bads"?* 5–16, 19–20. London.

————. 1979. *Against inflation*. London.

————. 1981. Economics and political economy. *American Economic Review* 71 (May suppl.): 1–10. Reprinted in *An essay on the nature and significance of economic science,* 3d ed., xi–xxxiii. London, 1984.

Schönfeld-Illy, L. 1924. *Grenznutzen und Wirtschaftsrechnung*. Reprinted. Vienna: International Carl Menger Library, 1982.

Steadman, I. 1987. Wicksteed, Philip Henry. *The new Palgrave,* edited by J. Eatwell, M. Milgate, and P. Newman, 4:915–19. London.

Strigl, R. 1928. Die Produktion unter dem Einflus einer Kreditexpansion. *Schriften des Vereins für Sozialpolitik* 173.2:185–211.

Weber, M. 1947. *The theory of social and economic organisation* [part 1 of *Wirtschaft und Gesellschaft*]. Translated by A. R. Henderson and T. Parsons. London.

————. 1949. *The methodology of the social sciences*. Translated by E. Shils and H. Finch. Glencoe, Ill.

Wicksteed, P. H. 1910. *The common sense of political economy and selected papers and reviews on economic theory*. Edited by L. Robbins. London, 1933.

Wieser, F. von. 1889. *Natural value*. Translated by C. A. Malloch. London.

Comment on O'Brien's
"Lionel Robbins and the Austrian connection"

Mark Blaug

Denis O'Brien's paper on Lionel Robbins traces the sources of Robbins's ideas with marvelous subtlety. We have always known that Robbins was deeply influenced by the writings of Wicksteed and Wicksell on the one hand, and Mises, Hayek, Mayer, and Strigl on the other, but no one else has ever shown precisely how he wove these together. Virtually all the material for this paper is in O'Brien's recent book, *Lionel Robbins* (1988), but somehow Robbins's Austrian connections stand out better in this paper than they did in the book. Robbins was throughout all the interwar years the greatest and indeed the only Austrian economist outside Austria, having neither trained nor taught in Austria.

In reading a paper such as this there is little a discussant can say except Bravo! However, I am prompted to voice a slight caveat with reference to two topics. One is the repeated insistence by O'Brien that Robbins was a general equilibrium theorist. The other is the assertion that Robbins held the Austrian monetary overinvestment theory of the trade cycle but never expounded and hardly ever mentioned the concept of "the average period of production," which stood at the very center of the Austrian theory.

I understand exactly what he means by saying that Robbins consistently criticized Marshall's partial equilibrium analysis from the standpoint of general equilibrium and, in consequence, employed Wicksteed's alternative cost doctrine to disparage Marshall's "real cost" theory of value: instead of Marshall's two blades of a pair of scissors in which supply prices are interpreted as payments necessary to overcome physical limitations, alternative cost theory makes both demand and supply depend on subjective preferences by tracing all costs back to utilities forgone. Nevertheless this is not general equilibrium theory in the sense of Walras but rather what I choose to call "total equilibrium" analysis. By "total equilibrium" analysis I mean any kind of economics that stresses the interdependencies between different markets and particularly factor markets and product markets. What Walras did was to interpret total equilibrium analysis in a particular way: he conceived the question of the existence of multimarket equilibrium in a capitalist economy as being analogous to the mathematical problem of solving a set of simultaneous equations, and it is for this reason that he became so preoccupied with the counting of equations and unknowns. It is perfectly possible to theorize about total equilibrium without committing oneself to the Walrasian scheme, and this is precisely what the Austrians did.

Thus the Austrians at one and the same time rejected Marshall's partial equilibrium analysis and the kind of economics that Walras advocated, which was, in the first place, an economics explicitly formulated in mathematical terms and, in the second place, an "end-state" rather than a "process" economics, that is, one that focused attention on the nature of equilibrium outcomes and not on the process by which equilibria are attained. The Austrians had no sympathy for Walras's analysis of the existence and uniqueness of multimarket equilibrium in terms of the metaphor of simultaneous equations and even less for his discussion of multimarket equilibrium in terms of price adjustments to net excess demand. Indeed all the Austrians, including Wicksteed and Robbins, eschewed the very notion of a determinate theory of pricing and underlined discontinuities and indivisibilities, being perfectly content with a general tendency towards equilibrium that is never in fact completely realized.

It would clarify matters, therefore, to distinguish between one-at-a-time economics and everything-depends-on-everything-else economics, or partial equilibrium analysis and total equilibrium analysis. That would permit us in turn to contrast total equilibrium analysis with general equilibrium analysis. Thus in the great "socialist calculation debate" of the 1930s, the Austrian economists employing total equilibrium analysis were in fact vanquished by Oskar Lange and Abba Lerner employing Walrasian general equilibrium analysis. To speak of "Austrian general equilibrium" theory, as O'Brien does, confuses the issue in question in the socialist calculation debate, both sides making use of general equilibrium *reasoning* but by no means the same type of reasoning.

Turning now to the question of Austrian trade cycle theory, Hayek and Robbins as advocates of the Austrian theory were the two most conspicuous opponents of Keynes in the 1930s. It is a signal fact crucial to the unprecedented speed with which the Keynesian revolution conquered mainstream economics that its two principal opponents quit the battlefield in the crucial years 1936–39. Hayek having published *Prices and production* (1931) and *Monetary theory and the trade cycle* (1933) and Robbins having published *The Great Depression* (1934), neither of them made any further statement on the nature of the trade cycle (apart from one or two journalistic pieces) nor indeed on any of the contentious issues of macroeconomics until the 1940s.

Hayek has explained his own silence in those critical years as a reluctance to repeat his earlier experience of criticizing Keynes's *Treatise on money:* Keynes simply capitulated and sat down to write a new book, *The general theory;* Hayek thought that Keynes would eventually change his mind about this book as he had changed his mind about the earlier one, so that all he had to do was to wait. I think that this account, offered in 1947, is ingenuous, being a rationalization after the fact. What Hayek was really doing in the late 1930s was writing *The pure theory of capital* (1941), which proved to be much longer in the making than he had imagined and which he had hoped would finally establish Austrian trade cycle theory on a firm foundation. But the book failed to make any impact, in part because wartime circumstances turned the attention of economists away from purely technical problems in economic theory and in part because Hayek offered no solution to the *pons asinorum* of Austrian trade cycle theory, the measurability of "the average period of production"; indeed, he even went so far as to reject the very concept of the period of production or its corollary, the period of investment.

But Austrian trade cycle theory attributed slumps to overinvestment in the previous boom financed by credit expansion, or what they called the "undue lengthening of the period of production." Capital in Austrian theory is always a thing of two dimensions, magnitude and duration, and investment of capital means either more capital or more capital left in existing processes for a longer period of time. Now, as every clever student in the history of economic thought knows, Böhm-Bawerk, the inventor of the concept of the average period of production, never succeeded in defining the average period of production independently of the rate of interest; as Wicksell showed, it was itself a function of the interest rate and hence could not be employed to explain the determination of the rate of interest. In short, the average period of production is not an adequate measure of the capital intensity of an economy, and hence we never can say unambiguously that there is an increase of capital in a boom—and even if we could, we never can say that this implies a longer period of production in response to a fall in the rate of interest. In the absence of an adequate metric of capital, the Austrian theory of the trade cycle is simply empty at its very center. (That was the point of Kaldor's savage critique of Hayek's book in the pages of *Economica* in 1942.)

I believe that Hayek failed to engage Keynes after the publication of *The general theory* because he could not formulate an Austrian counter-theory of the slump that was proof against technical objections. And I am equally sure that Robbins likewise saw no way of relaunching the Austrian theory of the trade cycle and, for that reason, held back in attacking Keynes, hoping perhaps that Hayek's *Pure theory of capital* would soon rehabilitate the Austrian theory. A glance at the pages of

The Economic Journal in the years 1936–39 should have revealed the extraordinary interest that *The general theory* had aroused, particularly among younger economists, and of course Robbins was only too aware that several of the most promising members of the department at the London School of Economics, such as Hicks, Kaldor, Lerner, and Shackle, had become converted to the new economics of Cambridge. It is extraordinary that Robbins's *Autobiography of an economist* (1971) drew a veil of discretion over his reactions to Keynesian economics in the years before the outbreak of World War II, other than a simple confession of past errors. Both Hayek and Robbins badly miscalculated the swiftness of the Keynesian revolution and hence never did succeed in mounting any attack, much less a successful attack, on the house that Keynes had built. The Austrian research program failed because it contained a fatal logical flaw, a flaw that is even more apparent today after the switching controversies of the two Cambridges than it was in the 1930s. Robbins may have suspected that flaw all along—hence his silence about the period of production. One reason, therefore, that Keynes won over Hayek and Robbins was that he offered a way out of the cul de sac that was the Austrian theory of the trade cycle.

From Hayek to Menger:
biology, subjectivism, and welfare

Jeremy Shearmur

As a people attains higher levels of civilization, and as men penetrate more deeply into the true constitution of things and of their own nature, the number of true goods becomes constantly larger, and as can easily be understood, the number of imaginary goods becomes progressively smaller. It is not unimportant evidence of the connection between accurate knowledge and human welfare that the number of so-called imaginary goods is shown by experience to be usually greatest among peoples who are poorest in true goods.

—CARL MENGER

. . . it is probably no exaggeration to say that every important advance in economic theory during the last hundred years was a further step in the consistent application of subjectivism.

—F. A. HAYEK

The question whether, if we had to stop at our present stage of development, we would in any sense be better off or happier than if we had stopped a hundred or a thousand years ago is probably not answerable. The answer, however, does not matter. What matters is the successful striving for what at each moment seems attainable. It is not the fruits of past success but the living in and for the future in which human intelligence proves itself. Progress is movement for movement's sake.

—F. A. HAYEK

I. *Introduction*

There are many important points of continuity between the work of Carl Menger and of F. A. Hayek.[1] In this paper I am concerned with a point

1. Epigraphs are from Menger, *Principles of economics* (New York and London: New York University Press, 1981), 53–54; Hayek, *The counter-revolution of science* (Indi-

of discontinuity. Menger was in many ways a subjectivist. But his account of goods relates them back to human needs and ultimately to human nature. And as Hayek and Kauder have told us, Menger's later years were spent, in part, in investigations into psychology and ethnography, in which he wished to ground his economics.[2] Within his economic writings, however, his views also differ from those of later writers in the Austrian subjectivist tradition, notably in his distinction between true and false goods.[3]

Menger defines a good in terms of the following conditions all being present: a human need; such properties as render a thing capable of being brought into a causal connection with the satisfaction of this need; human knowledge of this causal connection; and command of the thing sufficient to direct it to the satisfaction of the need.[4] He allows, however, that other things—imaginary goods—may derive a "goods-like character" from properties that they are imagined to possess or needs merely imagined by men.[5] Menger further relates his distinction to a view of the connection between human civilization and welfare, in a passage that I have quoted in an epigraph to this paper.

These are elements of Menger's work from which Ludwig von Mises explicitly dissented.[6] At one level, Mises's dissent is completely in order (indeed it parallels Menger's own critique of "The so-called ethical orientation of political economy" in Appendix 9 of his *Investigations*). If we are interested in the demand for goods at any one time, we do not need to know whether or not individuals are correct in their beliefs about the properties that they impute to those goods. In addition we must surely be less sanguine than was Menger as to whether the links that he discerned between the growth of civilization and preferences for real goods over imaginary goods are correct.

anapolis: Liberty Press, 1979), 52; and Hayek, *The constitution of liberty* (London: Routledge & Kegan Paul, 1960), 41. On the continuity, cf., for example, my "The Austrian connection," in *Austrian economics,* ed. W. Grassl and B. Smith (Beckenham, Kent: Croom Helm, 1986), and Karen Vaughn's contribution to the present volume.

2. See F. A. Hayek, "Carl Menger," republished as the Introduction to Menger, *Principles;* E. Kauder, *A history of marginal utility theory* (Princeton: Princeton University Press, 1965); and R. Fabian and P. M. Simons, "The second Austrian School of value theory," in *Austrian economics,* ed. Grassl and Smith, 37–101.

3. At the conference, Peter Rossner drew my attention to his unpublished paper, "To what extent was the Austrian School subjectivist? A note on Carl Menger," which discusses Menger's distinctive view of needs in some detail.

4. See Menger, *Principles,* 52.

5. See Menger, *Principles,* 53.

6. See especially Ludwig von Mises, "Remarks on the fundamental problem of the subjective theory of value," in his *Epistemological problems of economics,* trans. G. Reisman (New York and London: New York University Press, 1981), 167–82. See also the most interesting discussion of this aspect of Mises's work in Paul Silverman's 1984 University of Chicago Ph.D. dissertation, "Law and economics in interwar Vienna."

As a result, while there is a contrast between the work of Menger and that of Mises, Hayek, and later "Austrian" writers in this respect, the reader might well judge that it marks a move that was well made.[7] Should not Menger's distinction between true and imaginary goods— which he developed with respect to Aristotle—be dropped as unnecessary metaphysical baggage? And, along with Hayek in another epigraph to this paper, should we not welcome such a move as a step in the consistent application of subjectivism—and an important advance in economic theory?

In this paper I argue that while the subjectivism of the later members of the Austrian School has contributions to make of great importance, we should not follow it all the way. Rather, we should move back a little from Hayek to Menger and look again at two ideas suggested by Menger's work. The first is the idea that our concern with welfare issues may be taken beyond a concern with subjective satisfaction. The second is that we should also make something of Menger's concern with human nature—which I here suggest may fruitfully be interpreted in terms of a link with biology.

Such a case may be made at three levels. First, within economics, Menger's ideas about goods can be compared with Becker's ideas about Z-goods. This suggestion was put to me by David Levy, on hearing about the topic of the present paper. I have subsequently discovered that the link has also been suggested by Tyler Cowen.[8] I am happy, however, to leave the development of this point in the hands of these writers, who have a competence to which I cannot pretend in this field.

Second, it is of relevance in a field in which both Mises and Hayek have written extensively: the theory of understanding. Here, as I shall argue, a biological approach to the subjective can make an interesting contribution and can serve to strengthen some of Mises's and Hayek's insights. While my argument will be developed in the form of a critique, I do not imagine—in view of Hayek's own interest in matters biological—that he would object too strongly to the points that I make on this subject, insofar as they are cogent.

In the third area—the theory of welfare—things are perhaps different. My argument here is that to do justice to Hayek's own concerns, and to Mises's and Hayek's arguments about the significance of markets, it is necessary that claims about human welfare be made in terms that go beyond subjectivism. I start my argument with this issue.

7. Cf., for example, Lawrence White's endorsement of Mises's critique in his introduction to the 1985 New York University Press edition of Menger's *Investigations*.
8. George Stigler and Gary Becker, "De gustibus non est disputandum," *American Economic Review* 67 (1976): 76–90. See also Tyler Cowen, "Are all tastes constant and identical?" *Journal of Economic Behavior and Organization* 11 (1989): 127–35.

II. *Subjectivism and welfare*

In his inaugural address at the London School of Economics in 1933, "The trend of economic thinking," Hayek said:

> It is probably true that economic analysis has never been the product of detached intellectual curiosity about the why of social phenomena, but of an intense urge to reconstruct a world which gives rise to profound dissatisfaction. This is as true of the phylogenesis of economics as it is of the ontogenesis of probably every economist.[9]

He also quotes Pigou:

> It is not wonder, but social enthusiasm which revolts from the sordidness of mean streets and the joylessness of withered lives, that is the beginning of economic science.[10]

It is clear enough that in referring to this practical and reformist impetus in the ontogenesis of the economist, Hayek also refers to himself. He has written, about his return to Vienna after the First World War:

> We felt that the civilization in which we had grown up had collapsed. We were determined to build a better world, and it was this desire to reconstruct society that led many of us to the study of economics. Socialism promised to fulfil our hopes for a more rational, more just world.[11]

Hayek has not written much about the specific views that he held as a socialist; but he was influenced by Walther Rathenau,[12] and the general character of his early views is hinted at in the following brief comments about his choice of a teacher of economics:

> I was . . . a pupil of . . . Friedrich von Wieser. I was attracted to him . . . because unlike most of the other members of the Austrian School he had a good deal of sympathy with [the] mild Fabian Socialism to which I was inclined as a young man. He in fact prided himself that his theory of marginal utility had provided the basis of

9. "The trend of economic thinking," *Economica* (May 1933): 122–23. For some further discussion see my University of London Ph.D. dissertation, "The political thought of F. A. Hayek," 1987.

10. "Trend of economic thinking," 123, quoting from Pigou, *The economics of welfare,* 4th ed. (London: Macmillan, 1932), 5.

11. F. A. Hayek, Foreword to Ludwig von Mises, *Socialism* (Indianapolis: Liberty Classics Edition, 1981), xix.

12. I would like to thank Hayek's biographer, W. W. Bartley III, for discussion on this point.

progressive taxation, which then seemed to me one of the ideals of social justice.[13]

Hayek, it need hardly be said, is not today known for his socialism. There is in fact little mystery as to what happened: circumstances led him to work with Mises, and the combination of Mises's personal influence and Mises's published critique of socialism led Hayek towards a radical change in his views: "*Socialism* shocked our generation, and only slowly and painfully did we become persuaded of its central thesis."[14] After a recent rereading of the book he wrote: "I was surprised . . . by how many of its arguments which I had initially only half accepted, or regarded as exaggerated and one-sided, have since proved remarkably true."[15]

A measure of Hayek's reaction at the time can be gathered from his inaugural address—the first work in which he displayed Mises's impact upon these aspects of his views in general terms. What becomes clear from his text is that Mises had convinced him that it was *only* by means of the competitive processes of the market that economic coordination could be effected: "the wisest thing [which the intelligent planner] could do would be to bring about, by delicate regulation, what is accomplished spontaneously by competition. . . . [However,] he would lack the most important guide to such action which the competitive system affords."[16]

What is noticeable about Hayek's inaugural address, however, is the way in which he emphasizes his continuing attachment to the broad concerns about human welfare which had initially led him to socialism. He shows his unease at, as it were, finding himself in bed with conservatives, and he goes out of his way to stress that it is not his ethical concern for the relief of misery that has changed, but his views about how this may best be done.[17]

Indeed, one important strand in Hayek's work thereafter might be described as the elaboration of just this idea—from his development of the argument about economic calculation under socialism, through his discussion of issues in public policy in *The constitution of liberty,* to his critique of Galbraith on the "dependence effect" and his arguments about competition as a discovery procedure.[18]

13. See Hayek, "Coping with ignorance," in his *Knowledge, evolution and society* (London: Adam Smith Institute, 1983), 17.

14. Hayek, Foreword to Mises's *Socialism,* xxi.

15. Ibid., xxiii.

16. Hayek, "The trend of economic thinking," 132.

17. Ibid., 135–37.

18. F. A. Hayek, *The constitution of liberty* (London: Routledge & Kegan Paul, 1960); "The non sequitur of the dependence effect," in *Studies in philosophy, politics and economics* (London: Routledge & Kegan Paul, 1967); and "Competition as a discovery procedure," in *New studies* (London: Routledge & Kegan Paul, 1978).

However, these developments are paralleled by his own espousal of subjectivism and his rejection of the idea that one can make interpersonal comparisons of utility. He does this a little tentatively.[19] But it is hardly surprising that he took the view that he did, given the emphasis placed on this point by both Mises in Vienna and Robbins in London.

Subjectivism has considerable merits in other areas of economics and much of importance to contribute to the discussion of welfare issues. However, subjectivism does not, of itself, provide an adequate basis upon which Hayek could make his important points about the welfare characteristics of a market-based economic system. In his inaugural address he was concerned with human misery and its relief. This is a concern that is perfectly proper—and indeed worthy—although one might ask the theorist who expresses this concern whether he is also attached to other values, such as individual freedom of choice, individual autonomy, or the realization of specific cultural ideals, and also individual rights, and how tradeoffs are to be made between them. Once such matters have been explicated, much can be said about the alternative choices that are open to us, and their advantages and disadvantages. Indeed Hayek's own work contains a great deal of importance on these issues.

But what does welfare economics look like from a subjectivist perspective?

The purest attempt at a subjectivist theory of welfare is probably Murray Rothbard's theory of "demonstrated preference."[20] His reinterpretation of the theory of utility and of welfare economics takes seriously the idea that there can be no interpersonal comparisons of utilities. He also takes seriously the subjectivist idea that we do not have access to other people's preferences except insofar as they reveal them to us. The "very fact that an exchange takes place," he writes, "demonstrates that both parties benefit (or more strictly, expect to benefit) from the exchange. . . . The free market is the name for the array of all the voluntary exchanges that take place in the world. Since every exchange demonstrates a unanimity of benefit for both parties concerned, we must conclude that the free market benefits all its participants."[21]

But there are three problems concerning Rothbard's view—and related views which have been upheld by other economists in the modern Austrian tradition. The first is that his argument will shift our attention to the basis on which exchanges are to be judged voluntary, and on which we are to judge whether or not negative externalities can legit-

19. See Hayek, *The constitution of liberty,* 309, 517 nn. 8 and 10.
20. Murray Rothbard, *Toward a reconstruction of utility and welfare economics* (New York: Center for Libertarian Studies, 1977).
21. Ibid., 26–27.

imately be imposed upon others, i.e., to a theory of rights. But in discussing such different theories, and their pros and cons, we presumably cannot have recourse to considerations about the consequences of different courses of action, except insofar as these too can be discussed in purely subjectivist terms.[22]

Second, Rothbard's argument is at its weakest in just those circumstances with which Hayek has been most concerned. Hayek has made much of the way in which markets can assist us in situations in which we are ignorant. But when individuals are ignorant or have incorrect expectations it is by no means clear that the product of free exchange will in fact be a situation in which each is actually better off even in their own terms, even though each party may, as Rothbard says, have expected to benefit. Thus, while there are good cases of "praxeological" welfare, in which if two well-informed people exchange with one another both will be better off, this model seems severely restricted in its scope.

Third, Hayek has written of markets as examples of "spontaneous orders." (While his work and that of others interested in this topic—not least Carl Menger—has been suggestive,[23] much work on the identification and characterization of such orders still has to be done.) But we need, in the context of Rothbard's idea, to look closely at what we mean by "order." Rothbard's approach seems to suggest that the *only* question that we can ask, of some state of affairs, is whether it came about as a result of voluntary exchanges between consenting agents. In that case to call the result a "spontaneous order" is to say no more than that it is the unintended consequence of such voluntary activity. But to call something an "order" is suggestive of a contrast with "chaos." If we are saying something *more* about certain of the products of voluntary human activity than that they are the product of voluntary human activity, we are using a criterion to appraise them *other* than that suggested by Rothbard.

One additional point might be made by the Hayek of the inaugural address. The very starting point of Rothbard's approach seems to rule out, as beyond the scope of economics, the very thing that was Hayek's concern: human misery and what might be done towards its alleviation. From Rothbard's starting point it would seem as if one could not say that someone (other than, possibly, oneself) was in a condition of misery. This, to be sure, is in its way a dramatic solution to the problem of human misery. But it is hardly the one for which Hayek was looking.

22. On this cf. also Robert Nozick, "On Austrian methodology," *Synthèse* 36 (1977): 353–92.

23. See Norman Barry, "The tradition of spontaneous order," *Literature of Liberty* 5.2 (Summer 1982): 7–58. See also the discussion of Barry's paper by various authors in *Literature of Liberty* 5.4 (Winter 1982): 5–18.

An alternative theory of welfare that is open to the subjectivist is that of the Pareto criterion. I do not deny that there is theoretical interest in the study of Pareto optimality and of the conditions under which it might be realized.[24] However, what does seem strange is that so much attention is paid to it in general discussions of welfare issues in political economy. I also find strange the supposition—that still seems widely shared—that if something is a Pareto improvement, it is uncontentiously desirable.

First, virtually all *actual* economic activity—not least in a market economy—involves phenomena which do not satisfy the Pareto criterion. (Consider actual competition, in which some are successful and others are not, or learning by trial and error, or virtually anything involving innovation or the activities of government.) All this should hardly be news to the economist. After all, Adam Smith was well aware that some people lost out in, say, the move from a hunter-gatherer society to a society of herdsmen. Argument about the pros and cons of commercial society and their relation to other matters of human concern was for a long time the very stuff of argument in political economy, and a topic upon which we could well seek illumination from economists. But if they restrict themselves to what satisfies the Pareto criterion, they remove themselves from this discussion entirely.

What of Pareto improvement per se? Is it always uncontentiously desirable? I suggest that it is not. First, it is not obvious that the satisfaction of people's desires is necessarily of moral significance. Imagine that a person were, one day, to visit a room in which a number of people were engaged in a variety of activities in an apparently purposive manner, but he could not tell what they were each doing. It appeared, for example, as if they were performing actions that related to properties that they seemed to suppose that objects possessed, but which those objects did not seem to him to possess. In addition their plans and projects, insofar as he could discern them, seemed inchoate and fleeting. While they exhibited a propensity to truck and to barter, and exchanged things with one another, they would sometimes be observed to exchange much the same things back again, a little later. (He would, in effect, have viewed the room's occupants as the subjectivist views all human action.)

Now suppose that someone were to tell our visitor that it was of some

24. I would like to thank Mark Blaug for correcting an incautious statement in my verbal presentation at the conference which suggested otherwise, and also for some other important criticisms of ideas on welfare economics in an earlier version of this paper. He is, of course, in no way to blame for errors which may still remain. For a most interesting treatment of these issues—which is much deeper than that attempted here—see Charles Rowley and Alan Peacock, *Welfare economics: a liberal restatement* (New York: John Wiley, 1975).

moral significance—that it was better—that these individuals whom he was observing should be free to conduct these "exchanges" but that the only rationale offered for this judgment was that at the time at which these individuals made the "exchanges" in question, they wished to behave in this way. He might well take the view that on the basis of the information that he had so far, it was a moot point whether these exchanges were of any moral significance, or even whether they contributed to the well-being of those who made them. There seems no reason why he should judge that the satisfaction of their desires was of any moral significance, not least as he had no information whether there was a link between these people's activities and wider considerations of their well-being, or their pursuit of significant ends and goals, to say nothing of the well-being of others.

A lot would depend on what other information he could gather. If it turned out that our visitor was making his first visit to the stock exchange, then these activities and people's freedom to engage in them assume great moral significance. If, on the other hand, he was watching people in a nursing home for the senile, it would be appropriate if nursing assistants were, from time to time, to restrain these people's pursuit of their preferences and instead make sure that they were fed and washed and that they slept. But his—the subjectivist's—judgment would seem neutral between these two descriptions.

To put this point in more general terms, individuals may have preferences. But this fact in itself says nothing about how other people should react to them. It is, I would suggest, because we can link those preferences to something that is of value—such as the well-being of the individual with the preferences; the consequences for himself and others of his being free to act on the basis of them; or their rights—that we accord them ethical significance.

Second, what of Pareto improvement? Let us suppose that we do indeed take individuals' preferences seriously as an indication of their well-being. Should we not, then, welcome *any* Pareto improvement as desirable? I would suggest not. Consider a society that includes three people, two of whom are already in very comfortable circumstances and one of whom is in misery. Consider next a reallocation of resources such that the first two people become better off and no other member of the society is made worse off. The younger Hayek—as we have seen from his inaugural address—could well respond: but in this setting what matters is the alleviation of the condition of the person who is in misery. The gains made by the other people may be to their satisfaction; but there is no reason why an impartial spectator should agree that the condition after the reallocation of resources is better than it was before.

It might here again be questioned whether we can judge that the "unfortunate" individual is indeed in misery. Would not to attribute any such condition to him be to break with the idea that there can be no intersubjective comparison of utilities? To this it could be responded: such intersubjective comparison is not necessary—we are merely responding to our belief that the individual is at a low point on his own scale of well-being. However, this in itself would seem of no necessary ethical significance. Unless we were to interpret his being in that situation as unpleasant—in much the same sense as something is unpleasant for us—it is not clear why we would be concerned about it at all.[25]

Someone might deny that we can have such knowledge. But this seems to me to deny the obvious. Lest, however, this judgment seem simply a personal prejudice, let me call upon the testimony of a distinguished economist whose views might be of interest in this field, Lionel Robbins: "in daily life we . . . continually assume that [inter-personal comparisons of utility] can be made."[26] Robbins, however, goes on to argue that such claims "cannot be justified by appeal to any kind of positive science" and that there is a need for "a substantial curtailment of the claims of what now assumes the status of scientific generalization in current discussions of applied Economics."[27]

Now, while Robbins was arguably correct in his rejection of the specific work in welfare economics with which he was taking issue,[28] it seems to me that the basis on which he argues is less convincing than he—and many economists who have followed him—have supposed.

As Robbins himself noted, common sense is against him. We readily attribute well-being and its absence to other people. If we are told that there is a famine in some part of Africa, or that an aunt has been stung by a wasp, other people would quite properly wonder what was going on if we did not take this information as also informative about the victims' well-being. Our reaction would depend on our knowledge of them as members of the human species, tempered with knowledge about what they were used to and of local peculiarities (one's aunt might be allergic to wasp stings). Further, we all know that individuals' reactions to circumstances may be different—that some people are more sensitive to stimuli than are others; that other people make a greater fuss about

25. Of course, someone's being in a condition in which they should feel miserable but do not in fact do so may be an indication that they require the assistance of others that much more urgently; but this opens up issues that I cannot pursue here.

26. Lionel Robbins, *The nature and significance of economic science*, 2d ed. (London, 1935), 140. See also the first part of Ilmar Waldner, "Bare preference and interpersonal utility comparisons," *Theory and Decision* 5 (1974): 313–28, and Amartya Sen, *On ethics and economics* (Oxford: Blackwell, 1987), esp. ch. 2.

27. Robbins, *Economic science*, 141.

28. Cf. Robert Cooter and Peter Rappoport, "Were the ordinalists wrong about welfare economics?" *Journal of Economic Literature* (June 1984): 507–30, and the ensuing discussion.

their well-being. And we may know, further, that it may sometimes take a bit of time and trouble to sort out which are which.

To depart from this in the direction of a general skepticism about our knowledge of others' well-being clearly requires an argument. But there are some problems for the skeptic about interpersonal comparisons in making such arguments.

First, what is the status of claims about the intersubjective comparison of utilities? Robbins himself suggested that we imagine that "the representative of some other civilization were to assure us . . . that members of his caste . . . were capable of experiencing ten times as much satisfaction from given incomes as members of an inferior caste."[29] He argues that while we might be affronted by such a claim, we cannot refute it.

But this seems to me too quick. The people making the claim seem to believe in intersubjective comparisons of utility—as that is what their claim is about. We might ask them more about their claim and about whether, in their view, it could be tested. For example, is the difference innate? If so, what if babies were exchanged at birth? (They might have some local equivalent of the story of the princess and the pea.) Alternatively, the claim might rest on some theory of the cultural formation of taste. Either claim might, of course, be true. There is no reason why the defender of interpersonal comparisons must claim that each person has an equal capacity for pleasure. Robbins, however, might well retort that all this gives us no reason to suppose that such claims will in fact be open to refutation.

But is this true? Economics is, after all, dealing (for the most part) with the activities of members of our own biological species. And even if our experiences are not plausibly to be identified with properties of our physiology,[30] they are nonetheless closely dependent upon them. If someone were, say, to lay claim to an extreme subjective sensitivity, it would surely be strange if this were unrelated to *any* physical characteristics whatever. Thus when Robbins writes that "there is no means of testing the magnitude of A's satisfaction as compared to B's. If we tested the state of their blood streams, that would be a test of blood, not satisfaction,"[31] he would seem correct only if satisfaction were a purely mental state, with no physiological dependencies or concomitants. But as, after all, that which is giving rise to satisfaction will act through

29. Robbins, *Economic science,* 140.

30. Cf. K. R. Popper and J. C. Eccles, *The self and its brain* (New York: Springer International, 1978). See also Popper's discussion of the difference between scientific and philosophical reductions in "A realist view of logic, physics and history," in his *Objective knowledge* (Oxford: Clarendon Press, 1972).

31. Robbins, *Economic science,* 139–40.

various states of a person's physiology, this would seem rather strange. (At the same time, there may be greater problems about making inter-personal comparisons of utility between members of different species. But even this may not be impossible, as I shall suggest later.)

To sum up on this point: I do not wish to deny that it may be difficult to make judgments about others' well-being. But the idea that we cannot make intersubjective comparisons of well-being at all seems to me incorrect, especially when—as in the area of Hayek's interest in his inaugural address—we are concerned with their misery rather than their pleasure. Given the variety of human values and interests, and of our reactions to the various different situations in which we may find our-selves, it may well be that we cannot produce a "scientific" welfare economics involving interpersonal comparisons of utility after the fash-ion of, say, modern welfare economics or social choice theory. But this is, I would have thought, not necessarily to be regretted, just insofar as these disciplines seem able to contribute so little towards any real-world problems of political economy. (Or, insofar as non-Paretian approaches are used in welfare economics to deal with practical issues, important questions about subjective well-being, distribution, and the variety of human concerns are simply begged.) I wish to argue, however, that it is possible to develop theories and to argue in a nonarbitrary way (i.e., such that our claims are subject to criticism, formal argument, and empirical tests) about major issues of human welfare. Such discussion must take into account the various different dimensions of our concerns and the tradeoffs between them. It is a discussion from which econo-mists have excluded themselves, in their professional capacity, for far too long.

It might be thought, however, that my argument has been much too quick. For while there is not, in Hayek's work, an extensive discussion of the interpersonal comparison of utility, there is certainly a detailed discussion of subjectivism. This he develops especially in relation to problems of methodology and the theory of understanding. But if we were to accept a full-fledged subjectivism there, we might find ourselves led back to premises that conflict with the approach towards issues of welfare that has here been urged upon Hayek.

III. *Subjectivism and the theory of understanding*

One characteristic of the work of some of the best-known writers in the Austrian tradition after Menger is their concern for methodology and the philosophy of social science. They followed Menger not only in the fact that they spent so much time on the topic but also in some aspects of their substantive views. Menger himself argued that the physicist, when using such terms as "atoms" or "forces," is dealing with things with which he does not have direct experience—in Menger's view, these terms signify "merely unknown causes of real motions."[32] With this he contrasted the situation of the social scientist: "It is otherwise in the exact social sciences. Here the human individuals, and their efforts, the final elements of our analysis, are of empirical nature, and thus the exact social sciences have a great advantage over the exact natural sciences." Hayek, who himself cited this material from Menger, has written: "The physicist who wishes to understand the problems of the social sciences with the help of an analogy from his own field would have to imagine a world in which he knew by observation the inside of an atom."[33] But of just what does this "knowledge" consist, and what use is to be made of it?

Ludwig von Mises argued that there should be a methodological dualism between the social and the natural sciences and that human action should be understood as subjectively rational.[34] Hayek, in his arguments against the physicalism of some members of the Vienna circle, emphasized that we should understand human action as orientated towards objects as they are understood by human agents. These objects should be understood in terms of the classificatory schemas that the agents are using and as possessing properties that they take those objects to have—although they might well be in error—rather than, say, as having the properties that might be imputed to them by a physicist.

To understand actions in such terms requires that we understand what the categories are that our agents are using. I do not wish to claim that this necessarily poses a major practical problem. (Although there has, for example, been considerable controversy as to whether or not chimpanzees and gorillas are able to use a form of American sign language, or whether something more mechanical was going on.[35] And it is striking that we may come to classify as meaningful what may at first seem not to be a form of meaningful action, such as the contortions and groaning of a spiritualistic medium going into a trance.)[36]

---

32. Carl Menger, *Investigations into the method of the social sciences with special reference to economics* (New York: New York University Press, 1985), 142. Compare the discussion—and defense—of this view in Hayek's "Scientism and the study of society," n. 32, in which Hayek also refers to this view as found in the work of Lionel Robbins. For a criticism of this aspect of Robbins's and Hayek's work see my "Common sense and the foundations of economics: Duhem versus Robbins," forthcoming in *Philosophy of the Social Sciences*.

33. F. A. Hayek, "Scientism and the study of society," in *The counter-revolution of science,* 41.

34. Mises, *Epistemological problems of economics.*

35. Cf. Eugene Linden, *Apes, men, and language* (Harmondsworth, Middlesex: Penguin Books, 1976), and *Silent partners* (New York: Ballantine Books, 1987).

36. One might conjecture, however, that the historical origin of this behavior was in fact the attempt to simulate the appearance of an epileptic fit. But the behavior is now a matter of tradition, with no conscious links back to its origin—if this be such.

However, at a theoretical level things may be more problematic. Subjectivism as a theory of understanding emphasizes the rationality of an action, as opposed to the rationality of the theory or view of the world on the basis of which the individual is acting.[37] But to understand something as an action involves our taking the view that there is indeed some purpose to it. And subjectivism does not, of itself, give us any suggestion as to how we can discover what actions are in fact taking place.

Hayek has offered us a detailed account of the basis upon which human beings experience the world—of how the world as we experience it differs from the world as it is explained and classified by the physicist.[38] But if this account is true, it is certainly something that we cannot know directly to be true of ourselves—or of any other individual whom we happen to encounter: this is certainly not knowledge that we have by acquaintance.

In his methodological writings Hayek offers us a complimentary account, in which these problems are addressed more directly:

> [social phenomena] are accessible to us only because we can understand what other people tell us, and can be understood only by interpreting other people's intentions and plans . . . the elements from which we reproduce them are always familiar categories of our own mind.[39]

The reference here to "our own mind" is to be taken seriously. Hayek has elsewhere written:

> When we speak of mind, what we mean is that certain phenomena can be successfully interpreted on the analogy of our own mind, that the use of the familiar categories of our own thinking provides a satisfactory working explanation of what we observe.[40]

And he continues, writing of the scope and limitations of this approach:

> it is the only basis on which we can ever understand what we call other people's intentions, or the meaning of their actions; and certainly the only basis of all our historical knowledge . . . as we pass from men of our own kind to different types of beings we may, of course, find that what we can thus understand becomes less and

37. Cf., for example, I. Jarvie and J. Agassi, "The problem of the rationality of magic," in *Rationality*, ed. B. Wilson (Oxford: Blackwell, 1970).

38. See, notably, *The sensory order* (London: Routledge & Kegan Paul, 1952), essays in his *Studies in philosophy, politics and economics* (London: Routledge & Kegan Paul, 1969), and *New studies* (London: Routledge & Kegan Paul, 1978).

39. Hayek, "The facts of the social sciences," in *Individualism and economic order* (London: Routledge, 1948), 75.

40. "Scientism and the study of society," 77.

less. And we cannot exclude the possibility that one day we may find beings who, though perhaps physically resembling men, behave in a way which is entirely unintelligible to us. With regard to them we should indeed be reduced to the "objective" study which the behaviourists want us to adopt towards men in general.

Hayek's analysis is notable for the sharp dichotomy that he draws between the objects of human activity and the physical, and also for the sharpness of the discontinuity that he draws between them:

> The kind of objects of human activity which constantly occur in the social sciences . . . abstract from *all* physical properties of the things themselves. They are instances of . . . "teleological concepts," that is, they can be defined only by indicating relations between three terms: a purpose, somebody who holds that purpose, and the object which that person thinks to be a suitable means for that purpose.[41]

In our attempt to understand such actions, he stresses, further, that "no superior knowledge the observer may possess about the object, but which is not possessed by the acting person, can help us in understanding the motives of their actions."[42]

Hayek's view is interesting. And he is correct that we impute meaningful behavior to others on the basis of what makes sense to us in familiar terms. However, this imputation might seem to run the risk of being subjective in a pejorative sense—of being simply an exercise on our part, bearing no relation to what is actually going on. (At the same time, one might wonder why, in Hayek's view, we cannot impute states of well-being to others on precisely the same basis as we do meaningful behavior, on his account.)

I wish to argue that we have something important here to learn from Carl Menger's concern with human nature. Such a concern can assist us in relation to the problem of how we can come to understand the subjectively meaningful actions of other people. In addition it can help us to overcome the rigidity of Hayek's dichotomy between the physical and the meaningful. It also suggests that there can be more to our understanding of the behavior of other people than our projecting onto them the categories in terms of which we understand the world.

My starting point is a suggestion made by Peter Winch at the end of his "Understanding a primitive society."[43] In that essay, which is a

41. "The facts of the social sciences," 59.
42. Ibid., 60.
43. See Peter Winch, "Understanding a primitive society," in *Rationality,* ed. B. Wilson (Oxford: Blackwell, 1970). See also *The idea of a social science* (London: Routledge & Kegan Paul, 1958).

development and application of the approach of his *Idea of a social science* to a problem in interpretative anthropology, it seemed to most readers that in explicating his own views Winch generated a form of cultural relativism which would render intercultural understanding impossible. However, towards the end of the essay Winch, citing T. S. Eliot, suggested that a path into the understanding of a culture different from our own might be provided by the common human experiences of "birth, copulation and death."[44] It seems to me that he might be understood as suggesting that these stand as external reference points, in relation to which human culture and actions may be understood as having a significance.

This is clearly a departure from a purely internalist approach like that of subjectivism, for it suggests that there is an external standpoint in relation to which actions can be understood and, to a degree, evaluated. What is more, this external viewpoint is to serve as a point of reference in understanding the subjective. Such points of reference, however, can take us beyond our own species. We may understand, say, the behavior of animals by understanding its biological function. Even their more strange behavior and rituals can be understood (as in the theory of sexual selection) in terms that relate back to biology. In this respect our understanding can go beyond understanding people who have minds that are, in some sense, like ours—for example, as this is described in Hayek's *Sensory order.* We can even understand what a spider (or a fly or an ant) is up to by understanding its behavior in its biological context.[45]

Of course this approach is something to which we will need to have recourse only insofar as our intuitive ideas about what is going on prove unsuccessful, or to test those ideas. The biological thus offers us a level of understanding between the physical and the fully meaningful. It allows us to comprehend the actions of members of species other than our own. It also plays a role in enabling us to understand other cultures and subjectively meaningful action.

Suppose—to give a somewhat extreme example—we were to come across, in some other part of the universe, a species different from our own but which appeared to possess a culture. By what means could we try to discern whether, indeed, this was a culture, and then understand it? We should start with their biology—or, more properly, their biology and its relation to their ecology—and seek to understand what seemed to be their culture in terms of their biology, or as a cultural response to their biology and ecology. (I have said "what seemed to be their cul-

44. Winch, "Primitive society," 108.
45. I am not claiming that all animal behavior is biologically functional in the narrow sense of well-adapted.

ture," just because we might, say, find that we were confronted with something more like a beehive and the behavior of bees than human culture.)

If indeed it is a culture, we would have to understand it qua response to the biology and ecology of the species in question. (The approach could also be seen as a development of Adam Smith's ideas about understanding a society's institutions in relation to its mode of subsistence.) Eliot's list is—in rough terms—a description of some of the salient features of our biology which should be of concern to members of some other species trying to make something of us. It is, of course, somewhat crude. (It would not—I hope—get our aliens far in understanding the proceedings of an academic conference!) But we would have to start with something similar if, say, we were to try to come to grips with the culture of a species which was parasitic upon others; or the young of which grew up independently of their parents; or which did not engage in sexual reproduction, or whatever.

I would even suggest that we should not rule out the possibility that we could make some intersubjective comparisons of utility upon an interspecies basis. Insofar as we can understand our subjective experience in biologically based terms, and in its relation to our physiology, we might also be able to make some comparative judgments—at least in the sense of being able to criticize some claims that may be made about the experience of other species, or its qualities. At the same time, our ability to do this might be very limited: could we tell, say, from the purely "external" investigation of the physiology of our own species that toothache would be *that* painful?

Be that as it may, I think that at the level of understanding we have something to learn from the reinterpretation of Menger's concern for human nature in terms of the biological. What we have to learn is that there is something between the physical and the social or cultural, and that our path to the understanding of the social or the cultural may be built upon a biological basis.[46]

The biological gives us only a limited amount of information. While, as it were, we can understand the point of some activity in terms of its relation to an organism's biological needs—and, at a more sophisticated level, to the characteristics of its cognitive and sensory apparatus—this does not tell us much. Even our feelings for the "merely" biological aspects of ourselves are, clearly, mediated by a complex apparatus, and by culture, such that—as Hayek suggested—the objects with which we

46. There are connections between my point here and the view of the relation between consciousness and biological phenomena that Popper develops in his contributions to *The self and its brain*. To look at either meaning or consciousness primarily in terms of machines and their behavior may be a mistake.

interact are perceived as culturally constituted. And there is no way in which a complex human courtship ritual, or our enjoyment of a symphony, or our sense of wonder at a brilliant sunset, can be treated adequately *just* in terms of biology and ecology. However, biology does offer us a way in: we would simply not see the point of much human activity unless we had the ability to understand the apparatus upon which our cultural tunes are played.[47]

To draw some conclusions: My argument here is that it is important that we recognize the existence of something between the physical and the meaningful, namely the biological. This provides an initial toehold through which we can come to understand the meaningful behavior of other people, something that we need to do in order to judge that it *is* indeed meaningful behavior (although, of course, we may in some cases judge that it *probably* is, even if we cannot understand it as such). *Pace* Hayek, such a path to understanding is not, prima facie, restricted to those with whom we share particular biological or psychological characteristics. We can understand, say, the behavior of a cat as purposive, rather than just as a bundle of physical reactions, without committing ourselves to the view that its mind is, in some sense, like ours. There may, or may not, be some deep sense in which Hayek is correct about understanding and shared categories. My argument here is that this seems an (interesting) point in speculative metaphysics, rather than something that need be our concern in methodology, or in our attempts to understand the behavior of others.

What is more, such a level of understanding also allows us a point of entry with respect to judgments of well-being. This, it seems to me, is just as true for my cat as it is for a fellow human being. In both cases I can make informed judgments about the well-being of the creature in question which may be tested on the basis of biologically grounded knowledge. There is, however, a significant difference in respect of the human being. It is possible for me—in a way in which it is not possible for my cat—to understand that I am overweight and that I should diet and thus, as a matter of choice, undertake behavior which an external observer could correctly understand as unpleasant because I feel that I ought to do so. I might, alternatively, decide to fast during Lent for religious reasons. In such a setting I would imagine that someone might correctly be able to say to me, from an "external" perspective: you are unpleasantly hungry. However, I might well respond that while that is the case, I have chosen to be hungry, and explain to him the religious significance of my choice.

47. See C. S. Lewis, "Transposition," in *The weight of glory and other addresses* (Grand Rapids, Mich.: Eerdmans, 1965). For a discussion of some problems of responding appropriately in the absence of some elements of the usual biological basis for behavior see John Reid, *The best little boy in the world* (New York: Ballantine Books, 1977), ch. 4.

In making this point I wish to suggest that it is perfectly possible for us to say something about the well-being of other people from an "external" perspective. Indeed if we could not do this, we would, I think, be unable to learn a shared language with which to talk with other people about all kinds of "subjective" matters. And this in turn gives some weight to my claim that we can say rather more about human welfare than a pure subjectivism would allow.

IV. *Hayek on welfare theory*

A critic might, however, claim that Hayek hardly stands in need of the ideas about welfare that I am pressing upon him, on the grounds that he has some perfectly good ideas of his own. These I must therefore discuss, briefly.

Hayek has sometimes argued for the advantages of markets in relation to the desirability of the coordination of people's expectations.[48] This is an interesting idea, insofar as it shows a concern with welfare issues relating to dynamic processes in which people discover that their expectations do not cohere and must then revise those expectations if their behavior is later to be in better coordination. Hayek's ideas are suggestive, and it would be interesting to see how they might be characterized in more detail. (There is, on the face of it, a considerable difference between discoordination of a kind that might be dealt with by the arbitrage activities of a Kirznerian entrepreneur[49] and, say, that which would require more radical changes to be made.)

However, if we consider the revision of expectations and actions in the face of a lack of coordination, what may matter from the point of view of welfare is how these revisions take place and to what result, rather than just that the result involves (better) coordination. Suppose, say, that initial discoordination resulted from people not being willing to give me as much for my services as I felt that I deserved. Suppose that revision then takes place within a "black box"; and afterwards that they give me everything that I want. We must surely inquire what went on and how the result relates to human well-being if we are to judge the development from the point of view of welfare. If, say, in the "black box" the other people were menaced by my assistants, it is clear that we should not regard the outcome as an improvement. But on just what basis is it that only some kinds of transformations are to be counted legitimate? After all, we are not here dealing with anything like Pareto improvement, but rather with a process of adjustment, in which one—or more—of the parties will be revising their plans and expectations, in ways that

48. Cf. Hayek, *Law, legislation and liberty* (London: Routledge & Kegan Paul, 1976), 2:ch. 10.
49. See I. Kirzner, *Competition and entrepreneurship* (Chicago: University of Chicago Press, 1973).

may well promise them less satisfaction than they were hoping for before.

One response here might be to have recourse to some theory of rights, implicit or explicit. But Hayek is somewhat guarded on this topic. Insofar as there is such a theory in Hayek, it seems to rest either on a bare assumption of the undesirability of coercion, or on a form of indirect utilitarianism.[50] But the former certainly does not follow simply from subjectivism. (After all, I may have a taste for the coercion of others.) And insofar as there is an appeal to broadly utilitarian concerns, we must ask whether the argument involves intersubjective comparisons of utility, and also whether it works.[51]

One other criterion for the judgment of social systems that is sometimes offered in Hayek's work is his version of a veil-of-ignorance argument: an appeal to the idea that we should appraise a society in terms of the well-being of a member of that society chosen at random within it.[52] But if this judgment is to reflect more than our purely subjective preferences, it is not clear how the different elements in the randomly chosen individual's situation are to be weighted against one another. And if the judgment is to be just a matter of our personal preferences, it is not clear on what grounds we should accept the morally loaded idealization that Hayek wishes us to use, rather than judging, say, how we, or the particular people and causes that we favor, might fare in one rather than another such society.

Two other discussions by Hayek also merit consideration here. First, there is Hayek's exchange with Galbraith on the "dependence effect." Hayek there discusses Galbraith's argument that—as Hayek puts it—"the great part of the wants which are still unsatisfied in modern society are not wants which would be experienced spontaneously by the individual if left to himself but are created by the process by which they are satisfied."[53] Hayek, however, argues that this is true of the "amenities of civilization" and that we want these things because "they produce feelings or emotions which we would not know if it were not for our cultural inheritance."[54] He then argues that consumers are not determined in their choices by the efforts of individual producers but rather are influenced by producers who compete with one another, and also by the choices made by their fellows.

Hayek's argument is compatible with subjectivism. But it seems to me that its rhetorical force is not. His references to civilization, to music and painting, and to his own literary tastes for Jane Austen or Anthony

50. Cf. John Gray, *Hayek on liberty* (Oxford: Blackwell, 1984).
51. On this cf. ch. 3 of my "Political thought of Hayek."
52. Cf. Hayek, *Studies in philosophy, politics and economics*, 173.
53. Hayek, "The non sequitur of the dependence effect," 313.
54. Ibid., 314.

Trollope carry with them the idea that these are tastes that it is desirable for him to have acquired. (A purely *subjectivist* argument would run, equally, if its author had listed only various works of pornography, devoid of literary merit.) Similarly, Hayek's writings on the theme of competition as a discovery procedure obtain their force from our reading into them the idea that what is being discovered is conducive to human well-being.

Of course, such claims may be contested. Indeed an important strand in the history of ideas since the mid-eighteenth century has been an extended discussion about the pros and cons of markets—and of alternatives to them. Much of the work of Hayek, and of other members of the Austrian School, seems to me a vital contribution to this debate.[55] But to take a purely subjectivist view of these matters—to accept that "progress is movement for movement's sake"[56]—is, in my view, to turn one's back upon this argument by suggesting that we cannot engage in it, rather than to contribute to it. Accordingly, in my view the Austrian tradition in political economy needs to return to Menger's concern with the relation between markets (and, more generally, voluntaristic institutions) and civilization, but to develop a more adequate and rich treatment of these matters than Menger's own.

One problem about such an attempt, however, is how we should deal with the important fact, upon which the subjectivist tradition has placed so much emphasis, that there is such a diversity of human ideals and concerns. While, say, it may be possible for any member of our species to discover that I am hungry or thirsty or sad, there would seem, prima facie, little chance for someone who did not know me well to realize that the fact that I did not seem happy might have something to do with an absence of tabby cats, Häagen-Dazs butter-pecan ice cream, pinball machines, or Tuborg Paaske-Bryg beer. How, once we have moved beyond biological necessities, can we say much about what society is a good society, given the diversity of human concerns?

One idea of which Hayek has made much in his more recent writings can be of assistance to us here: his emphasis upon the size of the population that a society could support.[57] It is not that Hayek's own treatment of this theme is something with which I have much sympathy.[58] While, as Adam Smith argued, we benefit from being members of a society in

55. On this theme cf. my "Hayek and the spirit of the age," in J. Burton et al., *Hayek's "serfdom" revisited* (London: Institute of Economic Affairs, 1984).

56. See the third epigraph of this paper.

57. I would like to thank Greg Christiansen, the discussant of my paper at the conference, for urging that I respond to Hayek's views about population.

58. See, notably, *The fatal conceit* (London: Routledge & Kegan Paul, 1988). Hayek's discussion there and elsewhere seems to me also to systematically conflate the idea that certain of our moral ideas may have survived because they led us to conditions that would support a large population, and that there is something good about such ideas or about large populations per se.

which the market is large and the division of labor is advanced, and while, if there is a large population, Hayek is correct in his insistence that their existence and well-being is a constraint on the activities of the rest of us, I find Hayek's case against neo-Malthusianism unconvincing. Furthermore, it seems to me that John Stuart Mill's remarks on this topic in his discussion of "the stationary state" in his *Political economy* were very much to the point: "It is not good for man to be kept perforce at all times in the presence of his species. A world from which solitude is extirpated, is a very poor ideal. . . . Nor is there much satisfaction in contemplating the world with nothing left to the spontaneous activity of nature."[59]

But why, then, do I consider Hayek's revision of Bentham (from the Greatest Happiness of the Greatest Number to the Greatest Number)[60] to be interesting? It is that in the face of the diversity of human ends or goals upon which the subjectivist insists, one must probably have recourse to a nonsubjectivist but human-related measure in order to discuss the comparative ability of societies to satisfy human well-being. And while the actual goal of sustaining a large number of people in an existence in which their biological needs can be satisfied seems to me an unattractive ideal, the potential to do this might be a revealing measure of a society's ability to generate human well-being.

I hope that by now the direction in which I am moving may be clear. It is to the claim that a pure subjectivism is insufficient as a basis upon which Mises and Hayek can make the claims that they want to make—and should make—about what we can expect from markets. Rather, the properties of markets with which they were concerned seem to me to be of importance largely because of the idea that, through them, human well-being is enhanced. And to argue in this way involves the elaboration of criteria external to markets, in the light of which markets and other forms of social organization can be compared.

I should stress, in view of my earlier emphasis upon the biological, that I do not mean to limit what we can say about human well-being to the biologically based. But the biologically based, it seems to me, is not a bad starting point. We can indeed talk about gains in well-being in terms of people's not being frustrated in their biologically based desires; or, if they wish not to eat, drink, live in decent conditions, and so on, of this being a matter of their choice, rather than something that is forced upon them by their circumstances. To admit such ideas is not in itself to advance a case for economic interventionism. It was against a context of such general ideas about human well-being that the young Hayek, and

59. John Stuart Mill, *Principles of political economy,* 7th ed. (London: Longmans, 1871), book 4, ch. 6, para. 2, p. 331.
60. As Jack Birner and Axel Leijonhufvud remarked at the conference.

before him Adam Smith, set out their case for the market. It is to this argument, in my view, that we should return.

Further, however, it seems to me that a main line of argument about markets should consider the relation between what people can produce within them (and the unintended consequences of ordering our affairs by means of markets) and human well-being. If *all* we have produced by markets is the creation and subsequent satisfaction of an unending but fleeting succession of subjective whims, then it is by no means clear why we should care much about them. Of course, other things being equal we may say that it is better that desires be satisfied than not; we may also have some strong theory about human rights which gives an import to the satisfaction of nonaggressive human desires, whatever they may be. However, defenders of markets—from Mandeville to Hayek—have fully admitted that markets have their disadvantages too. In assessing their pros and cons, those of us who have read and have been impressed with the work of Mises and of Hayek will do ourselves—and markets— less than justice if we try to argue their merits in purely subjectivist terms.[61]

V. *Conclusion*

My argument has thus been that we should return to Menger's concern with human nature, and with a conception of human well-being that goes beyond the purely subjective. It is only with such a theory that we can do justice to Mises's and Hayek's own arguments for markets. By saying this I do not wish to downplay the importance of the insights of subjectivism. But I do wish to argue that we can go further, in talking about human well-being, than pure subjectivism would allow. Some of the most important insights of the classical liberal tradition, to which Mises and Hayek have done so much to contribute, relate to the importance of private property and of markets, and the liberating of the human imagination and the learning that they make possible. For this case to be made properly and for those who are impressed with it to engage with those who have objections, it seems to me essential that a more powerful theory of welfare should be developed: one which can give weight to the biological, to the choices in which we put our particular human concerns above the biological, and also to our concern for individual freedom. And as part of this theory the insights of subjectivism should be recognized: it is important that individuals may prefer to choose not to eat or to copulate, and may even, in some circumstances, prefer to die.[62]

61. Any reader who might believe that it is only possible to treat of ethical judgments as undiscussible expressions of preferences should consult D. McNaughton, *Moral vision* (London: Blackwell, 1987).

62. This is a reference back to Peter Winch's list.

Finally, lest it has not been clear to the reader of this paper, I should stress that my point is to urge that creation of a more adequate welfare theory be placed on the intellectual agenda, rather than to offer one myself. The creation of such a theory would in my view require talents honed within several different intellectual disciplines—including not just economics, political science, and philosophy, but also history. For it is only, I believe, if we keep before us where we have come from that we can judge whether where we are now is an improvement over what has gone before. Indeed it is for this very reason that I would urge a concern with aspects of Menger's work upon his latter-day intellectual heirs.

I would like to thank my colleagues at the Institute for Humane Studies and also David Gordon, for their comments upon an early version of this paper, and participants in the conference—especially Greg Christiansen, Mark Blaug, Larry White, and Bruce Cald-well—for some very useful criticisms and suggestions. I would also like to thank partici-pants in a meeting of the Seminar for Austro-German Philosophy in 1982 for discussion of ideas that appear in the third section of this paper, Charles Rowley for discussion, and Tyler Cowen for criticisms and suggestions. Errors and confusions that remain are, emphatically, my own.

III. Methodology

Menger's methodology

Karl Milford

I

At the time Menger published his *Principles* (1871), the German economists had not only developed the basic elements of a subjectivist tradition in economics (see Hermann 1832); they also had sought to establish
their economic theories on a sound epistemological and methodological
basis. These methodological and epistemological theories were primarily developed by Roscher (1842, 1843), Hildebrand (1848), and Knies
(1853, 1930) in the early 1840s and 1850s and were well accepted by the
1870s. Their views may be characterized as a peculiar hodgepodge of
Hegelian, German romanticist, and collectivist ideas, which were supported by an organic theory of the state. Another strand of thought of
considerable influence was their belief that science is a kind of special
knowledge, i.e., certain or at least highly probable knowledge, and that
the empirical sciences are characterized by induction. Although the
views of Roscher, Knies, and Hildebrand differed to some extent, they
shared the opinion that the empirical basis of the theoretical social
sciences is the history of mankind or economic history and that any laws
economists might find have to be inferred from this basis.

Roscher, for instance, held that the aim of the theoretical social
sciences is to uncover historical laws of development and that economics is a kind of theory of history (1842, vii; 1843, iv; 1886, § 16). It
seems that he derived these methodological conclusions from considerations concerning the subject matter of the social sciences and the belief
that induction requires as a necessary precondition repeated observations. Roscher apparently thought that the natural sciences may apply
inductive methods quite easily, since their subject matter is characterized by a certain kind of uniformity or repetition in the occurrence of
phenomena (1886, § 26). The social sciences, however, he believed to
deal with a subject matter which is subject to change and therefore
renders the application of inductive procedures impossible. Since he
held that science attains empirical knowledge by induction, he thought
that the structural properties of the subject matter of the social sciences
raise rather awkward epistemological and methodological problems.

Roscher therefore sought to solve this problem by trying to argue that
the social universe is indeed governed by some kind of uniformity or

repetitiveness. This uniformity, he suggested, is revealed by comparative and holistic studies of the historical development of different nations, peoples, or economies; and he believed that from this basis social scientists may induce the historical laws of economic development (1843, iv; 1886, §§ 16, 26).

Roscher's solution to the methodological problem of an empirical and theoretical social science thus implies the assumption that nations, peoples, or economic systems are really existing entities and observable, similar to physical things. Such a collectivist theory, however, contrasts strangely with his subjectivism in economics, which places so much stress on subjective evaluations of individuals; and indeed it seems that he himself was somewhat uneasy with respect to this situation.

He therefore tried to reconcile his subjectivist and collectivist views, pointing out that individuals can only act within a certain framework or a given "whole." According to Roscher nations, peoples, and economic systems really exist and are not simply theoretical constructions built upon the basis of individual actions. Not surprisingly, he launched a vigorous attack on the principle of methodological individualism, criticizing the individualistic tradition and in this respect even Adam Smith, whom otherwise he highly esteemed as a forerunner of the Historical School. Although Roscher was ready to admit that any "ordinary economy"—he used this term in the sense of "economizing individual" as well as in the sense of "economic system"—tries to maximize its utility, he pointed out that at the bottom of this activity two spiritual mainsprings are working: self-interest and public spirit. He emphasized, however, that public spirit is much more important than self-interest, because it is public spirit that actually establishes the society. From these considerations he concluded that entities such as societies, nations, peoples, or economic systems are "wholes" which form the preconditions such that individuals may act or even exist (1886, §§ 12, 26).

Thus although Roscher admitted that evaluations of individuals are central within economic life, he also emphatically stressed that we have to be aware of a necessary precondition for the working of self-interest, i.e., public spirit. Accordingly we can never provide any satisfactory explanation of social or economic phenomena unless we analyze the preconditions of individual rational behavior. Whereas methodological individualism holds that social institutions are the undesigned results of rational individual behavior and therefore have to be explained through the rational behavior of economic agents in terms of aims, information, etc., Roscher held that it is precisely the other way round: we first have to analyze the prevailing social institutions by analyzing the laws of their historical development, because this will give us a true notion of their essence. Only after having explained their essence are we able to understand the historical situation in which individuals act.

II

Roscher's methodological and epistemological theories provided the writers of the Historical School with a basic epistemological framework, which by 1871 was well established. In 1871 German economics confronted Menger with a methodological and epistemological framework which embraced, apart from subjectivism, also inductivist, scientist, historicist, collectivist, and organicist theories. Its scientist and historicist theories committed the representatives of the Historical School to the idea that theoretical social science is some kind of theory of history; its collectivist theories committed them to the idea that nations, peoples, or other social institutions have to be perceived as real existing "wholes"; and its organic theory committed them to a view of social "wholes" as entities equipped with a spirit or will, which serve as the preconditions for individuals to act.

Menger thought these methodological beliefs most harmful to the progress of economics, particularly with respect to price theory. Like many German economists, he also thought that classical price theory was falsified. Yet he also believed that the German economists, despite their fruitful subjectivist beginnings, were not capable of solving the problem of developing a unified price theory, because of their peculiar methodological and epistemological views. Methodologically considered, Menger's *Principles* were an attempt to show the possibility of a theoretical economics which was capable of solving the urgent problems of economic theory, precisely because it was based on a new and totally different methodological principle: the principle of methodological individualism.

It is therefore not surprising that even in the preface of his *Principles* Menger concentrated on methodological issues. He not only praised the German economists for their contributions to subjectivism, but he also launched a rather harsh attack on their methodological and epistemological views. He pointed out that "past attempts to carry over the peculiarities of the natural-scientific method of investigation uncritically into economics have led to most serious methodological errors, and to idle play with external analogies between the phenomena of economics and those of nature" (1981, 47).

The methodological view that Menger criticized most forcefully in his *Principles* was the German economists' notion of a satisfactory explanation in the social sciences. In contrast to their scientist and organic theories Menger developed a new kind of explanation, designed to explain the origin and structural change of social institutions such as money, markets, or price structures. These explanations considered social institutions as the undesigned result of rational individual actions and therefore sought to explain these undesigned results as the outcome of preferences, information, evaluations, time, and error.

Menger developed this new way of explaining social institutions on two levels. In the first chapters of his *Principles* his concern was to develop a unified price theory on the basis of the idea that individuals try to achieve their aims in what to them seems the best possible manner. However, the decisive element in these explanations is that Menger perceived the economic agents not as passive, but as active, problem-solving individuals. He depicted a world in which individuals do not simply react to their changing surroundings in a passive way but try to discover new possibilities of improving their lives or simply of surviving. These individual agents continuously solve problems and have to choose between different ways of achieving their aims. They have to evaluate alternative means and ends, and since their knowledge is far from being perfect, they will err in this process. Moreover, the growth of (scientific) knowledge will constantly generate new situations and thus new problems which the individuals will have to solve by inventing new solutions. Although the social universe is man-made, it is not simply the product of man according to some plan or "production function." By trying to solve problems and by inventing new solutions individuals permanently change the world they inhabit. And since the situations in which individuals must act permanently change, they can cope with these new situations only by inventing new solutions to the problems which confront them.

While Menger tried to show that the principle that individuals try to achieve their aims in the best possible manner is vital for the explanation of changing price structures, he also showed that the same principle can be applied to the explanation of the origin of certain other institutions (1871, 1883). According to Menger, the weak spot of any organic theory of the state is that it cannot explain the origin of social institutions or the change of social structures. In effect the organic explanation simply points out that these institutions have developed organically together with the whole system. Menger stressed that such an explanation cannot be seriously regarded as an explanation. In his theory of money as developed in the *Principles* he therefore tried to show that the emergence of social institutions can be explained in the same manner and on the same principles as for instance the change or the emergence of a price structure (1871).

It seems that Menger's methodological attempt as set out in the *Principles* was not completely grasped by the German economists. Roscher, although he quite clearly seems to have perceived some of

Menger's new contribution to economics, such as the equimarginal principle, obviously did not understand Menger's criticism of the organic theory. Perhaps this was due to some kind of selective reading by the German economists. Their writings show that they recognized only Menger's contribution to subjectivism, not his contribution concerning money. Yet it is Menger's theory on money, his explanation of its origin as an institution, which most forcefully brings to light the role of the principle of methodological individualism and thus his criticism of the organic theory of the state.

III

Menger set out to clarify his methodological theory of explaining social phenomena by writing a new methodological book, the *Investigations* (1883). However, he set his discussion of what he regarded as a satisfactory explanation in the theoretical social sciences in a wider context, because he believed that many of the methodological views of the German economists were due to a simple misunderstanding of the aim and the task of any theoretical science and its epistemological foundation. Thus he primarily focused on problems such as the aim and the task of the theoretical social sciences, the structure of their explanations, issues concerning induction, and a sound epistemological justification of the social sciences qua theoretical sciences.[1]

Menger began his methodological analysis with considerations about the proper aim and task of science. According to him, the aim is to develop either historical or theoretical explanations. He introduced his analysis by writing:

> We understand a concrete phenomenon in a specifically *historical* way (through its history) by investigating its individual process of development, i.e., by becoming aware of the concrete relationships under which it has developed and, indeed has become what it is, in its special quality. (1883, 43)

However, in developing historical explanations we have to apply theories:

> The understanding of the *concrete* phenomena of economy *by means of the theory,* the application of theoretical economics as *means* for this understanding, the utilization of the theory of eco-

---

1. I would like to point out that this analysis contrasts strongly with the general reading of Menger's epistemological and methodological contributions, which rather try to trace philosophical influences in Menger's work. Authors who have traced the philosophical influences in Menger's writings include, e.g., Kauder (1958), Hutchison (1973), White (1977), Boos (1986), Dobretsberger (1949), and—according to Kauder (1962)—also some Japanese authors. Some of the most interesting research in this field has been done by Smith (1986).

nomics for the history of economy—all these are, on the contrary, problems for the *historian,* for whom the social sciences considered in this way, are *auxiliary sciences.* (46)

In contrast, however:

> We understand a concrete phenomenon in a *theoretical* way (on the basis of the corresponding theoretical sciences) by recognizing it to be a special case of a certain regularity (conformity to law) in the succession, or in the coexistence of phenomena. In other words, we become aware of the basis of the existence and the peculiarity of the nature of a concrete phenomenon by learning to recognize in it merely the exemplification of a conformity-to-law of phenomena in general. (44, 45)

Menger had two reasons for starting his methodological analysis with these considerations. First—as already mentioned above—he found that the methodological debate in economics was severely hampered by a general confusion of historical and theoretical explanations. He believed that some of the major assertions held by various members of the Historical School—for instance, that economics has to be regarded as a historical discipline—were entirely due to this confusion (1883, 45). At the outset of his analysis he therefore tried to outline the different aims and problems at issue in historical and theoretical explanations. Second, and more importantly, by explaining the structure of historical and theoretical explanations, he pointed out that theories, laws, and strictly universal statements were required for both kinds of explanations (and, as he later stressed, also for predictions) (45). It followed that the primary aim of any theoretical activity was to search for laws and propose theories and strictly universal statements. As shown by the entire argument of the *Investigations,* Menger concluded that any epistemological justification of theoretical science must by necessity amount to a justification of strictly universal statements, theories, or laws. He believed this question to be the main epistemological problem requiring resolution, which, when resolved, would establish the social sciences qua theoretical sciences. He emphasized that this problem still awaited satisfactory resolution, stating in the preface of his *Investigations:*

> The theory of economics, as the so-called classical school of English economists shaped it in the main, has not been able to solve the problem of a science of the laws of national economics satisfactorily. But the authority of its doctrine is a burden on us all and prevents progress on these paths on which a scholarly mind for centuries, long before the appearance of A. Smith, sought the solution of the great problem of establishing theoretical social science. (1883, 29)

Menger remained aware that his opinion—that the aim of the theoretical social sciences, especially economics, was to advance theories and strictly universal statements—received criticism. He pointed out that the question whether the social sciences may be regarded as theoretical disciplines had received five different answers corresponding to five epistemological positions, or as he put it, "orientations of research" (1883, 29):

1. "the physical or atomistic conception of theoretical science" (24)
2. "the organic understanding of social phenomena" (24, 127ff.)
3. "the national and historical conception of theoretical science" (24)
4. "the historical-philosophical and statistical-theoretical orientations of research" (25)
5. "the conception of political economy as a specifically historical science" (25).

According to Menger, representatives of the first position held that the aim of both the social and the natural sciences was to propose strictly universal statements or laws, since such statements were required for explanation and prediction. He supported this position and regarded the problem of justifying natural laws, in contrast to social laws, as already solved. However, he also pointed out that although logical similarities existed regarding the justification of natural and social laws, it would be a serious mistake to draw simple methodological analogies between the natural and social sciences. All justification of the social sciences qua theoretical sciences must be based only upon the social sciences themselves: the special circumstances which the social sciences have to deal with must also be considered in developing their justification.

This was precisely the reason why he rejected the second position. Adherents of this position believed that social systems operated like organisms. Therefore they drew the conclusion that the social sciences should propose strictly universal statements or laws similar to the laws proposed by disciplines such as physiology and anatomy. Menger argued that this analogy was not only totally misleading, but the kind of laws proposed by physiology and anatomy were natural laws, i.e., strictly universal statements, and these laws had to be justified similarly to natural laws. Hence nothing could be gained from the attempt to establish the social sciences qua theoretical sciences in this way.[2]

2. Thus Menger's criticism of the "organic theory" is twofold. First he approaches this problem by considering whether such a theory can deliver a satisfactory explanation of social phenomena. Secondly he points out that even if we were prepared to accept the "organic theory" as a satisfactory explanation of social phenomena, this would not solve the epistemological problem of justifying strictly universal statements or laws.

Representatives of the third position rejected the idea that the social sciences ought to find and propose strictly universal statements or laws regarding socioeconomic phenomena. They argued that it would be impossible for the social sciences to find such laws, because the empirical basis of the social sciences changes. All that the social sciences could ever hope to achieve would be spatiotemporally restricted laws valid only for certain societies in a given historical period. Menger admitted that some methodological assertions of this position were correct, but only when reinterpreted. In any case, as he carefully pointed out, this position must be rejected for specific epistemological reasons. If methodological reasons implied that the task of the social sciences was to propose strictly universal statements or laws, then any argument failing to justify such statements as strictly universal clearly fails to solve the epistemological task of establishing the social sciences qua theoretical science.

Whereas representatives of the third position tried to establish the social sciences by narrowing their major goals, representatives of the fourth position tried to establish the social sciences as the theory of history. They held that the social sciences proposed laws *sui generis,* that is, laws of historical development. Menger rejected this position by rejecting the idea of laws of historical development (1883, 119n.).

The last "orientation of research" Menger treated, the fifth position, held that the social sciences strove in vain to establish laws of any kind: they could only propose specific historical explanations, because social phenomena were far too complex to be explained by any kind of law. As already shown, Menger fully agreed with the notion of specific historical explanations, and he therefore only rejected this position because it substituted the theoretical aim of the social sciences with a historical aim. Besides—as also shown above—he stressed the need for strictly universal statements or laws even for specific historical explanations. Thus he pointed out that the problem of justification of such laws cannot be solved simply by trying to substitute the aims of the social sciences.

Although Menger dealt with the four latter positions to some extent, his theoretical argument focused on what he believed to be the fundamental methodological assertions shared by the last three. He summarized these fundamental methodological assertions and constructed from this summary an epistemological position which he called the Historical School. He then severely criticized this school before developing his own epistemological justification of the social sciences qua theoretical sciences.

IV

Menger's devastating, immanent criticism of the Historical School attacked what he perceived to be the school's two basic methodological assumptions, upon which its epistemological position rested. The first was that the "natural sphere" was governed by strictly universal laws; thus one could search for such laws, since at least the possibility existed of their being uncovered, although discovery could be a matter of luck. In contrast to the "natural sphere," however, the "social sphere" was governed by change; searching for strictly universal laws would be in vain. Thus if the social sciences could find laws at all, they had to be laws of "lesser strictness":

> among the methodologists no view is more widespread than the one that in certain realms of the world of phenomena, and predominantly in that of nature, strict types and typical relationships can be observed; in others on the contrary, and especially in that of social phenomena only those of lesser strictness can. In other words, "laws of nature" can be observed only in the first realm; only "empirical laws," on the contrary, can be observed in the latter. (1883, 50–51)

Menger considered this argument invalid. He believed that turning to experience, or to some observed properties of the natural and social sphere, merely begged the question requiring solution and thus could not yield a satisfactory answer to the logical question of justifying strictly universal statements. Such a justification could only be provided by correct logical and epistemological arguments or, as he put it, by a correct "orientation of theoretical research." He pointed out that the methodological assertion of the Historical School—that the social sciences could never find laws in the sense of strictly universal valid statements—simply confused two different questions: the logical question of justifying strictly universal statements and the (metaphysical) problem of whether the universe was really governed by laws of the type expressed in the form of strictly universal statements. This methodological assertion of the Historical School, "so frequently found in the general theory of knowledge, will prove erroneous in the sequel. [For it is due to the error that] . . . that which on close examination turns out to be the result of different *orientations* of theoretical research in the individual realms of the world of phenomena is construed as the result of the differing natures of the *phenomena*" (1883, 51).

The second main assumption of the Historical School was tantamount to the following: similarly to the procedure of the theoretical natural sciences, the theoretical social sciences generalized their results by repeated observations from an empirical basis. The Historical School thought that the empirical basis of the social sciences was the history of mankind and that, for economics, the basis focused particularly on economic history. Since it was held that scientific knowledge was absolutely certain knowledge, the truth of which had been proven, science had to start by constituting an absolutely certain empirical basis. In conjunction with the first methodological argument of the Historical School, however, the achievement of true generalizations seemed almost impossible. This was because a changing empirical basis involved a high risk of failure for every far-reaching generalization.

According to Menger, the Historical School therefore tried to avoid abstraction from the empirical basis, that is, from the "immediate given." Instead it tried to "investigate the types and the typical relationships of phenomena as these present themselves to us in their 'full empirical reality,' *that is in the totality and the whole complexity of their nature*; in other words, to arrange the totality of real phenomena in definite empirical forms and to determine of the latter the regularities of their coexistence and succession in an empirical way" (1883, 56). His objection to this research orientation was that if it were carried out uncompromisingly to its full extent, nobody could ever attain knowledge:

> close examination . . . teaches us that the above idea is not strictly feasible. Phenomena in all their empirical reality are, according to experience, repeated in certain empirical forms. But this is never with perfect strictness, for scarcely ever do two concrete phenomena, let alone a larger group of them, exhibit a thorough agreement. There are no strict types in "empirical reality," i.e., when the phenomena are under consideration in the totality and the whole complexity of their nature. This might be the case if each individual concrete phenomenon were set up as a particular type. By this the purpose and usefulness of theoretical research would be completely invalidated. The desire to determine strict categories of empirical forms comprising "all empirical realities" (according to their full content) is therefore an unattainable goal of theoretical research. (56, 57)

He concluded that "an abstraction from certain features of phenomena in their full empirical reality is unavoidable. . . . Even the most realistic orientation of *theoretical* research imaginable must accordingly operate with abstractions" (79, 80).

According to Menger's analysis, we therefore have to reject the epistemological position of the Historical School for both logical and specific epistemological reasons: logically, because it cannot be carried out; epistemologically, because it cannot explain why the social sciences have to propose strictly universal statements, laws, or theories.

V

Since the methodological assertions of the Historical School had to be rejected, Menger developed his own ideas about the foundation of economics. He approached the problem first by considering whether the social sciences could be established qua theoretical sciences from a position thoroughly adhering to the principle that empirical statements, whether singular or strictly universal, should be decided exclusively by experience. This principle, which followed from considerations about how empirical statements could be decided to be true or false, may aptly be called the "principle of empiricism" (Popper 1979). It seems that Menger regarded this approach as the logical consequence of his logical and immanent epistemological criticism of the Historical School. For as we have seen, he only rejected the "naive empiricism" of this school, not its basic tenet, which was that empirical statements had to be decided by experience. Moreover, I believe that Menger would have been willing to admit that not all members of the Historical School supported naive empiricism.

Menger called the epistemological position which strictly adhered to this principle of empiricism the "realistic-empirical orientation of theoretical research" (1883, 54). He examined this epistemological position primarily with respect to two problems: the problem of concept formation and the problem of justifying strictly universal statements. To him, both problems seemed closely related, because he thought that they shared a similar logical structure. It seems, however, that in general he regarded the problem of concept formation, or that of analyzing terms or concepts, to be somewhat less important than the problem of justifying strictly universal statements. For instance, he pointed out that

> theoretical economics has the task of investigating the *general nature* and the *general connection* of economic phenomena, not of analyzing economic *concepts* and of drawing the logical conclusions resulting from this analysis. The phenomena, or certain aspects of them, and not their linguistic image, the concepts, are the object of theoretical research in the field of economy. (1883, 37 n. 4)

Concepts and terms are instruments, appropriate or inappropriate, but they will never, taken by themselves, yield knowledge of any significant interest:

> The analysis of the concepts may in an individual case have a certain significance for the *presentation* of the theoretical knowledge of economy, but the goal of research in the field of theoretical economics can only be the determination of the general nature and the general connection of economic *phenomena*. (1883, 37 n. 4)

Although Menger thought that concept analysis was not too important, he nevertheless tried to clarify the problems of the formation and status of scientific concepts within the social sciences. In dealing with this problem he seems to have been influenced by one of the most cherished methodological beliefs held during his time. According to this belief, science starts with meticulous descriptions of observed phenomena and thus requires, above all, precise definitions of the terms applied. Any such definition consists of two major parts: the term to be defined (the *definiendum*), and the definition formula which explains it (the *definiens*). (There is a third part to the definition, the *copula,* which is irrelevant to this discussion.) Now, according to Menger, the definiens provides a description of a "type" of phenomena. For instance, in defining the chemical concept of "gold" (definiendum), "gold" is defined as "a class of all objects with such and such chemical properties" (definiens). Menger's theory explaining how we form such classes or types of objects or phenomena is that we may actually observe such types in reality: "Experience teaches us . . . that definite phenomena are repeated, now with greater exactitude, now with lesser, and recur in the variation of things" (1883, 36). He thus reasoned that repeated observation of phenomena revealed certain similarities according to which phenomena should be grouped into classes or types by a process of abstraction. The term "gold" is simply an abbreviation of the class or type of objects which have certain chemical properties in common.

Menger emphasized, however, that we have to be aware of two important points when applying this method of concept formation. The first is that this method only yields "real concepts," "real types," "real forms," or "empirical forms" (1883, 105). I believe that by "real types" or "real concepts," etc., he simply meant "individuals" or "particulars." If, for instance, we use this method, we are only allowed to assert that the type or the class of golden objects refers only to objects observed at certain spatiotemporal points. Thus the real concept "gold" is defined as a class of objects with such and such chemical properties observed at point k and at time t. To give an example, the real concept of "gold" refers only to "the class of all golden objects at 10 A.M. in Vienna," which is clearly a particular.

Menger's second point concerned the application of the "realistic-empirical" method of concept formation. He acknowledged that with regard to the formation of real concepts, there would be no problem with "a theoretical science, whose field of research would comprise phenomena that exhibit no changes in any phase of their existence . . . since anyone who might have recognized the nature and laws of such phenomena at a definite moment would have recognized them in general" (1883, 105). He accentuated, however, that social phenomena do change in the course of their history. He freely admitted that some disciples of the Historical School, such as Knies, were correct to consider this point. Historical development must be considered when one forms the real concept of, for example, "worker" or "commercial crisis" or any similar concept. Menger explained that "if we want to get the real concept of 'worker' we must consider him not merely at the height of his development, but also in his period of development and in the period of the decline of his abilities" (1883, 105) and that "we can . . . make an analogous observation with respect to that development of economic phenomena which we have designated as one of *empirical forms*" (106). Menger therefore defined "real types" as "basic forms of real phenomena, within the typical image of which, however, a more or less broad scope is given for particularities (also for the development of the phenomena!)" (57).

My conjecture that Menger meant individuals or particulars by the term "real concepts" is supported on two grounds. The first is his considerations about the scientific character of "strict" or "exact types." The second is his method of dealing with the justification of universal statements within the epistemological position of the "realistic-empirical orientation of theoretical research." Menger started this analysis with an observation regarding the logical similarities pertaining to the problem of justifying strictly universal statements and the problem of concept formation on the basis of a "realistic orientation of research" (1883, 57). Referring to the logical situation of forming "real concepts," he said that this situation also prevailed "with respect to the second problem of theoretical research: the determination of typical relationships, *laws* of phenomena" (57).

He specified that laws based upon observations can never be claimed to be strictly universally valid. With regard to the justification of strictly universal statements within the "realistic-empirical orientation of theoretical research" he virtually offered Hume's argument against induction, although strangely without quoting him:

If the world of phenomena is considered in a strictly realistic way, then laws of the latter signify merely the actual regularities, determined by way of observation, in the succession and in the coexistence of real phenomena which belong to certain empirical forms. A "law" obtained from the above point of view can in truth only state that in reality, regularly or without exception, phenomena belonging to the empirical form C have followed the concrete phenomena belonging to the empirical forms A and B or that they were observed coexistent with them. The conclusion that the phenomenon C follows the phenomena A and B *in general* (that is, in all cases, even those not observed!), or that the phenomena under discussion here are *in general* coexistent, transcends experience, the point of view of strict empiricism. From the standpoint of the above manner of consideration it is *not strictly* warranted. (1883, 57)

Menger used the term "empirical laws" to refer to numerically universal statements, the truth of which is inferred from the truth of singular observational statements. These "empirical laws" are simply summaries of singular statements describing past observations. However, since these statements "are based on . . . observation . . . the criterion of their truth is accordingly experience" (1883, 70; my translation), and we may therefore test the statements in accordance with the principle of empiricism. Yet it is obvious that Menger's idea of testing does not correspond to the modern meaning of the term. For him, a contradiction between an empirical law and a new observation carried no methodological importance. Empirical laws only can be claimed to be true within a particular spatiotemporal domain, that is, set up only by those singular statements which the empirical law summarizes. Outside this domain, the empirical law claims neither to be true nor false, and—as Menger noted—contradictions of facts and empirical laws occur.

Menger concluded that the "realistic-empirical orientation of theoretical research" was logically sound. From an epistemological point of view, however, this position must be rejected, as it cannot establish strictly universal statements or laws: *"the realistic orientation of theoretical research excludes in principle, rather, in all realms of the world of phenomena the possibility of arriving at strict (exact) theoretical knowledge"* (1883, 58).

Thus the problem of establishing the social sciences qua theoretical sciences was still open. Yet Menger did seem to believe that there must be some solution to the problem, since the social sciences do propose laws claiming strict universality. Moreover, he believed that the social sciences must propose laws of this kind, as he tried to show by his analysis of the structure of the theoretical and historical explanations. He furthermore held that the problem of establishing the natural sciences as theoretical sciences had already been solved satisfactorily. Nevertheless, if "[the realistic-empirical orientation of theoretical research were the] only . . . orientation of theoretical research, or if it were the only justified one, . . . then the possibility of or the justification for any research aimed at exact theories of phenomena would a priori be out of the question" (1883, 58). Thus Menger believed it impossible that the only orientation for doing theoretical research could be the "realistic-empirical" one.

VI

Menger approached the problem of the possibility of a "strict" or "exact" orientation of theoretical research" by considering the formal requirements needed to establish the social sciences qua theoretical sciences. As with the "realistic-empirical orientation of theoretical research," he examined the question of concept formation and the problem of justifying strictly universal statements, which in this case he called "exact laws" (1883, 60ff.). His brief account of these formal conditions, provided here in its entirety, reads:

> The only rule of cognition for the investigation of theoretical truth, which as far as possible is verified beyond doubt not only by experience but simply by our laws of thinking, and which is of utmost fundamental importance for the *exact* orientation of research, is the statement that *whatever was observed in even only one case must always put in an appearance again under exactly the same actual conditions*; or, what is in essence the same thing, that strictly typical phenomena of a definite kind must always, under the same conditions, and, indeed in consideration of our laws of thinking, simply of *necessity,* be followed by strictly typical phenomena of just as definite and different a type. Phenomena A and B *must* under the same conditions always be followed by the strictly typical phenomenon C insofar as A and B are thought of as strictly typical and the succession of phenomena under discussion here has been observed even in only a single case. This rule holds true not only of the *nature* of phenomena but also of their *measure,* and experience not only offers us no exception to it, but such a thing simply seems inconceivable to the critical mind. (1883, 60; my translation)

I would like to point out that in this passage Menger discussed three different but closely related issues. First he stressed that the phenomena A, B, and C have to be "thought of as strictly typical" and thus was concerned with problems of concept formation, i.e., the problem of constituting "strict" or "exact types." Second, he also dealt with the question of justifying strictly universal statements, the "exact laws." While these two issues relate to the proper function of the rule of cognition, the third issue relates to the justification of the rule of cognition itself. His ideas concerning these issues are elaborated below.

For Menger the proposal of "strict" or "exact laws" presupposed "strict" or "exact types." But in contrast to the formation of "real types," which have the status of particulars, we arrive at "exact types" only by abstracting from all empirical peculiarities of the phenomena under investigation. These peculiarities comprise special properties arising from the phenomena's special situations in space and time. The definition of "exact types" therefore has to abstract from all special spatiotemporal circumstances, such that an "exact," or "strict," or "pure" term may come to comprise the class of all objects with such and such properties—whether they have been observed or ever will be observed. To refer to the example of "gold": "gold" is a strictly universal term, because contrary to the realistic concept of "gold," the definition of the "strict" or "exact" concept of "gold" is not restricted by any principles of individuation such as space and time. On this basis, it is suggested that Menger's "strict" or "exact types" may be perceived as universal terms.

It is interesting to note that Menger strictly differentiated "realistic types" and "exact types." Although he explained that the formation of "exact types," or concepts, is preceded by a "partially empirical-realistic analysis," he stressed that it is nevertheless "only a partially empirical-realistic analysis, i.e., [an analysis] without considering whether these [types are] in reality . . . present as *independent* phenomena" (1883, 60). However, as he pointed out, the "realistic orientation of theoretical research can only lead to 'real types' " (58) and thus to particulars. Hence he did not commit the error of the traditional school's logic in deriving universals directly from the particulars. According to the latter view, it is possible to arrive at universals by developing a hierarchy of terms simply by a generalization from individuals or particulars, i.e., by enlarging the range of a term and thereby diminishing the specificity of its content. Yet, as already shown (Popper 1979, 1984), this view is mistaken because it confuses the relative distinction between class and element on the one hand, with the absolute distinction of universals and particulars on the other. From this absolute distinction between universals and particulars it follows that there are two logical, mutually exclusive hierarchies of terms: one relating only to particulars and one only to universals.

Although Menger adhered to the absolute distinction between universals and particulars, he nevertheless admitted that the formation of exact types also had to proceed by a partially realistic empirical analysis. Thus he needed a theory that explained the transition from "real types," or particulars, to "exact types," or universals. He obviously believed that the rule of cognition provided such a link. This rule of cognition stated that *"whatever was observed in even only one case must always put in an appearance again under exactly the same actual conditions"* (1883, 60). Thus it is permissible to omit principles of individuation, such as space and time, from the definiens. However, since this procedure may occur at any level in the hierarchy of particulars, Menger tried to restrict this procedure to the most generally stated particulars, i.e., to the terms that are at the top of the hierarchy and characterized by a maximum of range and minimum of specific content. He believed that such terms define the simplest elements of everything real. In his argument against the attempt to avoid all abstraction he presumably used the phrase "simplest of everything real" in contrast to the phrase "the full complexity of reality." The "full complexity of reality" may only, according to Menger, be captured by terms of a very large content and a rather small range, i.e., by terms which lie at the very bottom of the hierarchy of terms. He therefore concluded his deliberations on how to arrive at "exact types" by stating that this analysis

> seeks to ascertain the *simplest elements* of everything real, elements which must be thought of as strictly typical just because they are the simplest. It [theoretical research] strives for the establishment of these elements by way of an only partially empirical-realistic analysis, i.e., without considering whether these in reality are present as *independent* phenomena. . . . In this manner theoretical research arrives at empirical forms which *qualitatively* are strictly typical. (1883, 60)

Turning to the problem of justifying strictly universal statements, or "exact laws," Menger emphasized again the logical similarities between this and the former problem. Referring to the problem of the formation of "exact" or "strict types," he pointed out that "in a similar way exact research solves the second problem of the theoretical sciences: the determination of the typical relationships, the *laws* of phenomena" (1883, 61). By "similar way" it appears that he meant that the rule of cognition may easily be introduced as a type of induction principle. His analysis of the "realistic-empirical orientation of theoretical research" showed that "empirical laws" cannot be claimed to be strictly universal, yet he also argued that no serious problems arose with respect to decisions concerning the truth value of an empirical law. In fact, he believed that empirical laws could easily be verified. However, a true empirical law conjoined with a true principle which asserts that "*whatever was observed in even only one case must always put in an appearance again under exactly the same conditions*" (60) yields a strictly universal statement or an exact law which is true. But Menger restricted the application of this rule: only the fundamental propositions of economics—for instance, that people usually try to achieve their goals in the best possible manner—could be transformed into exact laws. Economic theorists thus begin by depicting only simple situations on the basis of such propositions, then seek to ascertain the laws that prevail within such situations, and, lastly, analyze more complicated situations.

According to Menger, the exact laws were true by virtue of the truth of empirical laws and the induction principle; he furthermore thought that both kinds of statements were true beyond doubt. He believed that there was no difficulty in proving the truth of empirical laws; and the rule of cognition is, as he stated, "verified beyond doubt" and any exception to it "seems inconceivable to the critical mind." Hence in his analysis any contradiction between facts and exact laws was without any methodological significance. As for the truth of exact laws:

the law that the increased need for an item results in an increase of prices . . . is not true—is unempirical, when tested by reality in its full complexity. But what else does this prove than that the results of exact research do not happen to find their criterion in experience in the above sense? The above law is true in spite of all this, absolutely true . . . as soon as it is merely considered from the point of view which is adequate for exact research. (1883, 71–72)

Therefore, "testing the exact theory of economy by the full empirical method is simply a methodological absurdity, a failure to recognize the basis and presuppositions of exact research" (69).

Thus Menger was of the opinion that the "exact orientation of theoretical research," that is, strictly universal theories, can only be formulated at the expense of empiricism. If we establish strictly universal statements by way of the rule of cognition, then we have to reject the principle of empiricism. Either we adhere to the principle of empiricism and reject the principle of theoretism, or we adhere to the principle of theoretism and reject the principle of empiricism. Logically, there seems to be no other way out of this situation (Popper 1979, 43).

VII

Menger's solution of finding a sound epistemological justification of the theoretical social sciences can be depicted with the help of a diagram (figure 1).[3] The five key features may be elaborated as follows:

(a) Menger's principle of empiricism:
   Since all empirical statements "are based on . . . observation . . . the criterion of their truth is accordingly experience" (1883, 70; my translation).

(b) Menger's principle of theoretism:
   "We understand a concrete phenomenon in a *theoretical* way (on the basis of the corresponding theoretical sciences) by recognizing it to be a special case of a certain regularity (conformity to law) in the succession, or in the coexistence of phenomena" (44–45).

(c) Menger's objection to induction:
   "The conclusion that the phenomenon C follows the phenomena A and B *in general* (that is, in all cases, even those not observed!), or that the phenomena under discussion here are *in general* coexistent, transcends experience, the point of view of strict empiricism. From the standpoint of the above manner of consideration it is *not strictly* warranted" (57).

3. Such diagrams have been used by Popper (1979) and Nelson (1962).

PREMISES

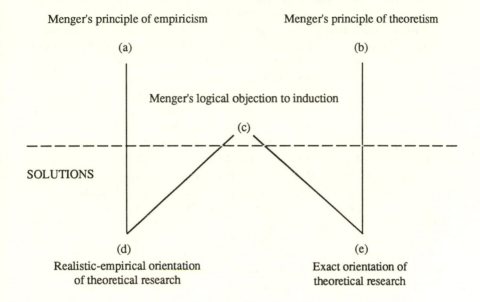

Figure 1.

(d) From (a) and (c) follows (d), the realistic-empirical orientation of theoretical research:

"If the world of phenomena is considered in a strictly realistic way, then laws of the latter signify merely the actual regularities, determined by way of observation, in the succession and in the coexistence of real phenomena which belong to certain empirical forms" (57).

(e) From (b) and (c) follows (e), the exact orientation of theoretical research:

"[An exact] law is true, absolutely true . . . as soon as it is merely considered from the point of view which is adequate for exact research" (72).

It has been shown that Menger believed that the "exact orientation of theoretical research" was based on the rule of cognition. Thus the question arises in what way he could have justified this rule; for if this rule could not be justified, the "exact orientation of theoretical research" and the exact laws have to be rejected as unfounded. He then would have had to admit that he was unable to achieve what he wanted: to establish the social sciences qua theoretical sciences.

Although the justification of the rule of cognition is vital for Menger's "exact orientation of theoretical research," he was remarkably brief about its justification. He simply stated that the rule of cognition "is verified beyond doubt not only by experience but simply by our laws of thinking" (1883, 60). He also seemed to have some kind of necessity in mind with respect to this rule, when he wrote: "experience not only offers us no exception to it but such a thing seems inconceivable to the critical mind" (60). Because he failed to provide any further argument for the foundation of the rule of cognition, the question arises whether he could have justified it and escaped the fatal consequences for attempting to establish the social sciences qua theoretical sciences.

However, any attempt to justify an induction principle either by experience or as a kind of synthetic a priori principle is bound to fail for logical reasons (Popper 1979, 70). Menger's attempt to justify the "exact orientation of theoretical research" therefore has to be rejected. Moreover, since the "exact orientation of theoretical research" can not clarify the possibility of a theoretical science claiming to be strictly universal and empirical, it has to be rejected not only for logical but for epistemological reasons as well.

It seems that Menger himself felt uneasy with his justification of economics. Although he considered unbridgeable the logical gap between the "realistic-empirical orientation of theoretical research" and the "exact orientation of theoretical research," he still tried to force an explanation because he emphasized the claim of the social sciences to explain reality, rather than an a priori fantasy world. Because of his emphasis on social science's ability to explain reality, he almost certainly felt the necessity of explaining this claim (1883, 55).

Since Menger admitted that there cannot be a satisfactory logical solution, he referred to what he described as "scientific usage," in which science uses both methods simultaneously when presenting and developing theories. This of course could lead to confusion because of the extreme difficulty in separating "exact laws" from "empirical laws," since these may appear highly similar. However, Menger stressed that this usage did not invalidate the logical argument concerning the two different epistemological foundations of economics (1883, 67).

VIII

The German economists (for instance, Roscher and Schmoller) quite clearly did not understand the methodological problems Menger had tried to solve in the *Investigations*. However, when the *Investigations* appeared in 1883 they certainly did realize his intention to launch a devastating attack on their methodological positions. Roscher, who had mentioned Menger's *Principles* in quite friendly terms in his *Geschichte der Nationalökonomie* (1874) and also in the twelfth edition of his textbook *Grundlagen der Nationalökonomie* (1875), now turned completely hostile. In the eighteenth edition of his textbook, published in 1886, he reviewed Menger's *Investigations* as follows:

> C. Menger's *Untersuchungen über die Methode der Socialwissenschaften und der polit. Oekonomie insbesondere* (1883) as a matter of fact only attacks the historical method, asserting not only the complete uselessness of the historical method for political economy, but also a complete misunderstanding of the essence of history. It seems that this ridiculous little piece of work is rather wasted in achieving its primary aim of destroying this pernicious method; however, involuntarily it is all the more instructive and typical for the older method, which abstracts from all reality and fails to recognize the organic whole of the economy and the life of a people. (1886, 62)

He also explicitly praised Schmoller's review of the *Investigations:* "cf. Schmoller's brilliant, and also for the general methodology important review in his yearbook N.F., Heft 3, 239ff." (62). Yet precisely this review quite clearly shows that Schmoller did not grasp Menger's ideas: he neither grasped Menger's point that naive empiricism has to be discarded for logical reasons, nor did he grasp Menger's logical argument against induction and its epistemological consequences.[4]

Although Menger's solution of finding a sound epistemological justification for economics of course cannot be regarded as satisfactory, it is most important to notice that he not only provided the Austrian school of economics with a most fruitful economic research program but also established a certain epistemological and methodological tradition. This tradition became the starting point for quite a number of methodological and epistemological investigations by Austrian economists. Apart from Menger various representatives of the Austrian School, such as Böhm-Bawerk, Wieser, Schumpeter, Machlup, and Hayek, not only developed the research program which Menger had provided for economics but

---

4. Schmoller writes: "The discrimination of the two orientations of research from which he [Menger] proceeds, doubtless is of some justification. . . . But this contrast must not be interpreted as an unbridgable gap" (1883, 977). He also believes that what Menger calls the "realistic-empirical orientation of theoretical research and the theoretical-exact orientation of theoretical research" is "nothing else but what is generally called inductive and deductive procedures" (978). Schmoller virtually holds a position which can be called "naive inductivism," i.e. an epistemological position which does not consider Hume's and also Menger's logical argument against induction.

also contributed to the methodological and epistemological tradition he established.

In effect Menger's epistemological and methodological considerations set out two central problems with which the Austrians have grappled ever since. The first of these concerns the question of the methodological or epistemological status of economic theories. Austrian writers have tried to resolve the question of distinguishing economics from other areas of inquiry, such as the natural sciences, mathematics and logic, morals and ethics, and philosophy and metaphysics. The question they put forward was whether economic theories may be regarded as empirical theories which are decided by experience, or as systems of implicit definitions which instead share the status of logic or mathematics. Alternatively, they considered the possibility that economic theories have to be regarded as a special kind of theory, a "theory *sui generis*" which shares neither the epistemological status of empirical theories nor those of logic. This question was of course the central issue in the *Methodenstreit,* because the falsification of classical price theory had led to methodological discussions of the role of experience with respect to social and economic theories.

Nevertheless, although Menger, Böhm-Bawerk, Wieser, Schumpeter, Mises, and also Hayek shared this interest in solving this problem, which, following Popper, may be called the demarcation problem in economics, they provided different solutions for it. As we have seen, Menger held that economic theories may be either empirical or a priori valid, depending on the method of their justification. Mises (1933, 1940) believed that economic theories are not only genetically, or psychologically, a priori but also a priori valid; Schumpeter's (1908) orientation was to consider economic theories in terms of implicit definitions, and Böhm-Bawerk (1924, vol. 2) apparently believed that economic theories are empirical theories which are decided solely by experience. In contrast, Hayek puts forward quite a different solution. Like Böhm-Bawerk, he holds that economic theories are empirical theories, i.e., theories which may be decided by logical argument and experience. But he also stresses that economic models can only yield negative knowledge, i.e., that they can only exclude certain classes of events but can never be verified (1952). According to Hayek, who in this respect is influenced by Popper (1984), models remain conjectures, open to improvement.

Hayek's view that models can only yield negative knowledge and are always open to improvement constitutes a major difference from the methodological views of Menger, Mises, and Schumpeter and perhaps to a lesser extent from those of Böhm-Bawerk. The aim of these writers was to find a sound (i.e., a sure) epistemological justification for economic or social theories. Their attempt to solve the demarcation problem was led by the quest for certainty. Menger tried to establish the conditions for certain knowledge by distinguishing between an "empirical orientation of theoretical research" and an "exact orientation of theoretical research"; but he believed that both orientations may yield certain knowledge if applied properly. Mises's aim was to find a source of knowledge which yields certain knowledge, knowledge which is not only genetically or psychologically a priori but also valid a priori. Schumpeter sought certainty within a system of implicit definitions which cannot be refuted. Böhm-Bawerk, apparently deeply impressed by the fallibility of human knowledge, sought to substitute for full certainty some kind of partial certainty. Hayek, however, deeply influenced in this matter by Popper's solution of the problem of induction and the problem of demarcation, a solution which shows the futility of striving for certainty or partial certainty, abandons this quest for certainty. His solution differs from the others' in that he does not try to provide an epistemological justification for economic theories. For although he believes, like Mises, that introspection is most important for the development of a new theory or model within the social sciences, in contrast to Mises he does not draw any conclusion as to the validity of such a model from this source of knowledge (see Hayek 1952).

The second fundamental problem the Austrians have dealt with, which is closely connected to the first one, concerns the aim and the task of the social sciences and thus what kind of explanation may be regarded as a satisfactory explanation in the social sciences. However, while their solutions to the demarcation problem differ to a considerable extent, there is a general agreement on what can be regarded as a satisfactory explanation in the social sciences. Accordingly the aim and the task of the theoretical social sciences is to explain social and economic phenomena or institutions as the unintended consequences of individual rational actions. Society or social institutions are the result of human action but not a product of human design, because the interplay of rational individual actions constitutes an always new world of structural relationships, which is, although it is man-made, largely autonomous. The philosophical background of this thinking ranges back to Mandeville, Hume, Smith, and Ferguson. However, this tradition was most forcefully developed and revived by Menger. Considering the state of the methodological and epistemological tenets with regard to the social sciences held by the German economists of his time, I would like to suggest that Menger's approach to economics was truly revolutionary.

My cordial thanks go to Pam Hottenstein, Werner Neudeck, Barry Smith, and David Miller and to the members of the Department of Philosophy of the University of Warwick, for their most generous help during my stay in the winter term of 1987.

References

Boos, M. 1986. *Die Wissenschaftstheorie Carl Mengers*. Graz.

Böhm-Bawerk, E. von. 1924. *Gesammelte Schriften von Eugen von Böhm-Bawerk*. Edited by Franz X. Weiss. Vienna.

Diehl, K. 1908. Die Entwicklung der Wert- und Preistheorie im neunzehnten Jahrhundert. In *Die Entwicklung der Volkswirtschaftslehre im neunzehnten Jahrhundert: Gustav Schmoller zur siebzigsten Wiederkehr seines Geburtstages*. Leipzig.

Dobretsberger, J. 1949. Zur Methodenlehre C. Mengers und der österreichischen Schule. In *Neue Beiträge zur Wirtschaftstheorie: Festschrift anlässlich des 70. Geburtstages von H. Mayer*. Vienna.

Hayek, F. A. von. 1952. *The counterrevolution of science*. Glencoe, Ill.

Hermann, F. W. 1832. *Staatswirthschaftliche Untersuchungen*. Munich.

Hildebrand, B. 1848. *Die Nationalökonomie der Gegenwart und Zukunft*. Frankfurt am Main.

Hutchison, T. W. 1973. Some themes from investigations into method. In *Carl Menger and the Austrian school of economics,* edited by J. R. Hicks and W. Weber. Oxford.

Kauder, E. 1958. Intellectual and political roots of the older Austrian School. *Zeitschrift für Nationalökonomie* 17.

———. 1962. Aus Mengers nachgelassenen Papieren. *Weltwirtschaftliches Archiv* 89.

Kerschagl, R. 1925. *Einführing in die Methodenlehre der Nationalökonomie*. Vienna.

Keynes, J. N. 1891. *The scope and method of political economy*. London.

Knies, C. 1853. *Die politische Oekonomie vom Standpunkte der geschichtlichen Methode*. Braunschweig.

———. 1873. *Geld und Kredit*. Berlin.

———. 1930. *Die politische Ökonomie vom geschichtlichen Standpunkt*. Leipzig.

Mangoldt, H. von. 1863. *Grundriss der Volkswirthschaftslehre*. Stuttgart.

Menger, C. 1871. *Grundsätze der Volkswirthschaftslehre*. Vienna. Translated as *Principles of economics*. New York, 1981.

———. 1883. *Untersuchungen über die Methode der Socialwissenschaften und der politischen Oekonomie inbesondere*. Leipzig. (*Gesammelte Werke,* edited by F. A. von Hayek, vol. 2. Tübingen, 1969.) Translated and edited by L. Schneider as *Investigations into the method of the social sciences with special reference to economics*. New York, 1985.

Mises, L. von. 1933. *Grundprobleme der Nationalökonomie*. Jena.

———. 1940. *Nationalökonomie*. Genf.

Nelson, L. 1962. Fortschritte und Rückschritte der Philosophie. *Gesammelte Schriften in neun Bänden,* edited by Paul Bernays, Willy Eichler, et al., vol. 7. Hamburg, 1977.

Popper, K. R. 1961. *The poverty of historicism*. London.

———. 1979. *Die beiden Grundprobleme der Erkenntnistheorie*. Tübingen.

———. 1984. *Logik der Forschung*. 8th ed. Tübingen.

Rau, K. H. 1841. *Lehrbuch der politischen Oekonomie*. Heidelberg.

Ricardo, D. 1817. *On the principles of political economy and taxation*. London.

Ritzel, G. 1950. *Schmoller versus Menger*. Frankfurt am Main.

Roscher, W. 1842. *Leben, Werk und Zeitalter des Thukydides*. Göttingen.

———. 1843. *Grundriss zu Vorlesungen über die Staatswirtschaft nach geschichtlicher Methode*. Göttingen.

————. 1874. *Geschichte der National-Oekonomik in Deutschland*. Munich.

————. 1875. *Grundlagen der Nationalökonomie*. 12th ed. Stuttgart.

————. 1886. *System der Volkswirthschaft*. Vol. 1. Stuttgart.

Schlick, M. 1925. *Allgemeine Erkenntnistheorie*. Berlin.

Schmoller, G. 1875. *Über einige Grundfragen der Rechts- und der Volkswirthschaft*. Jena.

————. 1883. Zur Methodologie der Staats- und Sozialwissenschaften. *Jahrbuch für Gesetzgebung, Verwaltung und Volkswirthschaft 7*.

————. 1884. Antwortbrief. *Jahrbuch für Gesetzgebung, Verwaltung und Volkswirthschaft 8*.

————. 1908. *Grundriss der Allgemeinen Volkswirthschaftslehre*. Leipzig.

Schumpeter, J. von. 1908. *Das Wesen und der Hauptinhalt der Nationalökonomie*. Berlin.

————. 1986. *History of economic analysis*. London.

Smith, A. 1776. *An inquiry into the nature and causes of the wealth of nations*. London.

Smith, B. 1986. Austrian economics and Austrian philosophy. In *Austrian economics: historical and philosophical background*, edited by W. Grassl and B. Smith. London.

Streissler, E. 1987. Carl Menger der deutsche Nationalökonom. Manuscript. Vienna.

Wieser, F. von. 1884. *Über den Ursprung und die Hauptgesetze des wirthschaftlischen Werthes*. Vienna.

White, L. 1977. *The methodology of the Austrian School economists*. New York.

A roundabout solution
to a fundamental problem in Menger's
methodology and beyond

Jack Birner

It pays to study Carl Menger's methodology of economics because he addresses problems that are still relevant today. One of these concerns the relation between explanatory general theories and empirical models. Menger does not solve this problem. I shall sketch the setting of Menger's formulation of the problem and show how his theory of knowledge prevents him from solving it. Then I shall discuss a later attempt to solve a generalized version of Menger's problem from a different, more promising epistemological perspective. But it turns out that this attempt fails too, because it takes too little notice of the idealizing character of general theories, a point which was elaborated extensively by Menger. Finally, a third solution will be discussed, one which combines features of both previous attempts.

Carl Menger wrote two full-size books: *Principles of economics,* of 1871, and *Investigations into the method of the social sciences,* which was published in 1883.[1] The books not only differ in content, but there is a marked difference in style as well. *Principles,* which contains his economic theory, is a very diplomatically written book. Although it contains an economic theory that is introduced as an alternative to the theory of the Historical School, it is nevertheless dedicated to Wilhelm Roscher, the protagonist of the older Historical School. Menger goes out of his way to present his own theory in as polite and inoffensive a form as possible. The conciliatory tone is radically abandoned in *Investigations,* Menger's book on the methodology of social science "with special reference to economics," as its subtitle says. Whereas *Principles,* though critical of the accepted, classical economic theory, is largely constructive, *Investigations* is an extensive critical comment on a variety of methodological positions, which Menger lumps together under the name of "Historical School." The polemical character of the

---

1. I have used the English titles in general discussion and also when specifically referring to the standard published English translations (see Menger 1981, 1985). Otherwise I have used German titles for specific citations and quotations—references are to Hayek's edition (Menger 1968)—including translations that are my own.

latter book makes it much harder to understand what the substance of Menger's own methodology is. It is only rarely that he states his views in a direct way; most of the time we have to deduce, or guess, from his criticism what his positive ideas are.[2]

It has often been observed that in order to understand Menger's methodology of social science one has to study his economic theory as well. This is true in the sense that for Menger, his writings on methodology were a means of pursuing the diplomatic offensive which he had begun in the field of economic theory, but then by different means. *Investigations* is, among other things, a weapon in a partisan war.[3] It was written when Menger discovered that his economic theory did not meet with the recognition he was convinced it deserved. In *Investigations,* and in later methodological writings,[4] he defended, by means of a methodological justification, the type of economic theory he had developed in *Principles:* a very general and abstract theory, which unifies all true fragments of existing economic knowledge. He argues that this approach deserves a place side by side with others, such as empirical and applied economic theory. We may say that Menger wanted to solve a demarcation problem: not in the sense that he wanted to show that the methods of the Historical School were unscientific, but rather that he wished to clarify the fundamental differences between its approach and the one he had followed in his *Principles*.

My observation about the strategic character of *Investigations* is not meant to imply that it does not reflect ideas on method that Menger truly held, or that it is a shallow book, because that is not true. But if one wants to understand its structure, it helps to keep in mind the place it

2. *Investigations* is generally considered to be a difficult book because of its style. I beg to disagree. Granted, it contains a lot of repetition, but every once in a while Menger adds to previous remarks, thus enabling us to get a better understanding of what he is trying to say. The style reveals his skill and experience as a journalist: the book reads like a newspaper article. What has probably fooled many a reader is the irony, a rhetorical style not expected from a German-language scholar. But then Menger was not a German but an Austrian, and not even an ordinary Austrian but an inhabitant of Vienna.

The failure to recognize the irony is one reason why the standard English translation is very unreliable. Let me mention just one blunder: Menger argues that it is wrong to criticize economists, as the Historical School does, for their belief that the economic motive is the only factor that accounts for human behavior. He quotes the examples of several economists who did not hold this narrow view, one of them being Adam Smith. To drive this point home, he ironically remarks: "Hat der letztere doch eine eigene Theorie des Gemeinsinnes geschrieben!" (*Untersuchungen,* 80; "The latter has even written a theory of moral sentiments of his own!"). The translators render this in a way that implies the opposite meaning of the original and betrays a staggering ignorance of the material: "If the last of these had only written his own theory of public spirit!" (*Investigations,* 88).

3. Cf. Clausewitz 1832, 34: "Der Krieg ist eine blosse Fortsetzung der Politik mit anderen Mitteln" ("War is a mere continuation of politics by different means").

4. *Grundzüge einer Klassifikation der Wirtschaftswissenschaften* (1889) is the most important of these. I draw on this publication too, as it contains a more detailed elaboration of some of Menger's ideas.

occupies in Menger's work, and especially the way in which it is related to *Principles*.

The methodology of *Investigations* can be summarized in one brief maxim: "To each goal its method." According to Menger, there are different goals of science, and a method that is conducive to attaining one goal is not appropriate to others. Menger defends a strong type of methodological pluralism. The structure of the book is dictated by Menger's distinction of the goals of science—of *all* science, that is, not only of social science.[5] The classification of the goals of science follows from the differences between types of knowledge in general: knowledge of the individual or concrete phenomena in time and space, and knowledge of the phenomena in their regular recurrence. To each goal corresponds one type of science: the study of individual phenomena is the domain of the historical sciences; the tools for studying phenomena that display regularities are provided by the theoretical sciences.

Mature scientific disciplines are characterized by the existence of the following subdisciplines:[6]

1. The historical sciences study the individual or concrete phenomena,[7] the individual essence, and relations. They comprise (1.1) statistics, which studies the static aspect[8] of the concrete phenomena of the real world, and (1.2) history, which studies the concrete phenomena of the real world in their development.

2. Some theoretical sciences comprise morphological sciences, whose object it is to provide knowledge of the essence of generally determined phenomena (or what is the same, the general types[9] of the phenomena, or typical phenomena) by means of the analytical-compositive method. This method consists of an analytical dissection of complex real phenomena into their elements and a subsequent reassembly of these into the elementary factors of one particular discipline.[10] The morphological sciences pave the way to theoretical science,[11] though not all theoretical sciences have a separate morphological branch.

3. The theoretical sciences provide "knowledge that transcends immediate experience."[12] They study the relations and the inter-

5. *Wissenschaft* means more than "natural science." It denotes all scientific disciplines in the broadest sense. I translate it as "science."

6. *Grundzüge*, 4.

7. And are thus purely descriptive.

8. "Unter dem Gesichtspunkt der Zuständlichkeit." It is hard to believe the choice of the word *statistics* for the static approach is accidental.

9. Menger uses "Gemeinbilder."

10. This point is elaborated below.

11. Menger dedicates paragraph 4 of *Grundzüge* to the question whether morphology is an independent subdiscipline of economics.

12. *Untersuchungen*, 50.

nal structure[13] of the generally determined phenomena, that is, their laws. They yield nomological knowledge of the general essence of phenomena, that is, of typical phenomena.

To this classification Menger adds:

4. The practical sciences. They aim at discovering the principles and procedures that are required for shaping the phenomena according to predetermined objectives. "It is their task . . . to determine the principles that, given the circumstances, make it possible to pursue definite objectives. They teach us what, given the circumstances, *ought to be* the case in order for definite human goals to be reached."[14]

In the natural sciences the development that has led to this diversification has largely been completed, as is the case in *Staatswissenschaften* and *Jurisprudenz*. But economics has lagged behind in its development,[15] and the categories are still confused. This confusion and lack of diversification is typical of a young and immature discipline. In Germany the lack of progress in economics is due to the mistaken methodology of the dominant Historical School. It wrongly claims that the historical method is capable of producing universally valid laws and that the truth of empirical laws is more justified than the truth of purely theoretical or exact laws.

Menger gives what amounts to a reductio ad absurdum of the former claim.[16] In order to be general, a theory has to abstract from nonrelevant and secondary factors; general theories are theories of the relations between typical phenomena. Menger observes that it would be possible to derive universal laws by means of the methods of the realistic-empirical approach, to which the historical method belongs, only "if each individual concrete phenomenon were set up as a particular type."[17] But then such knowledge would not be of any *general* use. This does not mean that Menger thinks historical knowledge is useless. On the contrary, historical knowledge is valuable, but only in its appropriate context.

If economics is to develop into a mature science, it has to be reorganized along the lines of the above division of labor. Therefore, Menger sees it as his primary task to make "the community of writers on economics recognize . . . the significance of this systematization for the *exposition* and more in particular the *understanding of the internal*

13. "Innere Zusammenhang."
14. *Untersuchungen*, 7.
15. *Grundzüge*, 5.
16. *Investigations*, 56–57.
17. *Investigations*, 57.

structure of the results of scientific research, and [to make] . . . the students of our discipline fully realize the impossibility of a systematic (in one system!) presentation of the results of the different epistemological approaches."[18]

Theoretical economics

The classification of scientific disciplines serves as a general framework for Menger's main objective: to show that his economic theory of the *Principles* delivers what the Historical School has so far failed to supply: a general, universally valid theory. In order to be universally valid, a theory must be true without exceptions. Both requirements, generality and universal validity, can only be met by idealizing theories of a particular kind. In order to show that his economics fulfills these requirements, whereas the theory and the method of the Historical School do not, Menger introduces a further distinction within theoretical economics. He distinguishes two directions of research: the *exact* orientation, which studies the laws of *Wirtschaftlichkeit* ("economicity"), i.e., the laws governing *ideal* economic phenomena; and the *realistic-empirical* branch, which studies the regularities in the succession and coexistence of *real* phenomena.[19] In scientific practice empirical and exact science are usually intertwined. Menger sets them up as *ideal types* so as to be better able to separate them.

In terms of this classification, the economic theory of *Principles* is an *exact* theory. So by his own standards Menger has accomplished no mean feat: he has elevated economics to the methodological status of physics and the other mature sciences. By comparison the Historical School has done less well; all *it* has attained so far is *historical* knowledge, and theoretical knowledge of the *empirical* variety. Menger introduces the exact approach, with its exact laws, as distinct from the historical and the empirical approach with their historical and empirical laws, which are not universally valid, in order to maximize the distance between his exact approach of the *Principles* and the type of theory of the Historical School.

Menger seeks a solution to his strategical problem along systematic or methodological lines. But this in its turn creates the logical or epistemological problem of what the relationship between empirical and exact theoretical research is. Menger explicitly recognizes this as a problem; the discussion of the characteristics of these two directions of research and their relations occupies much of *Investigations*. He has great difficulty explaining how they are related. This is hardly surprising. The problem is a general one: it is raised every time an idealizing theory is

18. *Grundzüge*, 6.
19. *Untersuchungen*, 5.

claimed to be relevant for understanding reality. And it is a difficult problem, as witnessed by the fact that despite extensive discussion it has not been solved to this very day.[20]

The methodological problem

Most students of Menger have neglected the systematic or methodological aspect of the problem.[21] Apparently it is assumed that the methodological relation between exact and empirical theories stands in no need of elucidation. I do not agree; there is a problem which remains to be solved. The solution which I propose offers a coherent interpretation of everything which Menger says on the methodological relation between exact and empirical theories. Thus many passages which seem obscure can be given a straightforward interpretation.

In order to arrive at an explication of how the empirical and exact theoretical sciences are related methodologically, I take as my guidance the few explicit observations that Menger makes about the relations between the various types of discipline. He says that the historical sciences study *all* sides of *certain* phenomena.[22] The theoretical sciences study *certain* sides of *all* phenomena.[23] But this goes for both the empirical and the exact theoretical sciences, and Menger does not specify how these two are related. I propose that we extend or extrapolate his classification by adding that the exact theoretical sciences are about *certain* sides of *all* phenomena *in abstraction from disturbing factors*.

This extrapolation is in exact keeping with a methodological distinction between two sorts of abstraction which is basic to *Investigations,* though Menger does not make this distinction explicit in general terms. It is precisely this lack of explication on his part that makes it so difficult to grasp the relationships between exact and empirical theoretical science.

Most methodological precepts have their roots in ontological considerations, and Menger's are no exception. He believes in the existence, in reality, of several fundamental motives for human behavior, which he calls alternately "influences" (*Einflüsse*), "goals" (*Bestrebungen*), "drives" (*Triebe*), "forces" (*Kräfte*), and "fundamental tendencies of human nature" (*Grundtendenze der Menschennatur*).[24] The particular drives that he mentions are the economic drive (which he considers by

20. The discussion has taken a new turn with the work of the Polish philosophers L. Nowak and W. Krajewski. For a discussion and an application of this work to an episode in recent economic theory development see Birner 1990a, 1990b.

21. Thus I find Milford's attempt (this issue) to look for a solution in Menger too one-sided in this respect.

22. *Untersuchungen,* 67; *Investigations,* 79.

23. Ibid.

24. *Untersuchungen,* 78.

far the most important), *Gemeinsinn* (which one might be tempted to translate as "common sense" but by which Menger means very clearly "moral sentiments" in the sense of Adam Smith),[25] altruism, and justice.[26] Menger firmly believes in the necessity for causal explanation: "Scire est per causas scire."[27] Ultimately all social phenomena can be reduced to the fundamental human drives. So these are the ultimate causes in social science. The methodological import of these basic drives is that they delineate the boundaries between scientific disciplines: economics, social philosophy (or perhaps sociology), ethics, and jurisprudence in the above cases. Each of these disciplines studies human behavior under one of these different aspects, to the exclusion of the others.

Within each discipline, the working of one fundamental drive can be studied in various degrees of purity, i.e., by abstracting in a greater or smaller degree from disturbing factors which are operative in reality. The more the disturbing factors are abstracted from, the stronger is the operation of the relevant fundamental drive brought to the fore.

For both an explicit distinction and a fortunate terminology describing exactly the methodological distinction that Menger has in mind, we have to turn to Friedrich von Wieser. Wieser distinguishes between *isolating abstraction* and *emphasizing abstraction*.[28] Wieser's concept of isolating abstraction is based on the ontological idea that there exist certain fundamental causes of whatever is observable. As in reality all these causes operate together, the theoretician has the task to single out the operation of one such cause in order to gain a better understanding of the reality behind the appearances.

For Menger, this is the crux of the analytical-compositive method, which in some sciences is delegated to a morphological subdiscipline.[29] The elementary forms or types which this science of morphology finds and without which theoretical laws could not be expressed, are "the result of a real analysis of the complex phenomena into their elementary factors and of the *isolating synthesis* of these."[30] However, the mere isolation of a single fundamental cause does not guarantee that we can study it in its pure form. For that purpose, we have to abstract from factors which inhibit the full working of that single cause. Exact theoretical science thus involves both types of abstraction.

Menger specifically mentions four disturbing factors which have to be

25. See note 2 above.
26. "Das reine Walten des Rechtsgefühls," *Untersuchungen*, 73. From the way these drives are introduced it is clear that to Menger's mind this enumeration is not exhaustive.
27. *Untersuchungen*, 87.
28. These are my translations of Wieser's "isolierende" and "hervorhebende Abstraktion." See Wieser 1914, 134–35.
29. *Grundzüge*, para. 4.
30. *Grundzüge*, 10, emphasis added.

Table 1.   Basic drives and disturbing factors

Disturbing factors (emphasizing abstraction)	Basic drives (isolating abstraction)				
	Economic drive	Morality	Altruism	Justice	etc.
Error	[Within each of the disciplines defined by one particular basic drive, the operation of that drive can be studied on various levels of emphasizing abstraction. Gradually abstracting from error, ignorance, etc., is something which recurs in each of the disciplines.]				
Ignorance					
Force					
Neglect					

abstracted from if we are to find the exact laws of economics:[31] ignorance, error, external force, and the degree in which people let themselves be guided by a fundamental drive (in the case of economics it is the degree to which people attend to their economic interests; for brevity's sake we shall call the absence of it "neglect"). Thus we obtain the matrix classification shown in table 1. Menger classifies disciplines that study, e.g., the economic aspect of *real* phenomena, i.e., abstract from the other fundamental aspects, without abstracting from error, ignorance, etc., as *empirical* theoretical disciplines. Disciplines that abstract *both* from the other fundamental aspects *and* from the disturbing factors are classified as *exact* theoretical disciplines. So, exact theories are even more idealized than empirical theories; they are about isolated aspects of *ideal* phenomena. This is what the *Principles* contains: a theory of purely economic goods, values, and exchange.

The logical and epistemological problem

The introduction of different goals of science with their corresponding scientific methods may contribute to solving Menger's strategical or methodological problem of justifying an approach along the lines of his *Principles,* but it does so at the price of introducing a different, though related, logical or epistemological problem.

Throughout *Investigations,* the idea is maintained that the various types of analysis, historical, practical, and theoretical,[32] have their place side by side as far as their usefulness is concerned. However, logically they are not all on a par; one discipline presupposes the results

31. Indeed, of *all* sciences of human behavior. Cf. *Grundsätze,* 78.
32. Morphological analysis in the sense used in Menger's methodology does not have a place that is independent of theoretical analysis. Cf. *Grundzüge,* para. 4.

of the others.[33] The system of economic sciences is ordered accordingly. Thus morphology yields the pure types whose relations are studied by theoretical analysis. In this sense we may speak of the types of analysis as levels of science. Menger does not make it clear whether this presupposition relation exists between exact and empirical analysis as well, although particular passages suggest this is the case. But even if empirical analysis presupposes exact analysis, Menger leaves no doubt about the idea that attempting to test the predictions of exact laws empirically[34] involves a category mistake and is a methodological absurdity.[35] If the test has a negative outcome, we must conclude not that the exact law is false, but merely that it is not applicable. Exact laws cannot be refuted by the results of empirical analysis. If a prediction of an exact law is not borne out empirically, Menger concludes:

> What else does this prove but that experience in the above sense [empirical evidence] is no test of the results of exact research (theorizing)? The above [exact] law is despite all this true, completely true, and of the highest significance to the theoretical understanding of price phenomena, provided one considers it [the law] under the point of view which is adequate for (in accordance with) theoretical research. If one looks at it from the point of view of realistic research, one runs into contradictions; however, in this case the mistake does not lie in the above [exact] law, but in the wrong way of looking at it.[36]

Menger even goes so far as to say, in *Principles,* that a negative test result is to be blamed on the pathology of the real economy, where ignorance, error, force, and sloppiness rule.[37] We can see here that Menger's pluralism is a very rigid one indeed, and that it may lead to instrumentalist conclusions.

On the other hand, Menger is a scientific realist: he maintains that both empirical and exact theories are descriptions of reality. The *Princi-*

---

33. Cf. *Grundzüge,* 9: "History and statistics, together with the common experience of life, are important foundations of the theoretical sciences, and the latter in their turn are the foundations of the practical disciplines," and 21: "History, morphology, and theory of economic phenomena are important and even indispensable auxiliary sciences of the practical sciences."

34. Apparently Menger believed that nonempirical tests are possible; cf. *Untersuchungen,* 43 n. 19: "The method of exact research, the part which experiment plays in it, its speculative element which transcends the experiment and all experience, particularly in the formulation of the 'exact laws,' is not the subject of our exposition in this work. Together with a critique of Baconian induction it will be explained separately elsewhere." The promised monograph on Bacon was never published and perhaps not even written.

35. *Untersuchungen,* 54.

36. *Untersuchungen,* 57.

37. *Grundsätze,* 201; *Principles,* 216.

ples is put forward as a theory which is to provide practically involved people with a scientific foundation for their conduct by laying bare the real causal laws of economics.[38] But the problem of the precise relationship between exact and empirical analysis is not solved.

For Menger (and his contemporaries)[39] the logical or epistemological problem of the relation between exact and empirical theory is a problem about the justification of knowledge: how can practical, historical, empirical-theoretical, and exact-theoretical knowledge be given a foundation that is true beyond doubt? Knowledge is certain knowledge, or has to be reducible, by infallible (logical) means, to certain knowledge. It is very important in assessing Menger's solution to his problem to keep this justificationist framework in mind.

The method by which knowledge about the world is to be achieved, is the method of induction. For Menger, context of discovery and context of justification are not separated.[40] How true one's knowledge is, is fully determined by the method one uses in obtaining it. Thus the exact method guarantees the truth of exact laws:

> The goal of this orientation, which henceforth we will call the *exact* one, and which is pursued in the same way in all domains of the world of phenomena, is the determination of strict laws of the phenomena, of regularities in the succession of phenomena. Not only do these laws appear to us as being without exceptions; by virtue of the epistemic ways by which we have arrived at them, they even bear the guarantee of being without exceptions. These laws are commonly called "laws of nature," but it is much more correct to call them "*exact laws.*"[41]

Menger's joint justificationist-inductivist theory of knowledge entails that abstraction is conceived of as a *process* rather than as the description of a set of hypotheses with particular properties, regardless of how they are arrived at.

But Menger is not a naive inductivist. He is well aware of the logical problem that arises if one maintains that general, universally valid laws can be derived from a finite number of observation statements.[42] His

38. *Principles*, preface.
39. With the possible exception of Whewell. Hansen (1968) makes much of the supposed connection between Menger's opponent Schmoller's ideas on the method of science and Whewell's. But I have been unable to find any "essential" relevant references to Whewell in Schmoller's published work.
40. Menger repeatedly speaks of "Bürgschaften der Wahrheit," guarantees of truth.
41. *Untersuchungen*, 38. The term "natural laws" is less appropriate, as it suggests that we are dealing with natural phenomena instead of the "moral" phenomena of human nature.
42. *Untersuchungen*, 34–35.

distinction between exact and empirical science would collapse if this were possible. But for a justificationist the recognition of the impossibility of justifying universal laws inductively raises the problem that he has to explain how universal laws *are* to be justified. Menger explicitly denies that they can be derived from a priori true principles,[43] and rejects the idea that universal laws can be found by means of conceptual analysis.[44]

But he also gives some positive hints as to how exact laws are found, by suggesting that it involves an act of mental construction.[45] "Pure types" need not have ontological correlates.

It [theoretical research] aims at establishing these elements by means of an analysis which is only in part empirical-realistic, i.e., without considering whether these elements occur in reality as *independent* phenomena, and even without considering whether they can be depicted at all in their full purity.[46]

The constructed nature of these pure types (*reine Typen*) emerges again in the next sentence:

In this way theoretical research arrives at phenomenal forms which are *qualitatively* strictly typical, at results of theoretical research which certainly may not be tested against full empirical reality (because the phenomenal forms that are here referred to, e.g., absolutely pure oxygen, alcohol, or gold, or a human being who pursues absolutely only economic goals, etc., *exist in part only in our idea*.[47]

In these passages Menger seems to come close to breaking out of the inductivist framework. But he does not take this decisive step. The problem is left unsolved, and Menger remains a reluctant inductivist.

Menger's position vis-à-vis exact laws finds itself caught in a fourfold predicament. Exact laws are: (1) not a priori truths; (2) nor the result of conceptual analysis; (3) nor are they empirical; (4) and they can be and must be justified. Item 3 seems to be unproblematic in view of Menger's idea that exact laws are laws of ideal phenomena. But this merely shifts the problem, because Menger thinks that (5) exact laws contribute to our understanding of the real world: there is an essential relationship

43. *Grundzüge*, 26–27.
44. *Untersuchungen*, 6 n.4.
45. Milford (this issue) has elaborated on Menger's solution of the problem of justifying exact laws. He makes it appear as though Menger chooses an inductivist and metainductivist solution. But this is not all there is to it. Menger makes it very clear that a constructive element is involved as well.
46. *Untersuchungen*, 41.
47. *Untersuchungen*, 41, second emphasis added.

between the idealizing laws of pure "economicity" (*Wirtschaflichkeit*) and the real economy. After all, the fundamental drives that figure in exact laws are real causes. Thus, at the conclusion of a section discussing real historical examples of monopolistic behavior, he writes: "the distribution of the goods is governed . . . in accordance with exact laws; and . . . the entire course of economic events is throughout not fortuitous but capable of being reduced to definite principles."[48] In addition, Menger observes that "What has been said here [about monopolies] is supported by experience and by history."[49]

Menger's justificationism-cum-inductivism makes it impossible for him to solve the epistemological level problem while at the same time maintaining both his methodological distinctions and his realism. For either exact theory is about empirical reality, but then it must have been derived from it in some way; or its basis is not empirical, but then it cannot be about empirical reality.

Social science without justification?

Could Menger have solved his problem of the relationship between exact and empirical theoretical social science if he had not been a justificationist-cum-inductivist? Counterfactual questions are notoriously hard to answer. But this one seems easier because some of its conditions have a factual counterpart. In the history of the philosophy of science there is a philosopher who addressed the problem Menger failed to solve, but in a different, antijustificationist and anti-inductivist framework: Karl Popper. He is the antijustificationist par excellence; he claims to have solved—or rather, dissolved—the problem of induction; and he is the author of *The poverty of historicism* and "The rationality principle," in which he tries to answer the question how general, idealizing theories and empirical models are related in social science.

But if your hopes for an answer have been raised by now, you're in for a disappointment: Popper, too, runs into great difficulties. Apparently, being a nonjustificationist is not enough.

I shall discuss Popper's analysis of theoretical explanation in the social sciences not only because of its connection with Menger's problem, but also because the problem is still, more than a century after it was first noticed, real, relevant, and unsolved. It continues to bother present-day methodologists of economics and of social science in general. After sketching Popper's analysis and its connections with Menger's problem, I shall discuss a third solution to the problem, one which takes us back, via a detour, to Menger.

48. *Principles*, 215.
49. *Principles*, 214.

Situational analysis

It is fair to assume that Popper derives his understanding of the structure of economics largely from Hayek. "Rationality principle" is Popper's rendition of the methodology of economics as he had learned it from Hayek. Hayek, in one of his methodological writings,[50] sketches a picture of empirical economics as being modeled around a "pure logic of choice." This terminology is echoed by Popper, who calls the method of economic analysis the "analysis of situations, the situational logic."[51]

Hayek is an intellectual descendant of Menger, so it might appear as if Popper were consciously trying to solve Menger's problem. However, there is no evidence for this. The only relevant reference to Carl Menger occurs in *Poverty,* where "the method of logical or rational reconstruction, or perhaps the 'zero method' " is said "partly to coincide with what has been called by Professor Hayek, following C. Menger, the 'compositive' method."[52] However this may be, a reading of Menger and Popper makes it unambiguously clear that they were both working on the same problem.

In his "Rationality principle," Popper addresses the problem of explanation in social science. He focuses on the question whether there are fundamental laws in social science, and if so, what their content is, what their methodological status, and whether they are true. I shall describe Popper's answers to these questions, and point to parallels and differences with Menger's position.

Are there laws of social science?

Popper is a methodological individualist; thus, if there are laws of social science, they must be, or be reducible to, laws describing the behavior of individuals. Popper states that there is one such law, which he dubs the *rationality principle*. It says that people act in accordance with their situation. The "situation" bears a great deal of the weight of explanations. Thus Popper writes: "we must remember, of course, that the situation, as I use the term, already contains all the relevant aims and all the available relevant knowledge, especially that of possible means for realizing these aims."[53] The rationality principle, however, is not to be conceived of as subjective or psychological; given the situation, there is only one rational course of action. Latsis called this type of explanation "single-exit explanations."[54]

50. Hayek 1937.
51. Popper 1945, 97.
52. Popper 1957, 141 n. 1.
53. Popper 1967, 359.
54. Latsis 1972, 211.

Menger too is a methodological individualist,[55] and we find in him the same antipsychologism and emphasis on the situation as in Popper. But Menger's fundamental law of economics is not identical with Popper's rationality principle. Rather, the rationality principle may be considered to be a generalization of Menger's "dogma of self-interest."

> The most original factors of human economy are the needs, the goods with which nature provides man immediately (both the consumption goods and the means of production), and the striving after as complete a satisfaction of needs as possible (after as complete a covering of the need for goods as possible). All these factors are ultimately independent of the whims of the human will; they are given by the situation that obtains: the point of departure and the aim of all economy (need and available quantity of goods on the one hand, and the extent to which the need for goods may be covered) are ultimately given to economizing man, and their nature and measure are strictly determined.[56]

For Popper, the application of the rationality principle involves the assumptions that subjects are fully rational and have perfect information. With a term borrowed from Marschak, he calls this the "null hypothesis":

> By this I mean the method of constructing a model on the assumption of complete rationality (and perhaps also on the assumption of the possession of complete information) on the part of the individuals concerned, and of estimating the deviation of the actual behaviour of people from the model behaviour, using the latter as a kind of "zero coordinate."[57]

As we have seen above, Menger gives a more complete list of idealizing assumptions. Besides full information on ends, means, and relevant economic mechanisms it includes the absence of external force and complete devotion to the pursuit of economic interests.

What is the methodological status of the law of social science?

According to Popper, the rationality principle has the same status as the fundamental laws of physics. It corresponds to Newton's laws of motion, and it serves to set the model in motion:

> Now if situational analysis presents us with a model, the question arises: what corresponds here to Newton's universal laws of mo-

---

55. See, for instance, *Investigations,* book 1, ch. 8.
56. *Untersuchungen,* 45.
57. Popper 1967, 141.

tion which, as we have said, "animate" the model of the solar system? Or in other words, how is the model of a social situation "animated"? . . . we need, in order to animate it, no more than the assumption that the various persons or agents involved act *adequately, or appropriately;* that is to say, in accordance with the situation.[58]

In Menger we find very much the same view. There is no structural difference between laws and explanations in natural and social science:

That exact research in the domain of human activity assumes a definite direction of will on the part of the acting individuals is not an exclusive characteristic of the exact social sciences. Thus, it does not constitute an essential difference between exact research in the natural and the social sciences, as the former also makes assumptions which show a formal analogy with the one discussed here.[59]

For Popper, the fact that we are directly acquainted with human behavior may be useful in the context of discovery, but it has no consequences for the justification of the rationality principle, as it does not confer a privileged epistemological status on it.

It is undoubtedly true that we have a more direct knowledge of the "inside of the human atom" than we have of physical atoms; but this knowledge is intuitive. In other words, we certainly use our knowledge of ourselves in order to frame *hypotheses* about some other people, or about all people. But these hypotheses must be tested, they must be submitted to the method of selection by elimination.[60]

For the justificationist Menger, on the other hand, the human nature of the "atoms" of social science does provide an advantage of the social over the natural sciences:

The ultimate elements to which the exact theoretical interpretation of natural phenomena must be reduced, are "atoms" and "forces." Both are unempirical. We cannot imagine "atoms" at all, and the forces of nature only by means of a picture, even though in reality we do not know what forces are; we merely use the name to designate the unknown causes of real motions. This leads, in the final analysis, to quite extraordinary difficulties for the exact interpretation of natural phenomena. In the social sciences it is dif-

58. Popper 1967, 358–59.
59. *Untersuchungen,* 260 n. 145.
60. Popper 1957, 138.

ferent. Here the last elements of our analysis, human *individuals* and their *strivings,* are empirical. Hence, the exact social sciences have a great advantage over the exact natural sciences.[61]

Has the law empirical content, and is it true?

For Popper the models that are built around the rationality principle have empirical content and may even be testable, though the principle itself is almost empty.[62] For Menger, on the other hand, "Testing the exact theory of economics against full empirical reality is . . . a methodological absurdity."[63] As to the truth status of the law, both Popper and Menger maintain that the law is not a priori valid,[64] nor is it derived by conceptual analysis.[65]

Popper says that the rationality principle is false,[66] "though a good approximation to the truth."[67] From the conjunction of this premise and his falsificationism, one would expect him to draw the straightforward conclusion to reject the rationality principle and look for an explanatory principle that is closer to the truth. But he does not. The reason he gives is: "We do not learn much in learning that this [the rationality principle] is not strictly true: we know this already."[68] Despite its falsity, it is advisable to maintain the rationality principle in order to prevent the models used in social science from becoming arbitrary.[69] Popper introduces this principle of tenacity in a rather ad hoc way, apparently because he values unifying power over truth. Menger, on the other hand, does not see an antithesis between unifying power and truth. Nor does he have to. His separation of the exact from the empirical level of economics sees to that. The exact law of economics is true and unempirical, and it is precisely its nonempirical character which accounts for its generality.[70] By the same token, it avoids the need for introducing a principle of tenacity separately.

Part of the explanation why Popper does not solve Menger's problem is that he does not take sufficient account of the idealizing character of theories and explanations. That for Popper the rationality principle is

61. *Untersuchungen,* 157 n. 51.
62. Popper 1967, 359.
63. *Untersuchungen,* 54.
64. Popper 1967, 360; Menger, *Grundzüge,* 26–27.
65. For Popper, as a general point of his philosophy. For Menger, see *Untersuchungen,* 6 n. 4.
66. Cf. Popper 1967, 360: "the rationality principle seems to me clearly false."
67. Popper 1967, 362.
68. Popper 1967, 362.
69. Popper 1967, 362.
70. "The fact that particular differences of the phenomena (deviations from their strictly typical character) appear to be irrelevant with respect to particular results . . . , allows of an incomparable extension to numerous domains of the phenomenal world" (*Untersuchungen,* 42).

part of an idealizing theory is confirmed by the fact that he thinks of it as applicable to *typical* initial conditions.[71] However, he seems to waver between two alternative approaches towards idealizing theories[72] without being able to make up his mind:

1. An idealizing theory is a *true* theory about *ideal* phenomena. This is Menger's position. It preserves the unity of science but leaves the problem of how to connect the ideal phenomena with empirical reality. At times Popper seems to realize the attractiveness of this view from a unificationist standpoint. I suggest that the unfalsifiability of laws describing ideal phenomena keeps him from wholeheartedly embracing this view. Instead he proposes the rationality principle as a methodological rule, precisely in order to preserve a certain degree of integration or unity of explanation in social science. The rule is introduced in a way which is ad hoc yet still does not avoid inconsistencies with the rest of his philosophy of science.
2. An idealizing theory is a *false* theory about *real or empirical* phenomena. This is Popper's view in the passages where he says of the rationality principle that it has empirical content but is a false hypothesis. It leaves him with the problem of finding a theory that is closer to the truth. But he does not advocate that, either, for fear of losing the unity of explanation.

Both authors run into problems, and neither solves them: Popper because he lacks an articulated metatheory of the character of idealizing theories, and Menger—although he stresses the idealizing character of theories—because his justificationist epistemology prevents him from explaining how theories on different levels of abstraction are related. Can a solution be found?

The long detour

There are several inconsistencies in Popper's account of the rationality principle. The rationality principle is a methodological principle, yet it is empirical; it has little empirical content, and it is false, though a good approximation of the truth; but despite its falsity it must not be rejected or replaced by a principle which is closer to the truth.

Noretta Koertge[73] tries to construct a consistent position out of this amalgam of incompatible assertions. She claims that the rationality principle is an empirical principle and that its content can be increased.

71. Popper 1967, 357.
72. The distinction is to be found in John Worrall's discussion of the ideal gas laws (1982, 218).
73. Koertge 1975, 1979.

She argues her case by sketching an explanatory scheme that takes several sorts of possibly disturbing factors into account:[74]

K1. *Description of problem situation.* A thought he was in problem situation of type C.

K2. *Dispositional law.* For all such problem situations A would use appraisal rule R.

K3. *Analysis of the situation.* The result of appraising C using R is *x*.

K4. *Description of agent's competence.* A did not make a mistake in applying R to C.

K5. *Rational appraisal principle.* All agents appraise their situations in a rational manner.

K6. *Explanandum 1.* Therefore A concluded that *x* was the rational thing to do.

K7. *Rational action principle.* People always act on the outcome of their rational appraisals.

K8. *Explanandum 2.* Therefore A did *x*.

Koertge claims that her scheme increases the empirical content of the rationality principle because the conjunction of the rationality principle with the auxiliary theories "rules out a large number of possible worlds."[75] She adds the crucial requirement that for each of the steps we be able to give independent evidence. If this condition is omitted, any explanatory failure can be explained away, and the explanation becomes ad hoc. The demand implies that an empirical failure of a prediction made with the help of this scheme should be attributable to one or more of the auxiliary assumptions by explaining why they failed to be true. The explanatory scheme treats all disturbing factors as explananda which can be subsumed under explanatory laws.

Compare Koertge's scheme to Menger's set of assumptions.[76] According to Menger, the conditions

that automatically follow from any systematic exposition of theoretical economics, are:

[M1] that all economic subjects considered here aim at fully observing their economic interests,

[M2] that in the field (or battle) of prices they are not in error about either the economic goals or the means needed to attain them,

[M3] that they are not unfamiliar with the economic state of affairs insofar as it influences the formation of prices,

74. See Koertge 1979, 91–92.
75. Koertge 1979, 89.
76. Koertge does not refer to Menger.

[M4] that no external force is exerted on them which harms their economic freedom (the pursuit of their economic interests).[77]

To M1, the assumption that all economic subjects aim at fully observing their economic interests, corresponds K5, the rational appraisal principle. To M2, the assumption that economic subjects do not err as to both the economic goals and the means for attaining them, corresponds K4, the description of the agent's competence. There is no single element in Koertge's scheme that corresponds to M3, the assumption that economic subjects know the relevant economic circumstances. What comes closest to it is an amended version of K1, i.e., that the subject correctly thought he was in a problem situation of a particular type. Then what corresponds to K2, the dispositional law, is Menger's "dogma of self-interest": man aims at the fullest possible satisfaction of his needs.[78] M4, the assumption of absence of external force, corresponds to an obvious presupposition of K7, the rational action principle. Finally, what corresponds to K3 and K7 together is Menger's theorem that all economic phenomena are strictly determined.

Koertge solves Popper's problem by making explicit a number of idealizing assumptions. This yields a classification which is very similar to Menger's. The difference with Menger is that Koertge empiricizes the assumptions along the lines of Wieser's method of decreasing abstraction. According to Wieser, all explanations start with extreme isolating and emphasizing abstractions. But there is more to explanation than this: "However, . . . he [the theoretician] cannot rest content with these extreme abstractions; if he did, he would not have made reality completely understandable. Rather, he must make his assumptions more concrete and more numerous, step by step, through a system of decreasing abstraction."[79] This is the way in which exact theories and empirical models are related. Wieser admits that because both deal with typical phenomena, one can never arrive at full reality by this method.

Menger's specification of the idealizing assumptions underlying exact predictions might have enabled him to follow Wieser's course. But he did not,[80] for fear of having to abandon the strict separation between exact and empirical laws. Allowing for the possibility of a connection between exact and empirical laws would open the door to the argument that history provides the material from which universal laws are built.

Koertge solves Popper's problems by reinventing a list of auxiliary

77. *Untersuchungen*, 56.
78. In *Principles* this is given as a definition of an economic subject.
79. Wieser 1914, 135, my translation.
80. Although he says that he follows the method of decreasing abstraction in *Principles*. But this is for expository purposes only.

assumptions that is very similar to Menger's. However, she follows the Wieserian road that Menger avoided by giving an empirical (instead of an exact) interpretation to the classification of disturbing factors that Menger abstracted from. Thus she does away with Popper's confusion between empirical laws and methodological principles. At the same time, by this long detour via Popper she gives a solution to Menger's problem of the relation between exact and empirical theories. Her solution obviates the need for Popper's ad hoc introduction of a principle of tenacity, and it blocks the way to the instrumentalist escape that Menger's conclusion[81] seems to suggest. Contrary to what Menger says, the falsification of an exact prediction is neither an indication that the relevant law has been wrongly applied, nor a methodological absurdity. It is an invitation to further research.

References

Birner, J. 1990a. Idealizations and the development of capital theory. *Poznan Studies*.
———. 1990b. Strategies and programmes in capital theory: a contribution to the methodology of theory development. Ph.D. thesis, University of Amsterdam.
Clausewitz, C. von. [1832] 1980. *Vom Kriege*. Ulstein.
Diemer, A., ed. 1968. *Beiträge zur Entwicklung der Wissenschaftstheorie im 19. Jahrhundert*. Anton Hain.
Hansen, R. 1968. Der Methodenstreit in den Sozialwissenschaften zwischen Gustav Schmoller und Karl Menger: seine wissenschaftshistorische und wissenschaftstheoretische Bedeutung. In Diemer 1968.
Hayek, F. A. 1937. Economics and knowledge. *Economica*.
Koertge, N. 1975. Popper's metaphysical research program for the human sciences. *Inquiry*.
———. 1979. The methodological status of Popper's rationality principle. *Theory and Decision*.
Latsis, S. 1972. Situational determinism in economics. *BJPS*.
Menger, C. 1871. *Grundsätze der Volkswirthschaftslehre*. Menger 1968, vol. 1.
———. 1883. *Untersuchungen über die Methode der Socialwissenschaften und der politischen Oekonomie inbesondere*. Menger 1968, vol. 2.
———. 1889. *Grundzüge einer Klassifikation der Wirtschaftswissenschaften*. In Menger 1968, vol. 3.
———. 1968. *Gesammelte Werke*. Edited by F. A. Hayek. Mohr.
———. 1981. *Principles of economics*. New York University Press.
———. 1985. *Investigations into the method of the social sciences with special reference to economics*. New York University Press.
Milford, K. 1989. Menger's methodology. *HOPE*, this issue.
Popper, K. R. [1945] 1973. *The open society and its enemies*. Routledge & Kegan Paul.
———. [1957] 1972. *The poverty of historicism*. Routledge & Kegan Paul.
———. [1967] 1983. The rationality principle. In Popper 1983.

81. Quoted above (see text at note 36).

———. 1983. *A pocket Popper.* Edited by D. Miller. Fontana Paperbacks.
Wieser, F. von. 1914. *Theorie der gesellschaftlichen Wirtschaft.* In *Grundriss der Sozialökonomik.*
Worrall, J. 1982. Scientific realism and scientific change. *Philosophical Quarterly.*

Aristotle, Menger, Mises:
an essay in the metaphysics of economics

Barry Smith

I. *Preamble*

There are, familiarly, a range of distinct and competing accounts of the methodological underpinnings of Menger's work. These include Leibnizian, Kantian, Millian, and even Popperian readings; but they include also readings of an Aristotelian sort, and I have myself made a number of contributions in clarification and defense of the latter.[1] Not only, I have argued, does the historical situation in which Menger found himself point to the inevitability of the Aristotelian reading;[2] this reading fits also very naturally to the text of Menger's works.[3]

The diversity of interpretations is not, however, entirely surprising. It is on the one hand a consequence of the fact that Menger broke new ground in economic theory in part by fashioning new linguistic instruments not yet readily capable of unambiguous interpretation. It reflects further a lack of knowledge on the part of historians of economic thought of the most recent scholarship on nineteenth- and twentieth-century Austrian philosophy and on the role of Aristotelianism therein.[4] Still more importantly, perhaps, it reflects the fact that Aristotelian ways of thinking were for so long alien to the modern philosophical and scientific mind. For non-Aristotelian readings were advanced above all

1. See the items listed in the bibliography, especially Smith 1986a and 1990; cf. also Fabian and Simons 1986.

2. Here we can distinguish as sources of Menger's Aristotelianism first of all the *Popularphilosophie* which was imposed on educational institutions throughout the Habsburg Empire and which incorporated, besides elements derived from the thinking of Leibniz and Wolff, also watered-down versions of Aristotelian and scholastic doctrines. Secondly, there is the nineteenth-century German and Austrian textbook tradition in the social sciences. Here Aristotelian elements played a crucial role not only in the textbook literature of economics (and not least in the work of Mischler, under whom Menger had studied) but in textbooks of history and legal theory and also, for example, in the writings on political householding of the cameralists (discussed in Silverman 1989). On Mischler see Streissler 1989.

3. Valuable source material in this respect has been assembled by Milford (1988), who however draws different conclusions from the cited texts, above all because he is concentrating on the implications of Menger's work for economic *methodology*. Here, in contrast, I am concerned with more basic matters of general philosophy.

4. The most relevant material is summarized in Grassl and Smith 1986. See also the papers collected in Nyíri 1986.

by those who would be charitable to Menger by stripping his ideas of what was held to be an unfashionable residue of metaphysics.[5]

There is one further reason for the diversity of interpretation, however, which reflects a recurring problem faced by those of us who work in the history of ideas in general and in the history of Austrian ideas in particular. This is the problem of how much credence one ought to award to self-interpretations when seeking an assessment of the nature and significance of a given thinker's achievements. For self-interpretations are very often flawed because their authors naturally give prominence to the detailed *differences* between their own ideas and the ideas of those around them; they pay attention, in other words, to what is original, quirky, or odd. That which they take for granted, and which they have imbibed from their surrounding culture, is thereby no less naturally and inevitably ignored. As anyone who has worked through the writings of Menger's Austrian philosophical contemporaries very soon becomes aware, the tacit intellectual background of educated Austrians in Menger's day and beyond was Aristotelian through and through—to such an extent that Menger himself might have felt the need to draw attention to this background only when attempting to explain his ideas to those, such as Walras, or his own son Karl, who did not share it.

Menger was otherwise relatively silent as far as methodological self-interpretation is concerned, at least in the sense that he did not ally himself explicitly, for example, with the Aristotelian camp.[6] Problems arise, however, when we consider the writings of those of Menger's Austrian contemporaries and successors—including Mises and Hayek as well as Karl—who sought self-interpretations of Menger at one remove. Such Austrian Austrians have been, I want to suggest, least likely to enjoy a conscious awareness of the essence of Austrian economic thinking. Their interpretations of Menger tend to pick out what is quirky, or especially modern, in Menger at the expense of the shared and therefore for practical purposes invisible background that holds his work together. And this background—as cannot be too often stressed— is Aristotelian, even if only in the watered-down sense that is still to be

---

5. Such misplaced charity is illustrated, for example, in the decision of Menger's translators to render the technical (and in Menger's usage Aristotelian) term *Wesen*, normally and correctly translated as "essence," with the more colloquial "nature." (The translations given here have been adjusted accordingly.)

For an illuminating discussion of an interestingly parallel case of misplaced charity in interpretation, see Meikle 1985 (esp. 8ff.), which rightly lays stress on the Aristotelianism at the core of Marx's thinking. Meikle's work is one among many indications of the extent to which, among philosophers at least, Aristotelian ideas are beginning once more to be taken seriously.

6. The *Investigations* are, as Alter rightly stresses (1989, 12–13), a critique of the methodological views of the German historicists. They are not the positive statement of Menger's own thinking in this respect (cf. Menger 1883, 43n.; 1985, 62).

more precisely specified. Indeed the Aristotelian background permeated Austrian thought to such an extent that even the newly burgeoning empiricism of the Austrian positivist movement was crucially colored by it.[7]

II. *The basic doctrine*

Those who have seen fit to advance an Aristotelian reading have of course themselves often left much to be desired in the way of precision and detail. Here, therefore, I shall do my best to set out the precise form of the Aristotelian doctrine that is relevant to the thinking of Menger and his Austrian contemporaries. I shall then go on to demonstrate how the Menger-Mises relation and the general issue of apriorism in economics might profitably be reexamined in its light.

I shall confine myself here to general philosophy: the ways in which Aristotle's ethics and politics filtered through into the thinking of the Austrians will not be of concern.[8] As will become clear, it is a highly refined and purified—and indeed simplified—version of Aristotle's general philosophy that is at issue when we are dealing with nineteenth- and early twentieth-century Austrian thought. It is an Aristotelianism shorn of all reference to, say, a passive or active intellect or to queer mechanisms for coming to know the world via a "making actual" within the soul of essences existing only "potentially" within things. Only as a result of more recent work on Austrian and German philosophy in general, and on the Brentano school and on the early phenomenologists

7. This thesis is defended at length in Smith 1987. I believe that the remarks in the text have important consequences also for the correct interpretation of Hayek's thinking. Thus John Gray's contention that Hayek's "central theory" is fundamentally Kantian in nature, a thesis based on part on Hayek's own retrospective self-interpretation, is otherwise supported by very little evidence in either the spirit or the letter of Hayek's writings. Gray particularly cites a passage from Hayek's *Sensory order* as marking the Kantian strain in Hayek's thought: "The fact that the world which we know seems wholly an orderly world may thus be merely a result of the method by which we perceive it" (Hayek 1952, 8.39; cf. Gray 1986, 12)

When taken in its context, this passage is part of the physiological argument of *The sensory order*—an argument in the spirit of Mach—to the effect that it is the physical similarity of stimuli and their relative frequency of occurrence which gives rise to the order of our sensations. Like other relevant writings of Hayek, such as his "Rules, perception and intelligibility" of 1962, it presents a picture of a philosopher allied with Mach and the early precursors of what later came to be called Gestalt psychology, a picture which is supported also by a historical examination of the influences on Hayek's thought at the time when the first version of *The sensory order* was being written. For both Hayek and Mach, now, there is no distinction between the phenomenal and noumenal world. Indeed there is no transcendentalism of any sort in either thinker. Yet Kantianism, as one normally conceives it, is characterized precisely by the presence of such a transcendental dimension.

8. See the relevant section of Alter (forthcoming), and also the material collected in Grassl and Smith 1986 for a treatment of this issue in relation to Menger. For the views of the Brentanists on ethics and the theory of value see Kraus 1937.

in particular, has clarity as concerns the nature of Austrian Aristotelian-ism become possible. And this allows also a move beyond such earlier defenses of an Aristotelian interpretation of Menger's work as were advanced for example by Kauder and Hutchison, which based them-selves on little more than superficial analogies.

What then is the basic doctrine of Austrian Aristotelianism that is shared, above all, by Menger, Brentano, and their immediate followers? If, at the risk of a certain degree of painful obviousness, we attempt an assay of the common axis running through a number of otherwise disparate modes of thinking, the basic doctrine might be said to embrace seven theses.

1. *The world exists, independently of our thinking and reasoning activities.* This world embraces both material and mental aspects (and perhaps other *sui generis* dimensions, for example of law and culture). And while we might shape the world and contribute to it through our thoughts and actions, detached and objective theorizing about the world in all its aspects is nonetheless possible.

2. *There are in the world certain simple "essences" or "natures" or "elements," as well as laws, structures, or connections governing these, all of which are strictly universal.* Strictly universal, both in that they do not change historically and in the sense that they are capable of being instantiated, in principle (which is to say, if the appropriate conditions are satisfied), at all times and in all cultures. The fact that the simple essences and essential structures do not themselves change or develop implies in addition that historical change is a matter, not of changes in the basic building blocks of reality, but of changes in the patterns of their exemplification and in the ways in which they come together to form more complex wholes.

Propositions expressing universal connections among essences are called by Menger "exact laws." Such laws may be either static or dynamic—they may concern either the coexistence or the succession of instances of the corresponding simple essences or natures. It is exact laws, as Menger sees it, which constitute a scientific theory in the strict sense. The general laws of essence of which such a theory would consist are subject to no exceptions. In this respect they are comparable, say, to the laws of geometry or mechanics and contrasted with mere statements of fact and with inductive hypotheses. The aim of the "exact orientation of research" is, as Menger puts it, "the determination of strict laws of the phenomena, of regularities in the succession of phenomena which not only present themselves as exceptionless, but which, when we take account of the ways in which we have come to know them, in fact bear within themselves the guarantee of their own exceptionlessness" (1883, 38; 1985, 59, translation corrected).

3. *Our experience of this world involves in every case both an individual and a general aspect.* As in Aristotle himself, so also in Menger and in the work of other Aristotelians such as Brentano and Reinach, a radical empiricism hereby goes hand in hand with essentialism. The general aspect of experience is conceived by the Aristotelian as something entirely ordinary and matter-of-fact. Thus it is not the work of any separate or special faculty of "intuition" but is rather involved of necessity in every act of perceiving and thinking—a fact which makes itself felt in the ubiquitous employment of general terms in all natural languages. Thus the general aspect of experience is as direct and straightforward as is our capacity to distinguish reds from greens, circles from squares, or warnings from congratulations.

For Menger, as for Aristotle, what is general does not exist in isolation from what is individual. Menger is, like other Aristotelians, an immanent realist.[9] He is interested in the essences and laws manifested in *this* world, not in any separate realm of incorporeal Ideal Forms such as is embraced by philosophers of a Platonistic sort. As Brentano formulates the matter in his study of Aristotle's psychology:

> the scientist wants to get to know the crystals and plants and other bodies that he finds here on earth; if therefore he were to grasp the concepts of tetrahedra and octahedra, of trees and grasses, which belong to another world, then he would clearly in no way achieve his goal. (1867, 135; 1977, 88)

Things are no different even in the case of mathematical knowledge:

> The individual straight line which is in the senses, and the being of this line which the intellect grasps, are essentially identical. One is therefore not allowed to suppose that the intellect should grasp something more immaterial than sense, that it should take into itself something incorporeal or at least something non-sensory. No: the very same thing which is in the intellect is also in the senses, but related to other things in different ways. (135; 88)

As Menger puts it: "the goal of research in the field of theoretical economics can only be the determination of the general essence and the general connection of economic *phenomena*" (1883, 7 n. 4; 1985, 37).

The theoretical scientist, then, has to learn to recognize the general recurring structures in the flux of reality. And theoretical understanding of a concrete phenomenon cannot be achieved via any mere inductive enumeration of cases. It is attained, rather, only by apprehending the

9. See the discussion of universals *in re* in Johansson 1989, e.g., 11, 147, and also Mäki 1989.

phenomenon in question as "a special case of a certain regularity (conformity to law) in the succession, or in the coexistence of phenomena. In other words, we become aware of the basis of the existence and the peculiarity of the essence of a concrete phenomenon by learning to recognize in it merely the exemplification of a conformity-to-law of phenomena in general" (1883, 17; 1985, 44–45).

4. *The general aspect of experience need be in no sense infallible (it reflects no special source of special knowledge) and may indeed be subject to just the same sorts of errors as is our knowledge of what is individual.* Indeed, great difficulties may be set in the way of our attaining knowledge of essential structures of certain sorts, and of our transforming such knowledge into the organized form of a strict theory. Above all we may (as Hume showed) mistakenly suppose that we have grasped a law or structure for psychological reasons of habit. Our knowledge of structures or laws can nevertheless be exact. For the quality of exactness or strict universality is skew to that of infallibility. *Episteme* may be ruled out in certain circumstances, but true *doxa* (which is to say, "orthodoxy") may be nonetheless available.

5. *We can know, albeit under the conditions set out in thesis 4, what the world is like, at least in its broad outlines, both via common sense and via scientific method.* Thus Aristotelianism embraces not only commonsense realism but also scientific realism, though Aristotle himself ran these two positions together in ways no longer possible today.[10] The commonsense realism of Menger (as of all Austrian economists) is seen in his treatment of *agents, actions, beliefs, desires,* etc. In regard to these sorts of entity there is no opposition between reality as it appears to common sense and reality as revealed to scientific theory. Menger's (or the Austrian economists') scientific realism, on the other hand, is revealed in the treatment of phenomena such as spontaneous orders and invisible-hand processes, where common sense diverges from the fine structures disclosed by theory.[11]

Taken together with thesis 3, this aspect of the Aristotelian doctrine implies that we can know what the world is like both in its individual and in its general aspect, and our knowledge will likely manifest a progressive improvement, both in depth of penetration and in adequacy to the structures penetrated. Indeed Menger points at the very beginning of the *Principles* to a correlation between "the higher culture of a people" and the extent to which "human beings penetrate more deeply into the true essence of things and of their own nature" (1871, 4; 1981, 53).

10. On the opposition between commonsense and scientific realism from the point of view of contemporary philosophy see Devitt 1984. Cf. also the illuminating discussion of "level ontologies" in Johansson 1989, 26ff.

11. Cf. Mäki 1989.

6. *We can know what this world is like, at least in principle, from the detached perspective of an ideal scientific observer.* Thus in the social sciences in particular there is no suggestion that only those who are in some sense part of a given culture or form of life can grasp this culture or form of life theoretically. The general structures of reality are not merely capable of being exemplified, in principle, in different times and cultures; like the basic laws of geometry or logic they also enjoy an intrinsic intelligibility which makes them capable of being grasped, again in principle and with differing degrees of difficulty, by knowing subjects of widely differing sorts and from widely differing backgrounds. Indeed, because the essences and essential structures are intelligible, the corresponding laws are capable of being grasped by the scientific theorist in principle on the basis of a single instance.[12]

7. *The simple essences or natures pertaining to the various different segments or levels of reality constitute an alphabet of structural parts.* These can be combined together in different ways, both statically and dynamically (according to coexistence and according to order of succession). Theoretical research, for Menger, "seeks to ascertain the *simplest elements* of everything real, elements which must be thought of as strictly typical just because they are the simplest" (1883, 41; 1985, 60). The theorist must therefore learn to penetrate through the dross of ephemeral detail. He must seek to determine the elements "without considering whether they are present in reality as *independent* phenomena; indeed, even without considering whether they can at all be presented in their full purity. In this manner theoretical research arrives at *qualitatively* strictly typical forms of the phenomena" (41; 60).

Scientific theory results, then, at least in part, when means are found for mapping or picturing the composition of such simple and prototypical constituents into larger wholes. Thus the theoretical science of psychology, for Brentano, "seeks to display all the ultimate psychic components from whose combination one with another the totality of psychic phenomena would result, just as the totality of words is yielded by the letters of the alphabet" (quoted in Brentano 1982, x–xi). Such "combination" or "composition" is not simply a matter of heaping or gluing together. It is a matter of certain entities or features or properties of entities arising in reflection of the existence of special sorts of combinations of other sorts of entities. Thus, for example, a *good* exists as such only if the following prerequisites are simultaneously present:

12. Cf. Menger 1883, 40; 1985, 60 on the "rule of cognition" for the investigation of "theoretical truth": "There is one rule of cognition for the investigation of theoretical truths which is not only, as far as this is possible, verified by experience, but is verified in indubitable fashion by our very laws of thinking. . . . This is the thesis that *whatever was observed in even only one case must always come to appearance again under exactly the*

1. A need on the part of some human being.
2. Properties of the object in question which render it capable of being brought into a causal connection with the satisfaction of this need.
3. Knowledge of this causal connection on the part of the person involved.
4. Command of the thing sufficient to direct it to the satisfaction of the need.[13]

If a good exists, then as a matter of *de re* necessity, entities of these other sorts exist also. I shall return in the sequel to the treatment of such simple structures of *de re* necessitation. It is these structures, I want to claim, which lie at the core not only of Menger's work but of the entire tradition of Austrian economics.

III. *Aristotelianism versus accidentalist atomism*

Many of the above theses are of course thin beer and might seem trivially acceptable. Taken together, however, they do have a certain metaphysical cutting power. It is thesis 5, above all, which establishes the line between the Aristotelian doctrine and that of Kant (for whom there looms behind the world we know an inaccessible world of "things in themselves"). Theses 1 and 5 mark off Austrian Aristotelianism from all idealist doctrines of the sort which embrace the view that the world of experience or of scientific inquiry is somehow created or constituted by the individual subject or by the linguistic community or scientific theory, or what one will. Theses 2 and 6 distinguish the doctrine from all sorts of historicism, as also from hermeneuticist relativism and other modern fancies. And theses 2 and 5 tell us that, for the Aristotelian, scientific or theoretical knowledge is possible even of the structures or essences of the social world, a view shared in common by both Menger and Brentano and denied (in different ways) by historicists and relativists of differing hues.

Most importantly, however, the doctrine is distinguished via theses 3 and 5 from the positivistic, empiricistic methodology which has been dominant in philosophical circles for the bulk of the present century and which enjoys a position as the unquestioned background of almost all theorizing among scientists themselves. Positivism has its roots in atomism, the view that all that exists is atoms associated together in accidental and unintelligible ways and that all intelligible structures and all

---

same factual conditions. . . . This rule holds not only of the *essence* of phenomena, but also of their *measure*" (translation amended).

13. Cf. Menger 1871, 3; 1981, 52 (section 1, "On the essence of goods").

necessities are merely the result of thought-constructions introduced by man. The origins of the struggle between atomists and Aristotelians in ancient Greek thought have been well summarized by Meikle:

> On the one hand there were Democritus and Epicurus, who thought of reality as atomistic small-bits that combine and repel in the void, and who had a hard job accounting for the persisting natures of things, species and genera on that basis. On the other hand there was Aristotle, who realised that no account of such things could be possible without admitting a category of form (or essence), because what a thing is, and what things of its kind are, cannot possibly be explained in terms of their constituent matter (atoms), since that changes while the entity retains its nature and identity over time. (1985, 9)

Where the atomist sees only one sort of structure *in re,* the structure of accidental association, the Aristotelian sees in addition intelligible or law-governed structures that he can understand. Where the atomist sees only one sort of change, accidental change (for example, of the sort which occurs when a horse is run over by a truck), the Aristotelian sees in addition intelligible or law-governed changes, as, for example, when a foal grows up into a horse. Just as for the Aristotelian the intelligibility of structure can imply that there are certain sorts of structure which are intelligibly impossible—for example, a society made up of inanimate objects—so for the Aristotelian there are intelligibly impossible *changes,* for example, of a horse into a truck, or of a stone into a color. The presence of intelligible changes implies, moreover, that there is no "problem of induction" for a thinker of the Aristotelian sort. When we understand a phenomenon as the instance of a given species, then this understanding relates also to the characteristic patterns of growth and evolution of the phenomenon and to its characteristic modes of interaction with other phenomena.

IV. *The special doctrine: forms of Aristotelianism in the social sciences*

We have not yet gone far enough, however, in picking out the essence of the doctrine of Austrian Aristotelianism. For Aristotelianism played a crucial role also in the philosophy of German social thinkers such as Marx,[14] and many other German political economists and legal theorists

---

14. Cf. Gould 1978, Wood 1981, Sowell 1985, and above all Meikle 1985. In the light of thesis 6 it is worth pointing out that Marx embraces also the assumption that science is able to penetrate through the ideological obfuscations by which the commonsensical mind is (as Marx conceives things) of necessity affected.

of the nineteenth and even of the twentieth centuries could have accepted at least the bulk of what has been presented above.[15] The opposition between German and Austrian modes of thinking should not, in this respect, be exaggerated. Thus Brentano, normally and correctly regarded as the Austrian philosopher (and philosophical representative of Austrian Aristotelianism) par excellence, was in fact born in Germany. Moreover, his Aristotelianism was decisively influenced by the thinking of the great German metaphysician F. A. Trendelenburg. Equally, however, it would be wrong to ignore the crucial differences, above all as between Marx's methodology on the one hand and the basic doctrine of Austrian Aristotelianism on the other. Thus Menger's doctrine of the strict universality of laws was denied by Marx, for whom laws were in every case specific to "a given social organism."[16] Moreover, while Marx and Menger shared an Aristotelian antipathy to atomism, the holism or collectivism propounded by Marx was in this respect radically more extreme than anything that could have been countenanced by Menger.

Hegel too is correctly described as an Aristotelian in many aspects of his thinking. His case is somewhat different from that of Marx, however, since it seems that he denied thesis 1. More precisely, Hegel failed to draw the clear line between act and object of cognition which thesis 1 requires, and he refused to acknowledge any sort of independence of the latter from the former. As he himself wrote (in dealing with Aristotle): "thought thinks itself by participation in that which is thought, but thought becomes thought by contact and apprehension, so that *thought and the object of thought are the same.*"[17] Or as Allen Wood expresses it: "Marx parts company with Hegel precisely because Hegel makes the dialectical nature of thought the basis for the dialectical structure of reality, where Marx holds that just the reverse is the case" (1981, 215).

To specify, therefore, the exact nature of the Austrian Aristotelian view, it will be useful to add to our basic doctrine a number of additional theses—specific to the domain of social science—which are formulated in such a way as to bring out as clearly as possible the opposition between the Austrian view and views shared by the principal German social theorists who had been influenced by Aristotelian ideas.

8. *The theory of value is to be built up exclusively on "subjective" foundations, which is to say, exclusively on the basis of the correspond-*

15. The survival of Aristotelian ideas in contemporary German legal theory is illustrated for example by Karl Larenz's standard textbook of legal methodology (1983), e.g., in his discussion of the "legal structural types" which the legal theorist "discovers in reality" (p. 338).

16. Cf. Meikle 1985, 6 n. 4.

17. *Lectures on the history of philosophy,* trans. E. Haldane and F. Simson (London, 1894), 2:147, emphasis mine.

ing mental acts and states of human subjects. Thus value for Menger—in stark contrast to Marx—is to be accounted for exclusively in terms of the satisfaction of human needs and wants. Economic value, in particular, is seen as being derivative of the valuing acts of ultimate consumers, and Menger's thinking might most adequately be encapsulated as the attempt to defend the possibility of an economics which would be at one and the same time both theoretical and subjectivist in the given sense. Among the different representatives of the philosophical school of value theory in Austria (Brentano, Meinong, Ehrenfels, etc.) subjectivism as here defined takes different forms.[18] All of them, however, share with Menger the view that value exists only in the nexus of human valuing acts.

9. *There are no "social wholes" or "social organisms."* Austrian Aristotelians hereby—and leaving aside the rather special case of Wieser—embrace a doctrine of *ontological* individualism, which implies a concomitant *methodological* individualism, according to which all talk of nations, classes, firms, etc., is to be treated by the social theorist as an in principle eliminable shorthand for talk of individuals. That it is not entirely inappropriate to conceive individualism in either sense as "Aristotelian" is seen, for example, in Aristotle's own treatment of knowledge and science in terms of the mental acts, states, and powers or capacities of individual human subjects.[19]

Economics is methodologically individualist when its laws are seen as being made true in their entirety by patterns of mental acts and actions of individual subjects, so that all economic phenomena are capable of being understood by the theorist as the results or outcomes of combinations and interactions of the thoughts and actions of individuals. Such combinations and interactions are not mere "sums." Thus neither ontological nor methodological individualism need imply any sort of atomistic reductionism: the individual of which the social theorist treats is, as a result of different sorts of interaction with other individuals, a highly complex entity. He might more properly be conceived as something like a node in the various spontaneous orders in which he is involved. This is a familiar idea, which extends back at least as far as Aristotle.[20] As the Hungarian philosopher Aurel Kolnai put it in his defense of "conservative libertarianism" published in 1981:

Society is not only composed of various parts—it is composed of various parts in a multiplicity of ways; and consequently its compo-

18. On this see Smith 1986b and also the papers collected in Grassl and Smith 1986.
19. On methodological individualism in Aristotle see also Kraus 1905.
20. See Menger's discussion (1883, 267–70; 1985, 220–22) of the view attributed to Aristotle to the effect that the state is a phenomenon co-original with the existence of man.

nent parts cannot but *overlap*. In other words, it consists ultimately of individuals, but only in the sense that it divides into a multiplicity of individuals across several social subdivisions, such that it comprehends the same individual over and over again in line with his various social affiliations. (319)

Every individual therefore "embodies a multiplicity of social aspects or categories," and these play a crucial role in determining which sorts of essential structures the individual might exemplify.

10. *There are no (graspable) laws of historical development.* Where Marx, in true Aristotelian spirit, sought to establish the "laws of the phenomena," he awarded principal importance to the task of establishing *laws of development,* which is to say, laws governing the transition from one "form" or "stage" of society to another. He "treats the social movement as a process of natural history governed by laws,"[21] and he sees the social theorist as having the capacity to grasp such laws and therefore also in principle to sanction large-scale interferences in the social "organism." Marx himself thereby accepted both methodological and ontological collectivism; he saw social science as issuing in highly macroscopic laws, for example, to the effect that history must pass through certain well-defined "stages." The Aristotelianism of the Austrians is in this respect more modest: it sees the exact method as being restricted to certain simple essences and essential connections only, in ways which set severe limits on the capacity of theoretical social science to make predictions. The methodological individualism of the Austrians has indeed been criticized by Marxists as a branch of atomism, though such criticisms assume too readily that methodological individualism trades in "sums."

What, now, of the German historical economists? As already noted, Aristotelian doctrines played a role also in German economic science, not least as a result of the influence of Hegel. Thus, for example, Roscher not only accepted many of the tenets of the basic Aristotelian doctrine listed above, he also developed, as Streissler has shown, a subjective theory of value along lines very similar to those later taken up by Menger.[22] Such subjectivism was accepted also by Knies. Moreover, Knies and Schmoller agreed with the Austrians in denying the existence of laws of historical development. In all of these respects, therefore, the gulf between Menger and the German historicists is much less than has normally been suggested. The German historicists are still crucially distinguished from the Austrians, however, in remaining wedded to a

21. Passage cited by Marx himself in the Afterword to the second German edition of vol. 1 of *Capital* and adopted as a motto to Meikle 1985.
22. See esp. Streissler 1989.

purely inductivistic methodology, regarding history as providing a basis of fact from which laws of economic science could be extracted. For an Aristotelian such as Menger, in contrast (cf. thesis 3 above), enumerative induction can never yield that sort of knowledge of exact law which constitutes a scientific theory.

V. *Apriorism*

Austrian Aristotelianism as formulated above is first and foremost a doctrine of ontology: it tells us what the world is like and what its objects, states, and processes are like, including those capacities, states, and processes we call knowledge and science. More generally, it tells us what sorts of relations obtain between the various different segments of reality. The question of apriorism, on the other hand, which is skew to all such ontological concerns—even to concerns pertaining to the ontology of knowledge—relates exclusively to the sort of account one gives of the conditions under which knowledge is *acquired*.

Defenders of apriorism share the assumption that we are capable of acquiring knowledge of a special sort, called "a priori knowledge," via noninductive means. They differ, however, in their accounts of where such knowledge comes from. Two broad families of apriorist views have to be distinguished in this regard.

On the one hand are what we might call *impositionist views,* which hold that a priori knowledge is possible as a result of the fact that the content of such knowledge reflects merely certain forms or structures that have been imposed or inscribed upon the world by the knowing subject. Knowledge, on such views, is never directly of reality itself; rather, it reflects the "logical structures of the mind" and penetrates to reality only as formed, shaped, or modeled by a mind or theory.

On the other hand are *reflectionist views,* which hold that we can have a priori knowledge of what exists, independently of all impositions or inscriptions of the mind, as a result of the fact that certain structures in the world enjoy some degree of intelligibility in their own right. The knowing subject and the objects of knowledge are for the reflectionist in some sense and to some degree *pre-tuned* to each other. Direct a priori knowledge of reality itself is therefore possible, at least at some level of generality—knowledge of the sort that is involved, for example, when we recognize the validity of a proof in logic or geometry (where it is difficult to defend the view that the character of validity would be somehow imposed upon the objects in question by the epistemic subject).

This brings us to the principal argument of the reflectionist against all versions of impositionism, which we might call the argument from arbitrariness. Let us suppose, for the moment, that the impositionist is correct in his view that the a priori quality of laws or propositions is entirely a matter of impositions. Imagine, now, that the totality of all laws or propositions is laid out before us. Is it to be completely arbitrary which of these laws or propositions are to enjoy the "imposed" quality of aprioricity? A positive answer to this question is belied by the extent to which there is wide agreement across times and cultures as to which the candidate a priori laws or propositions are. A negative answer, on the other hand, implies that there is some special quality on the side of certain laws or propositions themselves, in virtue of which precisely those laws or propositions do indeed serve as the targets of imposition. Clearly, however, this special quality must itself be prior to any sort of mental imposition which might come to be effected, which means that the original impositionist assumption, to the effect that the a priori quality of laws or propositions is entirely a matter of imposition, turns out to be self-refuting.

The impositionist view finds its classical expression in the work of Kant (whose ideas may be safe against the argument just presented), and special versions of impositionism are to be found also in Hume (in his treatment of causality), in Mach (in his theory of thought economy), and in the work of the logical positivists. The reflectionist view, on the other hand, finds its classical expression in Aristotle; it was developed further by successive waves of scholastics extending far into the modern era and brought to perfection by Brentano and his successors, above all by Adolf Reinach and other realist phenomenologists in the early years of this century, the latter building on ideas set out by Husserl in his *Logical investigations*.

VI. *Against the Kantian confusion*

There are obvious affinities between the reflectionist view and the doctrine of Austrian Aristotelianism outlined above. Reflectionism can be made compatible also, however, with other, variant doctrines. Thus the theories of *Verstehen* propounded by Dilthey (traces of which are perhaps to be found also in Mises) can be said to result when the reflectionist doctrine is combined with a cancellation (for the social sciences) of thesis 6, which asserts the possibility of detached scientific theory.

For Menger, we have argued, at least some of the propositions of economics are a priori in the sense that the corresponding structures enjoy an intrinsic simplicity and intelligibility which makes them capable of being grasped by the economic theorist—in principle—in a single instance. Note again, however, that the fact that such structures are intelligible need not by any means imply that our knowledge of them is in any sense infallible or incorrigible, nor that it need in every case be easy to obtain or to order into the form of a rigorous theory. Indeed much confusion in the literature on Austrian methodology has arisen because the alien moment of incorrigibility, together with connotations of special mental processes of "insight" or "intuition," has come to be attached to the aprioristic thesis in a way which has made the latter seem eccentric and unscientific.

Still greater confusion has arisen, however, as a result of the no less pervasive assumption that all talk of the a priori must of necessity imply an impositionist or Kantian framework. For the apriorism lying in the background of Menger's thinking is quite clearly reflectionist. Menger believes that there are a priori categories ("essences" or "natures") in reality and that a priori propositions reflect structures or connections among such essences existing autonomously in the sense that they are not the result of any shaping or forming of reality on the part of the experiencing subject. The impositionist apriorist, in contrast, insists that a priori categories must be creatures of the mind. He therefore may hold that the issue as to which sorts of economic structures exist is a matter for more or less arbitrary legislation by the economic theorist, or a matter of the "conceptual spectacles" of the economic agent. No grain of such ideas is to be found in Menger.

Menger is working, rather, against the background of an assumption to the effect that the universals of economic reality are not created or imposed in any sense but are discovered through our theoretical efforts. Economists do not study concepts or other creatures of the mind. Rather, they study the qualitative essences or natures of and the relations between such categories as value, rent, profit, the division of labor, and money: "Theoretical economics has the task of investigating the *general essence* and the *general connection* of economic phenomena, not of analysing economic *concepts* and of drawing the conclusions resulting from this analysis. The phenomena, or certain aspects of them, and not their linguistic image, the concepts, are the object of theoretical research in the field of economy" (1883, 6 n. 4; 1985, 37).

Menger, we might say in this light, seeks to develop a categorial ontology of economic reality in just the Aristotelian sense, and in just the sense, too, in which Brentano sought a categorial ontology of psychological reality. He seeks to establish how the various different sorts of building blocks of economic reality can be combined together in different sorts of simple structured wholes, and to establish—through the application of what he himself called a genetico-compositive method—how such wholes may originate and how they may develop and become transformed over time into other kinds of wholes.

There is, however, one reason why an impositionist or Kantian reading of Menger's views has seemed so tempting to so many. This turns on the fact that Menger lays stress both on the subjectivism and on the methodological individualism of economics. Indeed, the status (and possibility) of economics as a theoretical science can be said to rest, in his eyes, precisely on the acceptance of the two theses of subjectivism and methodological individualism. For subjectivism implies that an economy is not an autonomous formation with unintelligible properties of its own. Rather one can *understand* the workings of an economy by coming to an understanding of how the value of goods at earlier stages in the process of production is derived from the value to actual consumers of the products of the later stages. Moreover, one can see why this same understanding must apply *ceteris paribus* to every economy in whatever time or place. Methodological individualism implies that the whole of economics can in principle admit of an understanding of this sort, that there are no economic structures that cannot be grasped at least in principle in the thought-experiments of the economist. The latter must, as it were, put himself into the shoes of the individual subjects whose processes of thought and action come together to exemplify the structures of which he treats.

None of the above, however, implies that the economist's understanding might flow from the fact that the propositions of economics reflect structures that have been imposed upon the world—in Kantian fashion—by either the economic theorist or the economic agent. That is, the intelligibility of basic economic structures does not imply ontological dependence of such structures on the mind along the lines suggested by the impositionist. Rather, Menger's view implies precisely that economic reality is such as to manifest certain simple intelligible structures in and of itself. Economic reality is built up in intelligible ways out of structures involving human thought and action. It is for this reason that we are able, by appropriate efforts, to read off these structures in and of themselves.

Such structures, because they are so simple, are (to different degrees) intelligible. But for the same reason they are also universal, in the sense that—because they are indispensable to every economic action as such, or to every instance of exchange, barter, rent, profit, etc.—they are manifested (in principle) in every economy. They are at least in principle intelligible to everyone who has dealings with the objects concerned (i.e., to every economic agent, to every observer of the behavior of markets). Yet this does not imply that it is in every case a simple matter to discover what such structures are; nor, a fortiori, does it imply that it is a simple matter to formulate workable theories about them.

Austrian economics is entirely comparable in this respect to the more recent "universals of language" research program in linguistics. Here too the assumption is made that there are structures in (linguistic) reality which are universal to all languages. Such structures are at least tacitly familiar to everyone who has dealings with the objects concerned (i.e., to every speaker of a language). Yet this does not by any means imply that it is a simple matter to discover what such structures are and to formulate workable theories about them. Nor, either, does it imply that the issue as to which sorts of linguistic structures are universal is a matter of the "logical structure of the human mind" or of the "conceptual spectacles" of the language-using subject. Nor, moreover, does it imply that this issue is merely a matter for arbitrary legislation by the linguistic theorist. Universals of language are not created by the linguist. They are discovered, through painstaking theoretical efforts.

Apriorism in economics, now, does not mean—any more than in the case of linguistic universals—that economic theory must be free of empirical components. Indeed it is a difficult matter to sort out precisely what the appropriate role for empirical investigations in economics (and in related disciplines) ought to be. This itself is not something that can be decided a priori. What is certain for apriorists of whatever hue, however, is that quantitative investigations in economics can be carried out coherently only on the basis of at least some prior understanding of the natures of the entities to be measured and compared. For otherwise the economist is not merely measuring in the dark; he is also without any means of tying down the results of his quantitative theorizing to economic reality itself. Pre-empirical (qualitative) categorizations of this reality must necessarily exist before empirical (quantitative) economics can begin. The only issue is the extent to which such categorizations are conscious and explicit.

The ontological grammar of economic reality that is sketched by Menger can be seen in this light as providing a pre-empirical qualitative framework in whose terms specific empirical hypotheses can be formulated and specific mathematical models be given concrete interpretation. Such a foundation cannot itself be derived, on pain of circularity, either from empirical investigations of the more usual sort or from mathematical analyses. It must rather be derived at least in part—or so the apriorist argues—from that familiarity with particular economic phenomena which we are all of us able to acquire as economic agents.

VII. *Mises, Kant, and positivism*

That the author of *Human action* sees his methodology primarily in terms recalling Kantian doctrines is seen, for example, in passages such as "The a priori sciences—logic, mathematics, and praxeology—aim at a knowledge unconditionally valid for all beings endowed with the logical structure of the human mind" (Mises 1966, 57).

We know now that there is an Aristotelian alternative to the Kantian form of apriorism. This alternative seems not to have been explicitly recognized as such by Mises; but this is hardly surprising, given that, for reasons pointed out above, the special nature of Austrian Aristotelian apriorism was appreciated by very few at the time when Mises was working out the philosophical foundations of his praxeology.[23]

Common to all aprioristic doctrines is a view to the effect that there are laws or propositions which are on the one hand universal and necessary and on the other hand intelligible (capable of being grasped by noninductive means). Kantian impositionism is the view that such a priori laws or propositions reflect categorial impositions of the mind. As a result of the influence of Frege and Wittgenstein, now, especially as filtered down through the logical positivism (logical atomism) of the Vienna circle, recent Kantian varieties of apriorism have tended to take an extreme form which sees such categorial impositions as effected always via logic or language. More specifically, a priori propositions are seen as being characterized by the fact that they can in every case be exposed—via a process of stripping out defined terms and replacing them with definiens consisting of more primitive expressions—as mere tautologies or analytic truths, entirely empty of content and consistent with any and every factual state of the world. "All bachelors are unmarried" is revealed as analytic in this way by being converted into "All unmarried men are unmarried," which is an instance of the logical truth: "All A's which are B are B."

Mises qua methodologist was very clearly tempted by the idea that the laws of praxeology should be analytic in this sense. The theoretical part of economics would then be a purely formal or analytic discipline whose principles would flow from the logical analysis of certain concepts. Consider, first of all, his assertion to the effect that the propositions of praxeology

> are not derived from experience. They are, like those of logic and mathematics, a priori. They are not subject to verification or falsification on the ground of experience and facts. They are both logically and temporally antecedent to any comprehension of historical facts. They are a necessary requirement of any intellectual grasp of historical events. Without them we should not be able to see in the course of events anything else than kaleidoscopic change and chaotic muddle. (1966, 32)

Here the (Kant- and Wittgenstein-inspired) positivist conception of analyticity is only latently at work. Almost all of the above would, if

---

23. Again, the work of the phenomenologist Adolf Reinach is especially important in this regard. For Reinach, who achieved for legal science what Menger and his school have achieved in the field of economics, was especially aware of the non-Kantian nature of his aprioristic views. See also ch. 2 of Max Scheler's *Formalism in ethics,* a work in part inspired by the reflectionist theory of the a priori defended by Reinach.

suitably interpreted, be perfectly consistent with a view of praxeology as an a priori discipline of economics conceived in reflectionist Aristotelian fashion. When we read on, however, we discover that Mises does in fact run together what is a priori with what is analytic. Praxeology, we are told, is like logic and mathematics in the sense that its content is a matter of empty tautologies: "Aprioristic reasoning is purely conceptual and deductive. It cannot produce anything else but tautologies and analytic judgments." Thus, for example: "In the concept of money all the theorems of monetary theory are already implied" (1966, 38).

Thus while impositionism is not explicitly defended by Mises qua methodologist, he does insist on the analytic character of all a priori propositions. The methodology which results is thereby rendered inconsistent with a reflectionist apriorism, since it implies that a priori propositions are empty of content, and clearly propositions that are empty of content are unable to picture anything (intelligible) on the side of the objects of the corresponding theory.

If, however, we wish to hold on to the view that all the propositions of praxeology are analytic in this sense, we shall have to insist that the whole of praxeology can be erected on the basis of premises involving at most one single primitive nonlogical concept.[24] For suppose that there were two such concepts, neither definable in terms of the other. Consider, now, the propositions expressing the nontrivial relations between these concepts. These cannot, *ex hypothesi,* be analytic, for there are now no defined nonlogical terms which could be eliminated in such a way as to reveal the corresponding statements as truths of logic, and no truth of logic contains a plurality of nonlogical terms in other than trivial ways. But nor, from the Misesian point of view, can they be merely factual (synthetic a posteriori). On the positivist reading of the aprioristic doctrine, however, no third alternative is available, which implies that the original assumption that there are two (or more) such concepts must be rejected.[25] This helps to make intelligible the repeated insistence of Mises and his followers (and critics) that there is but one single

24. We shall need, too, some criterion as to what is to count as a nonlogical concept. Consider, for example, the concept *part of.* This is a formal concept, in the sense that it can be applied, in principle, to all matters without restriction. But it is not treated as a logical concept in the standard textbooks, and nor can it be defined in terms of the logical concepts which are standardly recognized as such. Indeed it seems that the concept *part of* is a nonlogical primitive concept. Consider, now, the proposition "If A is part of B, and B is part of C, then A is part of C," which asserts that the corresponding relation is transitive. This proposition is not analytic, for there is no law of logic to which it would correspond as a substitution instance. Hence it must be synthetic. But it is surely also a priori, and indeed a priori in the (reflectionist) sense that it pictures the (intelligible) way in which part-whole relations are nested together in the world, independent of our thoughts and actions.

25. I have developed this argument at greater length in Smith 1986a.

nonlogical concept (or "category" or "essence") of the praxeological discipline, the concept *human action,* from which all propositions of the discipline would somehow be derived:

> The scope of praxeology is the explication of the category of human action. All that is needed for the deduction of all praxeological theorems is knowledge of the essence of human action. . . . The only way to a cognition of these theorems is logical analysis of our inherent knowledge of the category of action. . . . Like logic and mathematics, praxeological knowledge is in us; it does not come from without. (Mises 1966, 64)[26]

VIII. *Mises the Aristotelian*

When once we examine Mises's *practice,* however, a quite different picture emerges, and we discover that Mises too was not at his best in his methodological self-interpretations. For we are forced to recognize that there is a veritable plenitude of nonlogical primitive concepts at the root of praxeology. Indeed, Mises's descriptions of this plenitude in his actual practice in economics, and also in occasional passages in his methodological writings,[27] can be seen to represent one of the most sustained realizations of the Austrian Aristotelian idea in the literature of economic theory.

Action, we are told by Mises, involves *apprehension of causal relations and of regularities in the phenomena.* It presupposes *being in a position to influence causal relations.* It presupposes *felt uneasiness.* It involves the *exercise of reason.* It is a *striving to substitute a more satisfactory for a less satisfactory state of affairs.*

Acting man *transfers the valuation of ends he aims at to the means he anticipates utilizing.* Action *takes time,* which like other *scarce factors* must be *economized.* Action presupposes *choosing between various opportunities offered for choice.*

Action involves *the expectation that purposeful behavior has the power to remove or at least alleviate uneasiness.* It presupposes the *uncertainty of the future.* It involves *meanings which the acting parties attribute to the situation.* A thing becomes a *means* only when reason *plans to employ it for the attainment of some end and action really employs it for this purpose.*

Certainly some of the concepts involved in the above may reasonably be counted as logical concepts; others may no less reasonably he conceived as being introduced by definitions formulated in terms of other,

---

26. See also Rothbard 1957.
27. Consider, for example, the paragraph beginning "The most general . . ." in Mises 1981, 24.

more primitive concepts. Consider, however, the concepts *causation, relative satisfactoriness, reason, uneasiness, valuation, anticipation, means, ends, utilization, time, scarcity, opportunity, choice, uncertainty, expectation,* etc., etc. The idea that one could simultaneously and without circularity reduce every one of the concepts in this family to the single concept of action, that they could all be defined by purely logical means in terms of this one single concept, is decisively to be rejected.[28]

How much better would it be to accept that we are dealing here with a family of a priori categories and categorial structures which would be, in the jargon, not analytic but synthetic. The laws governing such structures can almost all of them be very easily expressed in the form of what linguists like to call "implicative universals," which is to say principles to the effect that, if instances of some given species or category K_1 exist, then as a matter of necessity these and those other categories $K_2, \ldots, K_n$ must be instantiated also. Instances of the necessitating category K_1 are then said to be one-sidedly dependent upon instances of the necessitated categories $K_2, \ldots, K_n$. The formal ontological theory of such dependence relations has been worked out in some detail.[29] It can be illustrated in Menger's already-mentioned account of the essence of goods at the beginning of the *Principles:* "If instances of the species *good* exist, then there exist also instances of the species *need, human being, causal connection, knowledge, command,* etc." And it is to be found at work also in the context of Misesian praxeology, for example in laws such as: "If instances of the species *action* exist, then there exist also instances of the species *choice, apprehension of causal regularities, felt uneasiness,* etc. If instances of the species *choice of ends* exist, then so also do instances of the species *apprehension of causal regularities,* etc."

We might represent the a priori relations between such species (relations of *de re* necessitation) in diagrammatic form, employing links connecting broken to solid walls of adjacent frames to represent relations of one-sided dependence between the entities concerned (figure 1). A diagram of this sort is, we might say, a picture of an a priori structure in the sphere of human action. Similar diagrams can be produced also—following indications set out by Reinach in his monograph on speech act theory of 1913—for the a priori necessitation structures exemplified by speech acts of the various different types,[30] and I have sought elsewhere

28. Hoppe 1988, to which I hope to return elsewhere, is an interesting defense of a purportedly Kantian reading of Mises which seeks to break through the opposition between impositionism and reflectionism set out above.

29. See Smith, ed., 1982; Simons 1987, part 3; and Johansson 1989, ch. 9.

30. Compare the papers collected in Mulligan 1987.

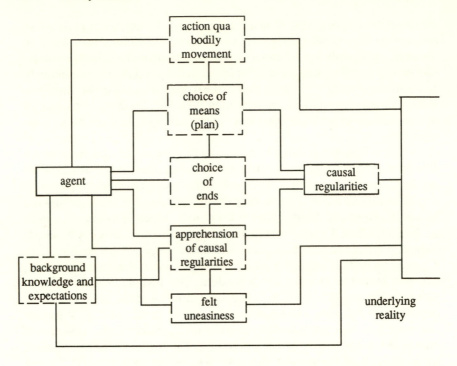

Figure 1.

to show how they can be extended also to the structures of entrepreneurial perception analyzed by Israel Kirzner.[31]

IX. *If Austrian economics did not exist,*
would it be necessary to invent it?

Austrian economics, we have said, is both theoretical and subjectivist.
Neoclassical economics, in contrast, is neither the one nor the other.
For it rests on the positivist thesis that economic reality lacks intrinsic
intelligibility *tout court,* so that no nontrivial part of economic theory
could be a priori in any of the senses distinguished above. The propositions of economics are mere inductive hypotheses, and the method of
economics consists in the building of testable models, selection among
which is effected, at least in principle, on the basis of relative predictive
strength. Because realism (in the reflectionist sense) falls out of account
as a criterion of selection, such models are repeatedly threatened with

31. See, e.g., Kirzner 1979 and Smith 1986a. Marx too utilized necessitation structures
of exactly this sort, for example in his analysis of human work in chapter 5 of Book 1 of
Capital. On this see Smith 1988.

becoming shorn of their relation to those basic everyday categories in which the science of economics has its roots. Austrian economics, in contrast, is marked by a willingness to sacrifice both the goal of predictive power and the mathematical tools associated therewith precisely in order to come to an understanding of these basic categories themselves.

The contrast here has seemed to many to justify the striking of pugilistic attitudes. From the Aristotelian apriorist perspective, however, it might begin to appear as if the principles underlying both sorts of economic methodology might possess some grain of truth. For Austrian economics might then be conceived not as an alternative to the economics of model-building and prediction but as a preliminary activity of establishing this missing connection to ground-level economic realities. Austrian economics might, in other words, be conceived as a safe harbor for a practice which at present takes place among neoclassicists only surreptitiously and unsystematically—a practice sometimes referred to under the rubric of "taking subjectivism seriously." This practice might also be conceived as the attempt to exert control—in the direction of greater commonsensical realism—over the model-building tendencies of mathematical economists. The exercise of such control might lead—from this admittedly somewhat idealized perspective—to the construction of different kinds of models. But then also it may even be that empirical and mathematical economics will in certain circumstances lead to results which constrain a revision of Austrian economics itself. A view of this sort can be found in germ already in the work of Wieser.[32] He too saw economic theory as beginning with the description—based in part on introspection, as he saw it—of the simplest structures of economic reality, a description which may then be supplemented and to some extent corrected by empirical research into the various ways in which these simple structures may come to be affected contingently, e.g., in different social and historical contexts.

For the moment, though, I am suggesting merely that we consider a thought experiment, or pipe dream, to the effect that Austrian economics might be seen as providing a certain sort of foundation for empirical-mathematical economics in something like the way in which geometry provides a foundation for the discipline of physics. We have said that from the Aristotelian perspective a proposition's being a priori

32. Wieser 1927, 5ff. It may be less at home in Menger's own thinking. For Menger the idea of "testing the exact theory of economy by the full empirical method is simply a methodological absurdity, a failure to recognize the basis of presuppositions of exact research" (1883, 54; 1985, 69). Examining Menger's account of the ways in which exact types are painstakingly extracted from the realm of economic phenomena by the economic theorist suggests, however, that he too might have assented to something like the retroactive control that is here described. On this whole issue see Menger's promissory note in *Investigations* (1883, 43; 1985, 62).

signifies that it (or the structure which makes it true) enjoys some degree of intelligibility. What it does not signify is that our knowledge of such a proposition must be in any sense incorrigible or infallible. Indeed the idea that empirical discoveries might lead in principle to a correction of the a priori foundation of the economic discipline opens up the exciting prospect of something like a *non-Euclidean* Austrian economics, perhaps even a family of such non-Euclidean disciplines, each of which could claim some degree of a priori support. I must confess at once, however, that I have no notion as to how such disciplines might look.

References

Alter, M. 1989. What do we know about Menger? *Working Paper Number 71*, Duke University Program in Political Economy.
————. Forthcoming. *Carl Menger and the origins of Austrian economics*. Boulder: Westview Press.
Brentano, F. [1867] 1977. *Die Psychologie des Aristoteles insbesondere seine Lehre vom nous poietikos*. Mainz: Kirchberg. Reprinted. Darmstadt: Wissenschaftliche Buchgesellschaft, 1967. English translation by R. George as *The psychology of Aristotle*. Berkeley and Los Angeles: University of California Press, 1977.
————. 1982. *Deskriptive Psychologie*. Edited by R. M. Chisholm and W. Baumgartner. Hamburg: Meiner.
Devitt, M. 1984. *Realism and truth*. Oxford: Blackwell.
Fabian, R., and P. M. Simons. 1986. The second Austrian School of value theory. In Grassl and Smith 1986, 37–101.
Gould, Carol C. 1978. *Marx's social ontology: individuality and community in Marx's theory of social reality*. Cambridge, Mass., and London: MIT Press.
Grassl, W., and B. Smith, eds. 1986. *Austrian economics: historical and philosophical background*. London and Sydney: Croom Helm.
Gray, John. 1986. *Hayek on liberty*. 2d ed. Oxford: Blackwell.
Hayek, F. A. von. 1952. *The sensory order: an inquiry into the foundations of theoretical psychology*. London: Routledge & Kegan Paul.
————. 1962. Rules, perception and intelligibility. *Proceedings of the British Academy* 48. Reprinted in Hayek's *Studies in philosophy, politics and economics*, 43–65. London: Routledge & Kegan Paul, 1967.
Hoppe, H.-H. 1988. *Praxeology and economic science*. Auburn: The Ludwig von Mises Institute.
Husserl, E. 1900–1901. *Logische Untersuchungen*. Critical edition, Dordrecht: Nijhoff, 1975, 1984. [A = first edition]. English translation of 2d ed. by J. N. Findlay as *Logical investigations*. London: Routledge & Kegan Paul, 1970.
Johansson, I. 1989. *Ontological investigations: an inquiry into the categories of nature, man and society*. London: Routledge.
Kirzner, I. 1979. *Perception, opportunity and profit: studies in the theory of entrepreneurship*. Chicago: University of Chicago Press.
Kolnai, A. 1981. Identity and division as a fundamental theme of politics. In *Structure and Gestalt: philosophy and literature in Austria-Hungary and her successor states*, edited by B. Smith, 317–460. Amsterdam: John Benjamin.
Kraus, O. 1905. Die aristotelische Werttheorie in ihren Beziehungen zu den modernen Psychologenschule. *Zeitschrift für die gesamte Staatswissenschaft* 61:573–92.

————. 1937. *Die Werttheorien: Geschichte und Kritik.* Brünn, Vienna, and Leipzig: Rohrer.

Larenz, K. 1983. *Methodenlehre der Rechtswissenschaft.* 5th ed. Berlin, Heidelberg, New York, and Tokyo: Springer.

Mäki, U. 1989. The best way forward: scientific realism. *Duke University Working Papers in Economics.*

Meikle, S. 1985. *Essentialism in the thought of Karl Marx.* London: Duckworth.

Menger, Carl. [1871] 1981. *Grundsätze der Volkswirthschaftslehre.* Vienna: Braumüller. Translated by J. Dingwall and B. F. Hoselitz as *Principles of economics.* New York and London: New York University Press, 1981.

————. [1883] 1985. *Untersuchungen über die Methode der Socialwissenschaften, und der politischen Oekonomie insbesondere.* Leipzig: Duncker & Humblot. Translated by Francis J. Nock as *Investigations into the method of the social sciences with special reference to economics.* New York and London: New York University Press, 1985.

Milford, K. 1988. Menger's solution of the problem of induction: on the history of methodological thought in economics. Department of Economics, University of Vienna, Working paper no. 8806.

Mischler, P. 1857. *Grundsätze der National-Oekonomie.* Vienna: Friedrich Manz.

Mises, L. von. 1966. *Human action.* 3d rev. ed. Chicago: Henry Regnery.

————. 1981. *Epistemological problems of economics.* New York and London: New York University Press.

Mulligan, K., ed. 1987. *Speech act and Sachverhalt: Reinach and the foundations of realist phenomenology.* Dordrecht, Boston, and Lancaster: Martinus Nijhoff.

Nyíri, J. C., ed. 1986. *From Bolzano to Wittgenstein: the tradition of Austrian philosophy.* Vienna: Hölder-Pichler-Tempsky.

Reinach, A. 1911. Kants Auffassung des Humeschen Problems. *Zeitschrift für Philosophie und philosophische Kritik* 141:176–209. Reprinted in Reinach 1988. English translation by J. N. Mohanty in *Southwestern Journal of Philosophy* 7 (1976):161–88.

————. 1913. Die apriorischen Grundlagen des bürgerlichen Rechts. *Jahrbuch für Philosophie und phänomenologische Forschung* 1:685–847. Reprinted in Reinach 1988. English translation in *Aletheia* 3 (1983): 1–142.

————. 1988. *Sämtliche Werke.* Edited by K. Schuhmann and B. Smith. Munich and Vienna: Philosophia.

Rothbard, Murray N. 1957. In defense of "extreme apriorism." *Southern Economic Journal* 23:315–20.

Scheler, Max. 1973. *Formalism in ethics and non-formal ethics of value.* Translated by M. S. Frings and R. L. Funk. Evanston: Northwestern University Press.

Schönfeld-Illy, L. 1924. *Grenznutzen und Wirtschaftsrechnung.* Vienna. Reprinted. Munich: Philosophia, 1983.

Silverman, P. 1989. Antecedents in the works of Sonnenfels and Kudler. *Duke University Working Papers in Economics.*

Simons, P. M. 1987. *Parts: a study in ontology,* Oxford: Clarendon Press.

Smith, B. 1982. Introduction to Adolf Reinach, "On the theory of the negative judgment." In Smith, ed., 289–313.

————. 1986a. Austrian economics and Austrian philosophy. In Grassl and Smith, 1–36.

————. 1986b. The theory of value of Christian von Ehrenfels. In *Christian von*

Ehrenfels: Leben und Werk, edited by R. Fabian, 85–111. Amsterdam: Rodopi.

———. 1987. Austrian origins of logical positivism. In *Logical Positivism in Perspective,* edited by B. Gower, 34–66. London and Sydney: Croom Helm.

———. 1988. Practices of art. In *Practical knowledge: outlines of a theory of traditions and skills,* edited by J. C. Nyíri and B. Smith, 172–209. London, Sydney, and New York: Croom Helm.

———. 1990. On the Austrianness of Austrian economics. *Critical Review* 4.

Smith, B., ed. 1982. *Parts and moments: studies in logic and formal ontology.* Munich: Philosophia.

Sowell, T. 1985. *Marxism: philosophy and economics.* London: Unwin Paperbacks.

Streissler, E. 1989. The influence of German economics on the work of Menger and Marshall. *Duke University Working Papers in Economics* no. 72.

Wieser, F. von. 1927. *Social economics.* New York: Adelphi.

Wood, A. 1981. *Karl Marx.* London: Routledge & Kegan Paul.

Mengerian economics in realist perspective

Uskali Mäki

I. *The perspective*

It is now almost a commonplace to declare that Carl Menger was an economist with a self-proclaimed interest in the "Natur und Wesen" of economic phenomena. While this view is no doubt correct, it remains insufficient as such. The metaphysical notions of nature and essence as well as their implications in regard to the content of economic theory have been left largely unanalyzed. The first purpose of this essay is to provide a richer and more accurate outline of the metaphysics of Mengerian economics, using aspects of Menger's theory of money as an illustrative case. The array of metaphysical categories will be extended beyond those of nature and essence so as to include those of nominal and real essence, universal, causal power, and necessity. The second aim of the essay is to show that given the metaphysical structure of Mengerian economic theory, it is conceivable to view the theory as being both apparently unrealistic and nonetheless ambitiously realistic as a representation of the market economy. This presupposes a revision of some standard conceptions of those features that make an economic theory realistic or unrealistic.

Accordingly, by using a selected set of metaphysical categories and a few semantic, ontological, and epistemological notions, I propose an interpretation of Mengerian economics from a realist perspective. More specifically, I try to show that it is in many ways sensible to see Mengerian economics as exemplifying a version of essentialist realism. Now that essentialism is once more back in fashion within general philosophy, an attempt to lay down the conceptual foundations of a tradition in economics in essentialist terms is an especially exciting exercise.

"Realism" is a name for a family of philosophical doctrines usually thought of as being opposed, on various dimensions, to such other doctrines as idealism, nominalism, phenomenalism, conventionalism, instrumentalism, operationism, and so on. In later sections I deal with some of these doctrines and oppositions. Here I begin by pointing out three roles that realism may have in regard to Mengerian economics.

First, we can investigate the doctrinal background of achievements within the Austrian tradition and try to point out how, if at all, Menger and other Mengerians were influenced by realist ideas developed by some of their predecessors or contemporaries in philosophy or elsewhere. The role of realism here is descriptive, and the perspective is prospective.

Second, various insights of modern and classical versions of essentialist realism can be used in constructing a framework for interpreting past achievements within the Austrian tradition. Such a framework of our own making can be employed in pursuit of an interpretive analysis of the presuppositions, elements, structure, and dynamics of the concepts, theories, and research practices of Menger, Wieser, Böhm-Bawerk, Mises, Hayek, and others. The role of realism here is primarily descriptive, and the perspective is retrospective. The problem is to discover to what extent and in what ways Austrian theories and economists can be understood as representatives of what we regard as realism in different guises.

Third, realism can be given a normative and programmatic role in regard to Austrian economics. Realist insights can be used in formulating guidelines for future work in economics. The role of realism here is primarily prescriptive and the perspective is prospective. The problem is to discover the consequences of some realist commitments with respect to basic ideas and practices within Austrian economics. There are three possible prescriptive outcomes: go on as before, revise some of the premises or practices, or reject the whole tradition.

The focus of this paper is primarily on the second role, but there is no doubt that the interpretive analyses that follow do have prescriptive implications as well. In fact the dividing line between interpretive description and programmatic prescription tends to vanish once we realize that, when providing interpretations of Menger and other Austrian economists and their theories, we may pursue correct interpretations and/or fruitful interpretations without being able to make a sharp distinction between the two. In this essay I have the minimum aim of attaining fruitful interpretations in the sense that they might help Austrian economists see and employ the whole potential of their inherited theoretical and methodological resources. For the most part I am prepared to defend my interpretations as correct ones as well. One criterion of success that might be favorably applied to my suggestions is the ability to create a unified picture of the views under interpretation. To name the kind of analysis pursued here, I would use the term *reconstructive interpretation*.

When outlining a realist interpretation and reconstruction of aspects of Mengerian economics, I have kept in mind contrasting metatheoretical orientations within economics. One of them is composed of predictivist and formalist versions of the instrumentalist view, popular among mainstream economists; another is a kind of encompassing empiricism, characteristic of some streams in historicist and institutional economics. In opposition to predictivist and formalist instrumentalism, Mengerian realism emphasizes veristic and explanatory ambitions in economic theorizing. In contrast to encompassing empiricism, it encourages the employment of strong isolations and abstractions in search of comprehension of what is not accessible to ordinary commonsense experience.

The primary object of the interpretive analyses that follow consists of Carl Menger's explicit and general metatheoretical pronouncements together with ingredients from his theory of money. The conceptual tools employed for these analyses include the metaphysical notions of essence, universal, causal power, and necessity, as well as a few semantic and nonsemantic notions of what I call (un)realisticness, and the partly epistemological notion of explanation as reductive redescription, all conceived in a realist fashion. The discussion integrates and develops suggestions made in earlier works (Mäki 1986, 1989, 1990a, 1990b, 1991) and introduces a few new ideas.

II. *Realism and realisticness*

There prevails a widely established but most unfortunate habit among economists and methodologists of economics of talking about the "realism" of economic theories and their assumptions. To help avoid confusion, I have suggested (in Mäki 1989) that we make a distinction between realism and realisticness (respectively, between nonrealism and unrealisticness). According to that suggestion, *realism* (as well as nonrealism and antirealism) should be used as a name for a family of philosophical doctrines, while *realisticness* (and *unrealisticness*) should be taken as designating a family of characteristics that we may wish to attribute to economic theories and their constituent statements. Consequently, *realism* should be eliminated from the expression "realism of assumptions" and replaced by *realisticness*. Another point to make in this connection is to emphasize that both realism and realisticness divide into several specific variants. Some of these will be mentioned in a moment.

Many commentators on neoclassical economic theories, friends and foes alike, are prepared to think that the "assumptions" of these theories are "unrealistic," and some have concluded that for this reason a nonrealist attitude towards neoclassicism is in order. This view has received expression in the Friedmanian and other forms of economic instrumentalism (for qualifications, see Mäki 1990b). Many would also argue that Austrian theories, although being a bit more "realistic" than standard neoclassical theories, are still on the "unrealistic" side of the dividing line, at least when compared to American institutionalism or to

Menger's actual opponent, German historicism. These sorts of assessment seem to be rooted deep in ordinary economists' unreflected intuitions. Therefore it may be hopeless to fight against them without a systematic metatheoretical framework. By means of an outline of such a framework, I hope to show that a case can be made for Austrian theories being realistic in a very ambitious sense and that therefore a radically realist view of Austrian economics is defensible.

I will now provide a list of a few relevant kinds of realism in condensed form (see Mäki 1989).

Ontological realism has the general form of the statement "X exists" or "Xs are real." "X" is a variable that can be given many qualitative values, such as the world, universals and particulars, physical objects and mental states, etc. What will interest us in particular is the existence of essences, universals, powers, necessities, and material, mental, and social entities, as well as their economic exemplifications. Of course, "exists" is also ambiguous. In section III, I provide three specifications for the concept of existence.

Semantic realism is concerned with the semantic ties of language—such as reference, representation, and truth—to those entities that are regarded as real. Accordingly, semantic realism divides into three subspecies. *Referential realism* is the statement that linguistic entities can be used to refer to real entities, these being independent of the referring linguistic entities. *Representational realism* says that representations are about the real features of existing entities, that is, of entities to which those representations refer. *Veristic realism* is the thesis that certain linguistic representations, namely meaningful statements and their configurations, are true or false of those real entities to which they refer.

Corresponding to forms of semantic realism, we may formulate kinds of *semantic realisticness and unrealisticness,* attributable to representations. A representation is *referentially realistic* if it refers to real existents, and *referentially unrealistic* if it fails to refer to what is real. A representation is *representationally (un)realistic* if it represents (fails to represent) features of existing things. Finally, a representation is *veristically realistic* if it is true of what it refers to, and *veristically unrealistic* if it is false of it. These varieties are interconnected so that if a representation is true or false, then it has to be both representationally and referentially realistic.

It seems clear that for the most part Austrian economists have subscribed to ontological and semantic realism and consequently have provided (descriptive and normative) assessments concerning semantic realisticness within economics. In particular most Austrian economists have thought that the economy exists, that economic theories about it are true or false, and that true theories are to be preferred to false ones. Of course there are complicated issues at stake here, and they cannot be settled in these simple terms. We need more categories to refine our statement.

Let us define *commonsense realism* as the view that everyday experience has access to what is real and that the semantic resources of commonsense frameworks enable one to put forth representations that are semantically realistic. *Scientific realism,* in contrast, is the view that there exist entities in the world to which common sense does not have access but which can, in principle at least, be truly represented by scientific theories. With these minimal formulations, I argue that Mengerian economics subscribes to both commonsense realism (in its conception of economic agents) and scientific realism (in its conception of the invisible hand).

Realisticness and unrealisticness, as properties attributable by economists to economic representations, have several other forms besides the simple and straightforward semantic ones (see Mäki 1989, 1990b). Of these, I here mention only those directly related to the theoretical operation of *isolation.* When carrying out an isolation, an economist picks out a limited set of elements in a total situation and excludes the rest from consideration. In popular parlance, the stronger an isolation involved in a representation (i.e., the larger the number of the excluded features in proportion to all features of a situation), the more unrealistic is the representation, and vice versa. In this particular sense of the term, historicist and institutionalist representations of the economy are more realistic than Austrian ones, which in turn are more realistic than standard neoclassical theories.

Isolation is often confused with abstraction, by economists and others. For the sake of clarity I suggest that *abstraction* be understood as a subspecies of isolation, related to representing universals. In an abstraction a universal feature of a thing is isolated from its other features.

I argue that in its theories Mengerian economics attempts to combine unrealisticness based on isolation and abstraction with semantic (referential, representational, veristic) realisticness, this combination being based on the tenets of essentialist realism.

III. *Existence*

Any formulation of ontological realism (and, by implication, of forms of semantic realism) involves the problem of specifying the meaning of "exists." In the case of a realist reconstruction of Austrian economics (indeed, of social science in general) this appears to be especially important. I suggest three specifications of descending strength for "X exists."

The strongest specification is "X exists independently of the human mind." This gives us a concept of *independent existence*. This formulation excludes from the realm of real existents such things as people's thoughts and feelings or, in general, mental entities belonging to human beings. It also excludes anything that is dependent on the mental, such as social norms, institutions, and processes. Only material (natural, physical) entities like plants and planets, photosynthesis, and gravitational fields exist in the required sense. The notion of independent existence leads to a materialist or physicalist realism.

Sometimes "X exists" is specified as "X exists externally to the human mind." What follows is a notion of *external existence* which, if incorporated into the formulation of ontological realism, will again make realism about mental entities an impossible option. Compared to physicalist realism, the scope of ontological realism would be widened, however, so as to include social entities along with material entities as real existents. As will be clear from discussion in later sections, social entities or, roughly, entities that involve the mechanism of the invisible hand, can exist externally even though their existence is causally dependent on the human mind. Any realism of the social sciences has to acknowledge the possibility of external existence.

The weakest specification of the meaning of "exists" is "X exists independently of and unconstituted by particular representations of itself." This leads to what may be called the notion of *objective existence*. This notion of existence is relative to particular representations in that something may exist objectively only relative to certain representations about that something. It excludes from the scope of ontological realism only those entities that are constituted by representations of themselves. It should be clear that, along with material and social entities, mental entities (such as the valuations, expectations, and purposes of economic agents, as represented by economists) can also exist objectively.

It seems to me that Austrian economics can be viewed as subscribing to ontological (and semantic) realism under all three specifications of "exists." In particular I argue that Menger's theory of money involves ontological realism about mental entities (existing objectively), social entities (existing both objectively and externally), and material entities (existing independently as well).

If it is correct to say that many Austrian economists are realists in the above senses, then it is also correct to say that they are objectivists. This may sound puzzling, since Austrians usually declare themselves to be champions of subjectivism. These two characterizations are easily reconcilable by formulating their combination as that between what may be called ontic subjectivism and ontological objectivism. *Ontic subjectiv-*

ism says that the economy is at least partly constituted by individuals' subjective valuations, expectations, purposes, etc. *Ontological objectivism* says that the economy as the object of economic theories is unconstituted by those theories and exists independently of them.

IV. *Universals*

Universals are features (properties, kinds, relations) shared by many particular objects. Universals are general; particulars are individual. In traditional terms a universal is the one, and particulars sharing it are the many. The age-old issue concerns the question whether universals have a nonlinguistic and nonmental existence. Realists about universals think they exist at least objectively. Nominalists and conceptualists think they do not exist except in language or in human minds thinking about them. At most, nominalists and conceptualists are realists about particulars. It is my view that Menger can be interpreted as a realist about universals.

Menger was no Platonist or transcendental realist. Instead he held an Aristotelian view of universals. According to this view, the existence of universals is dependent on that of particulars. Universals exist in the particulars that instantiate them, not somewhere else, in an independent realm of Platonic Forms. This is Aristotle's solution to the problem of the existence of universals; they do exist, but not separately from particulars. The one exists only as instantiated in the many (*Metaphysics* 7). Let us call this view *immanent realism* about universals (see Armstrong 1978).

That Menger was an immanent realist rather than a nominalist or a conceptualist is brought out clearly by the following statement: "The phenomena, or certain aspects of them, and not their linguistic image, the concepts, are the object of theoretical research in the field of economics" ([1883] 1963, 37 n. 4). Indeed, universals are objectively existing aspects of particulars according to immanent realism.

Menger formulated his view of theoretical economics by saying that it is an "exact science" that studies "exact types" and "exact laws." The sentence quoted just above gives an excellent clue to specifying these notions. If theoretical economics has as its object the universal aspects of particular phenomena, and if it also studies exact types and exact laws, then we may conclude that the latter are universals. More precisely, exact types are first-order universals, while exact laws are second-order universals: they are about the connections between exact types. Economics as an exact science, then, is a theoretical study of universals, conceived in an immanent realist fashion. (For details of this interpretation see Mäki 1986.)

Not just any universal can count as an object of economic theory. I suggest that those which count be called *economic universals,* i.e., universals involving economizing action on the part of human individuals. Exact or strict types such as economizing action itself, economic price, and money are among the economic universals. They can be claimed to exist at least objectively, but only as instantiated in particular episodes of human action, in particular prices in the market, and in particular instances of money. We employ in particular the idea that the money universal is the one that is exemplified by the many money particulars (this coin in my hand, that bank note over there, etc.).

If universals exist only as aspects of particular things and phenomena, mixed with particulars and other universals, they are not directly observable in a "pure" form. In order to have them as objects of theorizing, they have to be "abstracted from the full empirical reality" (Menger, [1883] 1963, 62). Another term that Menger uses in this connection is "isolation." Thus we may specify that theoretical economics represents economic universals as real objects that the cognitive mind has abstracted from particulars and isolated from other (also noneconomic) universals with which they exist in combination.

Economists often use the adjective "abstract" interchangeably with "unrealistic" when characterizing certain economic theories. Typically in these cases the precise meaning of the expression remains obscure. We are now able to suggest a rough specification for "is abstract." Loosely, a representation is abstract if it is about universals, and concrete if it is about particulars. More precisely, abstractness and concreteness constitute, not a dichotomous pair, but rather something like a continuum of characteristics of representations (for instance, representations of what Menger calls "real types" are more abstract than representations of particulars, but less so than those of exact types). However, for the sake of relating (un)realisticness to abstractness, let us stick to the simplified dichotomous specification.

Whether a representation is to be regarded as semantically realistic or unrealistic in the sense related to abstractness depends on one's theory of universals. If you are a realist about universals, then you have to think that an abstract representation (having a universal as its object) can be semantically realistic. If you are a nominalist, then you have to think that a concrete representation (having a particular as its object) can be realistic, while an abstract one is necessarily referentially unrealistic (because there are no extralinguistic universals, in your opinion). If you are a transcendental (Platonic) realist, then you have to think that only abstract representations can be realistic; concrete ones are always referentially unrealistic (because there are no particulars, according to your view). If you are an immanent realist, then you regard it conceivable that both abstract and concrete representations can be semantically realistic (because you think both universals and particulars are real).

If Menger and many other Austrian economists are immanent realists, then they view representations of both the money universal and its particular exemplifications as possibly being semantically realistic. On the one hand, the fact that a statement in economics is abstract does not preclude its being realistic in the sense that it may refer to and truly represent objectively existing aspects of the economy. On the other hand, the real extension of Austrian economic theory encompasses particulars too, since universals cannot exist without them.

The discussion above suggests that in his distinction of kinds of types and in his characterization of competing "orientations" in economics, Menger's choice of terms may be misleading. First, he contrasts "exact types" to "real types," although, were he to be read as an immanent realist, exact types are no less real than the "real" ones. Second, he labels the historicist approach "realistic," while in fact his own "exact" approach is realistic as well, albeit in a different sense. To avoid unnecessary confusions I suggest that, in Menger's terminology, "real type" be replaced by "empirical type" and "realistic orientation" by "empirical orientation."

V. *Essence*

It is often customary to think of essence in terms of the Lockean distinction between nominal and real essence (Locke [1690] 1959, 2:25–30). The distinction (but not the nominalist and skeptical connotations that Locke attached to it) is employed in what follows, as it suits our reconstructive purposes. The *nominal essence* of a thing consists of the manifest or observable properties by means of which it can be identified as a thing of that kind. However, if we want to explain the properties the thing manifests, we have to penetrate deeper and reveal the inner constitution of the thing. This is the *real essence,* and it is causally responsible for the thing's having the manifest properties that belong to its nominal essence. Locke himself put this idea of the relation between the two essences as follows in the case of gold, a chemical substance that will be of some interest to us: "it is the real constitution of its insensible parts [i.e., its real essence], on which depend all those properties of colour, weight, fusibility, fixedness, &c. . . . which makes it to be gold, or gives it the right to that name, which is therefore its nominal essence" (27).

Locke himself was skeptical of ever discovering the real essences, so he thought that only clusters of readily detectable properties and powers can serve as criteria for recognition and classification of things. Now that science has progressed in leaps and bounds, we do seem to have access to some of the real essences; there should be no obstacle now to using them, too, for classifying things as instances of kinds. This has been evidenced, for example, by "the substitution of chromosome counts for anatomical examination in determining the sex of an athlete" (Harré and Madden 1975, 17).

It seems that we have to have our essentialism with a dose of relativism or ontic pluralism; we have to relativize essences to points of view, explanatory questions, disciplinary interests, practical contexts. For example, the (nominal and real) essence of a particular sample of matter may be related to its being gold or its being money (or a ring, or an artificial tooth), depending on our point of view. To preserve the realist character of our essentialism, we are not allowed to think that essences are ontically dependent on epistemic points of view, i.e., that points of view or conceptual frameworks create essences. In a sample of matter there may in fact, objectively, inhere a number of essences—and hence ontic pluralism about essence is justified. Each relevant epistemic point of view, instead of generating an essence, turns our attention to it, helps uncover it. Plurality of existence and relativity of cognition may go hand in hand without violating the tenets of realism.

In section IX, I will show how the notion of essence can be used for interpreting the Mengerian notion of money. To anticipate: viewed from the economic standpoint, the nominal essence of a particular piece or sample of matter can be related to its being an instance of the money universal, and if this is correct, then its real essence has to be characterized in terms of the notion of the invisible hand.

VI. *Power*

Causal powers find a role in the ontic furniture of Mengerian economics together with essences, universals, particulars, and necessities. Powers are needed to put the economy into motion. Powers are properties that can be attributed to things. They come in many guises.

> Thus we say, Fire has a power to melt gold, i.e. to destroy the consistency of its insensible parts, and consequently its hardness, and make it fluid; that the sun has a power to blanch wax, and wax has a power to be blanched by the sun, whereby the yellowness is destroyed, and whiteness made to exist in its room. . . . Power thus considered is two-fold, viz. as able to make, or able to receive any change. (Locke [1690] 1959, 1:308–9)

Following Aristotle (*Metaphysics* 8.1), Locke calls the one active power and the other passive power. Often "power" is used to refer solely to active powers. There are also expressions that relatively unambiguously refer to passive powers, such as "disposition," "capacity," "liability."

The following analysis of the notion of power ties a power of a thing to its nature or real essence (Harré and Madden 1975, 86):

(P)   "X has the power to A" means "X can or will do A, in the appropriate conditions, in virtue of its intrinsic nature."

This notion involves the distinction between *intrinsic* and *extrinsic* conditions. The former consist of those features that constitute the nature or real essence of a thing. The latter consist of those circumstances that may change without the thing being changed. (P) says, in effect, that if both intrinsic and extrinsic conditions are appropriately materialized, then the power will manifest itself.

Harré and Madden make the further distinction between *enabling* conditions and *stimulus* conditions. The satisfaction of enabling conditions ensures that the thing is in the state of readiness to act so as to manifest the power. Fulfilling the stimulus conditions amounts to triggering the power so as to bring about the relevant action of the thing as a response.

Furthermore, it is often important to make a distinction between *internal* and *external* conditions of the manifestation of a power, and to keep this separate from the distinction between intrinsic and extrinsic conditions. "Internal" and "external" refer to spatial attributes, to the "inside" and "outside" of the spatial envelope of a thing. It is noteworthy that intrinsic conditions do not have to be internal to a thing, nor extrinsic conditions external to it (Harré and Madden 1975, 87–88).

Only particulars have powers to act; universals do not. "Powerful particular" is the basic constituent of the world in Harré and Madden's ontology. This is another reason to avoid transcendental realism and adopt immanent realism about universals: particulars have to exist for there to be powers. As will be seen, real causal powers seem to be important for the Mengerian vision of the economy.

Money particulars have many powers and capacities, such as those of enabling purchases of goods in the market, measuring and preserving value, increasing and decreasing in value, bringing about depressions. Take the power of a money particular to purchase goods. It has this power by virtue of certain intrinsic conditions, its real essence. As we shall see, these conditions are not internal to the money particular; for instance, they do not lie in its molecular structure. An external enabling condition for a note of one Soviet ruble to manifest its power to purchase goods is that it is used in the Soviet Union. A stimulus condition for the power to manifest itself is that somebody uses the money particular for purchasing something in the market. All powers and capacities of money particulars are rooted in the real essence of money, but the other conditions of their manifestation may vary from power to power.

Money would have none of the properties mentioned above were there not acting human agents with certain dispositions and powers such as the Mengerian drive to economize or the post-Mengerian entrepreneurial alertness. I have suggested elsewhere (Mäki 1991) that entrepreneurial alertness, as characterized by Israel Kirzner in particular (e.g., 1979, 1985), is a causal power, a power which pushes economizing agents into action. External enabling conditions of the manifestation of this power include free market order. Appearance of a profit opportunity is a stimulus condition for entrepreneurial alertness to manifest itself in economic action. It is noteworthy that intrinsic enabling conditions of entrepreneurial action are left untheorized in Austrian economics. In principle, they could lie either internal to individual actors (in their genetic codes, for instance) or external to them (e.g., in their cultural surroundings). I return to this in section X.

VII. *Necessity*

Any sample of gold has properties that are part neither of its nominal nor of its real chemical essence. To these belong its shape and size; relational properties, such as a sample's having a certain spatiotemporal location or being owned by someone; its use for some particular purpose, etc. These are unstable properties that vary from one sample of gold to another. The nominal essence of gold includes properties like color, weight, ductility. It is by these features that a sample can be recognized (at least by experts) as an instance of a natural kind, of gold. Further, gold has those manifest properties by virtue of its intrinsic structure, its real essence, expressed in its atomic number. The inessential or accidental properties of a sample of gold, such as its specific shape due to a jewelry designer, are not determined by its chemical real essence (although it is clear that its chemical constitution sets limits to its possible shapes).

The notion of real necessity can be incorporated into this picture in at least two different ways. Both are accompanied by *modal realism,* as necessity is taken as a feature of objective reality.

First, *de re* necessity is often regarded as a modality that characterizes the relationship between essential properties and their possessors that prevails by virtue of the structure of the world (not by virtue of how we decide to use words; this would lead to *de dicto* necessity). Depending on one's approach to the notion of essence, necessary or essential properties of things may be conceived as being those of its nominal essence and/or those of its real essence. For example, being liquid at certain temperatures, being colorless, and being tasteless (features characterizing the nominal essence of water), and/or being made of the combination of hydrogen and oxygen (characterizing its real essence) may be thought of as properties that water has necessarily, this being a matter of *de re* necessity.

Kripke (1980), for instance, thinks that only properties constituting real essences can be possessed necessarily: unlike any of its phenomenal features, being made of H_2O is the only necessary property of water. As will be seen, there is no reason to follow Kripke's principle in the case of money, insofar as a reconstruction of the Mengerian theory of money as an explanatory theory is pursued (the case of water may be similar in this regard). In other words, no division between nominal and real essence should be drawn on the basis of the *de re* necessity of the respective properties.

The second way of conceiving necessity is relevant for understanding explanatory theories. In Lockean terms, it characterizes the nomic connection between the nominal and real essence of a thing, and in terms cultivated by Harré and Madden, a relation of natural necessity prevails between the powers and the nature of a thing. The idea is that an entity with this nature or real essence *must* exhibit that behavior as a manifestation of its powers and capacities, under suitable conditions. A thing tends to behave in a certain way necessarily because it is what it is, i.e., it behaves in a way dictated by its nature, given appropriate conditions.

De re necessity thus conceived does not dictate that a thing's powers will necessarily be exercised in a definite way with unequivocal manifest effects irrespective of the circumstances. The idea is that a thing necessarily *tends* to behave in a certain way by virtue of its real essence. It is always possible that various countervailing powers and tendencies and circumstances modify the thing's behavior to a lesser or greater extent.

Menger's notion of "exact law" can be interpreted as depicting *de re* necessities of the above nomic sort. As I said in section IV, exact laws can be interpreted as second-order universals that connect exact types. It is these connections in the social world that can be viewed as involving alleged real necessities. The idea is that because the first-order universals (such as economizing action and money) are what they are, their connections are necessarily such and such. (For details see Mäki 1986.)

The instances of money have the powers and capacities they do by virtue of the real essence of money. I next introduce a notion that is needed to represent the real essence of money.

VIII. *The invisible hand*

Central to my reconstructive interpretation of Mengerian economics along realist lines is a conception of the structure and functioning of the invisible hand. I think it is correct to view the notion of the invisible hand and its relatives (such as those of spontaneous order, unintended consequences, organic evolution, etc.) as being constitutive of the whole enterprise of the theoretical social sciences. Mengerian economics is no exception in this regard.

It is hard to imagine an intentionally performed act that has only intended results as its consequences, i.e., that has no unintended consequences whatsoever. Usually such an act has both intended and unintended consequences. If it lacks one of them, it is most probably the intended results that fail to materialize. I have elsewhere (Mäki 1991) introduced the notion of the *sphere of intendedness,* which denotes the set of states of affairs that an acting agent intended to bring about by his or her act, irrespective of whether he or she was successful in the effort. The notion of an unintended consequence denotes a residuum; all consequences of an act by an agent that the agent did not intend to bring about are the unintended consequences of the act. The notion of an unintended consequence is a necessary ingredient in the notion of the invisible hand, but it does not suffice to define the latter.

The following seem to belong to the set of necessary conditions of the emergence of an invisible-hand consequence (see Mäki 1991). First, the item has to be a causal consequence of self-interested human actions. Second, actions of individual people belonging to a large collective are required. Third, the consequence must not emerge as an intended result of the actions of the collective or any of its individual members, i.e., it must not lie within any individual's or any collective's sphere of intendedness. Fourth, there has to exist a social mechanism of interaction, e.g., a market mechanism, that transforms individual actions into social consequences (phenomena, patterns). Fifth, the consequence has to be in the interests of the members of the collective. This last feature is part of the classical notion of the invisible hand; by dropping it, the notion can be generalized considerably. The Austrian view of the invisible hand or spontaneous order insists on keeping it, however. As Menger put it, the task of theory is to help answer the question, "How can it be that institutions that serve the common welfare and are extremely significant for its development come into being without a *common will* directed toward establishing them?" ([1883] 1963, 146).

Using the terminology of powers, in the market mechanism there seems to inhere a causal power, namely that of bringing about invisible-hand consequences. The market mechanism looks like a structural entity with a distinct power of its own. Another way of conceiving its character, indeed one that would be more compatible with Austrian individualism, is to think that it is agents who have the relevant power, namely the power to bring about invisible-hand consequences in the presence of the social conditions of the market.

Menger's theory of the genesis of money is a paradigmatic case of invisible-hand explanation in Austrian economics (Menger 1892; also [1883] 1963, [1871] 1976). It is an evolutionary account of a spontaneous process in the course of which direct exchange in pure barter becomes transformed into indirect exchange with an institutionally established medium of exchange. The point, of course, is that money as the generally accepted medium of exchange does not emerge as a result of an act of legislation or the like, but as an invisible-hand consequence of individuals' self-interested actions.

As Menger says, "The theory of money necessarily presupposes a theory of the saleableness of goods" (1892, 243). According to "the very nature of things," goods are blessed with "different degrees of saleableness (*Absatzfähigkeit*)" (242). In the terminology of the present essay, the marketability or saleability of a good is a capacity characterizing its nominal essence. Menger mentions a number of conditions that affect this capacity and its manifestation (246–47). Some of them are clearly internal to those goods as physical objects, such as their divisibility and durability.

In the course of the invisible-hand process, individuals are led to exchange less saleable goods for those that are more saleable. As an outcome of the process, the most saleable goods become established as money. It is precious metals that become selected, for reasons such as "their low cost of transport as compared with their value, and, on the other hand, . . . their unlimited durability and the relatively slight cost of hoarding them" (253).

In the invisible-hand process that leads to the emergence of money, it is not the case that "*by chance* a specific alternative becomes more often practiced (or is perceived as being more often practiced) than others" (Vanberg 1986, 92, emphasis added). As we just learned, in Menger's view it is not an outcome of a random process that precious metals adopt the role of generally accepted medium of exchange. Differences in saleability between various useful goods constitute a nonrandom factor that gives direction to the invisible-hand process. These differences are, to some extent at least, based on the inherent characteristics of the goods. These inherent characteristics are based on their physical and chemical real essences, which are irreducible to their economic real essences. As we learned from Locke, the manifest properties of gold depend on "the real constitution of its insensible parts." It is the real essence of gold, expressed in its atomic number, that is, in part at least, causally responsible for its excellent saleability, based on its manifest properties. It is not by chance but rather by virtue of its chemical real essence that gold becomes selected as a generally accepted medium of exchange. This conclusion suggests that Menger's theory of the genesis of money, through its constituent subtheory of the saleability of goods, is dependent on *realism about chemical real essences* as well. These entities exist independently of the human mind.

It seems to me that the notion of the invisible hand, in the form of a metaphorical expression, denotes a mechanism that is usually believed by Austrian economists to be a real aspect of the market economy, existing externally to human minds but not independently of them. Thus Austrians tend to be realists about the invisible hand and its theoretical representations. A further specification is needed here. The structure and workings of the invisible hand lie beyond an epistemic access based on common sense. To common sense, invisible-hand consequences usually appear as results of deliberate design. Commonsense representations are then not semantically realistic with respect to the invisible hand. Epistemic access to the invisible hand can be pursued only by means of scientific representations. This means that the Austrian realism about the invisible hand has to be *scientific realism*.

IX. *Theoretical redescription*

This section gathers some of the threads introduced in previous sections and shows how the structure of some simple elements of the Mengerian theory of money, conceived as an explanatory theory, can be reconstructed in terms of the notions of essence, universal, power, and necessity.

I pick something out of my pocket. I pretend to be ignorant about what it is and start describing some of its observable characteristics. It is a piece of matter that has a flat and round shape, with a diameter of 1.8 centimeters; it is relatively hard; it is reddish in color; it has the number 5 on it, etc. By describing such features I have not yet succeeded in telling what the thing is; I have not delivered any firm idea of its essence, nominal or real. For that purpose, the object has to be redescribed. To get deep into the essence of the object, the redescription has to be formulated in terms of a scientific theory; this is the scientific realist rule. It is scientifically warranted *theoretical redescription* that gives us the best possible clue as to what empirically described objects really are, what their nature or essence is.

As I have argued elsewhere (Mäki 1990a), the idea of theoretical redescription is vital for an essentialist realist notion of scientific explanation, a notion in terms of which I claim the Austrian notion of invisible-hand explanation can be fruitfully reconstructed. The central insight behind this notion of explanation is that *the way objects are* is dependent on *what those objects are*. If we have an idea of the essence of an object, we can pursue explanation of its behavior by redescribing it as a manifestation of the essence. In the course of explanation, theoretical redescription is substituted for empirical description, and the object of the latter is *ontologically reduced* to the object of the former.

Theoretical redescriptions are in part pragmatically conditioned, that is, they are relative to points of view, questions, purposes, etc. (this is what I called, in section V, relativity of cognition). A particular piece of matter in my pocket can be variously (but not arbitrarily) redescribed, depending on the pragmatic context. In the context of chemistry, for example, the redescription might go as follows. The piece can be empirically described as a relatively small, round, hard, reddish piece of matter with the power to conduct electricity. As the first step of its redescription, the particular piece of matter can be redescribed as an exemplification of copper, which is a universal and a natural kind, identified by means of features characterizing its nominal essence. In regard to its chemical nominal essence many characteristics of the piece under the empirical description are completely accidental, such as its being located in my pocket now, its shape and size, and its having the number 5 on it. As the second step, copper will be redescribed as a metal with a certain internal structure, expressed in its atomic number. At this level new universals are introduced, such as those of atom, neutron, proton, and electron—not only particular electrons inherent in our particular piece of copper, but electron as a kind. The atomic number of copper denotes the chemical real essence of the piece.

When my hand hit the piece of matter in my pocket, I was not visiting a chemical laboratory but instead strolling around a shopping mall with a newly emerged desire to have a candy bar in my mouth. This background sets another perspective from which to approach the question of what it is that my hand hit. I immediately recognize the piece as a coin, with certain figures on it, minted in copper; it is a five-penny coin in Finnish currency. Many years ago, it and other similar coins had the power to help purchase a whole candy bar, and also the power to make a beggar want it from me. Today its purchasing power is weak, and I have to add some other coins to get what I want and to make the beggar satisfied. Characterizations like these make it possible to recognize the particular piece of matter as an instance of money, of the generally accepted medium of exchange. Being an instance of the money universal is the nominal economic essence of the piece of matter in my pocket. Some of the characteristics of the particular piece are accidental in respect to its economic nominal essence, such as its spatiotemporal location (which is not among its essential properties), color and conductivity of electricity (which define its chemical nominal essence), and its atomic number (which is an expression of its chemical real essence). Its capacity to function in the role of a generally accepted medium of exchange constitutes its essential economic property that defines its economic nominal essence.

An essentialist realist is not content with revealing the nominal essence of money; the properties constituting the nominal essence have to be explained by referring to the real essence of money. It is here that the job of theoretical economics begins. We have to formulate, in theoretical terms, an answer to the question "What is money?" This can be accomplished by putting forth a statement about the causal history of money, namely that the money universal is an institutional form that is an outcome of a spontaneous social process dependent on the economizing and entrepreneurial action of human individuals. In other words, the money universal is a manifestation of the workings of the invisible hand. This is a condensed statement of what money ultimately is, of its real essence. As such, the statement enables us to give an account of the powers and capacities that instances of the money universal necessarily have.

Because of its real essence, samples of copper necessarily have the power or capacity to conduct electricity as well as some other properties. Similarly, by virtue of its real essence, instances of money have the power to act as a generally accepted medium of exchange, as a measure of value, etc. The task of theoretical monetary economics is to clarify the necessary relations between the nominal and real essence of money.

If we have to answer the question "Why is it that this flat, round, and reddish piece of matter can be used to acquire that candy bar over there?" we first have to answer the question "What is this piece of matter?" The answer must be given in economic terms. In answering the question the first step is the statement that the piece is an instance of a coin (of a "real type" in Menger's terminology). The second step is the statement that it is an instance of the money universal (of an "exact type"). The third step, one that belongs to theoretical economics proper, is the statement that the money universal is a necessary manifestation of the invisible hand (involving an "exact law"). These statements are needed to explain why the piece of copper has some of the powers it has.

Note that the third statement is about the structure of the money universal, not about its particular or generic instances. Indeed it would be incorrect to claim that the particular coin in my pocket is an outcome of an invisible-hand process; in fact it is a result of deliberate design. However, this fact is completely accidental in respect to the real essence of money.

We may say that a particular coin in my pocket now is both a spontaneous consequence of human actions and also an intended result of deliberate design. This sounds paradoxical, but the paradox disappears as we redescribe the coin in terms of immanent realism about universals. The particular in the coin is a result of design, while the universal in the coin, i.e., the economic kind that the coin instantiates, is an invisible-hand consequence (which constitutes its real essence).

There are differences in how the chemical and economic real essences of the copper coin are characterized. The chemical real essence of the copper coin is described in synchronic and nonmental terms (in terms of its atomic structure that contains no sentient elements), while the economic real essence of the copper coin is described in diachronic and partly mental terms (in terms of the genetic structure of the money universal, involving actions by sentient beings). An important thing is the peculiar spontaneous social origin of the money universal: the physical, industrial, and political origins of the particular copper coin in my pocket (having to do with such things as geological evolution, mining, minting, and legislation) are accidental in regard to its economic real essence.

The nominal essence of money, or the money universal, is recognizable by means of commonsense resources only. No scientific theory of money seems to be required. The abstraction that is involved in recognizing a particular piece of copper as money is something that we learn to accomplish as we grow up as members of Western culture. Thus the money universal seems to be a commonsense object. This seems not to be the case with the real essence of money. The fact that instances of money have the powers they have as media of exchange due to a spontaneous social process in which the subjects are economizing entrepreneurs is beyond any epistemic grasp based on common sense. No mere abstraction from accidental features is sufficient here. The limited perspective of common sense has to be surpassed by formulating a scientific theory that postulates the existence of a complicated social mechanism. The real essence of money is a scientific object.

Theoretical monetary economics in the Mengerian style claims to be able to explain why certain powers, tendencies, and capacities necessarily inhere in money. Explanations of actual monetary phenomena are pursued by theoretically redescribing them as manifestations of those powers and tendencies. Any particular manifestation, however, is "impure" in the sense that what it is a manifestation of is not restricted merely to those tendencies that inhere in the money universal, but embraces other factors as well. These other factors have been left out of the picture in the process of abstraction and isolation whereby the notion of money as an economic universal was formed. Mengerian theory is in this sense unrealistic. It is because of this kind of unrealisticness, i.e., because of the actual presence of those other factors, that no accurate *predictions* based on the theory alone are forthcoming. On the other hand, it is precisely because of the alleged semantic realisticness of the theory as a true representation of the nominal and real essence and their interrelationship that Mengerians claim to be able to provide successful *explanations* of monetary and other economic phenomena.

X. *Folk psychology*

I have argued that Mengerian economics subscribes to scientific realism in its conception of the existence and epistemic accessibility of the invisible hand. I now argue that this is accompanied by *commonsense realism* in the Austrian conception of economic agents. In particular my point is that the Austrian conception of agents is committed to so-called folk psychology.

Folk psychology is the conception of human action deployed by ordinary folk and also by scientists in ordinary life situations. This conception is formulated in a framework of minds with thoughts, emotions, desires, motives, intentions, beliefs. Within folk psychology, human action is explained and predicted as an emanation from these mental entities. Indeed mental entities are the ultimate explainers; they are not to be eliminated in favor of something else, unlike some radically materialist approaches that seek to substitute neurological or computational accounts for the intentional accounts of folk psychology (see, e.g., Churchland 1984, Stich 1983).

While it is clear that Austrian economics is not primarily interested in explaining individual action, it nevertheless contains a conception of human action that subscribes to the "commonsensism" of folk psychology: human action is characterized in such mental terms as valuation, purpose, expectation, alertness, etc.

Money and economizing action, the two universals at the two ends of the invisible-hand process, are not symmetrically treated by Austrian economics as to their explanatory reduction to real essences. Money is so reduced, as we have seen; money is identified with an invisible-hand consequence which gives the genetic structure of money. Entrepreneurial economizing, on the other hand, is not so reduced. Particular episodes of human action are redescribed as instances of the universal of economizing action, and particular agents as instances of the universal of economizing entrepreneur—just as particular coins are redescribed as instances of the money universal. But the real essence of these actor and action universals is not given, not even sought. No attempt is made to redescribe them further, for example, as manifestations of the genetic constitution of humans as biological creatures or of the cultural attributes of humans as social beings. Austrian economics pursues an account of why instances of money possess the powers and other properties they do, but not of why economic agents have the powers and other properties they are supposed to have. This is an implication of the commitment to the commonsense realism of folk psychology.

XI. *Why realism?*

I have argued that Menger (and probably many other Austrian economists) can be interpreted as espousing realism in different forms, such as ontological and semantic realism, commonsense and scientific realism, as well as essentialist, immanent, and modal realism. This means that Mengerian economics can be seen as pursuing realisticness in economic theory in some of its more demanding forms.

Conscious adoption of such a combination of realisms might enable Mengerian economists to engage in more accurate and fruitful self-reflection. A comprehensive realism of the kind outlined in this paper might serve as a basis for (1) interpreting past and present work within the Austrian tradition as well as for (2) providing recommendations for future activities within economics and its metatheory. Most of the discussion in the foregoing has dealt with the first task. I now make a few sketchy remarks about the second.

The combination of realisms outlined above may provide, for some audiences consisting of economists, a persuasive alternative to Friedmanian instrumentalism or any other metatheory of economics which fails to recommend the pursuit of semantically realistic theories and puts stress on predictive success at the expense of explanatory ambitions. These audiences may find a Mengerian type of essentialist realism an appealing option precisely because it is able to combine an insistence on realisticness with an ambitious notion of explanation by means of general theory. This combination has little resemblance to the canons of typical versions of historicism and institutionalism, often conceived as major representatives of the requirement of realisticness in economics.

Another audience, perhaps of minor importance to economists, might also find the suggested essentialist reconstruction interesting. This audience consists of philosophers who share the recent interest in, if not enthusiasm about, essentialism within general philosophy. If nothing else, this point could be used to give our efforts some extra credibility, perhaps a flavor of timeliness.

Essentialist realism of the Mengerian kind may also be found persuasive by audiences that do not regard economic theory as a neutral tool for advancing whatever goals (including radically interventionist ends) one happens to have, with the presupposition that the real world is malleable at will (a view well consistent with the instrumentalist conception of theory). Denial of such malleability would seem to presuppose acceptance of ontological and semantic modal realism: if there are real necessities in the economy, revealed by an economic theory, then that theory would seem to have the implication of proscribing policies that run counter to those necessities.

I have offered an outline of an essentialist reconstruction of Mengerian economics rather uncritically. I have done so to show that it seems possible to carry out a unified and coherent interpretation in these terms. There are two approaches that can and should be adopted in a critical inquiry into my suggestions. First, the fitness of the suggested general philosophical categories with Mengerian categories may be questioned. This concerns both the metatheoretical and the economic categories used by Menger and later Mengerians. Second, the philosophical categories and tenets of essentialism should not be taken as unproblematic. They are disputed by philosophers themselves, so they should be viewed as disputable. After all, by carefully scrutinizing one attempted application of those essentialist ideas, economic methodologists might be able to contribute to the ongoing philosophical discussion.

I am indebted to Bruce Caldwell for helpful comments.

References

Aristotle. 1960. *Metaphysics*. Ann Arbor: University of Michigan Press.

Armstrong, D. M. 1978. *Universals and scientific realism,* vol. 1, *Nominalism and realism*. Cambridge: Cambridge University Press.

Churchland, Paul. 1984. *Matter and consciousness*. Cambridge: MIT Press.

Harré, R., and E. H. Madden. 1975. *Causal powers*. Oxford: Basil Blackwell.

Kirzner, Israel. 1979. *Perception, opportunity, and profit*. Chicago: University of Chicago Press.

———. 1985. *Discovery and the capitalist process*. Chicago: University of Chicago Press.

Kripke, Saul. 1980. *Naming and necessity*. Cambridge: Harvard University Press.

Locke, John. [1690] 1959. *An essay concerning human understanding*. Vols. 1–2. New York: Dover.

Mäki, Uskali. 1986. Carl Menger's conception of economics as an exact science. Mimeo.

———. 1989. On the problem of realism in economics. *Ricerche economiche* 43.1–2:176–98.

———. 1990a. Scientific realism and Austrian explanation. *Review of Political Economy* 2.3:310–44.

———. 1990b. Friedman and realism. *Research in the History of Economic Thought and Methodology* 10.

———. 1991. Practical syllogism, entrepreneurship, and the invisible hand. In *Economics and hermeneutics,* ed. Don Lavoie. London: Routledge & Kegan Paul.

Menger, Carl. [1883] 1963. *Problems of economics and sociology*. Urbana: University of Illinois Press.

———. [1871] 1976. *Principles of economics*. New York and London: New York University Press.

———. 1892. On the origin of money. *Economic Journal* 2.

Stich, Stephen. 1983. *From folk psychology to cognitive science*. Cambridge: MIT Press.

Vanberg, Viktor. 1986. Spontaneous market order and social rules: a critical examination of F. A. Hayek's theory of cultural evolution. *Economics and Philosophy* 2.1:75–100.

IV. General themes

What do we know about Menger?

Max Alter

Introduction

Carl Menger was undoubtedly one of the most influential economists of all time. As he was a member of the founding trinity of neoclassical economics and founder of the Austrian school of economics, his ideas, so one would think, have significantly shaped the economic thought of the twentieth century. Such a characterization, however, ignores another superlative associated with his name: he is probably the least read and least understood, not only of the authors of the marginal revolution, but also of the first generation of Austrian economists. His work exerted its influence mainly through its reformulation in the writings of his followers and adherents, above all Friedrich von Wieser and Eugen von Böhm-Bawerk. But although their own thinking had been decisively shaped by Menger's *Grundsätze der Volkswirthschaftslehre* of 1871, they also gave his theory a direction which would ultimately take it far from his original aim.

The last two decades or so have witnessed a somewhat more differentiated approach to the famous writings of the 1870s. The process of dehomogenizing Menger, Jevons, and Walras has begun. More recently, with progress achieved in the understanding of Menger's work, the Austrian School itself has become the target of this critical approach. The disaggregation of the first generation of Austrian economists—Menger, Wieser, and Böhm-Bawerk—is beginning to show its first results.

The acquisition of the Menger archives by Duke University provides a welcome opportunity to reexamine the questions which have been raised about both the neo-classical and the Austrian triumvirates. To be able to take full advantage of the new material we ought to take stock of our current knowledge, above all, of Menger's theoretical and methodological contributions. Should there be any questions which are as yet unanswered, the focus provided by such questions will facilitate a structured evaluation of the new material.

One would have thought that over a century after the publication of both of Menger's main contributions, the *Grundsätze* of 1871 and the *Untersuchungen über die Methode der Socialwissenschaften, und der politischen Oekonomie insbesondere* of 1883, there should be few such questions. As we shall see in the next section of this paper, a bird's-eye survey of Menger scholarship reveals that there are, in fact, more questions than answers and such answers as there are often given conflicting interpretations of the same passages cited from his work. This is mainly due to the dual-track approach which the interpretation and analysis of his economic methodology and his economic theory have followed with scarcely any links established between the two strands of discussion. In the 1980s, however, another approach began to emerge. There, a synthesis in the interpretation of Menger's theoretical and methodological work has begun to open up the possibility of a more comprehensive understanding. Some of the questions raised by this synthetic interpretation, and their answers, are discussed in the two main sections of this paper.

In the first section we shall take a look at Menger's methodology and epistemology on the basis of a critical examination of his life's work as a whole and not only of the *Untersuchungen*. The central themes discussed there are the *verstehende* nature of Menger's methodology which ranks economics among the *Geisteswissenschaften*,[1] the problems encountered in Menger's introspectively conceived "exact" theory, and the status of his concepts of causality and of the unintended consequences of human action.

The same critical approach is then brought to bear on Menger's theoretical contributions. The second section focuses on the nature of his theory of value in contrast to his theory of price formation, on the implications of his basic assumptions of economic behavior, that is, of his hierarchically structured set of *Bedürfnisse*, and on the analytic problems resulting from his epistemologically based transformation problem. We shall also see that the existence of a transformation problem is not an accidental aberration. It is deeply embedded in Menger's

---

1. A number of German terms have been used in this paper to emphasize the specific intellectual tradition which is characteristic of Menger's world of thought. The two crucial terms are *Bedürfnis* and *Wissenschaft*, whose meaning encompasses far more than that of their English translations. On the problem involved in translating *Bedürfnis*, see Macpherson 1977. *Wissenschaft* is traditionally translated as "science," but it is more than that; it refers to any body of systematic knowledge allowing its critical examination. In German, literature and history can be dealt with "scientifically" without invoking any connotation of the methodology of the natural sciences. Since Menger inhabits this world of thought, the German terms have been retained throughout to act as a constant reminder of this fact. For the convenience of the reader who does not have ready access to a German-English dictionary I include the translation of these terms here (adjectival forms are listed in parentheses immediately after the noun): *Bedeutung*, meaning, importance; *Bedürfnis* (pl. *Bedürfnisse*), need or want; *Bedürfnisbefriedigung*, satisfaction of need or want; *Geisteswissenschaften* (*geisteswissenschaftlich*), humanities, moral sciences; *Geistesgeschichte* (*geistesgeschichtlich*), intellectual history; *Naturwissenschaften* (*naturwissenschaftlich*), natural sciences; *Verstehen* (*verstehende*), understanding; *Wesen*, essence, nature; *Wissenschaft* (*wissenschaftlich*), science; *Zusammenschau*, synopsis.

vision of the economic world. That will conclude the discussion of Menger's work in this paper.

A vast number of issues which are still largely unresolved are ignored here: there will be no discussion of Menger's theories of distribution or of capital and interest, or of the relationship of his theory of money with his theory of value. Neither will there be any investigations of his conceptions of entrepreneurship, of production, or of the role of institutions and of the invisible hand, nor will there be any attempts at assessing the claim that Menger's economic theory is above all a theory of economic development. The issues discussed in this paper are fundamental to an understanding of Menger's work and hence indispensable for a discussion of those just listed. Only a resolution of the problems posed by Menger's conception of value and of prices and of the way values and prices can be known by the economic agent and the observer will allow us to understand, for instance, how Menger approached the problem of capital. Only once these fundamentals have been clarified shall we finally be able to dehomogenize Menger, Jevons, and Walras and to disaggregate Menger, Wieser, and Böhm-Bawerk.

Some final remarks before we commence: A full demonstration of the results presented in the synthetic interpretation of Menger's work below would go well beyond the space available here. A full discussion is, however, available elsewhere,[2] and the reader will be directed to the appropriate place wherever necessary. This paper also presupposes a certain minimal acquaintance with Menger's *Grundsätze* and *Untersuchungen*. The analysis of Menger's work presented here is based on the original texts. Each reference to the original German also includes, however, a parallel citation to the standard English translation.

Menger in the literature

One vaguely representative, quantitative indicator of an economist's current popularity or, rather, current subjectively perceived importance is the frequency with which his work is cited in the relevant literature, and a very rough approximation of this indicator is a citation count in the *Social sciences citation index (SSCI)*. There, entries under Menger show citations by approximately two hundred authors since 1966.[3] Perusal of this literature brings a few interesting facts to light.

A large number of references are simply to Menger as an undifferenti-

2. See Alter 1990.
3. There is no mystical significance attached to the year 1966. It is simply the first year for which the information was available. Nor should too much importance be attached to the figure 200, since *SSCI* is not sufficiently comprehensive to be a reliable source for more than a first, superficial literature search. References there to citations of Menger contain some notable omissions, such as *Atlantic Economic Journal* 1978, Butos 1985, Hansen 1968, Hayek 1973, Karl Menger 1973, and *Journal of Austrian Economics*.

ated member of the founding trinity of neoclassical economic theory. Only relatively few contributions deal with specific aspects of Menger's economic theory, such as his theory of value and prices, his theory of capital, of distribution, and of markets. His theory of money is an exception here: not only have there been a number of papers explicitly devoted to Menger on money,[4] his analysis of money as medium of exchange may even be considered as state-of-the-art.[5] One comes across a number of bemusing aspects—for instance, Menger seems to be important enough to be called upon as an authority in a paper on the "economics of the Canadian Bishops,"[6] but he is not judged relevant enough to be listed in the index of a book devoted to an exploration of such Austrian themes as time, uncertainty, and disequilibrium in spite of the fact that he is cited by at least one of the contributors to the volume.[7] But there are also a number of puzzling aspects: some papers demonstrate the compatibility of Menger's analysis with the indifference-curves approach of later decades,[8] while others draw attention to the fact that Menger's hierarchy of needs engenders a lexicographic preference ordering.[9] Or, we are informed that Menger's theory does not contain a concept of entrepreneurial activity, only to learn less than a year later that Menger's concept of the entrepreneur is very much along Knightian lines.[10]

Most of the literature which mentions Menger but which does not deal with his theories or methodology directly does not tell us anything about Menger. If anything at all, then, it only tells us something about the state of ignorance in the economics profession at large as far as Menger's work is concerned. It will therefore be more fruitful to concentrate here on the small subset of the literature which discusses Menger's contributions to economic theory and methodology.

The discussion of Menger and his work has traversed two stages and has now entered a third one. The first stage started off with Karl Menger's introduction to the second edition of the *Grundsätze* and F. X. Weiss's essay on the differences between the 1871 and 1923 editions of that work.[11] It culminated via Hayek, Bloch, Stigler, and Knight in

4. Streissler 1973, O'Driscoll 1986; see also Hirsch 1928, Roll 1936. Most references in the English-language literature, however, are only to Menger's "On the origin of money" (1892).

5. See Jones 1976. Clower (1977) actually prefaced his paper with a quote from Menger's "On the origin of money"; indeed, "a sample from modern economic textbooks shows that the Mengerian conception is nowadays implicitly accepted" (Lagerspetz 1984, 3).

6. Block 1988.

7. See Rizzo 1979, where Menger is cited by R. Garrison on p. 216.

8. McCulloch 1977; implicitly also Scaparone 1986.

9. Apart from Ironmonger (1972) we find above all Georgescu-Roegen and his followers here; cf., e.g., Georgescu-Roegen 1968, Gowdy 1985.

10. See Kirzner 1978 versus Martin 1979.

11. Karl Menger 1923; Weiss 1924.

Kauder's *History of marginal utility theory* of 1965.[12] This literature brought together diverse strands of information about Menger—biographical, bibliographical, historical, philosophical, and theoretical—and attempted a first analysis and interpretation of Menger's work with varying degrees of success.

The second stage built mainly on the work done by Hayek and Kauder. Starting with Hansen in 1968, though without really following his lead, it lasted approximately a decade, witnessing two symposia dedicated to Menger in its course.[13] During this period the discussion of Menger and his work proceeded along two almost separate lines. Our understanding of Menger's methodology, of the *Methodenstreit,* and of its philosophical underpinnings was deepened by Hansen, Hutchison, and Bostaph.[14] Chronologically much later but belonging thematically to this period and to this line of argument are surveys of the literature on Menger's methodology by Cubeddu and Boos and an essay by White.[15]

Alongside the discussion of Menger's methodology developed the literature on Menger's contributions to economic theory. Here, above all, Streissler has begun to draw out the specific characteristics of Menger's theoretical work against that of Wieser and Böhm-Bawerk and to relate it to its socioeconomic environment.[16] Analyses of Menger's concepts of exchange and entrepreneurship not only widened the scope of this theoretical strand, they also drew more specific attention to the links of Menger's theory of value and prices with what has come to be called institutionalism.[17] At the end of this period we had at our disposal, on the one hand, a discussion of Menger's economic methodology and its philosophical origins and, on the other hand, a discussion of Menger's economic theory and its environment, including some pointers towards institutionalism. What was missing was an in-depth discussion relating these two strands in the literature on Menger, namely one which looked at Menger's theory in the light of his methodology and vice versa.

This was the point of departure of the third stage. Attempts at such a "unified," synthetic analysis, at discussing Menger's theories of value, prices, and capital in the light of his methodology and its philosophical origins, began emerging in the 1980s.[18]

Looking at the developments of the last decade and a half from the perspective of themes rather than chronology, we can see that advances

12. Hayek 1934, revised in Hayek 1968; Bloch 1940, but see also Bloch 1937; Stigler 1937; Knight 1950; Kauder 1958, 1959, 1962, 1965.
13. See *Zeitschrift für Nationalökonomie* 1972, reprinted in English as Hicks and Weber 1973, and *Atlantic Economic Journal* 1978.
14. Hansen 1968; Hutchison 1973, 1981; Bostaph 1976, 1978.
15. Cubeddu 1985; Boos 1986; White 1985.
16. Streissler 1969, 1972.
17. Exchange: Moss 1978. Entrepreneurship: Kirzner 1978; Martin 1979.
18. See Alter 1982, 1986; Butos 1985; Endres 1984, 1987.

in Mengerian scholarship have enlarged our understanding not only of both Menger's economic theory and his methodology but also of the interaction of these two, hitherto rather "specialist," areas of investigation. In the discussion of Menger's methodology virtually all the central themes have been picked up by all authors: the meaning and status of Menger's "exact" theory; Menger's essentialism and Aristotelianism; his rejection of mathematics; methodological individualism; and his conception of the unintended consequences of human action. But this does not mean that the interpretation of these themes has been unanimous throughout, or that the final word has been spoken on any of these issues as yet.[19]

The analyses of Menger's theory of value and prices covered the concept of economic rationality and the affinity of Menger's theory of value with institutionalist economics; Menger's theory of exchange; his concept of the entrepreneur; and, at long last, a very much overdue discussion of the difference between Menger's concept of capital and that of Böhm-Bawerk.[20]

The most obvious underlying theme in the literature listed here is, of course, that Menger was different from Walras and Jevons. But what was previously more a statement of an obvious, nonspecific condition is now given substance through synthetic investigation of Menger's work building on the two separate strands of Mengerian interpretation of the preceding stage. The dehomogenization process is finally maturing.

The picture of Menger which emerges from the literature is almost that of a great opportunity missed. If neoclassical economics had traveled the Mengerian road instead of the Walrasian one, the world—at least, when viewed from certain quarters—would have been a better place. Which are the features that make up our current image of this most obscure, neglected, and least read of the founders of neoclassical economics?

There seems to be no doubt about the impact of his achievements: without Menger there would have been no Austrian school of economics. There would not have been any of a large number of debates which were very much at the center of the development of economic theory at their time and which are by no means all resolved to date. The hallmarks of this school—methodological individualism, subjectivism, unintended consequences of human action, uncertainty, ignorance, the

19. For contrasting evaluations cf., e.g., Hutchison 1981 and White 1985. Against both of these cf. Hansen 1968.

20. Economic rationality: Alter 1982; Langlois 1985. Institutionalist economics: Endres 1984; Jaffé 1976; Streissler 1972; Streissler and Weber 1973; see also Butos 1985; Moss 1978; Pagano 1985, ch. 5; Vaughn 1978. Exchange: Moss 1978. Entrepreneur: Kirzner 1978; Martin 1979. Capital: Endres 1987.

quest for information, microanalysis, valuation at the margin, rejection of mathematics—all derive from the *Grundsätze* of 1871 and are accepted almost as articles of faith by its current adherents.

Some other features which have also almost achieved the status of slogans are not quite as undisputed as those of the first group. What precisely are we to make of Menger's essentialism? Does it or does it not matter for his economic theory? What does it mean to say that his concern is with the understanding of economic phenomena? In particular, is this understanding introspective or not? What is the status of his "exact" theory? Is it aprioristic? How do we have to understand his concept of genetic causality?

It is somewhat disconcerting that more than a century after the *Methodenstreit* these questions have not yet been answered satisfactorily. But if our doubts about the "correct" interpretation of his principles of economic methodology give rise to a certain amount of concern, this is still nothing compared to the headache imparted by a survey of the current state of interpretation of Menger's economic theory. Here the lack of agreement on what his central theoretical positions are is simply astounding.

Is valuation at the margin the core of his analysis or not? Can we define a conventional utility function on the basis of his verbal exposition? That is to say, does Menger assume a continuous and convex preference space, or are his preferences lexicographically ordered? Does he develop a theory of value, or of prices? If value and price are different concepts, what is the meaning of value? Does he jettison his principle of error, ignorance, and uncertainty in his theory of prices? What precisely does he mean by uncertainty if the preceding question is to be answered in the affirmative? Are his prices equilibrium prices in the Walrasian mold, or does he develop a theory of monopolistic pricing? Does he have a theory of entrepreneurial activity, or does he not? Does he advocate the roundaboutness of the methods of production and the concept of the period of production as the basis of his theory of capital? If not, what precisely is his theory of capital?

It is not difficult to find an advocate for any one of these alternatives in the literature on Menger.[21] And if anyone should become slightly worried that some of these positions are contradictory, not to say mutually exclusive, these worries are indeed justified. With such a large number of diverse interpretations of Menger's theory it almost seems as if we did not know anything at all about his economics. The pertinent question which arises out of this desperate situation is how can interpretations of one and the same book, namely the *Grundsätze* of 1871, arrive at

21. For a number of examples see the second part of the Introduction in Alter 1990.

conclusions which are so wildly disparate? Can we find an explanation for this puzzle? And can we find a way of deciding which interpretation is right?

In the remainder of this paper I try to answer both questions. To this end, I concentrate on a few central themes in Menger's theory and methodology which form the basis for an understanding of most subsequent issues.

The synthetic interpretation of Menger (part 1)

The most convincing explanation for the existence of a number of contradictory interpretations of Menger's economic theory is to be found, to my mind, in the obscurity of Menger's terminology. This terminology has nothing in common with that of twentieth-century neoclassical economics. Approaching Menger from the modern, Walrasian perspective must lead one astray because he inhabits a different world. His world is that of the nineteenth century—to be precise, that of nineteenth-century romantic-historicist thought.[22] Ideally we would need a guide not just to this world of thought but more specifically to Menger's understanding of it. That is to say, we would need a handbook to his philosophy of science. Unfortunately, although Menger intended to, he never published one, and there may be very good reasons for it, as we shall see later.[23] Nevertheless, if we approach the *Grundsätze* from this nineteenth-century romantic-historicist perspective, and if we search for Menger's conception of methodology and epistemology not only in his explicit statements about these subjects but in his implicit statements, that is, in the methodology and epistemology underlying his economic theory, we stand a fair chance of arriving at a consistent understanding of Menger's work.

Let me cite a few examples of where such an approach will take us. Menger's methodology, its components, their background, compatibility, and incompatibility have to be discussed on the basis of his theoretical writings as well as on his explicitly methodological works. The interpretation of his methodology occupies a central position in an understanding of his thought, since it is through the philosophy of science, that is, methodology and epistemology, that the scientific conception of social reality (the *geistesgeschichtliche* background) enters

22. For a detailed exposition see Hansen 1968 and Essay I in Alter 1990.

23. The *Untersuchungen* do not contain Menger's philosophy of science. They only contain a discussion of some of its elements, while crucial ingredients of Menger's epistemology (such as the role of induction in the establishment of "exact" theory) and methodology (such as the teleological nature of his conception of causality) have to be prized, indirectly, from his theoretical writings and their environment. The *Untersuchungen* are not, as some would like us to believe, an exposition of methodology. They are merely a critique of the historical economists' methodological aspirations.

the theory itself and, at times, even shapes the analytics of the argument.

This is the case, for instance, with Menger's concept of *Bedürfnis*. Needs and wants feature in all the early neoclassical authors, but it is above all in Menger's theory where they play the central role. Menger inherited this concept from German political economy. But it is only in German thought in general and Hegel's in particular that we can grasp the extent of its importance. There *Bedürfnis* and *Bedürfnisbefriedigung* represent the *loci classici* of economic activity and economic development in human life.[24] In Menger's system too *Bedürfnis* is the starting point of economic activity, and its satisfaction is its goal. The concept of *Bedürfnis* carries Menger's teleological conception of causality within his theory. It also carries his conception of time. In brief, it carries the characterization of his vision of the economic process.

The introduction of Hegel here is not nearly as farfetched as it may seem at first sight. We now know that notebooks on Hegel's philosophy exist among the Menger papers held at Duke University. But even a quarter of a century ago Kauder had reported Menger's interest in Hegel.[25] The interest of the later Menger in Hegel is, furthermore, not an isolated case. The later Dilthey, whose subjectivistic conception of *Verstehen* was not all that far removed from Menger's, had also turned in that direction.[26]

In the construction of his economic theory Menger utilized building blocks which he took from nineteenth-century German political economy and systematized their interaction on the basis of one unifying principle: valuation taking place at the margin of *Bedürfnisbefriedigung*. His essentialist, teleological, and time-based theory of value organizes a world full of ignorance and incomplete information (the world of Romanticism) and incorporates in its foundations concepts, such as expectations, which were to constitute major innovations for other neoclassical approaches. Indeed Menger's development of the theory in the *Grundsätze* can be traced right to the point where the essentialism of his conception of value becomes self-destructive because it poses a transformation problem from values to prices which remains insurmountable within his own methodological and theoretical framework. Menger's attempt to bridge the dualism between *Geisteswissenschaften* and *Naturwissenschaften,* which although always implicit in his work became explicit only in 1923, foundered at precisely the point where he tried to make value "true" and give the law of value the same status as the laws

24. See also the section "Menger's theory of value and German political economy" in Alter 1990.
25. Kauder 1965, 89 n. 27.
26. See also note 39 below.

of science—indeed linking it directly to biology—while retaining the historicist tradition in his theory of prices.[27]

These brief examples basically illustrate the answer to both questions posed at the end of the last section. The wild disparity of interpretations of Menger's theory is, to my mind, due to the fact that their proponents have taken the *Grundsätze* in isolation, referring neither to its *geistes-geschichtliche* background nor to its implicit methodology. In other words, they neglected what I call the synthetic approach to Menger's theory and methodology. And it is this approach that will provide the criterion with which we shall be able to answer the second question. Only a historic understanding of Menger's work will allow us to establish what he actually meant.

Such an approach requires, above all, that Menger's work be treated as an element of the history of economic thought, that is, as an element of intellectual history. We are thus engaging in historical work, or, to be more precise, we are embarking on hermeneutic research. We have a text at our disposal, and this text must be read within its own context. Its authenticity must be preserved. Therefore, if we are unable to understand the text authentically within our context we must reconstruct the text's own context. Only once we have understood the text in this way shall we be able, and free, to draw our conclusions about the value of the text for us.

It is very easy to be led astray and miss the meaning of the text when we approach the *Grundsätze*. The central example which springs to mind here is Menger's derivation of the marginality principle. It occurs in chapter 3 of the *Grundsätze* and can easily mislead the reader who approaches it with a Walrasian bend of mind (and here I refer to well-nigh all neoclassical economists, even those who profess Austrian affiliations like, for instance, Wieser, Böhm-Bawerk, and Hayek) to mistake this section as the core of the theory and to ignore all that went on before and afterwards in the development of Menger's argument. With this I mean, among other things, that one tends to read utility functions and traditional preference structures into a theory which simply does not satisfy the necessary axioms. One therefore overlooks the importance of Menger's concept of economic homogeneity, which has to be viewed in contrast to physical homogeneity, and one ignores the leveling effect the choice of a single commodity in his illustrative examples has on the hierarchically ordered *Bedürfnis* set which provides the basis of his theory. Finally, to preempt one of the conclusions to which these observations lead, one also misses one of the fundamental errors contained in the *Grundsätze,* namely that Menger addressed, within his own frame of reference, the wrong analytical problem.

27. A fully documented exposition of these arguments is presented in Alter 1990.

This brings us to another methodological point. The approach taken in this paper represents, above all, an internal critique of Menger's theory. Immanent criticism is here the first, necessary step if one wants to proceed any further. Questions of relevance of theory and critique of assumptions will only be briefly hinted at, if at all.[28]

Some commentators may object to the synthetic approach proposed here by pointing out that Menger's thought must have undergone a profound transformation since, in 1871, he had dedicated the *Grundsätze* to Wilhelm Roscher, the doyen of the German historical school of economics, whereas he attacked the very same school vehemently in 1883.[29] Furthermore, his conceptual apparatus of the second edition of the *Grundsätze,* published posthumously in 1923, differs significantly from that of the first edition.

A closer scrutiny of Menger's work will show that this objection to the synthetic approach cannot be upheld. On the contrary, we can demonstrate not only that Menger's thought did not undergo any transformation between 1871 and 1883 but also that the terminology of the second edition is much closer to the methodology and epistemology underlying the economic theory of the first edition than the terminology of the first edition itself. The theory itself remained unchanged between the first and the second editions.[30] We can, I believe, plausibly demonstrate that the only change that occurred between 1871 and 1883 was a change of heart towards the end of 1874, when Menger was upset by the lack of understanding Roscher displayed when reviewing Menger's contribution to economic theory in the latter's monumental *Geschichte der National-Oekonomik in Deutschland.*[31] To put it bluntly, Menger turned from liking to disliking the historical economists because they failed to appreciate his contribution to historicist theory.[32] The *Grundsätze* and the *Untersuchungen* sprang from the same mind and the same conceptual structure.[33] On this basis let us now turn to some elements of his explicit and implicit methodology.

Since general discussions of Menger's methodology exist and since the *Untersuchungen* are available in an English translation,[34] I confine

28. See Morgenstern 1972, 1165.
29. See, e.g., Hutchison 1973, 1981.
30. On this see, e.g., the editor's introduction to Karl Menger 1923.
31. Roscher 1874, 1040.
32. Before Popperians and Hayekians start hurling stones, they had better reflect that German historical economics has very much in common with today's institutional economics and, like all of nineteenth-century German historicism, shares very little, if anything at all, with the peculiar Popperian concept of the same name.
33. On this see also Menger's letters to Walras in Walras 1965. As space does not permit a more detailed exposition of these arguments, I have to refer the reader to Essays I and II and the appendix to Essay II in Alter 1990 for a fully documented discussion.
34. See Menger 1963/1985.

myself here to highlighting a number of problematic areas in Menger's methodology and epistemology.

Let us first look at the place of Menger's methodology and epistemology in the history of ideas. Menger's stated intention in the preface to the *Grundsätze* was to overcome the epistemological dualism of the *Geisteswissenschaften* and the *Naturwissenschaften*, on the one hand, and one-sided rationalism or positivism, on the other. He intended to achieve this by allowing for pluralism in method based on monism in epistemology.[35] What he meant by methodology, however, is revealed only by its use in the development of his economic theory: there he chose Aristotelianism as the vehicle to overcome the dualism and the rationalism at the same time; he thus chose the *geisteswissenschaftliche* tradition over the *naturwissenschaftliche,* Galilean tradition.[36] This is exemplified, for instance, by his choice of the fourfold Aristotelian conception of causality over the modern conception of efficient causality. In spite of his original intention the hermeneutic approach to his methodology thus reveals that he actually chose to associate with those who claimed at least different if not superior epistemological status for the humanities over the natural sciences. This is confirmed in the second edition of the *Grundsätze,* where he not only replaced the term "causality" used in 1871 and 1883 by the more appropriate one of "teleology" but also relocated economics from the *Socialwissenschaften* to the *Geisteswissenschaften,* thus publicly embracing the epistemological dualism.[37]

Further confirmation of this interpretation can be obtained by an investigation of the intellectual background to Menger's thought.[38] This makes it clear that Menger really belongs to the period immediately preceding the birth of the modern *Verstehen* doctrine, which was to receive its philosophical foundations only through Wilhelm Dilthey's "critique of historical reason" and which remained a preoccupation mainly of the German-speaking academic world well into the second half of this century.[39] One of Dilthey's forerunners had been the historian Droysen, who had designed a *verstehende* program for historical research and who had certainly also influenced Menger.[40] In a way, we can regard the *Untersuchungen* as Menger's preliminary (because nega-

35. This follows from his discussion of the structure of sciences and of the nature of "exact" theory in the *Untersuchungen.*
36. On this cf. Wright 1975, ch. 1.
37. See Menger 1923, 1.
38. See Essay I in Alter 1990, and Hansen 1968.
39. It is interesting to note that Menger's *Untersuchungen* and Dilthey's *Einleitung in die Geisteswissenschaften* were both published in 1883, both by the same publishing house, and they were both reviewed in the same famous review article by Schmoller (Schmoller 1883).
40. For a detailed discussion see Essay II in Alter 1990.

tively expressed, as a critique) formulation of a *verstehende* program for research in economics and the social sciences, in which he attempted a reconciliation of the controversy of the *Geisteswissenschaften* versus the *Naturwissenschaften* from a position within the *Geisteswissenschaften*. The economic theory of the *Grundsätze,* or, to be more precise, its first formulation of 1871, is in fact Menger's realization of his program for economic research.

Against this background the economic theory of the *Grundsätze* emerges as a *verstehende* economic theory. When Menger says in the *Untersuchungen* that *Verstehen* is "Erfassung des Wesens" (understanding as the grasping of the essence),[41] he merely spells out the methodological precept underlying his subjective moment of value. We, as human beings, can understand human action in a way we cannot understand nature. We can understand (economic) value because the meaning of the satisfaction of a *Bedürfnis* is not based on an objective, external property of the good consumed or the biological foundations of this act; rather, the satisfaction of the *Bedürfnis* has meaning *for us,* the economic agents. The observing economist can understand the action of an economic agent because the economist is likewise an economic agent. This is not just the inescapable starting point for a *verstehende* methodology; it is also clearly stated by Menger in the *Untersuchungen:*

> [In den exacten Socialwissenschaften] sind die menschlichen Individuen und ihre Bestrebungen, die letzten Elemente unserer Analyse, empirischer Natur und die exacten theoretischen Socialwissenschaften somit in grossem Vortheil gegenüber den exacten Naturwissenschaften. Die "Grenzen des Naturerkennens" und die hieraus für das theoretische Verständniss der Naturphänomene sich ergebenden Schwierigkeiten bestehen in Wahrheit nicht für die exacte Forschung auf dem Gebiete der Socialerscheinungen.[42]

In a nutshell, the *Geisteswissenschaften* are given priority over the *Naturwissenschaften* in the *Grundsätze* of 1871 and equally in the *Untersuchungen.*

Once Menger is located within the *verstehende* tradition of the nineteenth century, two questions become pertinent: What kind of *Verstehen* is implied by the *Grundsätze* of 1871 and the *Untersuchungen* of 1883? And how can we square *Verstehen* with Menger's methodological individualism?

The subjectivism of his value theory is founded not primarily on an atomistic vision of society and the requirements imposed by an analytical form, as was the case with Walras's development of marginal utility

41. Menger 1883, 14; 1963/1985, 43.
42. Menger 1883, 157; 1963/1985, 141–42.

theory (which really is an individualistic rather than a properly subjectivistic theory of value), but on the methodological precept of *Verstehen* in its empathic form, as we find it in, say, Savigny and Droysen, and in the explicitly subjective form given it by Droysen.

In his discussion of the subjective moment of value Menger develops his famous numerical table as a demonstration that the *Bedeutung* of the satisfaction of *Bedürfnisse* varies greatly.[43] The importance of this section of the *Grundsätze* for his economic analysis lies in his development of the lexicographic (or hierarchical) ordering of *Bedürfnisse*. For the interpretation of his methodology, the importance lies in his identification of the argument developed there with an "as yet unexplored area of psychology."[44] In his discussion of the objective moment of value he designates the process of identification of the *Bedeutung* of the satisfaction of a *Bedürfnis* (its value) with the satisfying capacity of a specific good (the value of the good) as transference (*Übertragung*), quite in keeping with the modern psychological meaning of the term,[45] and codifies this psychological process in his first principle of the explanation of value.[46]

This psychologistic interpretation is confirmed by Menger himself in two passages written in 1889, one published and the other one unpublished at the time. In his methodological essay of 1889 he defines the task of exact theory as the analysis of complex economic phenomena by means of the resoluta-compositive method, that is, of reducing them to their ultimate constituent elements and, above all, to their psychological causes.[47] In the same year he drafted an introduction to the planned new edition of the *Grundsätze*, in which he repeated this definition of economic theory as being based on psychology.[48] Thus in the same year that Wieser published his *Natural value*, Menger restated publicly a fundamental methodological precept which he had applied and also identified as such eighteen years previously.

The subjectivist conception of *Verstehen* is nevertheless not a necessary position which one has to take if one wants to adopt a *verstehende* methodology. It is merely a historically relative position.[49] It was, how-

43. Menger 1871, 90–95; 1950/1981, 123–28.
44. Menger 1871, 94; 1950/1981, 128.
45. See Menger 1871, 81 n. ** and 126 n.; 1950/1981, 116, 151–52.
46. Menger 1871, 107; 1950/1981, 139.
47. Menger 1889b, 2.
48. See Menger 1923, vii–viii.
49. This is attested by the *geisteswissenschaftliche* approach developed by the Italian philosopher Giambattista Vico at the beginning of the eighteenth century. Vico developed a *verstehende* methodology and epistemology which did not rely on empathy, subjectivism, or even introspection but on the *verum factum* principle: I can truly only know what I have made myself. Hence we can know history in a much superior way than we shall ever be able to know nature. Vico developed, to my mind, a methodology and epistomology far

ever, the first step which in the end would lead to the undoing of his philosophy of science as a whole, for Menger not only made the methodological claim for the fundamental role which psychology has to play in economic theory, he also postulated that psychology is a fundamental epistemological element. *Erkenntnis,* that is, achieving conceptual knowledge of the world around us, is nothing else but becoming aware of the effects which things have on ourselves. This is a very dangerous epistemological position. It echoes the Romantic conception of the unity of the microcosm with the macrocosm and moves perilously close to introspection as an epistemological postulate.

Menger's concept of methodological individualism has been so frequently discussed in the literature that there is no need for repetition. Suffice it to say that it is not only a fundamental methodological principle which is stated in the *Untersuchungen,* but its operation can also be traced without effort in the *Grundsätze.* Methodological individualism makes Robinson Crusoe the natural starting point for Menger's discussion of economic behavior and value formation in the same way that bilateral monopoly becomes the natural point of departure for his discussion of exchange and price formation. What has to be explained, however, is not what this concept means but why he uses it and how he could conceive of it as compatible with *Verstehen.*

This is a problematic issue because *Verstehen* has traditionally been associated with a holistic conception of reality. Menger breaks with this tradition and imposes methodological individualism on his psychologistic conception of *Verstehen,* thus creating an explosive mixture: *Verstehen,* subjectivism, psychologism, individualism—a specific kind of understanding which admits only of private experience as the basis of factual knowledge and restricts this kind of understanding to psychological facts and acts of individual persons only. In other words, if I want to know something essential about the social world I have to look into myself. Menger's methodological and epistemological practice in the *Grundsätze* imposes introspection as the only logically admissible epistemology on the researcher who wants to follow the path mapped out in Menger's economic theory. Menger himself never put it in these terms, but neither did he ever publish a final, positive statement of his methodology and epistemology, nor did he himself complete the second edition of the *Grundsätze.* An epistemology which ultimately admits only of introspection as the path to the discovery of knowledge is highly

---

superior to that of Menger. Be that as it may, this Vichian excursion serves merely to highlight the fact that Menger's philosophy of science is historically relative, very much an organic part of certain strands of the German *geisteswissenschaftliche* tradition, even though he was pursuing his own rather idiosyncratic way to disaster, as we shall see in a short while.

unsatisfactory, not to say a dead end, unless applied to a wholly solipsistic universe. However, Menger's interest in the analysis, that is, in the explanation and understanding of complex social phenomena, and his ontological realism are incompatible with the conception of a solipsistic world. I shall return to this argument in a moment.

We must here also take note that, for Menger, all these concepts are not just elements of his methodology but also have ontological standing. Methodological individualism is therefore not just a useful working hypothesis for the analysis of complex social and economic phenomena, it is a faithful reflection of the real structure of society and economy. In this sense Menger stands in direct opposition to the *verstehende*, historicist tradition. Individualism, or social atomism, is as a methodological concept traditionally associated with rationalism and the philosophy of the Enlightenment. Its central position in Menger's thought is certainly a puzzle given his own characterization of economic theory as a *verstehende* discipline and his extensive knowledge of the romantic-historicist tradition. Ideological motivation is definitely part of the explanation, as his remarks on Adam Smith in the *Untersuchungen* show, but there are also other factors which may play at least as important a part.[50]

The precise origins of Menger's *Zusammenschau,* his conceptual integration of *Verstehen* and methodological individualism, would be the subject of an intellectual biography. They remain untraceable on the basis of the sources cited in his currently published writings. But all is not lost as yet, because there are some particular facets of Austrian cultural history which may help to put this puzzle at least in a general context. I am referring here to the specifically Austrian interpretation of Leibniz's *Monadology,* which through an atomistic reinterpretation of the Leibnizian monad made the integration of romantic-historicist and rationalist elements of thought possible.[51]

The issue of the ontological basis of Menger's methodological principles and concepts has been raised above. We can try and clarify this issue by following Menger in his discussion of "exact" theory, because for him "exact" theory is the basis of all scientific knowledge of empirical reality. It is in this sense that Menger's "exact" theories are also empirical.

In the preface to the *Grundsätze* Menger sets out the epistemological and methodological basis of his economic theory. Economics is an empirical science just like the natural sciences but pursues knowledge

---

50. On this issue see above all his comments on Adam Smith in the *Untersuchungen* (1883, 200–208, esp. 208; 1963/1985, 172–77), esp. 177. Cf. also Menger's attempts to force Aristotle's conception of the state into a methodologically individualist form (1883, Anhang VII, 267–71; 1963/1985, Appendix VII, 220–22).

51. For a detailed discussion see Essay II in Alter 1990. See also Mülher 1948.

through a method *sui generis*. As in other empirical sciences, complex phenomena are analyzed by reduction to their simplest constituent elements and by subsequent recomposition in such a way that the complex phenomena are reconstituted by these constituent elements and their laws of development. The specificity of economics, like that of all the other empirical sciences, lies in the operation of the laws of development on the constituent elements; it is determined by their nature and finds its expression in the measure appropriate to these elements. In other words, the way in which these elements are measured cannot be determined from the outside, by a method imported from a different branch of knowledge, but must be determined from the inside. The measure is an essential, an organic part of the constituent elements.[52]

This is the core of Menger's methodology and epistemology. It contains a very complex network of interconnections between its constituent elements, and at the center of this network is Menger's analytic method, which Menger himself called variously analytic, analytic-synthetic, analytic-compositive, and, finally, "exact"[53] and which today is known by the name given it by Hayek, the resoluta-compositive method. Menger does not tell us directly how he can arrive at "exact" knowledge, but there are quite a few clues in the *Grundsätze* and the *Untersuchungen* which allow us to deduce his solution to this problem. It is important to note that this is not just a question concerning his methodology but addresses the very foundations of his epistemology. In the *Untersuchungen* Menger goes a little further in his description of "exact" knowledge, although he still does not provide us with a fully developed epistemological argument. There he tells us that "exact" theory is true by definition, that it is not amenable to verification or falsification against empirical reality. He postulates this for the "exact" theories of the *Naturwissenschaften* as well as for economic theory.[54] The only further qualification he provides is that the truth of "exact" theory is epistemologically necessary because it is epistemologically impossible for it to be otherwise.[55] The full explanation of this method and of its epistemological foundations was supposed to be provided in a separate treatise which was never written.[56]

What are we to make of these statements? Without further explanation they appear to characterize an extreme epistemological dogmatism.

52. Menger 1871, vii; 1950/1981, 46–47.

53. All these labels are listed by Menger in his letter to Walras (see Walras 1965, letter 602); see also Menger 1889, 1889a, 1891.

54. Menger 1883, 38, 43–44; 1963/1985, 59, 62.

55. See Menger 1883, 38; 1963/1985, 59.

56. Menger refers to his forthcoming "positive" philosophy of science in 1883 (43 n. 19; 1963/1985, 62 n. 19) and again six years later (1889; see Menger 1970, 3:212–13).

"Exact" theory is true because that is the way we know. If we want to arrive at an understanding of "exact" theory, one way, which seems to be the most reasonable and internally consistent, is to locate its meaning within Menger's Aristotelianism. However, we must remain fully aware that linking Menger's Aristotelianism to what we know about Aristotle today can only be done by analogy, because we may link directly only those elements of the history of ideas which we can demonstrate to be linked.[57] There are a large number of strands in the *Grundsätze* which testify to its Aristotelian character: the conception that knowledge is by causes, the teleological character of Menger's causality, his essentialism, the notion that each branch of knowledge is *sui generis* rather than being classified among either the *Geisteswissenschaften* or the *Naturwissenschaften,* as was the tradition in the German-speaking academic world in the nineteenth century, and his resoluta-compositive method. All these methodological elements of Menger's economic theory taken together testify to his fundamental Aristotelianism; each taken by itself may also be located in other *geisteswissenschaftliche* traditions.

We can show that Menger's references to the laws of thought make most sense if taken as reference to a kind of Aristotelian syllogism where "exact" theory furnishes the inductively derived premises or starting points from which the "exact" laws would be deduced. Menger's *Verstehen* can therefore be taken as an expression of Aristotle's concept of induction as the basis for the apprehension of "first principles." It is the epistemological basis which generates the simplest constituent elements in Aristotle's sciences that are grasped through inspection of simple facts. What we apprehend as first principles are, furthermore, true statements because scientific results are deduced from them. Since science is necessary knowledge of the true, the premises of the syllogism, the first principles, must also be true. Viewed in this light, Menger's insistence on the truth *per definitionem* of "exact" theories looks indeed less dogmatic and more amenable to epistemological analysis. It also explains why he never published his "positive" philosophy of science.

There is not enough space here to demonstrate in depth all the other problematic areas in Menger's methodology and epistemology. Let me therefore comment briefly on a few more central issues before turning to a discussion of his economic theory.

We have already seen that by causality Menger means teleology. His concept of cause is a veritable node in his methodology. Through it he unites influences from rationalist thought (through the references to the

---

57. For a fuller discussion of Menger's Aristotelianism see the section on "Menger and Aristotle" in Alter 1990.

natural sciences) and romantic-historicist thought (through his Aristotelianism). The romantic-historicist dimension becomes even more pronounced through his identification of causality with time.[58] He thus incorporates, on the one hand, the Aristotelian notion that time is merely the number of change,[59] and, on the other hand, he goes beyond it by locating the process of change in romantic-historicist thought through its identification with *Werden* and *Entstehen* (coming-into-being). Time is of the essence of the economic process, it is real, an element of the ontological basis of his economic theory, and it is fundamentally irreversible just as the teleological process is unidirectional and real.[60]

The methodological principle of unintended consequences of individual human action is the basis of Menger's theory of institutions, through which he attempts to explain how publicly beneficial institutions come into being without the intervention of a *Gemeinwille* (collective will).[61] According to Menger, "exact" social theory explains social institutions as the result of individualistic-teleological factors. Translating this statement into more familiar language, that is, analyzing it by reducing it to its ultimate constituent elements, we see that the application of the resoluta-compositive method to the complex phenomena of social institutions leads us to purposive human action of individuals as their ultimate constituent elements. In other words, the methodological postulate that organic social institutions are the results of the unintended consequences of individual human action, far from being a new and independent methodological insight, is the composite of teleology and methodological individualism in the romantic-historicist world, that is, in a world full of doubt and uncertainty. Unintended consequences of human action are therefore derivative of the most fundamental constituent methodological elements of the economic theory of the *Grundsätze*.

In this discussion of some of the central elements of Menger's methodology and epistemology we have seen that the methodology and epistemology implicit in the economic theory of the *Grundsätze* are part and parcel of the program of the *Geisteswissenschaften* in the second half of the nineteenth century. This program, spurred on by the rejection of rationalism and positivism and by the evident success of the *Naturwissenschaften*, attempted to establish the humanities as equally worthy of the epithet *Wissenschaft*. Within this *geisteswissenschaftliche* and especially historicist tradition, Menger adopted the Aristotelian conception of the science of man, the humanities, in close approximation of

58. Menger 1871, 21; 1950/1981, 67.
59. Menger 1871, 88; 1950/1981, 122.
60. Menger 1871, 128, also 22; 1950/1981, 154, also 67–68.
61. Menger 1883, 163; 1963/1985, 146.

Droysen's program for history. At the same time, however, Menger tried to remain with Aristotle's conception of knowledge and science in his aim to transcend the dualism of the *Geisteswissenschaften* and the *Naturwissenschaften*.

In his project, however, Menger was caught by the primacy his system afforded to the *Geisteswissenschaften* and by his admiration for the success of the *Naturwissenschaften*. He was thus forced to attempt the integration of the *Naturwissenschaften* into his conception of the *Geisteswissenschaften* if he wanted to arrive at a uniform basis for theoretical research in all empirical sciences. The result was a collapse of his methodological and epistemological strategy, at least as far as the *Grundsätze* are concerned, since his conception of induction, the postulate necessary for the immediate perception of the starting points of theoretical investigation, the essences, turned out to be introspection, the logical conclusion to be drawn from his psychologistic conception of *Verstehen* in liaison with his individualism and subjectivism. But Menger's essentialism penetrated his analysis to such an extent that, as we shall see below, he ended up with a formidable transformation problem of values into prices which he was unable to resolve because of the epistemological determination of values as essences and prices as appearances on the surface. An epistemological resolution of Menger's transformation problem would imply, among other things, that his position in the *Methodenstreit* was untenable and that Schmoller had been right all along.

The synthetic interpretation of Menger (part 2)

Let us now turn from Menger's methodology and epistemology to his economic theory or, rather, to the foundations of his economic theory. Menger's aim, in the *Grundsätze,* was to put economic theory on sound foundations by basing it on sound value theory and thus to enable economists to emulate the success of the natural sciences. This was to be achieved not by copying the methods of the natural sciences but by providing economics with "exact" foundations *sui generis*.[62] The conditions governing human activity geared towards the satisfaction of *Bedürfnisse* under conditions of scarcity constitute the core of these foundations. If this aim had been understood by commentators—theorists and historians of theory alike—in the way it was understood by its author, a great deal of misunderstanding could have been avoided and the *Grundsätze* would have been taken for what they were intended to be by the author: an exposition of principles underlying economic ac-

---

62. This is repeatedly stated in the preface to the *Grundsätze;* see Menger 1871, vii, ix, x; 1950/1981, 47–49.

tivity derived by an author who believed in an Aristotelian *Weltbild,* who believed that values were the subjectively and immediately known essences underlying rough, probabilistic phenomena such as prices, but who believed, above all, in the a priori truth of "exact essential laws" of any *Wissenschaft.* In his view the principles laid down in the *Grundsätze* were such laws derived for the realm of economic activity.

Menger develops his theory from a discussion of "things," that is, from a general theory of the conditions for human action. The story then moves from useful things to economic goods which are given value by the economic agent. This value is value only for the active subject; it does not exist in itself, nor is it a property of the good. Economic agents engage in exchange on the basis of their individual, subjective evaluations of the goods at their disposal. It is only at this stage that prices are introduced. These prices settle somewhere in the "feasible" region demarcated by subjective evaluation.[63]

What is his concept of value? Menger's general theory of human action as geared towards the satisfaction of *Bedürfnisse,* of needs and wants, becomes an economic theory under the condition of scarcity. In the course of this discussion he introduces the notions of uncertainty, information, unidirectional causality, and subjectivism, which serve to furnish his concept of value with its constituent elements. This concept is defined at the outset of the third chapter of the *Grundsätze:* ". . . es ist somit der Werth die Bedeutung, welche concrete Güter oder Güterquantitäten für uns dadurch erlangen, dass wir in der Befriedigung unserer Bedürfnisse von der Verfügung über dieselben abhängig zu sein uns bewusst sind."[64]

Value is the meaning and importance which concrete goods have for us inasfar as we are aware that the satisfaction of our *Bedürfnisse* depends on their availability for us. Immediately after stating this definition Menger emphasizes the human element in the relation between men and things under the condition of scarcity. This human element is the fundamental factor which not only precipitates economic activity but at the same time also provides this activity with the criterion (value) which gives it direction: *Erkenntnis,* the cognitive element in human activity, allows us to recognize scarcity of means in relation to ends (and hence makes us act to provide for the satisfaction of our *Bedürfnisse*) and, at the same time, furnishes us with a measure to judge the importance—in its quantitative as well as its qualitative dimension—of a good for our well-being (and thus makes us assign value to a good).[65]

One particular point must be kept in mind here: this definition of

63. See Menger 1871, x; 1950/1981, 49.
64. Menger 1871, 78; 1950/1981, 115.
65. Menger 1871, 79–81; 1950/1981, 115–16.

value, according to Menger, concerns the "essence" of the concept, its *Wesen*. It is thus fundamental to all economic activity, and without it we are unable to act in, nor will we be able to understand, the economic world. It is completely independent of any notion of price. Menger's concept of value, therefore, has nothing whatsoever to do with the traditional microeconomic concept of value as unit price. Nor is it identical to the traditional neoclassical concept of value as marginal utility, since the margin has not been introduced yet. The margin, in Menger's theory, is a consequence of the logic of his argument. It is not, as in Walrasian theory, an initial assumption, nor an instrumentalist behavioral hypothesis.

Valuation at the margin is the major result of Menger's development of economic theory. It follows as a logical step from the entire structure which he has built up.[66] Value, furthermore, is independent of the goods used in the satisfaction of *Bedürfnisse*. Goods enter the picture only in the second, the objective, aspect of value which contains the quantitative dimension. There Menger shows us how value is calculated. Successive satisfaction of *Bedürfnisse* leads from the satisfaction of the first, most important *Bedürfnis* through the structure of *Bedürfnisse* to the satisfaction of *Bedürfnisse* of ever decreasing importance by satisfying the first level of this structure—or hierarchy—up to a point where the first unsatisfied *Bedürfnis* of the next lower rung becomes more important to us than the next unsatisfied *Bedürfnis* of the higher rung. This leads to switching of satisfaction of one set of *Bedürfnisse* to that of the next lower one. This process operates as long as goods are available. The importance of the last *Bedürfnis* satisfied in this way, that is to say, its value to us, is what in traditional utility theory is known as marginal utility.[67]

We must also bear in mind that for Menger these assumptions also have ontological status. Here we can also see the fundamental difference between Menger and, for instance, Walras, for whom the economic margin has instrumental status arising out of the logic of the formalization of price theory and hence enters the substantive level of economic theory as an assumption. It is not, as in Menger's case, the result of the substantive economic argument.[68]

The derivation of value is enshrined by Menger in his five principles of value theory which lead from his definition of value to his derivation of value at the margin, that is, from the definition of value to its measure, and they encompass most of the methodological and theoretical ele-

66. See the discussion of the subjective aspect of value in Menger 1871, 88–95; 1950/1981, 122–28.
67. See Menger 1871, 95–114; 1950/1981, 128–41.
68. For a detailed discussion see Essay III in Alter 1990.

ments which later became to be associated with the characteristically Austrian approach to economic theory.[69]

Valuation takes place at the margin; this, in fact, is very much like the derivation of marginal utility. But we must be very careful here because Menger's "values" and traditional "marginal utility" have very little in common beyond their derivation at the margin. On the one hand, Menger's values are neither part of a utilitarian calculus nor can they be expressed in price terms (if we want to remain faithful to his conception, that is). He does not even use the term *Nutzen* (utility) except once or twice in his chapter on prices, where it takes the rather specialized meaning of "profit," as it occasionally still does in commercial jargon today.[70] If, on the other hand, we try and use "marginal utility" within Menger's framework, we equally run into problems of substance. Marginal utility divorced from prices becomes a rather ephemeral concept, while Menger's values nevertheless are still a statement of the opportunity-cost principle.

The state of Menger's theory just prior to the introduction of prices into the discussion can be summarized roughly along the following lines: Economic activity proper has been analyzed on the basis of a theory of human action—humans act purposely to satisfy their *Bedürfnisse*. This theory is placed within the scarcity relation between men and goods—scarce means are allocated to satisfy competing ends. *Bedürfnisse* are hierarchically structured; people act in a world full of uncertainty and on the basis of incomplete information. All activity takes place in real time; activity is therefore an irreversible process. Valuation—the assessment of an act of *Bedürfnisbefriedigung*—is entirely subjective in its qualitative as well as in its quantitative dimension. The existence of time and of uncertainty defines the current value of the means of production (goods of higher order) which are used for the production of future consumption goods (goods of first order) as expected value. Exchange, the interaction of two "individual economies" (*Einzelwirtschaften*), takes place within the limits prescribed by individual valuation such that both parties are better off after trading than they were before.

It pays to look back at the discussion of Menger's methodology and epistemology at this point. Menger believed in immutable, eternal and universal laws of economics—the laws derived from his "exact" theory, that is, his theory of value. We also know now that he believed "exact" theory to be true and certain: his theory of value was the truth without which the economic world could be neither analyzed nor controlled.

69. Menger 1871, 107–8; 1950/1981, 139.
70. See Menger 1871, 177; 1950/1981, 195.

Development and change, on the other hand, were not the realm of "exact" theory but of empirical-realistic theories, which only produced probable results. This is also the locus where the romantic-historicist influences surface in his theory. At the end of change and development in the economic world we find a fully developed monetary system. It is not by chance that Menger's chapter on money, which contains a truly historicist analysis, appears as the last in the *Grundsätze*. Nor is it misplaced in a book which sets off to explain the essence of economic behavior. For the point of transition from Menger's essentialist world of values to the romantic-historicist world of money is Menger's concept of price.

> Die Preise, oder mit anderen Worten, die im Tausche zur Erscheinung gelangenden Güterquantitäten . . . sind doch nichts weniger als das Wesentliche der ökonomischen Erscheinungen. Dieses liegt vielmehr in der durch den Tausch herbeigeführten besseren Vorsorge für die Befriedigung der Bedürfnisse der beiden Tauschenden. *Die Preise sind hiebei aber lediglich Erscheinungen, Symptome des ökonomischen Ausgleiches zwischen menschlichen Wirthschaften.*[71]

Prices are merely accidental phenomena, quantities of goods exchanged. They are symptoms of the essence of economic activity, that is, of the improvement in provision for the satisfaction of *Bedürfnisse* through exchange. This is the crux of Menger's theory and the point which almost all interpretations of the *Grundsätze* seem to have ignored, because they fail to account for this fundamental difference between price and value: in Menger's theory value is the essence of economic activity which manifests itself in the phenomenal domain through prices. For this theory, therefore, it does not suffice to treat prices as magnitudes which are simply calculated from values by setting price equal to value. Here we are dealing with fundamentally different spheres of discourse which obey different epistemological and methodological laws because these spheres are constituted of completely diverse elements. We are dealing with a transformation of values into prices in several dimensions—epistemological, methodological, and analytical. All this, of course, holds true only as long as we accept the rules of the game as defined by Menger.

In the chapter on prices in the *Grundsätze* Menger begins to shift ground. The opening section is still very much in the spirit of the preceding 170 pages, but with the discussion of the process of price formation the discourse shifts not only from values to prices but more

71. Menger 1871, 172 (emphasis added); 1950/1981, 191.

generally from essences to appearances, from the truth and certainty of "exact" theory to the probable results of "realistic-empirical" theory.

It is easy to identify the shift from essences (*Wesen*) to appearances (*Erscheinungen*), that is, to surface phenomena, because not only does Menger make it quite explicit in the opening paragraph of the chapter,[72] he also uses the simile of "deep essences" and "surface phenomena" in the introduction to his critique of all economists from Aristotle onwards who believed that prices are of the essence of exchange and that therefore only equivalents are exchanged.[73]

According to Menger, it is the task of a correct price theory to explain how economic man is led to exchange specific quantities of goods in order to achieve the highest possible satisfaction of his *Bedürfnisse*.[74] Consistent with his subjective value theory, he rejects the notion of exchange of equivalents because it is economically meaningless to exchange equal values for each other. An individual will only engage in exchange if a higher value can be obtained in exchange for the goods he gives up.[75]

A survey of Menger's theory of prices becomes rather unexciting after his theory of value. All his important theoretical insights have been developed only in the latter. And from the point of view of late twentieth-century neoclassical economic theory he has not produced anything which could equal Walras's grandiose scheme of the analysis of a general equilibrium set of prices for an economy composed of perfectly competitive markets. But Menger did not set out to do this in the first place, and he was very well aware of the difference between his own and Walras's theory.[76] Menger's economic universe was different from that of Walras, and it obeyed different epistemological and methodological laws. It is precisely here, in Menger's price theory, where the impact of his epistemology and methodology can be most closely observed, because it is here that we can discern at which point that universe falls apart.

The difference between Menger's and the Walrasian system or, at any rate, its post-Hicksian version, manifests itself not only at the methodological or epistemological level. Contained in Menger's concept of *Bedürfnisse* and their hierarchical structure is an inversion of the traditional textbook case of preference structures. The lexicographic preference structure, or *Bedürfnis* structure, underlying Menger's system is the rule and not an exception to be excluded for analytical convenience.

72. Menger 1871, 172; 1950/1981, 191.
73. See Menger 1871, 172–73; 1950/1981, 191–92.
74. See Menger 1871, 175; 1950/1981, 193–94.
75. See Menger 1871, 173–75; 1950/1981, 192–94.
76. See Menger's letters to Walras in Walras 1965.

And it renders the traditional derivation of demand functions impossible if we have more than one good and if these goods satisfy different *Bedürfnisse* in different *Bedürfnis* classes of the hierarchy to a different degree. In addition to the problem posed by the lexicographic ordering, there is also the problem of the mathematical representation of Menger's basic approach which divorces valuation from goods.[77]

The problem is, however, not entirely intractable. A first approximative solution was already available in the late 1950s, although it appeared in print only in 1972. I am referring here to Ironmonger's version of consumer technology, which not only allows us to derive all the basic well-known results of the traditional neoclassical theory of household behavior but also explicitly takes account of a hierarchical want structure akin to Menger's lexicographic structure of *Bedürfnisse* and of the separation of goods and values postulated by Menger.[78]

Adopting Ironmonger's system as the basis for the formalization of Menger's economic analysis imposes certain restrictions on Menger's economic process. These restrictions are entirely due to the application of linear programming as a tool and not substantively necessitated. Furthermore, the model is only capable of handling perfect competition. Monopolistic situations, where quantity could depend on price or on exogenous factors and thus open the door to indeterminacy, are ruled out. In contrast to Menger's theory, Ironmonger's model is also characterized by the absence of uncertainty and expectations. Still, Ironmonger's basic model combining the subjective and objective determinants of the individual's consumption decision, which are linked by the consumer technology matrix, with the hierarchy of wants and with scarcity expressed by the income constraint is the one extension of traditional neoclassical theory which comes closer to a larger number of the original analytic intentions embodied in Menger's theory than any other formalization developed so far. In addition Ironmonger also shows us in which direction the derivation and discussion of individual and market demand functions have to proceed so that, at least on analytical grounds, we do not have to give up Menger's approach as fruitless.[79]

The main reason why the implications of the lexicographic *Bedürfnis* structure of Menger's theory have gone largely unnoticed in the literature lies, to my mind at least, in Menger's technique of exposition. Menger does not derive theorems from axioms but represents the theo-

77. I am here abstracting from the problem that Menger refused any role for mathematics in his theory of value. This issue and the formalization rules for a mathematical representation of Menger's system are discussed in detail in the chapter "Neo-classical axiomatisation and Menger's theory of value" in Alter 1990.

78. Ironmonger 1972.

79. For a full discussion of these issues see the section "Extensions to neo-classical theory" in Alter 1990.

retical basis of his analysis in his "real life" illustrations. There he slips in one very special assumption without being aware of the consequences of this simplification: in each of them, he only deals with one commodity, corn or water, respectively.[80] The problem with this approach is, of course, that the assumption of only one commodity renders any hierarchical ordering (of his *Bedürfnisse*) indistinguishable from an ordering along the real line and thus renders his theory indistinguishable from the conventional utility theory approach. The assumption of a single, homogeneous good is, in fact, later on relaxed in the *Grundsätze,* when he allows for goods of different quality to be used in the satisfaction of a *Bedürfnis*.[81] There, however, he gets himself into a complete muddle failing to resolve this case. Any attempt to represent it formally would show that in his verbal statements he became entangled in mathematical contradictions. Fundamentally, Menger barked up the wrong tree because he allowed himself to solve the didactically easier case of determining the value of a single (homogeneous) good instead of following the route he had mapped out for himself. Along this route the interesting case is the analysis of the value of physically heterogeneous goods which are also economically heterogeneous, not only because along this line of reasoning the impact of the lexicographic ordering of the structure of *Bedürfnisse* on the derivation of value can be demonstrated but simply because his entire theoretical edifice rests on physical heterogeneity: the lexicographic structure of *Bedürfnisse,* the absence of overall substitutability, the establishment of suboptimal (in a universal sense) equilibrium positions of the individual due to absence of complete information and of frictionless and costless market adjustment.[82]

But let us now return to our discussion of the epistemological level of Menger's theory, because here, as has been repeatedly hinted at above, his whole construction falls apart. I am referring to the point of transition of values to prices with all its implications.

Menger's strict adherence to methodological individualism lets him commence the derivation of prices with the case of bilateral monopoly. Naturally, bilateral monopoly prices cannot be determined precisely but can only be located within a certain region of indeterminacy whose limits are given, in Menger's theory, by the subjective values of the participants in the exchange. In other words, although we are able to ascertain price empirically *after* the exchange, the theory cannot pre-

---

80. See Menger 1871 (and 1950/1981), ch. 3 passim.
81. Menger 1871, 114–19; 1950/1981, 141–45.
82. For a more detailed discussion of the issue of homogeneity/heterogeneity and its impact on Menger's analysis see the section "Neo-classical axiomatisation and Menger's theory of value" in Alter 1990.

dict this price, because price formation depends to a large extent also on noneconomic factors. The only variables which can be precisely determined by the theory *ex ante* are the subjective values.

This is not an alien argument for a modern economist at all, because current neoclassical theory too knows this region of indeterminacy. There both buyer and seller wish that the other end of the market was perfectly competitive, so that each seller could sell his own goods somewhere above his own marginal costs, in the region between the limits given by his own marginal revenue and the other's demand curve. The exact price at which they each will sell is left open by the theory and is determined by variables which are exogenous to the model.

This modern statement of bilateral monopoly differs in one fundamental aspect from Menger's case. The modern case is entirely formulated in terms of quantities of goods and prices, while Menger's case is formulated in terms of values, quantities of goods, and prices. Hence the additional concept of value in Menger's theory must be operationally meaningful within the framework of the theory or, by Occam's razor, it must be jettisoned. But this would be fatal for the theory, because it is the value theory which contains all the necessary and sufficient conditions for the explanation of economic behavior.

The problem which this issue raises is therefore the following: Menger was an essentialist and developed a rather idiosyncratic epistemology and methodology on that basis. Can we demonstrate within his own system of thought that values which are precisely determined are indispensable to an explanation of price formation and that they thus tell us more about actual prices than merely that these fall into a "feasible" region? For the case of bilateral monopoly, his theory can only tell us that there is a "feasible" region within which the price vector must be located. As both sides of the exchange grow in number and competition among buyers and among sellers therefore develops, the "feasible" region begins to shrink and, according to the operation of Menger's value theory, the limiting points move closer towards each other until the numbers of participants on both sides of the exchange have grown to such an extent that none of them have any freedom to influence the market price in their favor. But this limiting case is precisely the case of perfect competition. In other words, in the case of perfectly competitive markets, and only in this case, will prices be uniquely determined by subjective values. Thus Menger's theory is in all but the perfectly competitive case unable to lead us directly from values to prices and back again. It is befallen by a problem of the transformation of values into prices, which it cannot solve because the resolution of that problem depends on factors which are exogenous to the theory.

The transformation problem is crucial, it is not resolvable, and it is deeply imbedded in the foundations of Menger's theory. It is a logical outcome of his conception of a dichotomy of the theoretical universe into "exact" and "realistic-empirical" which, in turn, is based on his essentialist vision of the world. This essentialism in combination with the subjective character of his value theory creates a formidable episte-mological obstacle for any economist who wants to use Menger's theory for an analysis of economic events within the world of thought developed by Menger.

Menger's value theory is perfect *for the acting subject* (the economic agent). Immediately perceived valuation provides the foundations on which economic behavior rests in the real world: valuation according to Menger's principles gives the acting subject firm guidelines for action when faced with market prices. The problem for the theory arises when the *acting subject* is different from the *knowing subject,* that is, when the *acting subject* becomes the *object of investigation* of the knowing subject (that is, of the inquiring economist trying to gain some knowledge). Although the enquiring subject (the economist) knows his own value structure, he has no means of knowing the acting object's value structure if this acting object is another person than himself. Hence he does not know how to interpret the objectively ascertainable market prices with respect to the limits given by valuation peculiar to the acting object. In other words, save for the case of perfectly competitive markets, Menger's theory of value is of no use to the knowing subject (the inquiring economist) if the latter wants to explain precisely why prices are what they are.

This fundamental problem is all the more important for Menger not only because bilateral monopoly is the archetype of price formation in his theory but also because he gives hardly any consideration to the case of perfect competition in the *Grundsätze*. Nevertheless he regarded his exposition of the "essence" of economic activity as complete. But—and here the story takes an almost macabre twist—we also have every reason to believe that Menger was aware of the existence of this transformation problem, for why else did he originally plan to say something about the relationship of values to prices in the second edition of the *Grundsätze*?[83]

Are there any consequences of this problem for the theory? There are indeed, and to say the very least, they seriously shake the foundations of

83. A remark by the editor of the second edition lends support to this interpretation of Menger's theory of value and prices. It emerges quite clearly from this remark that Menger himself was aware that in the first edition of the *Grundsätze* he had failed to provide an exposition of the link between his theory of value and his theory of prices. Although planned, this exposition was never completed: "Geplant, aber nicht ausgeführt wurde . . . eine Bemerkung, welche die Verbindung von Wert- und Preislehre herstellen sollte" (Menger 1923, xvii).

Menger's theoretical edifice. We have seen that Menger's transformation problem is due to his essentialism and the subjectivism of his value theory. One could therefore conceive of two different approaches to try and resolve it. On the one hand, one could give up his essentialism, but then the character of his value theory would change drastically. It would mean a recasting of his epistemology and methodology, a rethinking of his aims of economic theory, and eventually also an admission that Schmoller's critique was justified. On the other hand, one could first jettison the subjectivism of his value theory and then try, in one way or another, to make it more objective while still hanging on to essentialism and the rest of his epistemology and methodology. But this second approach would not only open up his theory immediately to Schmoller's accusation of "deductivism" and "speculation," it would also question within his own epistemology the justification for the postulate that results of "exact" theories are true, certain, and immediately accessible.

In either case Menger's original position is untenable. And as we have arrived at the concept of speculation, let me speculate a little and say that Menger must have been aware, in one way or another, of the scenario described here. For why else did he neither authorize a reprint or a translation of the *Grundsätze* nor complete the second edition during his lifetime? Why did he want to "clarify" the relationship between prices and values but not do so? Because he knew that, after everything was considered, his ultimate answer had to be to withdraw the theory from circulation because it did not, it could not, within the frame of reference which he had mapped out himself, answer the questions he had posed in 1871 and 1883. And if all this was true, should we really expect him, above all after the *Methodenstreit* had broken out, to throw overboard his theory and his *wissenschaftliche Weltauffassung* just because there was a transformation problem? Or should we not more reasonably expect him to show tenacity in view of the difficulty which had befallen his research program and try and rescue it? After all, his theory had introduced many innovations to economic analysis: it did solve the paradox of value in a nonmechanistic way; it posed the question of value from the outset in an intertemporal framework without assuming certainty and complete information; and it did not adopt perfect competition as the paradigm for analytic work. Certainly from today's perspective, it was a very unorthodox theory, and many of its features were not understood by those who claimed to be his successors or to be working within the research program he had established.

Conclusion

What is left of the traditional image of Menger and his theory after this discussion? Certainly not a great deal if we expected to find only confirmation of what we thought we knew about his theory, methodology, and epistemology. But the synthetic interpretation of his work may help us to reassess not only his theoretical contributions and the meaning of his methodology, it may also, with any luck, demonstrate to more than just a highly specialist audience to what extent methodological and epistemological factors influence theorizing, at times even down to the level of choice of analytical tools, and that the adoption of a particular theoretical approach is always a choice and thus an exclusion of alternative approaches. Above all, it ought to alert theorists and historians of theory alike to the fact that economic theory is a product of the human mind, that the interpretation and application of theory is part of intellectual history, that therefore the forces which operate on the world of ideas also operate on the formation of economic theories, and, finally, that concepts do not always mean what we want them to mean.

Apart from such general reflections, what can we take with us from Menger's thought after the exposition presented here? Above all, that his methodology and epistemology, taken as a whole, are not acceptable; they must be abandoned, at least as understood in this paper, because an approach that insists on introspectively derived knowledge of truth does not satisfy the canons of scientific work of whatever persuasion. But once we abandon the epistemological foundations of Menger's theoretical edifice the field is open for anyone to pick and choose those constituent elements of his economic thought which suit them best. Although this appears at first to reduce this issue to a question of personal style, the stakes are much higher, as we shall see in a moment. If you consider certainty, full information, and absence of time a justifiable abstraction or simplification of a world described in terms of uncertainty, error, and irreversible processes, then the general equilibrium approach has currently more to offer than Menger's theory. If, on the other hand, purposive human activity fumbling in an uncertain world seems a more attractive basic assumption than the mechanistic interaction of human atoms, then Menger's approach may offer a great deal more insight than the Walrasian approach. The main drawback of Menger's approach is that we have not even begun to explore where it would lead us, while the general equilibrium model has certainly produced a few powerful results. Still, there exist at least a few results which have been derived from assumptions very much akin to some of Menger's. Lexicographic preferences are a particularly good example, with work by Georgescu-Roegen, Ironmonger, and others having at least begun to shift the emphasis from all too bland neoclassical *homo oeconomicus*.

But all this is confining the lessons we can learn from Menger almost entirely to the neoclassical world. Once we have started questioning assumptions, who is to say where it will stop? We may even question the appropriateness of fundamentals such as methodological individualism. This, though, is a much trickier business, because here we openly enter the political battlefield. Could we indeed learn something from Menger's erstwhile friends and later enemies, the historical economists, and from their descendants, today's institutionalist economists? And if we think we could learn something from institutional economics, then what about learning something from some even more radical approaches? This may nevertheless be asking almost too much, because at bottom this implies that we critically question the foundations of our thinking, something Menger certainly appears to have done; but in the end the costs of drawing honestly and openly the conclusions from his questioning seem to have been more than he could afford.

All the claims about Menger which have been put forward in this paper have been derived from a critical examination of his published work. The archives of Menger's unpublished manuscripts will certainly reveal a great deal about his life, his thought, and his intellectual development. I do not think that they will prove wrong the fundamental results presented here. But this is precisely the use to which they should be put: a critical reexamination not only of Menger's work but also of the origins of the Austrian School and of neoclassical economics. It could be an occasion to carry out an analysis of competing economic methodologies—positivist, hermeneutic, dialectic. The manuscripts should definitely be made available, if possible in a printed, critical edition, to as wide an audience as possible so that competing confessions—Austrian, Walrasian, institutionalist, Marxist—could start shedding some light from different angles on the thought of the Austrian School. If finance for such a project could be found, it is not only economics which would stand to gain from it.

I want to thank Dr. J. M. Albala-Bertrand for his comments on the first draft of this paper.

References

Alter, Max. 1982. Carl Menger and *homo oeconomicus:* some thoughts on Austrian theory and methodology. *Journal of Economic Issues* 16 (March): 149–60.

———. 1986. Carl Menger, mathematics, and the foundations of neo-classical value theory. *Quaderni di storia dell'economia politica* 4.3:77–87.

———. 1990. *Carl Menger and the origins of Austrian economics.* Boulder, Col.: Westview Press.

Atlantic Economic Journal 6.3 (September 1978). Special edition devoted to Carl Menger and the Austrian school of economics.

Bloch, Henri-Simon. 1937. *La théorie des besoins de Carl Menger.* Paris: Librairie Générale de Droit et de Jurisprudence.

———. 1940. Carl Menger: the founder of the Austrian School. *Journal of Political Economy* 48.3:428–33.

Block, Walter. 1988. Economics of the Canadian bishops. *Contemporary Policy Issues* 6:56–68.

Boos, Margarete. 1986. *Die Wissenschaftstheorie Carl Mengers: biographische und ideengeschichtliche Zusammenhänge.* Vienna: Hermann Böhlaus Nachf.

Bostaph, Samuel Harvey. 1976. Epistemological foundations in economics: the case of the nineteenth-century *Methodenstreit.* Ph.D. dissertation, Southern Illinois University.

———. 1978. The methodological debate between Carl Menger and the German historicists. *Atlantic Economic Journal* 6.3:3–16.

Bucharin, Nikolai. 1966. *Das Elend der subjektiven Wertlehre.* Reprint of *Die politische Ökonomie des Rentners.* Frankfurt: Verlag Neue Kritik.

Butos, William N. 1985. Menger: a suggested interpretation. *Atlantic Economic Journal* 13.2:21–30.

Clower, Robert W. 1977. The anatomy of monetary theory. *American Economic Review* 67.1:206–12.

Cubeddu, Raimondo. 1985. Fonti filosofiche delle "Untersuchungen über die Methode der Socialwissenschaften" di Carl Menger. *Quaderni di storia dell'economia politica* 3.3:73–158.

Dolan, Edwin G., ed. 1976. *The foundations of modern Austrian economics.* Kansas City: Sheed & Ward.

Endres, Anthony M. 1984. Institutional elements in Carl Menger's theory of demand: a comment. *Journal of Economic Issues* (September): 897–903.

———. 1987. The origins of Böhm-Bawerk's "greatest error": theoretical points of separation from Menger. *Journal of Institutional and Theoretical Economics* 143:291–309.

Georgescu-Roegen, Nicholas. 1968. Utility. In *International encyclopedia of the social sciences,* edited by David L. Sills, 16:236–67. New York: Macmillan and Free Press.

Gowdy, John M. 1985. Utility theory and agrarian societies. *International Journal of Social Economics* 12.6–7:104–17.

Grassl, Wolfgang, and Barry Smith, eds. 1986. *Austrian economics: historical and philosophical background.* London: Croom Helm.

Hansen, Reginald. 1968. Der Methodenstreit in den Sozialwissenschaften zwischen Gustav Schmoller und Karl Menger—seine wissenschaftshistorische und wissenschaftstheoretische Bedeutung. In *Beiträge zur Entwicklung der Wissenschaftstheorie im 19. Jahrhundert,* edited by A. Diemer, 137–73. Meisenheim: Verlag Anton Hain.

Hayek, Friedrich A. 1934. Carl Menger. In *The collected works of Carl Menger,* 1:v–xxxviii. Reprints of Scarce Tracts in Economics and Political Science, 17. London: The London School of Economics and Political Science. Reprinted in Carl Menger, *Principles of economics,* translation of Menger 1871 by James Dingwall and Bert F. Hoselitz, 11–56. New York: New York University Press, 1981.

———. 1968. Einleitung. In Menger 1871, vii–xxxvi.

———. 1973. The place of Menger's *Grundsätze* in the history of economic thought. In Hicks and Weber 1973, 1–14.

———. 1988. *The fatal conceit: the errors of socialism.* Vol. 1 of *The collected works of Friedrich August Hayek,* edited by W. W. Bartley, III. London: Routledge.

Hicks, J. R. 1975. The scope and status of welfare economics. *Oxford Economic Papers* 27.3:307–26.

Hicks, J. R., and W. Weber, eds. 1973. *Carl Menger and the Austrian school of economics*. Oxford: Clarendon Press. (See also the discussion which followed the symposium on Menger, published in *Zeitschrift für Nationalökonomie* (1972): 111–50.)

Hirsch, Willy. 1928. *Grenznutzentheorie und Geldwerttheorie* (unter besondere Berücksichtigung der "österreichischen Schule"). Jena: Fischer.

Hutchison, Terence W. 1973. Some themes from *Investigations into Method*. In Hicks and Weber 1973, 15–37.

———. 1981. Carl Menger on philosophy and method. In *The politics and philosophy of economics*, 176–202. Oxford: Basil Blackwell.

Ironmonger, D. S. 1972. *New commodities and consumer behaviour*. London: Cambridge University Press.

Jaffé, William. 1976. Menger, Jevons and Walras de-homogenized. *Economic Inquiry* (December): 511–24.

Jones, Robert A. 1976. The origin and development of media of exchange. *Journal of Political Economy* 84:757–76.

Kauder, Emil. 1958. Intellectual and political roots of the older Austrian School. *Zeitschrift für Nationalökonomie* 17.4:411–25.

———. 1959. Menger and his library. *The Economic Review* 10.1:58–64.

———. 1962. Aus Mengers nachgelassenen Papieren. *Weltwirtschaftliches Archiv* 89:1–26.

———. 1965. *A history of marginal utility theory*. Princeton: Princeton University Press.

Kirzner, Israel M. 1978. The entrepreneurial role in Menger's system. *Atlantic Economic Journal* 6.3:31–45.

Knight, Frank H. 1950. Introduction. In Carl Menger, *Principles of economics*, translated and edited by J. Dingwall and B. F. Hoselitz, 9–35. Glencoe, Ill.: The Free Press, 1950.

Lagerspetz, Eerik. 1984. Money as a social contract. *Theory and Decision* 17:1–9.

Langlois, Richard N. 1985. Knowledge and rationality in the Austrian School: an analytical survey. *Eastern Economic Journal* 9.4:309–30.

McCulloch, J. Huston. 1977. The Austrian theory of the marginal use and of ordinal marginal utility. *Zeitschrift für Nationalökonomie* 37.3–4:249–80.

Macpherson, C. B. 1977. Needs and wants: an ontological or historical problem? In *Human needs and politics*, edited by R. Fitzgerald, 26–35. Rushcutters Bay: Pergamon Press.

Martin, Dolores Tremewan. 1979. Alternative views of Mengerian entrepreneurship. *HOPE* 11.2:271–85.

Menger, Carl. 1871. *Grundsätze der Volkswirthschaftslehre*. Reprinted in *Gesammelte Werke*, vol. 1. 2d ed. Edited by F. A. Hayek. Tübingen: J. C. B. Mohr (Paul Siebeck), 1968.

———. 1875. Wilhelm Roscher. *Wiener Abendpost*, 26 January, 4–5.

———. 1883. *Untersuchungen über die Methode der Socialwissenschaften, und der politischen Oekonomie insbesondere*. Reprinted in *Gesammelte Werke*, vol. 2. 2d ed. Edited by F. A. Hayek. Tübingen: J. C. B. Mohr (Paul Siebeck), 1969.

———. 1884. *Die Irrthümer des Historismus in der deutschen Nationalökonomie*. Reprinted in Menger 1970, 1–98.

———. 1888. Zur Theorie des Kapitals. Reprinted in Menger 1970, 135–83.

———. 1889a. Grundzüge einer Klassifikation der Wirtschaftswissenschaften. Reprinted in Menger 1970, 187–218.

————. 1889b. Nationalökonomische Literatur in Oesterreich. *Wiener Zeitung*, 8 March, 2–4. (Contains the review of Rudolf Auspitz and Richard Lieben, *Untersuchungen über die Theorie des Preises*. Leipzig: Duncker & Humblot, 1889.)

————. 1892. On the origin of money. *Economic Journal* 2:239–55.

————. 1923. *Grundsätze der Volkswirtschaftslehre*. 2d ed., "aus dem Nachlass herausgegeben von Karl Menger." Vienna: Hoelder-Pichler-Tempsky A.G.

————. 1970. *Gesammelte Werke*, vol. 3. 2d ed. Edited by F. A. Hayek. Tübingen: J. C. B. Mohr (Paul Siebeck).

————. 1950/1981. *Principles of economics*. Translated by J. Dingwall and B. F. Hoselitz. Glencoe, Ill.: The Free Press, 1950. Reprinted with an introduction by F. A. Hayek. New York: New York University Press, 1981.

————. 1963/1985. *Problems of economics and sociology*. Edited with an introduction by Louis Schneider. Translated by Francis J. Nock. Urbana: University of Illinois Press, 1963. Reprinted as *Investigations into the method of the social sciences with special reference to economics*, with a new introduction by Lawrence H. White. New York: New York University Press, 1985.

Menger, Karl. 1923. Einleitung des Herausgebers. In Carl Menger 1923, v–xviii.

————. 1973. Austrian marginalism and mathematical economics. In Hicks and Weber 1973, 38–60.

Morgenstern, Oskar. 1972. Thirteen critical points in contemporary economic theory: an interpretation. *Journal of Economic Literature* 10:1163–89.

Moss, Laurence S. 1978. Carl Menger's theory of exchange. *Atlantic Economic Journal* 6.3:17–30.

Mülher, Robert. 1948. Ontologie und Monadologie in der österreichischen Literatur des XIX. Jahrhunderts. In *Die österreichische Nationalbibliothek*, Festschrift, 488–504. Vienna.

O'Driscoll, Gerald P., Jr. 1986. Money: Menger's evolutionary theory. *HOPE* 18.4:601–17.

Pagano, Ugo. 1985. *Work and welfare in economic theory*. Oxford: Basil Blackwell.

Punzo, Lionello F. 1988. Von Neumann and K. Menger's mathematical colloquium. In *Von Neumann and modern economics*, edited by S. Chakravarthy, M. H. Dore, and R. M. Goodwin. Oxford: Oxford University Press.

Rizzo, Mario J., ed. 1979. *Time, uncertainty and disequilibrium: exploration of Austrian themes*. Lexington, Mass.: Lexington Books.

Roll, Eric. 1936. Menger on money. *Economica*, n.s. 3 (12):455–60.

Roscher, Wilhelm. 1874. *Geschichte der National-Oekonomik in Deutschland*. Munich: Oldenbourg.

Scaparone, Paolo. 1986. La teoria austriaca del consumo e dell'utilità: un'interpretazione. *Quaderni di storia dell'economia politica* 4.3:147–56.

Schmoller, Gustav. 1883. Zur Methodologie der Staats- und Sozialwissenschaften. *Schmollers Jahrbuch*, n.s. 8.3:239–58. Reprinted in Schmoller, *Zur Litteraturgeschichte der Staats- und Sozialwissenschaften*. Leipzig: Duncker & Humblot.

Schumpeter, Joseph A. 1954. *History of economic analysis*. London: George Allen & Unwin.

Stigler, George J. 1937. The economics of Carl Menger. *Journal of Political Economy* 45.2:229–50.

Streissler, Erich. 1969. Structural economic thought: on the significance of the Austrian School today. *Zeitschrift für Nationalökonomie* 29:237–66.

————. 1972. To what extent was the Austrian School marginalist? *HOPE* 4.2:426–41.

————. 1973. Menger's theory of money and uncertainty—a modern interpretation. In Hicks and Weber 1973, 164–89.

Streissler, Erich, and Wilhelm Weber. 1973. The Menger tradition. In Hicks and Weber 1973, 226–32.

Vaughn, Karen I. 1978. The reinterpretation of Carl Menger: some notes on recent scholarship. *Atlantic Economic Journal* 6.3:60–94.

Walras, Léon. 1965. *Correspondence of Léon Walras and related papers.* Edited by W. Jaffé. Vol. 2. Amsterdam: North-Holland.

Weiss, Franz X. 1924. Zur zweiten Auflage von Carl Mengers *Grundsätzen. Zeitschrift für Volkswirtschaft und Sozialpolitik,* n.s. 4:134–54.

White, Lawrence H. 1985. Introduction to the New York University Press Edition. In Carl Menger, *Investigations into the method of the social sciences with special reference to economics,* vii–xviii. New York: New York University Press.

Wright, Georg Hendryk von. 1975. *Explanation and understanding.* London: Routledge & Kegan Paul.

Restoring an "Altered" Menger

Lawrence H. White

As I understand it, Max Alter's paper makes two key claims: first, that Menger's methodology is "untenable"; second, that Menger's value theory "falls apart." In this comment I contest both claims. But much as Alter spends the first third of his paper on a review of the Mengerian literature which is irrelevant to arguing these claims, I begin with stylistic criticism which is irrelevant to rebutting them.

Alter's paper, regrettably, is more than normally difficult to translate into propositions that I can comprehend. Indeed this is so mild that it is almost an understatement. Here I paraphrase the remarks of Menger's translators (1981, 38; 1985, xix) about Menger's writing style. To be fair, Alter is probably not quite as bad a stylist as Menger. Nock reports that Menger offered sentences in the *Investigations* of eighteen and twenty lines. Alter's are not that long. But they are often long and convoluted enough to obscure his argument.

Alter chooses to seed his paper with German-language terms like *Bedürfnisse* ("wants") rather than to use their English equivalents. He does so, he says, in order "to emphasize the specific intellectual tradition which is characteristic of Menger's world of thought." He also quotes passages from Menger in the original German rather than in English translation. To a bilingual reader this is probably not an annoyance. But to me, I confess, it is (despite Alter's providing a glossary). It gives the paper an air of pseudoprofundity. More importantly, it promotes the dubious idea that Menger's ideas cannot be properly discussed in English.

Alter's choice of words and phrases creates obscurity which could have been avoided. A writer on abstruse methodological topics owes his readers the courtesy of using terms as plain and unsubtle as possible, so that the readers can penetrate as far as possible to his argument. Alter too often leaves the reader in a fog with phrases like "the subjective moment of value" (what does "moment" mean here?) and "the specifically Austrian interpretation of the Leibnizian monad" (to what on earth does that refer?).

It is a merit of Alter's paper that it advances bold claims about Menger. It is a demerit, and a repeated source of frustration to the reader, that these claims are often left unsupported. In lieu of a supporting argument the reader is referred to Alter's forthcoming book for details. It would have been better for the paper to have advanced fewer claims with more support.

I make these criticisms for the following reason. If I am guilty in what follows of misunderstanding Alter's substantive arguments, I hope the foregoing evidence of contributory negligence on his part will persuade the court to be lenient toward me.

Methodology

Alter offers what he calls a "synthetic" interpretation of Menger's methodology and theory. I agree with Alter that Menger's ideas on method cannot be adequately appreciated without reference to his theoretical works as well as to his explicitly methodological writings. I agree also that Terence Hutchison's hypothesis of a "break" in the continuity of Menger's thought between the *Principles* and the *Investigations* stands on weak ground.

I am less persuaded by Alter's contention that Menger's value theory cannot be adequately appreciated except in the context of Menger's views on methodology. Perhaps Alter is only saying, correctly, that the methodological context may help us to identify the *explananda* of Menger's theories (what his theories were being proposed as theories *of*). But whatever Menger's vision of the philosophy of science might have been, his economic theory of a given phenomenon can be appraised by the standards appropriate for all economic theories. What we can learn from Menger's theoretical work, the value of his contribution for us, does not largely depend on a hermeneutic understanding of what he "really meant to say."

The first of Alter's key claims is that Menger suffers "a collapse of his methodological and epistemological strategy" because his "exact" theorizing rests on introspection. Menger's practice in the *Principles,* it is said, "imposes introspection as the only logically admissible epistemology on the researcher who wants to follow the path mapped out in Menger's economic theory." And this is said to be inconsistent with theorizing about real-world social phenomena: "An epistemology which ultimately admits only of introspection as the path to the discovery of knowledge is highly unsatisfactory, not to say a dead end, unless applied to a wholly solipsistic universe."

Alter makes a valuable doctrine-historical contribution by pointing out that introspection plays a role in Menger's method of exact theorizing. An implication of Alter's insight is that the explicit emphasis placed on introspection by later Austrians, particularly Wieser and Mises, was a natural outgrowth and not an innovation, as secondary accounts have sometimes suggested (e.g., White 1984, 12).

Alter's description of Menger's overall position, however, is misleading. As Alter of course recognizes, Menger endorses a "realistic-empirical" conception of economic theory as well as an "exact" conception. An implication which Alter appears not to recognize is that Menger is far from admitting "only of introspection as the path to the discovery of knowledge." Menger describes the task of realistic-empirical theory as follows: "The realistic orientation of theoretical research has the double problem of investigating the types and the typical relationships (the general nature and the general connection) of *real* phenomena. It is supposed to make us aware of the empirical forms (the types) and the repeated relationships (the empirical laws) of real phenomena" (1985, 105, emphasis his). We might describe this task today as the search for "stylized facts," and might question whether it is properly classified as *theoretical* research (White 1985, x–xi). But it is certainly clear that for Menger there is a nonintrospective path to knowledge.

Alter's rejection of Menger's use of introspection is unjustified. Menger's "exact" economic theory does appeal to introspection, in the sense that it makes use of the inside perspective on human action that we share in virtue of being human ourselves. It is patently wrong to say that such a theory applies only to "a wholly solipsistic universe." In a passage Alter himself cites, Menger argues that "the final elements of our analysis, human *individuals* and their *efforts,* are of an empirical nature" (1985, 142 n. 51). Menger does not argue that the final elements are the whims of our own mind, or are otherwise solipsistic. Introspection gives us access to useful and reliable knowledge (not an unlimited amount, but some) about other human individuals whose efforts are akin to our own. An introspectively based theory of real social phenomena, if successful, engages the inside perspectives of its readers. Thus it applies not to a "wholly solipsistic universe" but to a universe in which there is such a thing as a common sort of experience, like the experience of making a choice. It does not spin wheels which exist only in the mind of its author.

Use of introspective knowledge in building a theory is fully compatible (to say the least) with ontological realism and with the scientific explanation of real-world social phenomena. To turn Alter's assertion on its head, an epistemology which discards introspection as a path to the discovery of knowledge is highly unsatisfactory, unless applied to a universe devoid of other human minds.

Alter's rejection of introspection is based on sheer assertion. For example, we have the unsupported assertion that "an approach that insists on introspectively derived knowledge of truth does not satisfy the canons of scientific work of whatever persuasion." In fact there are respected methodological "persuasions" in which introspection can play a role in arriving at scientific truth. It will not do simply to dismiss them out of hand.

Even if Alter tried to support the claim that introspection is scientifically useless, it is difficult to imagine how he could succeed. To establish the claim that there is no such thing as introspectively derived knowledge of a scientific truth, he would have to consider concrete examples of economic principles that Menger (or other economists) claim to have deduced from an introspective starting point. Take the law of demand, which states that any individual, and any collection of individuals, demands successively less (or at least not more) of a good at successively higher prices (wealth held constant). Would Alter wish to argue that this is not true? Or that knowledge of its truth cannot be arrived at deductively? Or that the premises for the deductive argument (that individuals choose purposively, that choice involves a ranking of alternatives, etc.) are not introspectively apparent? These arguments could not, I believe, be sustained. The law of demand is true, deductive, introspectively derived, and scientifically useful. Thus it provides a counterexample to Alter's claim that the canons of scientific work rule out introspectively derived knowledge.

Value and price theory

Alter's key claim with regard to Menger's price theory is that Menger's "conception of value becomes self-destructive because it poses a transformation problem from value to prices which remains insurmountable within his own methodological and theoretical framework."

The use of the phrase "transformation problem from value to prices," together with the attribution to Menger of a view of "values as essences and prices as appearances on the surface," suggests that we have somehow veered into a discussion of Karl Marx rather than Carl Menger. But no, Menger is the subject. Alter is far from clear in identifying what the supposed "transformation problem" is. But the gist of the "problem" seems to be that in Menger's theory "prices cannot be determined precisely but can only be located within a certain region of indeterminacy" except in the limiting case of perfect competition. Alter regards this as a shortcoming because the theory, except in the limiting case, is "unable to lead us directly from values to prices and back again." Alter concludes: "In other words, save for the case of perfectly competitive markets, Menger's theory of value is of no use to the knowing subject (the inquiring economist) if the latter wants to explain precisely why prices are what they are."

These statements betray a very imperfect understanding of Menger's theory of price. In the *Principles* (ch. 5) Menger posits a finite number of buyers and sellers and a given total supply of a good that comes in discrete or "lumpy" units (his example is horses). The set of market-clearing prices is shown to constitute a range whose limits are determined by the valuations (maximum potential bids) that the marginal buyers and sellers place on the last unit available. These valuations reflect the subjective preference rankings individuals give to units of goods, rankings which are themselves derived from the priorities (or rankings in terms of perceived importance) that the individuals assign to the wants which the goods are believed to satisfy. For Menger, "value is . . . nothing inherent in goods, no [physical] property of them, but merely the importance that we first attribute to the satisfaction of our needs, . . . and in consequence carry over to economic goods as the exclusive causes of the satisfaction of our needs" (1981, 116). Values are carried over or imputed to goods and are not confined to wants. Thus Alter perpetrates confusion by his many statements (e.g., "Menger's basic approach . . . divorces valuation from goods") suggesting that values attach only to wants.

Price cannot fall below the the greater of the valuations of the least eager actual seller and the most eager excluded buyer, and cannot exceed the lesser of the valuations of the least eager actual buyer and the most eager excluded seller.[1] That the market-clearing price "cannot be determined precisely" by Menger (except in the unlikely event that the upper and lower limits of the range precisely coincide) is not a defect of his theory but rather *an inescapable feature of the situation* he chooses to analyze. There is not one and only one price which will in fact clear the market, but rather any price within a well-defined (and possibly quite narrow) range will do so. A theory which claimed to determine price uniquely in that situation would be *spuriously* "precise."

The situation Menger chooses to analyze is not uncommon in the real world. It is consequently a feature of some real-world prices that they could be moved up or down by a penny and would still clear the market. A theory which claims to "explain precisely why prices are what they are," i.e., to determine unique market-clearing prices, claims too much as applied to such real-world markets. "Imprecision" of prices is a feature of the real world.

In fact Menger's situation is more than common: it is well-nigh the universal real-world situation. Few goods (certainly in retail transactions) are treated as continuously divisible, and no earthly market has more than a finite number of agents. The mathematical assumptions apparently necessary to model rigorously a perfectly competitive situation, in which equilibrium price really is a *precisely* determined unique

1. The implications of Menger's approach are spelled out more completely by Böhm-Bawerk's chapters on price in *Positive theory of capital* (1959, 215–47).

point, are quite forbiddingly special. If I understand E. Roy Weintraub's discussion (1985, 37–41) correctly, there must strictly be a continuum (an uncountable infinity) of measure-zero (individually negligible) trading agents for perfect competition. Weintraub quotes Robert Aumann (1964, 39): "Indeed, the influence of an individual participant cannot be mathematically negligible, so long as there are only finitely many participants."[2]

Menger's theory is far from useless to economists. It provides an understanding of the process of price formation. Furthermore, all the usual comparative-statics exercises of supply-and-demand analysis can be performed with Mengerian step-functions. The use of smooth functions which overlap only at a single point perhaps makes the results appear in a tidier fashion, but it does not produce results which cannot be reached with a Mengerian apparatus.

Alter states that Menger "believed that values were the subjectively and immediately known essences underlying rough, probabilistic phenomena such as prices." This is at best put a bit unclearly. Marginal values, in the sense of the maximum bids that agents are prepared to make in light of their subjective rankings, exactly determine what Menger (1981, 248–50) calls "economic prices," that is, the prices that would emerge in a fully arbitraged equilibrium. Economic prices are not probabilistic and are "rough" only in the sense of having freedom to fall within a more or less narrow band as discussed above. Actual market prices conform to economic prices more or less closely as arbitrage is more or less complete. Thus actual prices are "governed" by marginal values (Menger 1981, 171).[3]

It is in this manner that Menger "transforms" values into prices. There is *no* "transformation problem" of the sort that bedeviled Marx, namely of a systematic tendency for relative prices to deviate from values. Menger's theory is *not* "self-destructive" in any apparent sense, least of all in the sense of harboring an inner contradiction as Marx's theory can be said to do (Böhm-Bawerk 1975).

There is an important effort to extend Menger's analysis which Alter fails to recognize, namely the article by McCulloch (1977). Alter cites the article, but only to say that it "demonstrate[s] the compatibility of

---

2. Alter observes that "current neoclassical theory, too, knows this indeterminacy region" that Menger discusses. But he does not recognize that neoclassical theory knows it as the contract curve of the Edgeworth-Bowley box, or as the "core" of an *n*-person game (see Weintraub 1985, 38–40). He inexplicably relates it instead to monopoly pricing.

3. Menger (1981, 197) expresses the conviction that under the impact of bargaining actual "prices will . . . have a tendency to settle at the average of the extreme possible limits," but this seems an arbitrary judgment and in any case is not an essential ingredient of his theory.

Menger's analysis with the indifference-curves approach of later decades." This suggests that Alter's reading of it is superficial at best. McCulloch shows that Mengerian analysis differs from the Hicks-Allen indifference-curve analysis in important ways. One obvious difference is that each of McCulloch's "indifference curves" goes through only a single bundle in discrete-commodity space (except with superabundant goods). More importantly, McCulloch shows that Menger's framework derives as theorems conditions which Hicks simply assumes. McCulloch persuasively attributes the superiority of the Mengerian approach in these respects to its introspective method: "The Austrian school [unlike the orthodox approach] realizes that there is nothing unscientific about attributing human-like motives to its objects of study" (1977, 270).

The Mengerian framework as extended by McCulloch is capable of handling multiple goods, including complements and substitutes. Thus Alter is simply wrong in labeling Menger's hierarchical structure of wants "an inversion of the traditional textbook case of preference structure." Alter is also wrong in saying that Menger's system is incapable of generating demand functions in the case of more than one good whose successive units intermingle in the preference hierarchy.

McCulloch also clears up a terminological confusion which has been promoted by the English-language phrase "marginal utility." A good's marginal *use* (the particular want-satisfaction to which the last unit of the good is applied) is distinct from its marginal *value* (the ordinal importance attached to the last unit, as imputed from the importance of that particular want-satisfaction). Alter indicates that Menger rarely used the term *Nutzen,* which is commonly translated as "utility," and lacked the term *Grenznutzen* introduced by Wieser, which is commonly translated as "marginal utility" but which McCulloch (1977, 253) insists should be rendered "marginal use."

An author fluent in German certainly cannot be accused by someone who is not of failing to understand the distinction between *Grenznutzen* and *Grenzwert*[*h*]. But Alter's claim that Menger's marginal utility concept is "divorced from prices" and "ephemeral" rests on *some* sort of confusion. Neither the marginal use nor the marginal value is an ephemeral concept. And neither is "divorced from prices," in the sense that both play a role as described above (the marginal use plays a role via the marginal value) in the process of price formation. Both concepts have applications apart from the analysis of price formation: they are useful for analyzing the allocation problem of a Crusoe. But a Mengerian agent facing market prices will most certainly not arrive at marginal uses and marginal values of the goods he consumes in a way "divorced from prices." Marginal values will be adjusted to market prices in conformity with the equimarginal principle (as applied to lumpy goods): quantities consumed will be adjusted such that an individual's last unit of good A will have a subjective value for him not less the subjective value of the additional units of alternative good B that he could have for the same price or less.

McCulloch's discussion allows us to answer the questions that Alter raises early in his paper. The Austrian theory does not have to *assume* that preferences over commodities are "convex" but rather can *demonstrate* that they are (or rather, to be precise, demonstrate that "indifference curves" are convex; preferences themselves are quasi-concave). The theory assumes that preferences are *not* continuous. Preferences are *not* "lexicographically ordered" in the sense that a unit of one good is categorically preferred to that of another no matter how many units of each are already owned, but preferences do consist of an ordinal ranking among a finite number of items.

We are also in a position to affirm, in answer to Alter, that Menger does "jettison . . . error, ignorance, and uncertainty in his theory of prices." Error and ignorance are excluded from economic prices, which are the prices that would prevail in a fully arbitraged (no-error) market. Error and ignorance play a role in actual prices only as the reasons for nonsystematic divergences from the band of economic prices. Menger comments that in pricing, "error and imperfect knowledge may give rise to aberrations, but these are the pathological phenomena of social economy and prove as little against the laws of economics as do the symptoms of a sick body against the laws of physiology" (1981, 216). Alter's characterization of Menger's value theory as inhabiting "a world full of ignorance and incomplete information (the world of Romanticism)" should be discounted heavily in light of the exclusion of these elements from his price theory.

The synthetic interpretation of Alter

Alter's claims can be, and have been here, assessed independently of any discussion of his reasons for making them. But it will help us to *understand* Alter's interpretation of Menger if we can place it within the context of his methodological agenda. This agenda is hidden until the concluding section of the paper. There Alter urges economists not only to reject introspectionism but also to question methodological individualism. (Oddly, Alter refers to this as a "political" battle, when in fact the phrase *methodological individualism* was coined precisely to distinguish it from other varieties of individualism, including the political variety.) Alter asks, with a seeming air of openmindedness, whether we could "learn something" from the historicists and institutionalists.

I hypothesize that Alter's ultimate aim is to rehabilitate the doctrines of the Historical School. Alter's judgment of Menger thus boils down to: well, he was better than Walras, but not quite as good as Schmoller. Once introspectionism and methodological individualism (and presumably classical liberalism) are discarded, other parts of Menger's thought are to be looted for historicist purposes: "once we abandon the epistemological foundations of Menger's theoretical edifice the field is open for anyone to pick and choose those constituent elements of his economic thought which suit them best."

This hypothesis accounts for several otherwise puzzling statements in the paper. It explains why Alter wishes to conclude from his critique of the "transformation problem" that "Schmoller had been right all along" on questions of method. It explains why Alter goes out of his way to speak of "the affinity of Menger's theory of value with institutionalist economics" and to praise Menger's theory of the origin of money as "a truly historicist analysis."

Other puzzles remain. Alter attributes the discovery of Menger's (supposed) affinity with historicism to papers by neo-Austrians like Kirzner, papers which actually are quite innocent of indicating any such affinity. One wonders whether it is these papers, or historicism and institutionalism, that Alter understands in an idiosyncratic way. To associate Menger's work with historicism and institutionalism in the usual senses (as represented by Schmoller and Veblen) is quite wrongheaded, because it is a far cry from the methods of those schools to provide *theoretical* accounts of economic institutions in a deductive-compositive way. Alter never tells us what he believes Schmoller's vindicated position on method to have been. In fact Menger's historicism is a "discovery" which, as far as I can tell, Alter may claim for himself.

References

Alter, Max. 1990. What do we know about Menger? *HOPE,* this issue.

Aumann, Robert. 1964. Markets with a continuum of traders. *Econometrica* 32:39–50.

Böhm-Bawerk, Eugen von. 1959. *Capital and interest.* Vol. 2, *Postive theory of capital.* Translated by George D. Huncke. South Holland, Ill.: Libertarian Press.

———. [1896] 1975. *Karl Marx and the close of his system.* Clifton, N.J.: Augustus M. Kelley.

McCulloch, J. Huston. 1977. The Austrian theory of the marginal use and of ordinal marginal utility. *Zeitschrift für Nationalökonomie* 37:249–80.

Menger, Carl. [1871] 1981. *Principles of economics.* Translated by James Dingwall and Bert F. Hoselitz. New York: New York University Press.

————. [1883] 1985. *Investigations into the method of the social sciences with special reference to economics*. Translated by Francis J. Nock. New York: New York University Press.

Weintraub, E. Roy. 1985. *General equilibrium analysis: studies in appraisal*. Cambridge: Cambridge University Press.

White, Lawrence H. 1984. *The methodology of the Austrian School economists*. Auburn: Ludwig von Mises Institute.

————. 1985. Introduction. In Menger 1985.

Understanding differently: hermeneutics and the spontaneous order of communicative processes

Don Lavoie

> The real meaning of a text as it addresses the interpreter does not just depend on the occasional factors which characterize the author and his original public. For it is also always co-determined by the historical situation of the interpreter and thus by the whole of the objective course of history. . . . The meaning of a text surpasses its author not occasionally, but always. Thus understanding is not a reproductive procedure but rather always also a productive one. . . . It suffices to say that one understands *differently when one understands at all.*
>
> —HANS-GEORG GADAMER[1]

Recently a group of Mengerian economists have taken up the banner of hermeneutics, referring to the philosophical views of Hans-Georg Gadamer, Paul Ricoeur, and others, and have started to develop a distinctive brand of the Austrian tradition on this basis. This reinterpretation of the school has arisen mainly under the influence of Ludwig Lachmann and has an enthusiastic following at one of the leading scholarly centers of Austrian economics, George Mason University.[2] It is too early to tell exactly what will come from this new turn in the Austrian School. One critic pointed out that "the hermeneutical revival has so far remained largely unsettled as to the precise contents of its message."[3] As one of the perpetrators of this re-vision of Austrian economics, I plead guilty.

---

1. From Gadamer 1960, 280, as excerpted and translated by Linge (1976, xxv). Note that what Gadamer says of understanding the meaning of a text is meant to apply to all attempts to understand.

2. Among the Austrian School economists to take up contemporary hermeneutics have been Richard Ebeling, Ludwig Lachmann, and myself. All of us have referred to the roots of hermeneutics within the Austrian School by way of Wilhelm Dilthey's influence on Mises's view of history, and by way of the interpretive sociologists Max Weber and Alfred Schütz. An attempt to reinterpret Mises's method in more hermeneutical terms was made in Lavoie 1986. Ebeling's work (1986, 1991) has drawn from Paul Ricoeur, and my own has taken inspiration primarily from Hans-Georg Gadamer.

3. See Mäki 1991, 5.

The present paper will only partially repair this, by trying to articulate what I take to be one of the central messages of hermeneutical philosophy, the idea of "understanding differently." Beyond clarifying what hermeneutics is, I would like to indicate one way that it might help economics, Austrian or otherwise.[4] It might help us to better appreciate how communicative processes work in economics and in the economy.

Hermeneutics is a general theory of understanding and can be considered as potentially useful at a number of different "levels." What might be called "exegetical-level" hermeneutics is probably the most obvious way the philosophy could have implications for any discipline, and my own discussion will misleadingly seem to take place only at this first level. On the surface I am only raising a question about how to interpret the texts of Carl Menger's economics. A second level will also arise here, however, which might be called "agent-level" hermeneutics, and which involves treating human actions as meaningful "texts" to be read.[5] At this level would be found not only the issue of how economists understand the actions of agents in the economy but also the issue of how agents come to understand one another. And then there could be still a third level of possible application, which might be called "social-level" hermeneutics. This level would treat the overall economy as a "text" to be read.[6]

I want to make it clear from the outset that the theory of understanding to be outlined here is of much wider significance for economics than as an aid to exegesis. To be sure, the tradition used to be rather narrowly focused on the interpretation of texts, and it still talks of the hermeneutical situation in terms of the "reading" of "texts." But the philosophy is no longer considered a method for interpreting written texts, nor even a method of the human sciences, but is thought to be, more broadly still, a philosophy of human understanding in all its modes. It is not merely an aid to the economists' talk about other economists' talk, a special case of the methodology of intellectual history. It is conceived as a general theory of how we understand anything, from a painting to a scientific

4. For more comprehensive summaries of hermeneutical philosophy see Bernstein 1983, Hekman 1986, Linge 1976, Madison 1986, 1988a, Mueller-Vollmer 1985, Rabinow and Sullivan 1979, and Warnke 1987.

5. In his written comments on the conference draft of this paper Richard Langlois persuaded me to clarify these different levels, and it is from him that I borrow the term "agent-level hermeneutics." Of course the idea of agent-level hermeneutics is well known in sociology. Max Weber—see especially Lachmann's interpretation (1971)—was trying to treat human action as meaningful texts in need of interpretation. For a useful elaboration of agent-level hermeneutics see Paul Ricoeur's classic paper "The model of the text" (1981).

6. Although I believe the social or "macro" level offers a very promising way of thinking about the study of economies, I confine myself here to the exegetical and agent levels.

paper, from a poem to a breakfast conversation. It uses the word "text" to stand not just for literal texts but for anything that has meaning to somebody, including, for example, the words of market negotiations or the prices decided upon in those negotiations.

Even in its answer to the exegetical-level question about how we come to an understanding of a literal text, hermeneutics takes itself beyond this level. Textual interpretation is itself modeled on the agent-level situation of verbal discourse, of the way we come to an understanding together in an everyday conversation.

This agent-level hermeneutical question, it would seem, could be a vitally important part of our substantive economics.[7] How do verbal communicative processes work within the economy? It can be argued that economists pay far too little attention to such agent-level hermeneutical questions and that when they do attend to them, their theory of the communicative process is oversimplified. Agents in economists' models are sometimes permitted to "copy" knowledge endowments from each other, but they don't seem to be able to engage in anything like human interpersonal communication. Economics is typically carried on at a level of abstraction at which nothing depends on assuming that its "agents" are able to engage in everyday discourse, either with one another or with the researcher. But in the real world everything agents do is connected to verbal discourses of various kinds. Contracts are negotiated, engineering designs are studied, marketing strategies are elaborated, advertising campaigns are formulated, stock market bids are decided upon, and profit/loss accounts are interpreted, in language. It is, I presume, what discourses like these *mean* to their participants and to others, which basically drives economic processes. Studying the economy, whether theoretically or empirically, would seem to require paying serious attention to these discourses of the business community, of the workplace, and of the policy arena. Yet that isn't what most contemporary economics looks like.

A dose of hermeneutics might help, not only to get economists to devote a larger quantity of their attention to agent-level communicative processes but also to improve the quality of the attention they do pay to them. Economics could use a richer theory of understanding, not only to help with exegetical questions about how to understand other economists but also to help with agent-level questions concerning how everyday verbal communication takes place among agents in the economy.

---

7. This is especially true of Mengerian economics, where the issue of knowledge-conveyance has become *the* central issue and the chief basis of its critique of mainstream neoclassical theory. See the paper elsewhere in this volume by Karen Vaughn for an account of how contemporary Mengerian economics found its way to the knowledge-conveyance issue.

The immediate question of the occasion for which this paper is written is: How do we understand Menger? But the more fundamental question hermeneutics raises is: How do we understand anything? I will suggest that the answer hermeneutics gives to this extremely general philosophical question happens to be quite "Mengerian" in spirit.

I. *Mengerian economics and the hermeneutical turn*

> In two letters to Walras, June 1883 and February 1884, [Menger] insisted that we are dealing not only with quantitative relationships but also with the "essence" of economic phenomena. . . . If it is permissible to equate the "comprehension of essence" with the "interpretation of meaning," we may conclude that Menger's intention in both letters was to defend the possibility of an economic theory designed to interpret meaning.
>
> —LUDWIG LACHMANN[8]

In the description of the themes of this conference the exegetical hermeneutical question is posed: What strands in the current Austrian tradition would be recognizable by Menger? For example: How would he feel about radical subjectivism, about apriorism, about interpretive or hermeneutical economics? I do think that the hermeneutical version of contemporary Austrian economics is "in the spirit" of the work of that great founder of the Austrian School. But I have to admit that the contemporary hermeneutical Austrians understand economics differently than Menger did and that it takes a nimble imagination to picture Menger, who saw economics as a matter of "exact laws," as endorsing hermeneutics.

One of the central messages of hermeneutical philosophy might be illustrated by noting how misleading this way of posing the exegetical question is. Whether our imaginary story has us going back in time to ask Menger, or has him coming ahead in time to tell us, it is still science fiction. Is this not a strange, even metaphysical, way of setting a standard for interpretation? If we cannot resist the temptation to imagine that Menger is still alive to tell us how he feels, it would be better to imagine him fully alive and open, for example, to all the new developments of this century, not frozen in some fixed point of view from the past. But once we describe the imaginary situation that way, it is clear

---

8. See Lachmann's 1966 paper "The significance of the Austrian School" (1977, 48–49).

that asking what Menger would think about contemporary Mengerian economics begs crucial questions about how he would interpret all the other developments that have taken place since his time. And how could we really answer such questions? Hermeneutics would say that our task is not best described as a reproduction of a psychological meaning that presumably once resided inside of the skull of a long-deceased Austrian economist. To be Mengerian is not to (mechanically) copy something as accurately as possible from Menger's head into our own but to (creatively) interact with and learn from his words. Our primary question is not What did Menger mean when he wrote his works? but What do his works mean to us now? We want not to cling rigidly to Menger's own intended meaning but, as hermeneutics would say, to place ourselves in the direction of Menger's words. We want to adhere not to the "letter" of his words but to their "spirit."

So, then, what does Menger's economics have to say to us today? Of all the things he said, what would be identified as his key, lasting contributions? I would say Menger had two related principles that continue to define the school: subjectivism and spontaneous order. Most modern followers of Menger would probably agree. Subjectivism was the point of the book *Principles* ([1871] 1981) with which Menger launched the Austrian version of the marginalist revolution, and spontaneous order was the point of much of his *Investigations* ([1883] 1985), with which he participated in the *Methodenstreit*. The school has evolved into apparently quite divergent branches, but the centrality among all of them of these two Mengerian themes is unquestionable. Two of Menger's most influential followers, Mises and Hayek, each emphasized one of these more than the other, but they saw the two principles as fundamental and interconnected. Mises's theory of entrepreneurship builds on subjectivism to understand the creative contribution of individual human actors to the market process. Hayek's elaborations of spontaneous order theory depict the market process as a creative discovery procedure. Both are, in my view, describing the same thing, a nonmechanistic process which generates order on the social level from the interplay of subjective perspectives on the individual level.

What is distinctively Mengerian is not just adherence to both of the principles in economic analysis but conceiving them in their synthesis. These principles are considered by Austrian economists to be interrelated and mutually conditioning, such that you cannot really have one without the other. The classic example of this synthesis is Menger's illustration of the evolution of money. The steps of this process are understandable as guided by self-interested actions based on subjective perceptions, but the overall order that results is not (and in many cases, could not have been) the direct product of anyone's design.

So if we take these principles to define what we mean by a Mengerian approach to economics, how Mengerian is the hermeneutical version of Austrian economics? I would like to argue that the hermeneutical Austrians are "in the spirit" of both of Menger's principles. Menger's point about subjectivism can be described as an obviously hermeneutical move. It was developed as an answer to objective value theory in classical economics, showing that value "is nothing inherent in the good itself" (1981, 58) but depends on its relation to subjective human needs. The subjectivist turn he gave to economics insists that what matters to the economist is not objective circumstances as such but the *meaning* they have to the agents involved. The Mengerian emphasis on the economy as shaped by human purpose, on value as determined by diverse subjective perspectives, would seem to be plainly a matter of agent-level hermeneutics.[9]

But the case of Menger's theory of the market as an "organic" institution, or as his modern followers call it, a spontaneous order, may not be so obvious.[10] His spontaneous order message is an answer to historicism, a philosophical position with which hermeneutics has been associated by some of its critics, so that, it could be argued, hermeneutics may not be compatible with Menger's approach to this issue.[11] Even if we leave aside the highly controversial question of whether hermeneutics is guilty of historicism, there would seem to be at least superficial plausibility to the charge that hermeneutics would necessarily fail to cope with spontaneous order. After all, if understanding is based on the

9. On the other hand, contemporary hermeneutics, with its critique of Cartesian thinking, suggests that some traditional writings on subjectivism are in need of reformulation. I have raised some questions about the way subjective costs are treated by some "radical subjectivists" in my paper on the Lester/Machlup debate (Lavoie 1989).

10. In a fascinating paper on the hermeneutics of G. H. von Wright, Uskali Mäki (1991) has argued, in effect, that while this form of hermeneutics has a definite role to play with regard to the "subjectivism" side of Mengerian economics, it is unable to help with the "spontaneous order" side. Since Wright's theory of understanding is strictly acausal, Mäki shows why it cannot help with the study of causal processes in economics, including spontaneous order processes. I agree, and would add that some other leading people associated with the name "hermeneutics," such as E. D. Hirsch, may also be guilty of leaving no room for spontaneous order. The versions associated with the names of Hans-Georg Gadamer and Paul Ricoeur, however, do not seem to be subject to the same argument. Their theories of understanding are not dichotomized from explanation but are taken to incorporate a notion of causal explanation within understanding. These versions do not concede positivism's view of causal explanation to the natural sciences, as Wright seems to do, but see a hermeneutical dimension to all attempts at explanation, whether natural or social-scientific. Thus much of the argument Mäki formulates against Wright may not be applicable to philosophical hermeneutics.

11. Contemporary hermeneutical philosophers vigorously deny this charge and have themselves offered critiques of earlier versions of hermeneutics for being historicist. The critique of the hermeneutical Austrians by Albert (1988) equates Gadamer's hermeneutics with J. G. Droysen's historicism, even though Gadamer specifically criticizes Droysen for his historicism in part 2 of *Truth and method* (1960, 1984).

traditional hermeneutical task of finding the meaning *intended* by the author of a text, it would seem to be inherently unequipped to deal with the theory of the market as a spontaneous order, a matter of *unintended* consequences.

Since this paper will not address social-level hermeneutics—which is clearly the level at which Menger's spontaneous-order analysis of markets is presented—it cannot directly respond to such critiques. It will try to provide an indirect response of a sort, instead, by arguing that even at the exegetical and agent levels, hermeneutics requires its own notion of spontaneous order. My claim here is not the defensive one, that hermeneutics merely *leaves room for* spontaneous order in social-level interpretation, although I believe such a defense can be made. It is that hermeneutics makes a certain sort of spontaneous-order process one of its own central themes, even where it is not specifically concerned with the social level. In its explication of why understanding a text or an agent's actions is not a matter of getting an exact copy of anything, hermeneutics renders the communicative process as a creative discovery procedure. It is the sort of process which Menger, if we can imagine him among us today, might call a spontaneous order.

II. *A critique of the copy theory of communication*

> Nowhere does understanding mean the mere recovery of what the author "meant," whether he was the creator of a work of art, the doer of a deed, the writer of a law book, or anything else. The *mens auctoris* does not limit the horizon of understanding in which the interpreter has to move, indeed, in which he is necessarily moved, if, instead of merely repeating, he really wants to understand.
>
> —HANS-GEORG GADAMER[12]

What might be called the copy theory of knowledge is all but universally rejected by modern philosophers and economists.[13] Our knowledge of the world is never a reproduction of it but is made up of descriptions from particular points of view, answers to questions previously posed, simplifications which deliberately abstract from certain aspects in order to emphasize others. As Heinrich Rickert put it,

It can be shown on the basis of general logical considerations that no knowledge can possibly provide a reproduction. This is because

12. See Gadamer 1976, 210.
13. Richard Rorty's fascinating book *Philosophy and the mirror of nature* (1979) is essentially an extended critique of the copy theory of knowledge.

every knowledge claim must take the form of a *judgment*. . . . The relationship between an original and its copy will never obtain between reality and the content of the judgments made about it. . . . If we reject the picture theory, however, it does not follow that knowledge is worthless because it is unable to incorporate the content of reality itself into its concepts.[14]

We economists don't talk about copies but rather models of economies, and few of us have any illusions that our models are in any sense copies of reality. These models will not directly tell us how the real world works; they need to be used, that is, interpreted, to see their significance.

Perhaps nobody really believes the copy theory of knowledge anymore, but what about the copy theory of communication? If the (now discredited) copy theory of knowledge takes, as its standard for judging a particular interpretation of the world, the simple question of how close a copy of the real world it is, the (not yet discredited) copy theory of communication holds a similar standard. An interpretation of a text is to be judged according to how close it comes to copying the original meaning that was intended by the author. This idea is so much a part of our ways of talking that it may sound nonsensical to challenge it. Whatever my understanding of the world is, even given that it's not itself a copy of the world, when I communicate that understanding to somebody else, surely I want him or her to get as close as practically possible to an exact copy of my understanding. To say you've understood me "differently" sounds like you've twisted my meaning, you've missed my point.

But many of the same reasons Rickert and other philosophers have given for why knowledge of the world is not a matter of copying anything would seem to apply to the issue of communication as well. Each of us in the communicative process sees different selected aspects of the world, each has different experiences to draw on, so that when we communicate with one another successfully we are not reproducing a fixed meaning but finding our own way to appropriate another's meaning for ourselves, to make it our own by relating it to what we already know.

The copy theory treats human communication as if it were telecommunication.[15] Bits of information are passed along from one agent to

14. See Rickert 1986, 43. Rickert's views on this point directly influenced the Austrian School by way of Max Weber and Ludwig Mises.

15. F. A. Hayek has made much of the analogy with telecommunication in the context of that human communication which takes place through prices. While I find the analogy useful for some purposes, I think it can be extremely misleading. Elsewhere I have tried to describe the price system as a communicative process that is analogous to verbal discourse (Lavoie 1987; 1990). For an interpretation of Hayek's approach which finds it exemplary of hermeneutics see Madison 1988b.

another as if people were connected to one another by computer wire. Data is "received" by the agent in the same way a computer peripheral scans a document. One person starts out with given knowledge K_1, which is taken to be itself a model (not a copy) of the objective world he inhabits. At some point he "communicates" this knowledge to another person, who receives a (more or less precise) "copy" of it: K_2.

Miscommunication, according to the copy theory, is a simple matter of K_2 turning out to be unequal to K_1, that is, a loss of some bits has occurred during the copying process. Protection against such miscommunication among human agents can presumably be secured in the same way it is among computers: by building in redundancy. A person can make sure his message has gotten through intact by accompanying it with a parity check, to see if a bit was lost, or by sending the message twice, or by having the recipient repeat it back to him. The only threat to successful communication is "noise" which makes for situations where K_2 no longer equals K_1. When computer buffs (like me) say our computers are "talking to one another" all we mean is that copies of strings of bits are allowed to pass unencumbered between our machines. Successful communication simply means that noise is not a practical problem and has been overcome, for example, by some redundancy technique. It is assumed that the only relevant difference here is that computers can read a text exactly, whereas getting what is inside somebody else's head can be more difficult. The interpretive standard for human communication, whether attainable or not, is thought to be the same: $K_1 = K_2$.

Hermeneutics constitutes a direct challenge to this copy theory of communication.[16] Understanding is not a reproduction of some original meaning-in-itself somehow mysteriously contained in texts but is always a *mediation* between a text and a reader. According to hermeneutics, successful communication necessarily takes place in such a way that one agent understands what is communicated differently than the other. Accuracy, strictly speaking, is not only impossible, it is not desirable.

This is not to say that anything goes, that you can read whatever you want into a text. Hermeneutics is not saying interpretation is easy because you can make a text say whatever you please. It is saying it's difficult, because being right is no simple matter of reproducing accurately from an already fixed meaning. It involves a creative act on the reader's part to develop a meaning from a certain sort of process of interaction with the text. Understanding another requires not a passive reproduction but an inventive production. The need for such creative

16. It is hardly alone among philosophical approaches in this regard. All the contemporary theories of discourse raise fundamental challenges to the copy theory of communication.

efforts is determined by the fact that there is a radical diversity of perspectives, which therefore require *translation*. And the task of the translator, as Gadamer puts it, "must never be to copy what is said, but to place himself in the direction of what is said (i.e. in its meaning)" (1976, 68).

A better exegetical reading, say, of Menger, is not the one that mechanically reproduces a static meaning that is thought to have been originally intended, but the one that advances what we see as the more promising strands of Menger's work. Understanding Menger's economics, to paraphrase Gadamer, necessarily means understanding it differently than Menger could have understood it when he wrote it. A scholarly attempt to do economics in the Mengerian spirit cannot be a mere backward-looking effort to recover the way he must have thought about economics. It should be seen as an attempt to open ourselves to the truth-claim we can discern in the Mengerian legacy.

Similarly if we ask an agent-level hermeneutical question about the meaning of an agent's action in the economy, we are not trying merely to reproduce what it meant to the agent. When, for example, we attempt to understand the actions of the Federal Reserve Board in September 1929, we had better take advantage of the fact which we know, and they did not, that the stock market crash was about to occur. If we were interpreting, say, a letter from Paul Warburg to J. P. Morgan about the state of the economy, wouldn't our account be shaped by our knowledge of the upcoming events? Shouldn't it? Shouldn't we try to take advantage of all sorts of things, including details of historical information and general insights from economic theory, much of which the author could not have had access to, in our effort to understand the historical meaning of the letter? Of course we cannot project our understanding to the agent, but every detail of our interpretation of the agent's purposes is shaped by our knowledge of subsequent events. Our questions might in fact be focused primarily on what key things Warburg did not seem to know that he should have, or what he did not do but could have, or other such questions which necessarily transcend the horizon of the author of the text.

The copy theory oversimplifies both the possibilities open to human communicators, whether economics professors or economic agents, and the obstacles in their way. On the one hand the obstacles to successful communication go way beyond what can sensibly be called noise problems, so that understanding may begin to seem rather difficult. But on the other hand, the ways available to get around the obstacles are more involved than is allowed in copy theories. Those would-be friends or foes of hermeneutics who only stress the additional obstacles to understanding and not the solutions may leave the mistaken impression that hermeneutics makes understanding out to be all but impossible.[17] On the contrary, the point of the philosophy is not *whether* understanding is possible, since we take it for granted that it happens all the time, but *how* it is possible. Properly understood, hermeneutics leads not to some kind of hopeless pessimism that we may never understand one another but to a better appreciation of how it is that we pull it off so easily, and so often.

But the challenge cuts more deeply than a mere elaboration of more obstacles to and solutions for communication. It involves a profound reappraisal of what human communication is. As hermeneutical philosophers put it, human communication is dialogical rather than monological. Computers copying files to one another can be said to be communicating in some sense, but they are not engaging in discourse. If human understanding involves a dynamic process of mediation between perspectives, the copy theory's presentation of communication as unidirectional and under the strict control of anyone, either senders or receivers, becomes problematic. Communication in the sense of the copy theory is a zero-sum game in which knowledge is not expanded but merely relocated. Human discourse, by contrast, is a *dialogue* of exploration which tries to discover or invent some common ground between diverse perspectives.

Gadamer is modeling all "reading," which might appear to be a strictly unidirectional process of extracting a fixed message, on what happens in a good conversation, on a dynamic, bidirectional process, a process of "give and take." And this process, like a good conversation, is taken to be exploratory and creative.[18] On this basis hermeneutics challenges the meaningfulness of the copy theory's standards for judging successful communication, that is, that the closer you can get to K_1 = K_2 the better. It claims that the message intended by the writer *never* "equals" the message understood by the reader.

The reason we necessarily understand differently is that understanding involves what hermeneutics calls an "applicative" moment: we understand something by making it our own, by appropriating it for ourselves, by applying it to our own context, by thinking of it in terms of examples with which we have experience. It is not so much the meaning

17. This may be due to confusing hermeneutics with at least some versions of deconstructionism, which seem to be saying that understanding is impossible. I think there is a sense in which hermeneutics shows understanding to be *easier* than many social scientists seem to think, and it is certainly not saying it's impossible. I'll leave it to those better able to understand Derrida than I to interpret his comment that all reading is misreading. Hermeneutics would definitely not want to relax, much less abandon, the scholar's effort to distinguish better from worse readings. It helps us to improve our ability to tell the difference.

18. I would like to thank Karen Vaughn for alerting me to this point about creativity.

the text or action has for its author that concerns us when we truly try to understand, but rather its meaning for us. And because we and our historical context are necessarily different from the author and his, we will understand his words and actions differently than he could have understood them himself.

According to the copy theory, if there has been a communication failure, the "agents" have no alternative but to repeat themselves, to send another copy. Human communication, by contrast, involves explication, elaboration, illustration, a process of questioning and answering which discovers new things that the original message did not clearly contain. We have recourse to more options than the computer has, to try to get the message right; we don't just ask for another copy, we ask, "What does this mean?" After all, the machines, which are able to "communicate" only in this copy sense, never really "understand" the messages they so rapidly move around but only make them more conveniently accessible to human agents. The human beings who program the machines, supply them with properly formatted inputs, and interpret their outputs are the ones who do all the cognitive work that needs to be done on these messages to make them meaningful.[19]

When a computer scans a document, the information is made to fit precisely into a context that is already given. Whenever a computer runs into inputs that don't fit its pre-given rules of format, it is helpless. The problem of finding an appropriate context simply doesn't come up for the machine, and is solved for it by human users. The "knowledge" communicated in the copy theory can be treated as separate and explicit pieces of data, simply bits speeding in one direction along a wire, all ready to be placed in their appropriate bins according to the programmer's formatting rules.

As researchers in the field of artificial intelligence have discovered the hard way, human intelligence works not by the exhaustive accumulation of particular details but by the grasping of whole patterns, as happens when we recognize a face without being able to identify its particular components. The copy theory imagines human discourse to work like a fax machine: a picture of a face is "communicated" by sending a matrix of bits representing shades of gray that include all the details of a photograph. The human on the other end of the fax machine, however, does not scan and record the bits, he or she sees the whole face. Admittedly humans are incomparably slower at moving and storing the thousands of details computers manipulate, but we effortlessly pull off a more amazing feat when we tacitly integrate those details as subsidiary

---

19. See Winograd and Flores 1986.

clues in the forming of a mental image of the face.[20] This is what hermeneutics discusses in terms of the "hermeneutical circle": we understand a part of a text, say, its first sentence, in terms of the whole, say an entire book, and yet we can only understand the whole book in terms of its parts. This kind of pattern recognition underlies a whole range of intellectual achievements from the most primitive perceptions to the most complex scientific theories and artistic creations. The grasping of wholes by means of subsidiary clues, the "seeing" of things in terms of their background context, is a tacit skill which enables our communicative powers to advance far beyond other animals' and, so far, computers'.[21]

The text copied is just passively received, and presumed already meaningful. It is simply allocated into preset storage files, as when a computer categorizes input data and stores it accordingly. The text understood may resist being pigeonholed in this way and may challenge the reader's existing categories. It needs to be actively integrated into a perspective in which, at first, it may seem to make no sense whatever. Cognitive work is required of the recipient to find a way to *give* meaning to what may at first be a foreign and inexplicable text. One has to find the right metaphors in terms of which to think of the phenomenon under examination. Or one has to choose the most apt way to tell the story of how some processes worked. The reader not only must be active in trying to apply the text to his own situation and fit it into the context of what he already knows, he must risk what he thinks he knows against the claim the text makes on him. The text copied is mastered by those who manipulate it. The text understood can always make a claim against the prejudices of the reader.

Not only is *a* context always needed to make sense of any given text, but there are generally several contexts or perspectives involved. Human communication faces the added challenge, not considered in the copy theory, that the background context which gives meaning to the text is not necessarily given at the outset but may need to be found. The initial context of the sender and receiver may radically diverge, and always diverges some. Thus at least two different background contexts or perspectives are relevant in any attempt to understand in the human sciences: that of the text and that of its reader. The copy theory implicitly collapses these two perspectives into one. The text copied is

20. This is what is meant by "seeing something in its context." It is the aspect of practical decision making which Hans-Georg Gadamer calls "grasp[ing] the 'circumstances' in their infinite variety" (1984, 21) and which Fritz Machlup calls "sizing up . . . the total situation" (1946, 534).

21. See Polanyi 1958.

assumed to mean the same thing to its generator as it does to its recipient. The text understood involves what Gadamer calls a "fusion of horizons" between two diverse perspectives. It involves *adding* to what is said through a mediation of the "horizons" of the interpreter and the interpreted, and this mediation calls on tacit resources supplied by the language-speaking community in which the reader participates.

I believe that this way of thinking about communicative processes is broadly consistent with the way everyday, verbal understanding occurs in the business world. More is going on out there than a mere copying of information sets. When businessmen communicate with one another over lunch in order to explore possible gains from trade, what we have is not a unidirectional passing of messages from a sender to a receiver, but an interactive process between diverse perspectives, an effort of translation between two languages, a creative dialogue.

III. *Understanding as a spontaneous order process*

> Gadamer's point in equating hermeneutic understanding with dialogue, then, is that the former is a learning experience. In attempting to understand a text or other aspect of the tradition, we both bring that object into our world, illuminate the meaning it has for us, and transform our own previous perspective. Hermeneutics involves mediation or, in other words, a capacity to see the significance of a truth-claim for our own situation. . . . In describing understanding as a form of dialogue, then, Gadamer is not suggesting that the successful outcome of a process of understanding favors either the initial claims of the interpreter or those of the object. Rather, just as the conclusion of a genuine conversation is not the sole property of either one of the dialogue-partners, the outcome of *Verstehen* is neither our own property, the result of the dominance of our prejudices, nor the property of the tradition, the result of its dominance. Instead, just as in conversation, the result is a unity or agreement that goes beyond the original positions of the various participants; indeed, the consensus that emerges in understanding represents a new view and hence a new stage of the tradition.
> —Georgia Warnke[22]

Those who adhere to the copy theory view, that the author's original intention should be the standard for exegetical interpretation, consider

22. See Warnke's excellent interpretation of Gadamer's philosophy, from which this quotation is taken (1987, 104).

Gadamer's approach to be a dangerous invitation to chaos. E. D. Hirsch, for example, argues that in allowing a reader to revise the author's own original meaning, Gadamer fails to sufficiently respect the author. Furthermore, by giving the reader license to reinterpret the author's original meaning, Gadamer opens the door to complete arbitrariness. The reader is free to see whatever he wants in the text, and the possibility of finding the "true" meaning is lost. Thus Gadamer's theory is disrespectful not only of authors, but even of the notion of "truth" itself. Gadamer's error, he says, is that he confuses the meaning of a text with its significance.[23] The meaning is set by the psychological intentions and specific audience of the author, and it never changes in subsequent interpretations. Only the significance of this fixed meaning depends on the reader. All that should be permitted to change in subsequent readings of the text is its significance, not its meaning.

Gadamer's response turns both of Hirsch's charges back on him. It is those who would fix the meaning of a text to the psychological meaning originally intended, who fail to sufficiently respect the author. And it is this "psychologism" that does disrespect to the notion of truth, by leaving aside the issue of the possible truth-claim the text may make. Psychologism reduces the text to something that merely tells us about the mental state of the author, instead of taking it seriously by treating it as something that tells us about the subject matter the author wanted to talk about. We are not really looking for what an author had in mind, but for the meaning—and possible truth—of what he said.[24]

If, for example, we restrict the meaning of the New Testament to what its authors had originally meant, then we do the authors "a false honor." In the face of modern science, the authors' intended meaning is often simply absurd to us, and the result of this way of reading would be an all too easy rejection. "Their honor," Gadamer insists, "should lie precisely in the fact that they proclaim something that surpasses their own horizon of understanding—even if they are named John or Paul" (1976, 210). To really respect an author is to allow him to speak *to us,* even if, like John or Paul, he could not possibly have imagined what we and our situation would be like. Hirschean hermeneutics leaves the text dead, where Gadamer's would ask the reader to breathe life into it, by allowing it to reexpress itself to a different context.

Gadamer and Hirsch agree that the significance of a text or ac-

---

23. See Hirsch's critique of Gadamer in Hirsch 1967, 245–64.

24. Since the days of what Gadamer calls Romantic hermeneutics it had been common for texts to be reduced to objects without a truth-claim on the reader. Gadamer credits Husserl's phenomenology with having shown why such psychologism fails to deal with meaning. What counts in interpretation is not mental states but the subject matter of the text.

tion must vary with the reader's situation.[25] But Gadamer would ask whether it makes any sense to separate the meaning of an action from its ever-changing significance. Understanding Paul Warburg's actions in 1929 and understanding their historical significance, as leading up to the stock market crash, are part of the same act.

The Hirschean approach privileges the author of a text, claiming that without fixing meaning to the author's intentions, the door is open to complete arbitrariness. The arbitrariness this approach fears, on the other hand, privileges the reader, permitting him to impose his own thinking onto the text. From Gadamer's standpoint interpretation requires avoiding either of these privilegings. The reader does need to truly respect the author, by opening himself to the possible truth of what is said, but he must also appropriate what is said for himself, see it in the context of what he already knows, relate it to his own situation. He should neither dominate over the text, forcing it into silence, nor capitulate to it, forcing himself into silence. He should promote a dialogue where both the text and its reader can speak, and where understanding can emerge as a beneficial unintended consequence of the process.

Though the meaning of a text or action is not under the control of its author, it is not thereby arbitrary and does not oblige us to give up on the idea of truth. There will be several different true meanings of texts or actions, of course, since according to Gadamer the meaning is partly determined by the reader and his situation. But this does not mean that any reading is as true as any other. Meaning is considered to be determined systematically in the dialogical process where divergent interpretations "play off" one another.

In Austrian economists' terminology, Gadamer's approach could be called a spontaneous order theory of understanding. Just as the fact that market processes are under no actor's deliberate control does not imply they are without order, so hermeneutics says the same in regard to the dialogical process. Market order can be seen as a special case of a more general category, spontaneous orders, of which, for example, crystal formation and biological evolution are treated as other cases.[26] Systematic order arises in these cases without being the direct product of anyone's design. Gadamer is saying essentially that understanding is another case.

25. As Gadamer put it in regard to agent-level hermeneutics, "understanding the historical significance of an action presupposes that we do not restrict ourselves to the subjective plans, intentions, and dispositions of the agents" (1976, 122).

26. See Hayek 1967, 1978. When Austrian economists refer to the thought processes of the mind as an example of a spontaneous order process, they are applying spontaneous order theory to what I am calling agent-level hermeneutical questions. See Hayek's *Sensory order* (1952).

The process of coming to an understanding goes beyond the control of its participants and exhibits a "buoyancy," an unintended order, of its own. Gadamer refers to the "ontology of play" or game-playing, by which he means that understanding is an orderly interplay of purposes which is not itself confined to any of those constituent purposes. He calls it a "to-and-fro movement which is not tied to any goal which would bring it to an end" and says that play "represents an order in which the to-and-fro motion of play follows of itself" (1984, 93–94).

In the dialogical process "it is no longer the will of the individual person, holding itself back or exposing itself, that is determinative" (Gadamer 1976, 66). Indeed this is precisely why dialogue is so creative. It is productive of knowledge that none of its participants had. As Gadamer says, "in genuine conversation, something emerges that is contained in neither of the partners by himself" (1984, 419). And "just as the relation between the speaker and what is spoken points to a dynamic process that does not have a firm basis in either member of the relation, so the relation between the understanding and what is understood has a priority over its relational terms" (1976, 50).

It is when Gadamer discusses the nature of language that the affinity of his theory to the Mengerian theory of spontaneous orders is the most evident. The decisive move hermeneutics makes, from the Mengerian standpoint, is to consider all understanding to have the same basic structure as verbal communication in language. Once this move is made, Mengerians will readily accept that, as Menger himself often pointed out, language is a good example of a spontaneous order process. The "user" of language is not in control of the process in which he participates but is taken up into a larger order and takes advantage of a rich background context stretching back to the historical discourses from which the current communicators evolved.

As Gadamer (1976, 87) emphasizes, it is not simply that we speak the language, there is a real sense in which the language speaks us. Speaking is more than a deliberate use of "tools" of communicating ideas, as if these were held within the mind independently of its culture and mode of expression. Rather, "When you take a word in your mouth you must realize that you have not taken a tool that can be thrown aside if it won't do the job, but you are fixed in a direction of thought which comes from afar and stretches beyond you" (1984, 496). Learning to speak inserts us into a communicative process which we both influence and are influenced by. Language supplies us with tacit "prejudices" which direct our attention, and through which we can come to understand one another and our world.

Understanding is not the deliberate achievement of an isolated individual but is a social process, a process of coming to an understanding together with other participants to the dialogue. There is order to this process, but it is an order that transcends the control of any of its participant individuals.

I am grateful for a National Endowment for the Humanities summer 1988 fellowship, which enabled me to write this paper. I should thank Uskali Mäki for a friendly challenge that got me thinking about the issues, and Jack Wiseman for setting up a seminar on hermeneutics and economics at George Mason University in the summer of 1988, at which I benefited from several other friendly challenges. Especially useful at that seminar were criticisms from Wiseman, Geoffrey Brennan, James Buchanan, and Karen Vaughn. Conversations with the various graduate students at GMU who have taken interest in these ideas, especially Pete Boettke, Steve Horwitz, Susanne Paine, Dave Prychitko, and Ralph Rector, have helped me enormously. For useful comments on earlier drafts I would like to thank Bruce Caldwell, Richard Langlois, Wade Hands, Warren Samuels, Jack High, and Arjo Klamer.

References

Albert, Hans. 1988. Hermeneutics and economics: a criticism of hermeneutical thinking in the social sciences. *Kyklos* 41.4:573–602.

Bernstein, Richard J. 1983. *Beyond objectivism and relativism: science, hermeneutics, and praxis*. Philadelphia: University of Pennsylvania Press.

Ebeling, Richard M. 1986. Toward a hermeneutical economics: expectations, prices, and the role of interpretation in a theory of the market process. In *Subjectivism, intelligibility and economic understanding: essays in honor of Ludwig M. Lachmann on his eightieth birthday*, edited by Israel M. Kirzner. New York: New York University Press.

———. 1991. What is a price? explanation and understanding (with apologies to Paul Ricoeur). In Lavoie 1991.

Gadamer, Hans-Georg. 1960. *Wahrheit und Methode: Grundzüge einer philosophischen Hermeneutik*. Tubingen: Mohr.

———. 1976. *Philosophical hermeneutics*. Berkeley and Los Angeles: University of California Press.

———. 1984. *Truth and method*. New York: Crossroad.

Hayek, Friedrich A. 1952. *The sensory order*. Chicago: University of Chicago Press.

———. 1967. *Studies in philosophy, politics and economics*. Chicago: University of Chicago Press.

———. 1978. *New Studies in philosophy, politics, economics, and the history of ideas*. Chicago: University of Chicago Press.

Hekman, Susan J. 1986. *Hermeneutics and the sociology of knowledge*. Notre Dame, Ind.: University of Notre Dame Press.

Hirsch, E. D., Jr. 1967. *Validity in interpretation*. New Haven: Yale University Press.

Lachmann, Ludwig M. 1971. *The legacy of Max Weber*. Berkeley: Glendessary Press.

———. 1977. *Capital, expectations, and the market process: essays on the theory of the market economy*. Kansas City: Sheed, Andrews & McMeel.

———. 1986. Economics as a hermeneutical discipline. Paper presented at the conference "Interpretation, Human Agency, and Economics," 28 March, George Mason University, Fairfax, Virginia.

Lavoie, Don. 1986. Euclideanism vs. hermeneutics: a reinterpretation of Misesian apriorism. In *Subjectivism, intelligibility and economic understanding: essays in honor of Ludwig M. Lachmann on his eightieth birthday,* edited by Israel M. Kirzner. New York: New York University Press.

———. 1987. The accounting of interpretations and the interpretation of accounts: the communicative function of "the language of business." *Accounting, Organizations and Society* 12:579–604.

———. 1989. Hermeneutics, subjectivity, and the Lester/Machlup debate: toward a more anthropological approach to empirical economics. In *Economics as discourse,* edited by Warren Samuels. Boston: Kluwer Academic.

———. 1990. Computation, incentives, and discovery: the cognitive function of markets in market-socialism. *Annals of the American Academy of Political and Social Science* 507 (January): 72–79.

Lavoie, Don, ed. 1991. *Hermeneutics and economics.* London: Routledge & Kegan Paul.

Linge, David E. 1976. Editor's introduction. In Gadamer 1976.

Machlup, Fritz. 1946. Marginal analysis and empirical research. *American Economic Review* 36 (September): 519–54.

Madison, G. B. 1986. Hans-Georg Gadamer's contribution to philosophy and its significance for economics. Paper presented at the conference "Interpretation, Human Agency, and Economics," 28 March, George Mason University, Fairfax, Virginia.

———. 1988a. Hermeneutical integrity: a guide for the perplexed. *Market Process* 6.1:2–8.

———. 1988b. How individualistic is methodological individualism? Groupe de recherche en épistemologie comparée, Working paper no. 8806. University of Quebec at Montreal.

Mäki, Uskali. 1991. Practical syllogism, entrepreneurship, and the invisible hand: the hermeneutics of G. H. von Wright. In Lavoie 1991.

Menger, Carl. [1871] 1981. *Principles of economics,* New York: New York University Press.

———. [1883] 1985. *Investigations into the method of the social sciences with special reference to economics.* New York: New York University Press.

Mueller-Vollmer, Kurt. 1985. *The hermeneutics reader.* New York: Continuum.

Polanyi, Michael. 1958. *Personal knowledge.* Chicago: University of Chicago Press.

Rabinow, Paul, and W. M. Sullivan. 1979. *Interpretive social science: a reader.* Berkeley and Los Angeles: University of California Press.

Rickert, Heinrich. 1986. *The limits of concept formation in natural science: a logical introduction to the historical sciences.* New York: Cambridge University Press.

Ricoeur, Paul. 1981. The model of the text: meaningful action considered as a text. In *Hermeneutics and the human sciences.* New York: Cambridge University Press.

Rorty, Richard. 1979. *Philosophy and the mirror of nature.* Princeton: Princeton University Press.

Warnke, Georgia. 1987. *Gadamer: hermeneutics, tradition and reason.* Cambridge: Polity Press.

Winograd, Terry, and Fernando Flores. 1986. *Understanding computers and cognition.* Norwood, N.J.: Ablex.

The Mengerian roots of the Austrian revival

Karen I. Vaughn

I. *Introduction*

The thesis of this paper is straightforward. The Austrian revival in the United States is the continuation of a research program begun by Carl Menger in 1870 but truncated in the early part of the twentieth century as the economics profession became more and more entranced first with Marshall and then with Walras. Despite the richness and complexity of Menger's economics, by the 1930s economists in the English-speaking world, at least, knew of Menger only indirectly through his students. If he was thought of at all, his contribution was considered to be little more than a nonmathematical version of marginal utility analysis. The real substance and importance of Menger's work had to be rediscovered by Friedrich Hayek in the middle decades of the twentieth century. Although at first the debt to Menger was often unconscious, the rediscovery of Mengerian ideas was the root of the revival of interest in Austrian economics by an increasing number of younger economists beginning in the 1970s. Further, Mengerian ideas form the basis for some of the most interesting aspects of current Austrian theory.

II. *Carl Menger and the incomplete subjectivist revolution*

After nearly one hundred years of his being identified with Jevons and Walras as marginal revolutionaries, the reevaluation of Menger's contributions to economics began in earnest in 1972. Erich Streissler's 1972 article "To what extent was the Austrian School marginalist?" was followed by Hicks and Weber's edited volume of essays, *Carl Menger and the Austrian school of economics,* in 1973 and by William Jaffé's "Menger, Jevons and Walras dehomogenized" in 1975. In 1978 an entire issue of the *Atlantic Economic Journal* was devoted to Carl Menger and included a piece by Ludwig Lachmann entitled "Carl Menger and the incomplete revolution of subjectivism." The point of all these essays was that Menger had been misrepresented by economists who thought of him as a marginal utility theorist who used words instead of mathematics. Streissler argued that Menger's *Principles* was really more a

379

treatise on economic development than on marginal utility theory (1972, 430). Jaffé showed the importance of ignorance and error in Menger's theory (1975, 521), and Lachmann argued that Menger's contribution had been more to begin a subjectivist revolution than to carry it out in full (1978, 59). These writers all helped to illuminate the aspects of Carl Menger that form the backbone of the Austrian revival.

The principle reason that Menger was for so long lumped with the "marginal revolutionaries" was that value indeed was the central unifying principle of his economics. Like Jevons in England and like the German Historical School, which for so many subsequent decades Menger regarded as the enemy, Menger was convinced that the labor theory of value of the Ricardian school was dangerously incorrect, yet unlike the German Historical School, he was convinced that a correct theory of value was a necessary prerequisite to any analysis of real, historical economic phenomena. Hence he set out in the *Principles* to develop a theory of value that began from the subjective valuations of individuals concerning the usefulness of goods for the purpose of fulfilling their needs. Like other discoverers of the principle of diminishing marginal utility, Menger proposed that people rank-ordered their needs and applied successive units of goods to satisfying less and less urgent needs. The value of any part of a stock of goods was equal to the least important use to which a portion of the stock was put (1981, 122–28). This theory, only later termed "diminishing marginal utility" by Wieser (1893), was what earned Menger the reputation of having been one of the co-participants in the marginal revolution.

Of course it was pointed out several times that Menger's formulation of diminishing marginal utility was imprecise.[1] The numerical scales of value that he included to illustrate why an individual would consume combinations of valued goods, rather than exhausting his desire for the most important before moving on to the less important good, were incomplete. Since he included no given income endowment, it was impossible from his table to figure out the equilibrium consumption basket. It was assumed that the many interesting examples of allocating increasing quantities of the same good to successively less important uses were just imprecise verbal elaboration on the same theme. Nevertheless, despite the supposed imprecision of Menger's presentation, at least he was credited with developing the basic idea, and that was that. The incredibly rich and suggestive context within which this admittedly

---

1. In fact Menger's translators, Dingwall and Hoselitz, felt compelled to point out Menger's "error" in a lengthy footnote on p. 126. I argue in Vaughn 1988, 440, that the scale of values tables that Menger includes in his text are meant only to be illustrative of a general principle and do not substitute for analysis. His genuine analysis of the principle of marginal use is found in the verbal discussion following the tables.

central part of Menger's theory was couched seems to have been overlooked by most of the subsequent evaluators of Menger's work until the reevaluation referred to above. Yet it is only when Menger's theory of value is read within the larger context of his *Principles* that one truly appreciates his greatness. And it is only then that it becomes apparent that differences between Menger and the neoclassical revolution are what is really important about him.

Three themes that recur throughout Menger's *Principles* form the basis of his particular view of economics. They are, roughly, (1) knowledge and plan, (2) the primacy of process, and (3) spontaneous order and the progress of civilization.

Jaffé argued that Menger, far from viewing man as a rational "lightning calculator," saw him as a "bumbling, erring, ill-informed creature, plagued with uncertainty, forever hovering between alluring hopes and haunting fears, and congenitally incapable of making finely calibrated decisions in pursuit of satisfactions" (1975, 521). One does not have to agree with Jaffé all the way in order to recognize an important truth in this description. To Menger rationality did not mean omnipotence or omniscience. Humans were born into ignorance and had as their primary task to learn the "causal connection between things and the satisfaction of their needs" in order to make reasonable decisions about their economic well-being. Further, they not only had to acquire knowledge, they also had to have the power to do something about their knowledge.[2]

Knowledge and power: throughout the *Principles* Menger stresses the importance of acquiring knowledge and power to economic behavior.[3] Economic life is built around gaining knowledge and power: knowledge of causal relationships between things and satisfactions (1981, 52), knowledge of the relationship between goods of a higher order and goods of the first order (56–57), knowledge of available quantities of goods (89), knowledge of trading opportunities (179), knowledge of the "economic" situation (224), and the power to make the best use of one's knowledge. The acquisition of knowledge was an integral part of the economic problem; it was not a problem to be assumed away in the confines of *ceteris paribus*.

This leads to the second theme of importance in Menger's *Principles*, the primacy of process. That man is ignorant and constantly must try to improve his knowledge implies that his economizing activities cannot be

---

2. Menger points out that useful things become goods when four conditions are met: there must be a human need, there must be a causal connection between the useful thing and the ability to satisfy the need, humans must know of this causal connection, and they must have command over the use of the good (1981, 52).

3. It should be noted that when Menger uses the term "power" in this context, he is referring to the power people can acquire over things and not power over other people.

passive and reactive. Insofar as men recognize their ignorance and try to overcome it, they must engage in some process that leads to a future different from the past. That process consists of either imagining a future different from the past or noticing something previously over-looked and taking steps to act on this new knowledge to one's advantage.[4] We see exactly such a process described in the introductory sections of Menger's much-celebrated theory of value.

Menger's theory of value was far more complex than simply a theory of how people make choices with given information. The theory of marginal use is preceded by a discussion of an individual's need to plan to meet his requirements for an uncertain future (1981, 80–84). In order to meet their requirements adequately, men must anticipate their needs and their resources over a planning period so that they can take steps to correct any potential shortfall in resources. The plan includes the recognition that, over time, needs may change; hence men must plan for a variety of contingencies. Once the estimation is made, they must then actively seek out additional resources if they believe their currently anticipated supplies are inadequate. Obviously Menger recognized that men live in time and must plan through time.[5] Economizing behavior is more than just allocating given resources among competing ends. In order to economize over time, men must seek out information and take action to improve their potential well-being. These actions include producing goods, seeking out sources of supply, and participating in economic institutions that gather information about the availability of goods.

The human being that is the subject of Menger's study is neither Veblen's lightning calculator nor a passive reactor to changing constraints. Certainly he cannot be summarized by a static and fully defined preference function. He is ignorant of the world around him, but he seeks to remove as much of that ignorance as he can. He is an active creator both of himself and of his world. And creation is a process rather than a state of affairs.

Menger fills his writing with examples of active processes. The most important of these, of course, is his theory of exchange. In the two chapters devoted to exchange and price formation it seems obvious that

---

4. Notice that both these ways of describing a process of introducing novelty into an economic system have recently been explored in the literature. Kirzner has consistently examined the relevance of entrepreneurial "alertness" to market processes (1973, 1979, 1985). Shackle has argued that in order for choice to be genuine, it must be an imaginative leap from the present to an as yet uncreated future (1972). Both these ideas are implicit in Menger's writings.

5. "The idea of causality, however, is inseparable from the idea of time. A process of change involves a beginning and a becoming, and these are only conceivable as processes in time. Hence it is certain that we can never fully understand the causal interconnections of the various occurrences in a process, or the process itself, unless we view it in time and apply the measure of time to it" (Menger 1981, 67).

Menger is not interested solely in deriving equilibrium prices for different market structures.[6] Rather, he describes a process whereby men seek out trading partners for the purpose of better satisfying their needs and then engage in a process of bargaining to get the best deal they can.

> The same principle that guides men in their economic activity in general, that leads them to investigate the useful things surrounding them in nature and to subject them to their command, and that causes them to be concerned about the betterment of their economic positions, the effort to satisfy their needs as completely as possible, leads them also to search most diligently for this relationship wherever they can find it, and to exploit it for the sake of better satisfying their needs. (1981, 180)

Menger's men are not simply solving a maximization problem. They actively search out trading partners and exploit the differences in valuation between them. And since the activity of trading requires knowledge and effort, not everyone will come to the same conclusions. Actual trades will depend on actual circumstances that will differ from individual to individual. The economist's job is to show the principles by which individuals bargain with one another once a trading partner is found, and to develop general principles for the formation of prices in more developed markets. Hence Menger's theory of price described the limits of economic prices and did not attempt to determine equilibrium prices.[7]

In a modification of typical neoclassical procedure Menger begins with isolated monopoly and then shows how the range of potential prices would narrow with increases in the numbers of buyers and sellers in the market. However, even here he was not so much deducing equilibrium prices under different market models as he was giving an analytic and a historical account of how increasing competition leads to lower prices, greater output, and the more complete exploitation of every economic opportunity. In fact Menger's chapter on price formation is more an analysis of the characteristics of economic progress than it is an analysis of equilibrium prices.[8]

I do not want to exaggerate the nonequilibrium character of Menger's work. He implies the notion of an individual equilibrium (1981, 74–76), and he uses the idea of an equilibrium between needs and requirements

6. Laurence Moss points out that Menger calls his theory a theory of price formation rather than price determination to underscore the indeterminateness of the outcome of exchange (1978, 26ff.).

7. It should also be pointed out that Menger consciously abstracted from error and ignorance in his theory of competitive price (1981, 224). The implications of this are discussed in Kirzner 1978, Moss 1978, and Vaughn 1978.

8. "The manner in which competition develops from monopoly is closely connected with the economic progress of civilization" (Menger 1981, 217).

as the goal of individual plans (97). Further, he makes passing mention of an equilibrium between future and present consumption (159n.) and describes prices as "symptoms of an economic equilibrium between the economies of individuals" (191). The whole notion of setting the limits to economic exchange implies some equilibrium toward which actions are progressing. However, economic equilibria are at best partial and ephemeral. The world is characterized more by constant flux than by equilibrium states, although equilibrium may obtain from time to time:

> the foundations for economic exchanges are constantly changing, and we therefore observe the phenomenon of a perpetual succession of exchange transactions. But even in this chain of transactions we can, by observing closely, find points of rest at particular times, for particular persons, and with particular kinds of goods. At these points of rest, no exchange of goods takes place because an economic limit to exchange had already been reached. (188)

While the passage above pretty clearly describes a notion of partial equilibrium, Menger also makes reference in his *Investigations* to "economic prices," a notion that bears some resemblance to prices in general equilibrium (1985, 71). Prices are "correct" to Menger only when everyone protects his economic interests, people have complete knowledge of their goals and means of achieving them, they understand the "economic situation" (all market opportunities are known and taken into account in personal calculation), and they have the freedom to pursue their goals.[9] However, he views economic prices as the benchmarks for measuring the deviations of real prices and as the direction toward which civilization is progressing, not as an underlying characteristic of the economy at any moment in time.[10] Menger seems to have believed that as civilization progressed, people's economic knowledge would improve so as to make real prices more closely approximate economic prices. In fact, so much of Menger's observations have to do with the way in which civilization progresses that I must agree fully with Streissler (1972) that Menger was fundamentally providing a theory of economic development in the *Principles* and not a theory of static

9. In Appendix 6 to the *Investigations* (1985, 216–19), Menger gives an account of the "economic situation" that amounts to a verbal description of constrained optimization. There he argues that given the goals of an individual and the constraints he faces, there is really only one theoretically correct economic solution. However, he also points out that real individual action will deviate from this solution for reasons of "volition, error and other influences" (217).

10. This is why Streissler wrote, "Menger's tâtonnement is a social process and a most laborious one to boot. One might, perhaps, condense the contrast between Menger and Walras thus: Walras's tâtonnement takes a minute; Menger's tâtonnement takes a century! Needless to say, with Menger we are most of the time out of equilibrium in the sense that the equilibrium price has not yet been found" (1972, 440).

economic allocation.[11] Once one reads the *Principles* with this purpose in mind, it is difficult to see how it could ever have been read in any other way.

The importance of knowledge and process come together in Menger's concern with progress and development. We see this in his identification of economic progress with the increase of human knowledge and with his persistent interest in the nature and origin of various phenomena from value to economic institutions. The opening paragraph of the *Principles* states the relationship between progress and knowledge very clearly:

> All things are subject to the law of cause and effect. This great principle knows no exception, and we would search in vain in the realm of experience for an example to the contrary. Human progress has no tendency to cast it in doubt, but rather the effect of confirming it and of always further widening knowledge of the scope of its validity. Its continued and growing recognition is therefore closely linked to human progress. (1981, 51)

Throughout the *Principles* we see repeated examples of how increasing knowledge of the causal relationship between goods and their ability to contribute to want satisfaction contributes to human progress. In fact Menger explicitly criticizes Adam Smith for too narrowly identifying the "progressive division of labor" as the source of wealth (1981, 72). Rather, Menger argues,

> The quantities of consumption goods at humans' disposal are limited only by the extent of human knowledge of the causal connections between things, and by the extent of human control over these things. . . . the degree of economic progress of mankind will still, in future epochs, be commensurate with the degree of progress of human knowledge. (1981, 72)

In fact, Menger's zealous adherence to the idea that economic progress was caused by the growth of knowledge has opened him up to the criticism by Lachmann (1978, 58) that he was not sufficiently subjectivist.

In one sense Lachmann is correct. Menger believed that there were objective laws of nature and that goods had objective properties that made them more or less capable of fulfilling human needs. Hence people need to learn of the causal relationship between the properties of a good

11. In this respect, Menger's *Principles* has far more kinship to *The wealth of nations* than to Ricardo, Jevons, or Walras. Menger himself seemed to be aware of the affinity since he criticized Smith on two key points—the causes of the wealth of nations (71–74) and the propensity to truck, barter, and exchange (175)—both issues that are central to Menger's theory of growth.

and its ability to satisfy needs. However, people could make mistakes about a good's properties. For instance, at a more primitive time people could believe that witch doctors cured disease, but with the advancement of knowledge they would come to realize that such a belief is in error. Hence Menger included in his lexicon the category of "imaginary goods" (1981, 53).

For a pure subjectivist this category is problematic. If goods are defined by individual subjective evaluations, why would any good be more imaginary than any other? The answer, it seems to me, is that Menger's theory of development required that he make room for error in perceptions and consequent learning, and this meant that he had to judge some past beliefs as mistaken if there were to be any meaning in the notion of improved knowledge. If one is going to talk about progress, one must be able to define it. Menger could not define it in terms of national wealth, since he did not think one could aggregate the wealth of individuals in a sufficiently precise way as to come up with a meaningful measure of national wealth (1981, 109–13). The measure of progress had to be an individual one, yet if one held that an individual's subjective evaluations could never be incorrect even in light of his own later knowledge, how could one ever speak of "progress"? Hence Menger took the position that people value goods according to their subjective assessments of the relationship between the good and the need it could satisfy, but that they can be mistaken in their understanding in the sense that once they acquire better information, they will recognize their mistake. Witch doctors objectively do not cure disease. Progress means that people come to realize this and, as a result, will substitute better forms of medicine. Here, then, Menger's theory of imaginary goods is not so much a truncating of subjectivism as it is an extension of subjectivism to knowledge.[12]

While Menger repeatedly identifies progress with the growth of knowledge, it is interesting that the process he describes by which much progress takes place is not necessarily an intentional one. Some economic progress emerges as the intentional outcome of individuals' seeking solutions to economizing problems by, say, organizing firms to collect information about availability of supplies (1981, 91–94). In other cases the individual search for economic improvement leads to the emergence of institutions that were planned by no one and yet serve the interests of all. This second kind of progress is the kind that Smith and the Scottish Enlightenment referred to as outcomes that were the prod-

---

12. That is, Menger does not assume that individuals have a direct pipeline to truth about the world around them. They form theories about the nature of the real world and act upon these theories. Eventually, Menger believes, these theories are either supported or falsified by experience.

uct of human action but not of human design and which Friedrich Hayek was later to refer to as a "spontaneous order."[13]

The most famous example of a spontaneous order in Menger is his theory of money. Money is the unintended outcome of individuals' attempts to improve their chances to get what they want through barter. They find that if they trade less marketable commodities for more marketable ones, they can increase the barter opportunities open to them. Eventually one commodity emerges as the most marketable and becomes institutionalized as money (1981, 257–60). Notice that this is a process in which the outcome is neither deliberately designed nor predictable in advance. An increase in knowledge results, but it is not knowledge that is searched for. Such processes are mentioned again and again in Menger.[14] The outcome of all of them is a new convention or institution that aids individuals to satisfy their wants better by following some new pattern. It is not an exaggeration to think of Menger as developing a theory of economic institutions grounded in a theory of individual economizing action.

Knowledge, process, and development: All are key concepts in Menger's work, and all had to be rediscovered in the twentieth century.

If this reading of Menger is correct, it is legitimate to ask why these major contributions were overlooked as neoclassical economics was undergoing its formation in the late nineteenth and early twentieth century. There are several convincing reasons to offer. First, Menger was known in the English-speaking countries primarily through the work of his colleagues Wieser and Böhm-Bawerk. Those two were most known for those aspects of their work that contributed to the growing neoclassical orthodoxy. Wieser developed the theory of marginal utility further and articulated the principle of opportunity cost to which it gives rise (Wieser 1893). He further worked on extending Menger's sketchy

13. Hayek 1973, 36ff. I am not claiming that the growth of the "professional class which operates as an intermediary in exchanges and performs for the other members of society not only the mechanical part of trading operations . . . , but also the task of keeping records of the available quantities" (Menger 1981, 91) is not also an example of the product of a "spontaneous order." The emergence of new market institutions must be viewed as such. However, there does seem to be a difference in that such institutions are the product of someone's deliberate idea that perhaps had some consequences not imagined but was still recognizable as part of the plan. Money, on the other hand, emerged purely as the unintended consequences of human action that no one planned or even could have envisioned before its emergence. These examples seem to be at two different places on a continuum of emergent institutions rather than being two different kinds of processes.

14. While the *Principles* is full of analysis of the "origin and nature" of various phenomena, in the *Investigations* Menger extends his notion of spontaneous orders to "law, language, the state, money, markets" (1985, 147) and in fact develops the theory of spontaneous order more fully than in the *Principles*. See book 3, ch. 2, "The theoretical understanding of those social phenomena which are not a product of agreement or of positive legislation, but are unintended results of historical development" (1985, 139–60).

notions of general equilibrium in a manner more consistent with Walras than with Menger's intent (Wieser 1927). Böhm-Bawerk became best known for his capital theory, which Menger regarded as a grave error because it reintroduced classical aggregative notions into economics.[15] Hence even the disciples chose to glean from Menger's work ideas that were not true to its overall thrust. And Menger could not speak for himself to the increasingly important English-speaking audience, for the *Principles* was not translated into English until 1950.

The second- and third-generation Austrians retained some of Menger's message, but in order to be part of the greater scholarly community they were increasingly obliged to develop their ideas in neoclassical parlance. Clearly this was true of Haberler, Machlup, and Morgenstern, for example. Schumpeter was an even more extreme case. While retaining much of the Austrian concern with process and institutions, he nevertheless embraced the static equilibrium economics of Walras as the epitome of economic science.[16] Even Ludwig von Mises, the most identifiably Austrian thinker of this period, was more concerned with equilibrium theorizing than Menger had been.[17] And Friedrich Hayek, who had been Mises's student in Vienna, went to England and tried to convey an Austrian theory of capital and the trade cycle in neoclassical terms.[18]

III. *Economic calculation and the rediscovery of Mengerian themes*

Modern Austrian economics owes its demise and rebirth to a putative failure: the debate over the economics of socialism.[19] This watershed event in the evolution of the Austrian tradition was a classic example of miscommunication in the economics profession. Interestingly, when he

15. Menger is reported by Joseph Schumpeter to have regarded Böhm-Bawerk's theory of the period of production as a grave error (1954, 847 n. 8). It is also interesting to note that Mises believed that Wieser never understood subjectivism (Mises 1978, 36).

16. This is Schumpeter's claim in his *History of economic analysis* (1954, 827). His enchantment with Walras is also evident in his assessment of the calculation debate, where he argues that "as a matter of blueprint logic, it is undeniable that the socialist blueprint is drawn at a higher level of rationality" (Schumpeter 1942, 185). This could only be said by someone who believed Walras's logic was somehow more "scientific" than Menger's.

17. I think this is true of the *Theory of money and credit* (1934), where Mises used a framework of analysis that was more neoclassical than Menger's framework had been. Despite the more Mengerian part to *Human action* (Mises 1966), it can also be read as another exercise in equilibrium theory.

18. Here I am referring to *Prices and production* (Hayek 1931).

19. For a full account of the debate from an Austrian perspective see Vaughn 1980, Lavoie 1985, and Kirzner 1988. See also the recent article by Caldwell (1988), in which he also argues that the calculation debate was instrumental in Hayek's "transformation." I see it not so much as a transformation as a rediscovery of what he learned from Menger through Mises.

technically started the debate in 1920 Mises believed that the arguments he produced to support his famous contention that economic calculation under a socialist regime was impossible, were not particularly Austrian but were simply good economic arguments. Perhaps even more than Mises, Hayek viewed himself as part of a broad scholarly community that had progressed beyond distinctions as to school and country of origin. Hence it was in a spirit of professional unity that Hayek in 1930–31 delivered a series of lectures on the topic of capital theory to an intrigued and receptive audience at the London School of Economics.[20]

At first after his arrival in London there was no small enthusiasm for Hayek's ideas. However, during the 1930s and early 1940s Hayek lost two important debates: first, he lost out to Keynes over the question of the trade cycle, and then, more important to our story, he lost out to Oscar Lange over the issue of the economics of socialism. That he lost out so completely was largely due to the fact that he had a fundamentally different understanding of market economies from his English colleagues. The economics profession during these years was becoming more and more entranced with Walras, while Hayek at root was a Mengerian—although it took him almost a decade to rediscover his Mengerian roots.

Perhaps it was easy for Hayek in the early "years of high theory" to believe he was part of one scholarly community when the questions under discussion were limited to how one defined capital or what the role of bank money was in a trade cycle. Differences of opinion are the stock in trade of science, and one expects to encounter opposition to new ideas and to argue hard for one's new theory. Besides, when arguing over specific pieces of theory, one generally assumes the basic framework. However, the debate over socialism was different. When arguing over the feasibility of replacing a market economy with a centrally planned economy, the totality of an economist's understanding of markets is called into play. It is not a surprise, then, that the very basic differences of world view between Hayek and the market socialists would hamper communication.

As is now well known, Mises began what was later referred to as the economic calculation debate by pointing out in an article in 1920 that Marxist plans to do away with markets, money, and prices in the post-

20. The demise of a particularly Austrian perspective is underscored in the volume resulting from that series of lectures, *Prices and production* (Hayek 1931). Because of the static equilibrium framework within which Hayek developed his theory in that volume, it reads more like a neoclassical rendering of some Austrian insights than a work in Austrian economics as we have come to think of it today. On Hayek's experiences in London see Hicks 1967. For an account of the effect of Hayek's capital theory debates on his professional development see O'Driscoll 1977.

revolutionary society were naive (see Mises [1920] 1935). Every economy required a set of market prices in order for economic calculation
to be possible. Without money or markets, Mises claimed, economic
prices could not be known, and hence socialist economies were doomed
to suffer inefficiency at best and chaos at worst.

Mises's challenge was taken up by a number of conventional English-
speaking economists, who first attempted various ways of solving the
pricing problem in central planning, ranging from estimating demand
and supply equations from empirical data in order to compute economic
prices to Oscar Lange's version of "market socialism."

Lange's market socialism attempted to answer Mises's criticism by
deriving shadow prices from market information in much the same way
that Lange believed it was accomplished in real markets. His scheme
(Lange and Taylor 1938) required that there be a real market in consumer goods but that all producer goods, "the means of production,"
were to be collectively owned. Prices for factor inputs would be decreed
by a Central Planning Board (CPB), and all production would take place
in state-owned firms. The managers of all state-owned firms would be
instructed to behave as perfect competitors and maximize profits based
on the prices dictated by the CPB.

The crux of Lange's plan, and the feature that won him the most
praise from his colleagues, was his plan for arriving at economic prices.
He imagined that actual pricing in real markets took place according to a
Walrasian *tâtonnement,* with the auctioneer arriving at the market-
clearing price by trial and error. Hence, Lange argued, the CPB would
act as an auctioneer and adjust prices according to trial and error as
well, increasing prices in response to shortages and decreasing prices
in response to surpluses. Information about shortages and surpluses
would be obtained from the managers of state-owned firms. Since Lange
believed his scheme duplicated all the important features of the market
(the parametric function of price, trial-and-error pricing, and profit
maximization), there was no reason to believe his brand of market
socialism would be any less efficient than capitalism. Hence he was able
to enlist neoclassical general equilibrium theory in the service of socialism.

Hayek first wrote on the economics of socialism in response to the
early plans to estimate demand and supply curves statistically. His
critique of market socialism continued after Lange published his work
and went on until about 1944. Over the course of these eight years he
became increasingly frustrated in his attempts to explain to his colleagues why he was convinced that their plans for redesigning society
would not succeed. All of his best arguments were considered either
trivial or irrelevant. It was not so much that the profession thought he

was wrong in anything he said. They just did not see how what he said mattered.

As one reads through the calculation articles of this period,[21] it becomes not entirely surprising that Hayek was not understood. Despite some extremely insightful comments, it seems obvious that Hayek was himself struggling with locating the theoretical source of his intuitive rejection of the market socialists' plan. His critiques are often poorly organized, almost musing in nature. Themes are introduced in one article only to be developed in later writings as their importance becomes clearer to him. Even more damning, his arguments were too philosophical or detailed to seem like good economic theory. In retrospect it is obvious that Hayek was not playing the game by the same rules as everyone else, and that he was himself unaware of the gulf that separated him from the rest of the profession.

All of Hayek's criticisms of market socialism center around two familiar Mengerian themes: the role of knowledge in society, and the dynamic nature of market economies. Neither of these was important to neoclassical economics at the time. Consider first his argument against the earlier socialist solution of estimating supply and demand equations statistically (Hayek 1935). At the time, Hayek was understood to have made a practical objection to such a plan—that it would be too difficult to make the required computations given the existing state of technology. What he was really arguing, however, was that one could not even set up such an estimation problem. First, he questioned the nature of the information required to set up the equation system. He argued that in trying to specify the goods to be priced, many important details automatically accounted for in market transactions would be lost. The goods specified would be aggregates rather than descriptions of the variety of attributes people actually value. In addition, the socialist presumption seemed to be that technological information was somehow available and given.

In response to this, Hayek argued that technological knowledge was dispersed among many minds and had to be discovered through competition. There was no relevant sense in which it was "there." Secondly, he argued that the equations solution to the pricing problem under socialism implied that prices were generally in equilibrium and did not change rapidly. In fact, he argued, markets are characterized by constant change:

The essential thing about the present economic system is that it does react to some extent to all those small changes and differences

21. All of the articles relevant to the calculation debate are collected in *Individualism and economic order* (Hayek 1948).

which would have to be deliberately disregarded under the system we are discussing if the calculations were to be manageable. In this way, rational decision would be impossible in all these questions of detail which in the aggregate decide the success of productive effort. ([1935] 1948, 156–57)

Hayek raised a number of other important questions in this article: Will the managers of state-owned firms behave as private entrepreneurs would? How can a regulator get enough information to regulate a state-owned firm? What are the criteria by which one allocates resources to state-owned firms, when much decision making must be based on estimates of future probability rather than past performance, and how can a regulator measure success or failure without genuine profits? While most critics took all of these objections to be concerned primarily with the question of incentives, in fact every one was a variation on the theme of knowledge and process. These themes reappeared again and again during the next decade in Hayek's writing.

Hayek explored these themes explicitly the next year in one of his most famous articles, "Economics and knowledge" ([1937] 1948, 33–56).[22] Here he began with an exploration of the meaning of "equilibrium" that in effect redefined the concept. Equilibrium for an individual, he argued, in order to have any meaning, had to refer to a consistent plan rather than a particular consumption basket. The implication of this, however, was that the concept of a social equilibrium was problematic, an idea Menger had lightly touched on in the *Principles*. Social equilibrium had to mean not a state of affairs but a set of mutually compatible plans. But in that case one had to ask what people had to know in order for mutually compatible plans to exist, and by what process they would come to know what they needed to know. This led him to the question of how people acquire knowledge in a market economy and to propose, as Menger had implied, that the crucial feature of markets was that they permitted individuals to take advantage of the existing division of knowledge.

In this discussion we see the beginning of the exploration of the connection between knowledge and process. Once it is recognized that knowledge is not a given but must be acquired, one cannot help but ask what are the implications of changing knowledge for social action. That leads inexorably to questions of process and the role of equilibrium theory.[23] Not surprisingly, in this article Hayek proposed a fundamen-

22. As Caldwell points out (1988, 513), Hayek himself regarded his essay "Economics and knowledge" as the beginning of his "transformation" from accepting pure technical economics to pursuing his life-long attempt to articulate the principles of a spontaneous order.
23. Here we see an intermediate stop between Menger and the modern controversy surrounding the proper role of equilibrium theory.

tally different notion of equilibrium from the static equilibrium assumed by his neoclassical colleagues. There seems to be no indication that he realized he was doing so.

Hayek continued to explore the implications of knowledge and process in his direct answer to Oscar Lange written in 1940, and in two culminating articles in 1945 and 1946, "The use of knowledge in society" (1948, 77–91) and "The meaning of competition" (1948, 92–106). Hayek's critique of Lange repeated some of his earlier objections to "statistical" socialism which Lange's scheme failed to address. Lange's plan still would require that products be defined in such a way as to obscure real market differences, and it still presumed that production functions somehow would be known, at least well enough for the CPB to be able to monitor the behavior of state firms. It also still presumed that equilibrium prices persist for long periods of time. Hayek, on the other hand, continued to argue that prices in real markets are always changing. Unless Lange's CPB would adjust all prices continuously in response to surpluses and shortages, it would have no hope of coming close to matching the efficiency of the market. Since surpluses and shortages would always need to be reported to the CPB before prices could change, it is obvious that CPB prices could never respond as quickly to changing demand and supply patterns as market prices could. Even more important, the need for firm managers to accept listed prices as parameters meant that under Lange's scheme "there will be less differentiation between prices of commodities according to the differences of quality and the circumstances of time and place" (1940, 192). In addition, unless it was recognized that many important managerial decisions are based on anticipations of the future that could never be second-guessed by the CPB, the chances of success for market socialism, Hayek concluded, were slim indeed.

Rather than writing in reaction to socialist plans, Hayek addressed the problem of knowledge head on in "The use of knowledge in society" ([1945] 1948, 77–91). There he redefined the economic problem so that instead of being a question of allocating known resources among known ends, it is "how to secure the best use of resources known to any members of society, for ends whose relative importance only these individuals know" (78). Economic efficiency required the greatest use of existing knowledge. The real questions were what kind of knowledge was usable and important and what kind of institutions were most likely to generate the knowledge necessary to act economically. Socialists seemed to think that only scientific knowledge matters, but in fact the market functions because people can profit from their particularized knowledge of special circumstances—knowledge of time and place, as Hayek called it. It was this kind of knowledge that was most important to everyday economic decision making. The socialists' failure to appreciate the importance of this kind of knowledge, Hayek charged, was directly linked to their assumption that change was infrequent in the market. In fact all real economic problems are problems of adjusting to change. Markets only function because of the constant deliberate adjustment to change that economic actors engage in. The only way to take advantage of the particularized knowledge of individuals that allows that constant adjustment to change take place is to use the decentralized decision-making feature of markets.

The following year Hayek published the final article in this nine-year series. In "The meaning of competition" ([1946] 1948, 92–106) he launched his final (albeit indirect) attack on the socialists, this time challenging their underlying assumptions about the nature of competition by offering his own alternative. Competition, he claimed, is the "moving force of life" (93), and yet it is completely omitted from economic models of perfect competition. It is a "dynamic process whose essential characteristics are assumed away" (94). The wishes and desires of consumers, including the kinds of goods and services they want and the prices they would be willing to pay for them, are not implications of some set of given equations. They are problems to be solved by competition. In the rush to homogenize and theorize, economists forget that the real world is characterized by diversity and personal relationships. The proper question for economists to ask is what institutional arrangements are required to get the most suitable people for each task. It is clear that Hayek believed the market economy goes a long way toward solving that problem.

In these last two essays, finally, the distinctive Hayekian (and not surprisingly, Mengerian) message emerges.[24] Markets are about knowledge and change. The knowledge important for market decisions is specialized, detailed, particularized according to time and place. It is also sometimes tacit and unreportable.[25] The information that is generally assumed in economic models is really the product of a market process in which competition is rivalry among partially ignorant suppliers who through a genuine process of trial and error seek to earn profits by learning about and providing information to partially ignorant consumers. Since even the best market socialists' plans assumed the

24. In fact the best statement of Hayek's view of competition was not published until 1969, the German version of "Competition as a discovery procedure." The English version did not appear until 1978, when Hayek published *New studies in philosophy, politics, economics and the history of ideas*. In this important essay he clearly and concisely expresses the central point of all the earlier articles on knowledge and competition published in the 1930s and 1940s: the main task of competition is to generate the knowledge that static equilibrium assumes is given (Hayek 1978).

25. Hayek was anticipating some of the arguments made by Michael Polanyi in *Personal knowledge* (1958). In fact the tacit nature of much market knowledge only came clear after Polanyi. It is necessary, then, to regard Polanyi as a major force in the development of the Austrian understanding of the knowledge problem.

existence of knowledge that was yet to be discovered and provided no satisfactory means to duplicate the market process in generating that knowledge, market socialism must be presumed to be unsatisfactory. Lange had not even touched the hem of the robe.

Unfortunately Hayek's critique of Lange was unappreciated by his colleagues.[26] They understood him to be claiming that incentive structures in bureaucratic firms might cause managers to shirk—a problem Schumpeter called political. They also believed he was making trivial criticisms by pointing to the specialized nature of many of the capital goods that would be priced by the CPB. His larger exploration of the problem of knowledge seemed to fall on deaf ears. His pointing to the difficulty of monitoring state-firm behavior when decisions had to be based on estimations of the future profitability of alternatives again was interpreted to be a matter of incentives. It is no wonder that Hayek ceased writing primarily for an audience of economists by the end of the 1940s. He was simply not in the same conversation as everybody else. He had to wait twenty more years for his message to be heard.

IV. *The quiet years*

To speak of an Austrian revival is to suggest an Austrian economics that was once at death's door. The patient went into cardiac arrest and was revived only by the workings of an outside force. That is an apt metaphor for the reawakening of interest in Austrian economics in the closing quarter of the twentieth century. By the end of World War II any kind of distinctively "Austrian" economics was certainly dead to the economics profession. The loss of the calculation debate was devastating. During the 1950s and into the 1960s, if not completely dead, Austrian economics was certainly comatose. Austrian economics became associated with failed arguments and outdated theories and methods.

After his intellectual losses to Keynes in the 1930s and to Lange in the 1940s Hayek left England altogether. He eventually joined the Committee on Social Thought at the University of Chicago, where he concentrated his efforts in the fields of philosophy, jurisprudence, psychology, and the history of ideas. While hindsight allows us to recognize that Hayek's excursions into these other fields were simply a further part of the intellectual inquiry he began in the socialism debate, at the time it seemed as if he had given up economics all together.[27]

26. See, for example, the summary review of the debate by Abram Bergson, in which he argues that Mises's original claim is totally without force, that Hayek had exaggerated the difficulties inherent in monitoring state firms, and that the questions about knowledge, while "a wholesome antidote to the tendency to regard a CPB as superman," probably did not imply too much limitation to the ability of socialist economies to plan (1948, 412, 335–37).

27. Caldwell (1988) also points out the continuity of Hayek's research after 1948. His work in psychology stemmed from his exploration of the knowledge problem, his work on

Although Hayek emigrated to America in the late 1940s, it was his older colleague Mises who was responsible for bringing Austrian economics to America. While I believe Hayek's ideas ultimately proved more important in shaping the Austrian revival, it was because of Mises that there was a revival at all. For that reason, a quick look at Mises's biography is in order.

Mises had been a student of Böhm-Bawerk's at Vienna.[28] Instead of joining the academy after his student years, he instead became a major economist for the Austrian Chamber of Commerce and Industry from 1909 to 1938. He claimed that an orthodox academic career was closed to him because of his outspoken antistatist views, so he chose a less orthodox route to carrying on his intellectual life. He became a *Privatdozent* at Vienna in 1913 and received the rank of associate professor in 1918. Although he served, unpaid, in this capacity throughout his life in Vienna, his real contributions as a teacher were made in the private seminar that he ran at the Chamber from 1920 until his departure from Vienna in 1934. His students included some of the most famous economists to have come out of Austria, including Gottfried Haberler, Friedrich Hayek, Fritz Machlup, Oskar Morgenstern, Paul Rosenstein-Rodan, and also the philosopher Alfred Schütz. This seminar apparently was all that kept the Austrian intellectual tradition alive during those years, even in Austria.

Mises was by his own account always an outsider to academic circles. The only formal teaching position that he ever held was as professor of international relations at the Institut Universitaire des Hautes Etudes Internationales in Geneva from 1934 to 1940. Despite his claim that he found the teaching there satisfying, his general despair at the political collapse of Europe in front of the Nazi invasions led him to emigrate to the United States in 1940.

In the United States, Mises once again secured an unofficial position with a university, this time with New York University, where he held a chair that was financed by the Volker Fund, a conservative organization that knew of his life-long antistatist fight. At NYU he conducted a weekly seminar which, along with the publications flowing from his pen during the two decades following 1945, *was* the Austrian School in the United States.

Although continuing to teach and write during this time, Mises was so far out of the mainstream of economic thought in the United States as to be virtually nonexistent. Perhaps this explains in part why his masterly

---

spontaneous social orders from his recognition of the dynamic nature of markets, and his political philosophy from his exploration of the shortcomings of planning.

28. Information about Mises's biography is taken from his own *Notes and recollections* (1978).

treatise, *Human action,* published in 1949[29] and serving as a complete summary of his lifework, attracted little more than a flurry of attention. It was a treatise in the grand style: comprehensive, philosophical, non-mathematical, deductive, explicitly critical of Marxist and interventionist ideology, and hence completely out of step with the times. Further, it was contemptuous of the currently fashionable positivist methodology and held instead that empirical data (or "history" as Mises referred to it) had to be organized according to a priori theory. While this is a more acceptable position to take today (and was also the position taken by Menger during the *Methodenstreit;* see Vaughn 1987, 443), at the time it seemed as if Mises was opposed to scientific method. His claim that praxeology, the science of human action, was not only a priori but apodictically certain did nothing to calm the scientific outrage of the economics profession. His insistence on the apodictic certainty of praxeological theory made it seem as if the superiority of the free market over interventionism was also apodictically certain and earned him the reputation of a conservative ideologue.

Unfortunately, because of the emphatic style Mises used in his writing and because of the insistence on the certainty of theory, he was read by some as doing little more than rewriting neoclassical economics in words rather than mathematics and as adding arcane philosophy and irrelevant observations about the human condition. This was particularly unfortunate because large sections of *Human action* are direct continuations and elaborations of Menger's ideas. Mises builds time, uncertainty, and process right up front in his system. He understands the problem of social cooperation in much the same way that Menger did, and expands on Mengerian insights in light of twentieth-century European philosophy.[30] Indeed Mises also made one tremendously important addition to Mengerian thought by insisting on the impossibility of economic calculation without money.[31] More than Menger, Mises integrated money into the theory of markets. While his theory of prices in chapter 16 does seem more determinate than Menger's, it is not so much so that.he deserved the superficial reading by contemporary eyes

29. *Human action* was a completely revised and rewritten version of a book Mises published in German in 1940 entitled *Nationalökonomie: Theorie des Handelns und Wirtschaftens.*

30. It is ironic that O'Driscoll and Rizzo's (1985) attempt to explore a Bergsonian notion of time to support Austrian economics garnered so much criticism when they were simply following up on a hint Mises has left in *Human action* (100n.).

31. Mises's claim that one cannot have economic calculation without money prices caused him to be held up to ridicule during the calculation debate, yet I think it is one of his most important contributions to economics. We have still to plumb the depths of its implications. Jack High (1983, 8–9) also recognizes the importance of Mises's integration of money into his theory of markets.

that he so often received.[32] In a way, he was suffering the same fate as Menger almost a hundred years earlier. He was read in light of what the profession as a whole already believed, and hence the interesting bits that did not fit into the neoclassical framework were ignored: the bits about the importance of time and process, about knowledge and ideology, about the meaning of action—the Mengerian themes that were also ignored in Menger.

Mises himself was partly to blame for this misreading. He did pay more attention to equilibrium theorizing than had Menger, and he was more concerned with the certainty of theory than with exploring the consequences of ignorance and error. While the knowledge problem may be in Mises implicitly, it is not an explicit concern of his. One has to know the Mengerian tradition in advance in order to find it easily in Mises. Like Hayek, he was presuming the ideas in that tradition rather than stating them for the uninitiated. To make matters worse, Mises was also drawing on a sophisticated European intellectual background that was totally unknown to his American audience. To this day, *Human action* strikes me as an odd mixture of polemic and dispassionate analysis. Mises was at once dedicated to *Wertfreiheit* and a passionate defender of the free market. This political stance, coupled with his unfamiliar understanding of economic theory, clearly estranged him from any potential professional audience in the 1950s.

Indeed, Mises's name primarily became associated with free-market causes and extreme conservative politics. Private foundations eager to keep alive arguments supporting free-market policies at a time when the profession was enamored of "indicative planning" and "fine tuning" supported Mises's work. He was touted by such diverse groups as the John Birch Society and the followers of Ayn Rand (who finally broke with Mises because his subjectivist economics seemed to contradict Rand's philosophy of objectivism). His seminar attracted a variety of people, from serious students of economics to political conservatives who saw Mises as an island of sanity in an increasingly insane world. And as the radical 1960s got under way, Mises became something of an underground hero to a group of "libertarian anarchists" who believed that his economics provided a complete and self-sufficient argument against all state intervention.

During the 1950s and 1960s, then, Austrian economics was understood mostly as odd methodology and free-market advocacy. Mises's writing during this time consisted of some methodological essays and

---

32. This misreading was not only the fault of hostile contemporaries. Mises's student Murray Rothbard, who was influential in the early days of the Austrian revival, wrote a textbook translation of *Human action* that reads very much like a rendition of neoclassical economics in nonmathematical language (Rothbard 1962).

some public policy articles.[33] In both of these his style seemed to get more and more polemical as he saw the statism he had unsuccessfully combatted in Europe taking over the intelligensia of his newly adopted country. This time it was Mises who was in the wrong conversation.

If Mises's seminar during these years *was* Austrian economics, at least in the United States, its future depended on the students who attended. The two most notable in the history of Austrian economics in America were Murray Rothbard and Israel Kirzner. Rothbard, himself a dedicated advocate of the free market, became Mises's faithful interpreter to the radical libertarian fringe, while Kirzner, against overwhelming odds, attempted to carry on Mises's work in the context of the mainstream academic community. Kirzner published three books during these middle years, and Rothbard two,[34] but other than that there was little professional scholarship in American Austrian circles. Certainly there was almost no communication with the rest of the profession. However, Mises, Rothbard, and Kirzner must have had something of importance to say, because despite the almost total professional silence about these Austrian economists, by the time the 1960s erupted into the early 1970s, there had emerged a host of young people, many of them free-market radicals, dedicated to economics but dissatisfied with the reigning orthodoxy, who had discovered the work of Mises (and to a lesser extent Hayek), who had listened to the Austrian folklore at Murray Rothbard's knee, and who were ready to change the world—as most young people were in those days.[35]

V. *The Austrian revival*

If one had to set a specific date for the Austrian revival in America, I would choose 1974, although rumblings of a reawakening of interest in Austrian economics were heard several years before. Specifically, in 1969 James Buchanan published *Cost and choice,* in which he claimed that the Austrians really had won the calculation debate because they

33. The two works that come to mind are *The ultimate foundations of economic science* ([1962] 1978) and *Economic policy: thought for today and tomorrow* (1979).

34. Kirzner's works during this time were *Market theory and the price system* (1963), *An essay on capital* (1966), and *The economic point of view* (1967), which was essentially an exploration in the history of economic thought. The history of thought is a convenient vehicle for airing unpopular views. Rothbard published *Man, economy and the state* (1962) and *America's Great Depression* (1963), an attempt to apply an Austrian theory of the trade cycle to that great American tragedy.

35. I can only offer personal testimony as to why the Austrian School attracted young followers in the late 1960s and early 1970s. As an undergraduate I was frankly attracted by the free-market message that I believed was inherent in Austrian economics. It was only much later, as the revival got under way, that I also began to be interested in Austrian economics as an intellectual system apart from policy or political philosophy. I suspect my experience was not unusual. Interestingly, I now find the "free-market" aspects of Austrian economics the least intriguing of all the intellectual challenges it offers.

understood the subjective nature of cost whereas the market socialists did not. This exploration of subjectivism for economic theory and policy was a shot across the neoclassical flagship's bow. In 1972 Erich Streissler's article on Menger was published in *HOPE,* and George Shackle, a sympathetic fellow traveler, published *Epistemics and economics,* which broke new ground in subjectivist theory and provided a set of problems for further Austrian research. In 1973 more help came from England: Sir John Hicks, having recently found some interesting bits in Menger concerning time, edited *Carl Menger and the Austrian school of economics,* and in the United States that same year, Israel Kirzner attempted to delineate an Austrian theory of market processes in *Competition and entrepreneurship.*[36] This was one of the first books by a committed Austrian that self-consciously tried to explain Austrian theory to the profession at large. It carved out room in neoclassical orthodoxy for entrepreneurship and change and raised a wealth of questions about the further implications of change for understanding markets. The publication of these books not only raised important questions but also made Austrian themes and ideas respectable again. In October 1974, when Hayek won the Nobel Prize in Economics (shared, ironically, with Gunnar Myrdal), the time surely seemed ripe for a revival of Austrian economics.

As important as these academic events were to the revival of Austrian ideas, the catalyst for the revival came from another source. In 1974 the Institute for Humane Studies sponsored a week-long conference on Austrian economics in South Royalton, Vermont.[37] This conference brought together a varied group of economists and current graduate students whose unifying characteristic was that they had expressed some interest in the work of Mises or Hayek. The main speakers were Murray Rothbard, Israel Kirzner, and Ludwig Lachmann, who was introduced to American Austrians for the first time at that conference. The papers were an odd mix. They ranged from the history of the Austrian School, its method, and particular characteristics, to policy and the ethical implications of Austrian economics.[38] The interesting feature of the papers, however, was the implicit assumption by all the

36. In this list of important books that heralded in the Austrian revival I should also mention *LSE essays on cost* (Buchanan and Thirlby 1973). This book traced a tradition of subjective cost theory that began in the 1930s at the London School of Economics as an outgrowth of the work of Hayek and Lionel Robbins and continued to survive into the 1970s through the writings of Jack Wiseman and G. F. Thirlby.

37. The Institute for Humane Studies ran two more conferences in Austrian economics over the next two years whose purpose was to articulate an Austrian research program. The third conference, at Windsor Castle, England, produced a volume entitled *New directions in Austrian economics* (Spadaro 1978).

38. The papers for this conference were collected and published by Edwin Dolan, who had organized it. The title was descriptive of what we all thought was being discussed there: *The foundations of modern Austrian economics.*

speakers and participants (with the possible exception of Lachmann) that Austrian economics was something given that had to be learned, rather than a line of inquiry that was to be developed and created.

Perhaps this was a necessary fiction in the early days of the Austrian revival, especially considering the composition of the revivers. With the exception of the three speakers, most of the enthusiasts for Austrian ideas at that conference (or anywhere else) were either graduate students or young assistant professors. Most young students of economics, no matter where they are educated, usually believe that they have discovered truth and that their job is to apply truth the world around them. This attitude was doubly evident at South Royalton, where the young Austrians also believed their truth was being unjustifiably ignored by a mistaken academic community. There was an aura of crusade enveloping South Royalton, and for years afterward even Austrian sympathizers were to comment upon the "siege mentality" of the young Austrians. In retrospect that attitude of virtue wronged was probably necessary in order to give these young, mostly unknown economists the courage to pursue an eccentric research program that flew in the face of received orthodoxy. It enabled them to undertake the difficult work of actually building a coherent Austrian paradigm. And, much in the same manner as Hayek explains the evolution of the common law, the attempt on the part of the young Austrians to "learn" the theory led inexorably to the emergence of new ideas.[39] It seems clear today that what has been happening over the last fifteen years has been a creative development, not a scholastic repetition, of a line of inquiry begun by Menger more than one hundred years before.

VI. *Modern Austrian economics: the market process*

From the beginning of the revival there was consensus on several cornerstones of Austrian economics. And since the revival was brought about by students of Mises, Mises's phraseology became the language

39. One good example of how new ideas grow out of attempts to restate the old is the writing of O'Driscoll and Rizzo's *Economics of time and ignorance* (1985). In 1980 O'Driscoll and Rizzo delivered a paper at the AEA meetings in Denver on the topic "What is Austrian economics?" There was a surprisingly large audience for their paper, indicating some widespread interest in Austrian themes. They argued that Austrian economics was subjectivist and paid attention to real time and to expectations, to heterogeneity of products, and to market processes rather than equilibrium states. As a result of that paper they commenced to write their book. They expected to have it finished in about a year, but instead it took about five years. Part of the trouble was simply the problem of trying to articulate what Austrian economics is. They began their project by thinking of it as something there that must be explained rather than as a theoretical system that must be developed. By the time of its completion, the book broke new ground in developing a coherent Austrian paradigm (and consequently was criticized by many Austrians who "knew" it wasn't faithful to Austrian principles); but the authors struggled precisely because they began by thinking they were reporting and articulating rather than creating.

of that consensus.[40] Where neoclassical economics was concerned with describing equilibrium states, Austrians were concerned with disequilibrium processes. Where neoclassical economics was static and timeless, Austrian economics took account of time and change. Where neoclassical economics was based on full knowledge and certainty, Austrians were interested in the implications of ignorance and uncertainty. As opposed to neoclassical beliefs in the importance of empirical testing of theoretical propositions, Austrians argued that theory was a priori and all testing was simply interpretations of historical data. Austrians rejected mathematical modeling because it limited the kinds of questions that could be asked and it necessarily abstracted away from too many real-world considerations. They rejected using macroeconomic aggregates because they tended to obscure the micro foundations of macro problems. And everyone agreed that government intervention was always worse than the market alternative.

Despite the initial agreement on basic propositions there was no clear understanding, it seemed to me, of what those propositions implied about how to do economics. One knew there was much wrong with modern economics, but one did not yet know how to put it right. It was necessary first to explore the propositions themselves for internal coherence and relative importance, and to figure out what difference this "Austrian perspective" made for understanding the real world. To the much-asked question "What is Austrian economics?" there was simply not a ready answer. It has taken almost fifteen years, and a growing body of literature, much of it produced by the young scholars from South Royalton, to begin to answer that question, and it is being answered in at least two different ways.[41]

40. Hayek was not mentioned very much at South Royalton except in the context of his capital theory. The reasons were partly that Murray Rothbard did not think much of Hayek's politics or economics and partly that the first volume of *Law, legislation and liberty* (1973) had not been out long enough to make an impact on the group. However, once Hayek won the Nobel Prize later on that year, he obviously came into the limelight. His works were discussed more and more as the Austrian conferences continued and as the group of participants became more immersed in the literature of Austrian economics.

41. The literature produced by the Austrian revival falls into three broad categories: intellectual history of the Austrian School, criticism of neoclassical economics, and some small amount of constructive theorizing. It is probably not surprising that so much of the work done so far has been in the first two categories. First, it was necessary to learn what the Austrian tradition was before one could presume to work in it. Also, given the problems of publishing unusual work in the major journals, doing history of thought was often the only way to get exposure for Austrian ideas. Criticism of the orthodoxy is also a necessary step in locating the distinctiveness of an alternative paradigm. It is also constructive in the sense that through the process of criticism one explores the robustness of one's own theory. Constructive theorizing is the most difficult and is only beginning to play a part in the Austrian literature. Examples of the latter type of work are of course Kirzner 1973, 1979, and 1985; Lachmann 1986; O'Driscoll and Rizzo 1985; and White 1984. Lavoie is currently reexamining the methodology of the Austrian School in light of modern

To draw the difference between the two answers with broad brush-strokes, one way of conceiving of the Austrian contribution is as a supplement to or a reinterpretation of neoclassical economics. Here the presumption is that neoclassical economics began on sound footing with its recognition of the subjective nature of value but then took a wrong turn towards overconcern with formalism, mathematical modeling, and macroeconomic aggregative reasoning. The task of Austrian economics is to make a midcourse correction by pushing conventional economics in the direction of greater attention to subjectivism and process. Equilibrium is a necessary construct as long as one does not concentrate exclusively on equilibrium conditions. Equilibrium theory must keep prominent all the variations of behavior and detailed adjustments that make equilibrium possible. And certainly, policy conclusions should not be based on too literal a translation of economic theory to economic reality. While many contemporary Austrians accept this view, it is probably best exemplified in the early work of Israel Kirzner.

In *Competition and entrepreneurship* (1973), for example, Kirzner focused on how entrepreneurial alertness to hitherto unnoticed profit opportunities would bring the system closer toward equilibrium, thus providing a supplement to conventional theory. In that volume his entrepreneur does not create or discover anything that is genuinely new. One can still think of a world of given tastes and given resources where the function of the entrepreneur is to notice that given resources are not being fully exploited. The entrepreneur may even be said to exploit differences in knowledge, but it is knowledge that in some sense exists. Hence Kirzner's entrepreneur supplies a moving force to bring the system from disequilibrium to equilibrium. While the later Kirzner (e.g., 1985) is willing to agree that the entrepreneur may in fact be said to discover opportunities, he does not believe this is in principle different from saying that the entrepreneur "notices" what already exists. Yet the difference between noticing what is already there and creating what is yet to be is the crux of the difference between the two ways of understanding Austrian economics.

The other interpretation sees Austrian economics as a radical departure from neoclassical economics. While still approving of the subjectivist revolution, this view does not think there is much salvageable in the basic framework of contemporary economic theory. This view, along with Shackle, is impressed with the "kaleidic" nature of reality and the genuine creativity of choice (see Shackle 1972). It also takes seriously

---

continental philosophy that carries forward the methodological positions taken by Menger and Mises. There are also several unpublished doctoral dissertations coming out of George Mason University that promise to add to the corpus of new Austrian theoretical works.

Lachmann's worry about the implications of the subjectivity of expectations and Hayek's admonitions about the subjectivity of knowledge itself. To this view, the implications of the problems of knowledge and process require a very different way of organizing our understanding of economic reality. The implication of "radical subjectivism" is to jettison the conventional notion of equilibrium in favor of some idea of ordered process. That is, to follow the implications of the Austrian insights into the human condition is to cease speaking of end states at all and to look only at processes.

This view of Austrian economics is more tentative and less coherent than the first. While it bespeaks a dissatisfaction with static, engineering notions of equilibrium, it has not yet developed an alternative organizing principle that is widely accepted. One attempt to develop an alternative is Lachmann's *Market as an economics process* (1986). Here, rather than trying to come up with a general theory of market behavior, Lachmann instead disaggregates markets and analyzes them according to such features as the importance of stocks versus flows, the kind of product sold, and the information characteristics of the particular market. Rather than trying to predict outcomes, to Lachmann the best the economist can do is to understand and describe "what men do in markets" (1986, 3). There is not even a presumption that all market activities will be coordinated, since "competitive market forces will cause discoordination as well as coordination" (5).

While Lachmann's work is insightful and largely convincing, it also is narrow in scope. Others have argued that Austrian economics need not stop with limited market studies; it can be folded into a more formal framework without doing violence to its understanding of human action. Specifically, Langlois (1983) and Boettke, Horwitz, and Prychitko (1986) have argued that an evolutionary framework is the most congenial setting for an Austrian theory of the market process. Biological evolution provides a model of ordered change where there are no predictable end states and no notion of an ideal outcome. Evolutionary theory rests on the basis of "three interrelated factors: selection, memory and variation or mutation." We can find the economic analogues to these in competition, habits, or institutions, and entrepreneurship and creativity (Langlois 1983, 5). Such an analogy allows us room to explore the origin and nature of institutions, the source of creative change, and the role of competition in good Mengerian and Hayekian fashion. Knowledge becomes not an addendum to the theory but the central element in the evolutionary process. This is perhaps what Hayek had in mind when he referred to the "twin concepts of evolution and spontaneous order" (1979, 258).

Interestingly, both paths of development of Austrian ideas have their roots in Menger. Certainly, the "Austrian economics as supplement to and conscience of modern economics" view can claim Menger as its legitimate ancestor. Menger did write of equilibrium states as well as processes, and his emphasis on knowledge can be interpreted as discovery rather than creation. Yet if the reading of Menger offered here is correct, it is the second vision of modern Austrian economics that seems more consistent with the spirit of Menger's inquiry. Once we examine Menger's concept of spontaneous order in the context of the problem of knowledge in society (as Hayek did in the 1930s and 1940s), we are led to recognizing just how deeply the problems of incomplete, decentralized, and inarticulate knowledge cut in the social world. The unraveling of the implications of the knowledge problem, both to people's intentional choices and to the unintended social consequences of human action, then becomes the main task of economics. We are led to construct theories of institutional emergence and development where the important questions are not ones of optimal end states but of the processes by which humans interact to create and adapt to their social environment. And we are inexorably led to asking, and with luck answering, the same question that moved Adam Smith and Carl Menger: what causes the growth and development of the wealth of nations?

References

Bergson, Abram. 1948. Socialist economics. In *A survey of contemporary economics,* edited by Howard S. Ellis, 1:412–48. Homewood, Ill.: Richard D. Irwin.

Boettke, Peter, Steven Horwitz, and David Prychitko. 1986. Beyond equilibrium economics. *Market process* 4.2.

Böhm-Bawerk, Eugen von. [1888] 1959. *The positive theory of capital.* Translated by George Huncke. South Holland, Ill.: Libertarian Press.

Buchanan, James M. 1969. *Cost and choice: an inquiry into economic theory.* Chicago: University of Chicago Press.

———, and G. F. Thirlby, eds. 1973. *LSE essays on cost.* New York: New York University Press.

Caldwell, Bruce J. 1988. Hayek's transformation. *HOPE* 20.4:513–42.

Dolan, Edwin G., ed. 1976. *The foundations of modern Austrian economics.* Kansas City: Sheed & Ward.

Hayek, Friedrich A. 1931. *Prices and production.* London: George Routledge & Sons.

———. 1935. *Collectivist economic planning.* London: George Routledge & Sons.

———. 1948. *Individualism and economic order.* Chicago: University of Chicago Press.

———. 1973. *Law, legislation and liberty.* Vol. 1. Chicago: University of Chicago Press.

———. 1978. *New studies in philosophy, politics, economics and the history of ideas.* Chicago: University of Chicago Press.

———. 1979. *Law, legislation and liberty*. Vol. 3. Chicago: University of Chicago Press.

Hicks, J. R. 1967. *Critical essays in monetary theory*. Oxford: Clarendon Press.

———, and W. Weber, eds. 1973. *Carl Menger and the Austrian school of economics*. Oxford: Clarendon Press.

High, Jack. 1983. The market process: an Austrian view. *Market Process* 1.1.

Jaffé, William. 1975. Menger, Jevons and Walras dehomogenized. *Economic Inquiry* 14.4:511–24.

Kirzner, Israel M. 1963. *Market theory and the price system*. Princeton: von Nostrand.

———. 1966. *An essay on capital*. New York: Augustus M. Kelley.

———. 1967. *The economic point of view*. Kansas City: Sheed & Ward.

———. 1973. *Competition and entrepreneurship*. Chicago: University of Chicago Press.

———. 1978. The entrepreneurial role in Menger's system. *Atlantic Economic Journal* 6.3:31–45.

———. 1979. *Perception, opportunity and profit*. Chicago: University of Chicago Press.

———. 1985. *Discovery and the capitalist process*. Chicago: University of Chicago Press.

———. 1988. The economic calculation debate: lessons for Austrians. *Review of Austrian Economics* 2:1–18.

———, ed. 1982. *Method, process and Austrian economics: essays in honor of Ludwig von Mises*. Lexington, Mass.: Lexington Books.

———, ed. 1986. *Subjectivism, intelligibility and economic understanding: essays in honor of Ludwig M. Lachmann on his eightieth birthday*. New York: New York University Press.

Lachmann, Ludwig M. 1978. Carl Menger and the incomplete revolution of subjectivism. *Atlantic Economic Journal* 6.3:57–59.

———. 1986. *The market as an economic process*. Oxford: Basil Blackwell.

Lange, Oscar, and Fred M. Taylor. 1938. *On the economic theory of socialism*. New York: McGraw-Hill.

Langlois, Richard N. 1983. The market process: an evolutionary view. *Market Process* 1.2.

Lavoie, Don. 1985. *Rivalry and central planning: the socialist calculation debate reconsidered*. Cambridge: Cambridge University Press.

Menger, Carl. [1871] 1981. *Principles of economics*. Translated by James Dingwall and Bert F. Hoselitz. New York: New York University Press.

———. [1883] 1985. *Investigations into the method of the social sciences with special reference to economics*. Translated by Francis J. Nock. Edited by Lawrence White. New York: New York University Press.

Mises, Ludwig. [1920] 1935. *Economic calculation in the socialist commonwealth*. In Hayek 1935, 87–130.

———. [1934] 1980. *Theory of money and credit*. Indianapolis: Liberty Classics.

———. [1949] 1966. *Human action: a treatise on economics*. 3d ed. New York: Henry Regnery.

———. [1962] 1978. *The ultimate foundations of economic science: an essay on method*. Kansas City: Sheed, Andrews & McMeel.

———. 1978. *Notes and recollections*. Translated by Hans F. Sennholz. South Holland, Ill.: Libertarian Press.

———. 1979. *Economic policy: thoughts for today and tomorrow*. South Bend, Ind.: Regnery/Gateway.

Moss, Laurence S. 1978. Carl Menger's theory of exchange. *Atlantic Economic Journal* 6.3:17–29.

Nelson, R. Richard, and Sidney G. Winter. 1982. *An evolutionary theory of economic change*. Cambridge: The Belknap Press of Harvard University Press.

O'Driscoll, Gerald P. 1977. *Economics as a coordination problem: the contributions of Friedrich Hayek*. Kansas City: Sheed, Andrews & McMeel.

———, Mario J. Rizzo. 1985. *The economics of time and ignorance*. Oxford: Basil Blackwell.

Polanyi, Michael. 1958. *Personal knowledge: towards a post-critical philosophy*. Chicago: University of Chicago Press.

Rizzo, Mario J. 1979. *Time, uncertainty and disequilibrium: exploration of Austrian themes*. Lexington, Mass.: Lexington Books.

Rothbard, Murray N. 1962. *Man, economy and the state: a treatise on economic principles*. Los Angeles: Nash.

———. 1963. *America's Great Depression*. Princeton: van Nostrand.

Schumpeter, Joseph. 1934. *A theory of economic development*. Translated by R. Opie. Cambridge: Cambridge University Press.

———. [1942] 1963. *Capitalism, socialism and democracy*. New York: Harper & Row.

———. 1954. *History of economic analysis*. Edited by E. B. Schumpeter. Oxford: Oxford University Press.

Shackle, George. 1972. *Epistemics and economics: a critique of economic doctrines*. Cambridge: Cambridge University Press.

Spadaro, Louis M., ed. 1978. *New directions in Austrian economics*. Kansas City: Sheed, Andrews & McMeel.

Streissler, Erich. 1972. To what extent was the Austrian School marginalist? *HOPE* 4.2:426–41.

Vaughn, Karen I. 1978. The reinterpretation of Carl Menger: some notes on recent scholarship. *Atlantic Economic Journal* 6.3:62–64.

———. 1980. Economic calculation under socialism: the Austrian contribution. *Economic Inquiry* 18:535–54.

———. 1987. Carl Menger. In *The new Palgrave: a dictionary of economics*, edited by John Eatwell, Murray Milgate, and Peter Newman, 438–44. London: Macmillan.

White, Lawrence. 1984. *Free banking in Britain: theory, experience and debate, 1800–1845*. Cambridge: Cambridge University Press.

Wieser, Friedrich von. [1893] 1971. *Natural value*. New York: Augustus M. Kelley.

———. [1927] 1967. *Social economics*. New York: Augustus M. Kelley.